ENCYCLOPEDIA OF
ANNUALS AND
PERENNIALS

ENCYCLOPEDIA OF ANNUALS AND PERENNIALS

FOG CITY PRESS

Published by Fog City Press
814 Montgomery Street
San Francisco, CA 94133 USA

Copyright © 2002 Weldon Owen Pty Ltd

Chief Executive Officer: John Owen
President: Terry Newell
Publisher: Lynn Humphries
Managing Editor: Janine Flew
Art Director: Kylie Mulquin
Editorial Coordinator: Tracey Gibson
Picture Research and Editorial Assistant: Marney Richardson
Production Manager: Martha Malic-Chavez
Business Manager: Emily Jahn
Vice President International Sales: Stuart Laurence

Project Editor: Bronwyn Sweeney
Designer: Kerry Klinner
Consultant: Geoffrey Burnie

ISBN 1 876778 66 0

Color reproduction by Bright Arts Graphics (S) Pte Ltd
Manufactured by Kyodo Printing Co. (S'pore) Pte Ltd
Printed in Singapore

A Weldon Owen Production

Contents

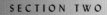

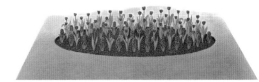

How to Use This Book

The *Encyclopedia of Annuals and Perennials* is designed to help, encourage, and inspire gardeners, both novice and experienced. It is packed with information about choosing and buying plants, planting, propagation, soil conditions, and cultivation. The book is easy to read and each page has colorful photographs showing how beautiful your garden can be. In addition, Sections Eight and Nine provide an encyclopedia of annuals and perennials to help you choose and identify them.

Each section is color-coded for easy reference.

General information about planting, propagating, and caring for your plants to get the optimum results.

The beginning of a new chapter within one of the nine major sections in the book. The line above is the section heading.

Helpful illustrations feature throughout the book.

Clear and simple step-by-step photographs, in this case to show you how to prepare a garden bed.

Colorful photographs give you guidance and inspiration in planning and planting your garden.

---

106 PREPARATION AND PLANTING

Getting the Soil Ready

Along with proper plant selection, preparing a planting bed so that it contains good, granular soil is critical to the success of your flower garden. If you do a thorough job at this stage, you will be rewarded by quicker plant establishment and less weeding later.

plastic. However, this can take weeks or more than a month depending on the weather—the hotter it is, the faster the plastic works. Then, when it has decayed.

Timing

If possible, start digging your new garden a season or a year before you intend to do your planting. That way, you can do a really thorough job of preparing the soil, and the soil will have a chance to settle before you plant. If spring typically is too wet to work the soil in your area, dig the garden in fall instead. If you can't prepare the soil ahead of time, you can usually get the bed ready and start planting in the same season. See "Planting Time" on page 114 for suggestions on the best time to actually plant.

Working the Soil

Once you've cleared the bed, break up the soil. Consider of tools carefully. Decades turned the soil with garden and other hand tools. In many have turned to rent machines can churn the (12.5 to 15 cm) of soil effort on your part. But always the best choice or tilling when the soil dry will break up the

Making New Beds

When you're digging a garden bed in a lawn, begin by marking the bed outline with rope, a garden hose, or string and stakes. Strip off the sod with a flat spade by cutting long, spade-width strips across the width of the bed. Slide your spade under the strips to sever them from the soil. Roll up the turf as you go or remove it in rectangles, and take the bundles to the compost pile. As an alternative, you can kill the grass by covering it with black

1. Set o... area...

Use a broadfork to prepare previously worked beds or to aerate compacted soil before planting.

SOME BA...

---

12 GARDENING WITH ANNUALS AND PERENNIALS

Some Basic Botany

You will probably choose the annuals and perennials for your garden on the basis of the color and fragrance of their flowers. But don't forget to also consider their attractive leaves for those times when they aren't in bloom, and the many decorative seedpods or useful fruits that appear when flowering time is over.

Knowing a little basic botany will not only help you to identify and select the plants that are best suited for your garden. It will also help you to understand how your garden grows, so you can maintain your plants most effectively.

Root System

A plant's root system is vitally important, and certain root systems may be better suited to your soil than others. Roots help to hold the plant firm and stable in the soil and provide it with a system for absorbing water and nutrients. They may also act as storage organs (root vegetables do this), holding nutrients for use during times of vigorous growth or flowering.

Most annuals have a fibrous root system (made up of many fine and branching roots), which does not penetrate deep into the soil. Rather, it tends to remain quite shallow. Because this type of root system does not penetrate particularly deeply, you will need to pay special attention to the water requirements of such plants when rain is scarce.

Some plants, including many of the perennials, have strong central roots, called taproots, that travel straight down in search of water and nutrients. The taproot is a single, thick, tapering organ (a carrot, for example, is actually an

The two basic types of root system: the taproot (left) and fibrous roots (right).

enlarged taproot) with thin branch roots at the side. Taprooted plants can more easily withstand fluctuating soil moisture conditions, but many are more difficult to transplant because their roots tend to penetrate more deeply into the ground and can be very sensitive.

Plant Stems

The stems of your annuals and perennials support the leaves, flowers, and seedpods, and also serve as pathways for movement of nutrients and water between roots and leaves. Just like roots, stems are storage organs, too. Bulbs and corms, from which tulips and gladioli grow, for example, are actually specialized storage stems.

Some plant stems are specially adapted for vegetative reproduction. Stolons (also known as runners) are stems that travel horizontally along the soil surface. At certain intervals along the stolon, new shoots and roots will form, and these give rise to new plants. Sweet violets and dusty miller are examples of plants that produce stolons. Plants such as irises form new plants from underground stems, which are called rhizomes.

anther
filament
stamen
stigma
pistil
style
petal
ovary
sepal
receptacle
peduncle
stem
internode
petiole
node
bud
leaf

Knowing some of the common plant parts, identified here, will help you understand the descriptions you read in books and catalogs.

Simple leaf

Compound leaf

Lobed

Toothed

Entire

Ovate

Linear

Many perennials and some annuals can be propagated by stem cuttings. Swollen buds, or nodes, located along the stems are the sites for new growth. When you take stem cuttings from your plants to make new plants, the new root systems form underground at active nodes on the cutting. See "Propagating Perennials" on page 164 for more on taking cuttings.

Foliage

Among annuals and perennials, you will find every shape, texture, and color of leaf imaginable. Leaves that are whole and undivided, like those of marigolds and coneflowers, are called simple. Leaves divided into two or more parts on the same stalk are called compound. The lacy, finely divided leaves of yarrow, cosmos, and love-in-a-mist are compound leaves. Leaf shape ranges from the long, thin, linear leaves of irises to the eye-shaped, elliptical leaves of petunias and the almost circular nasturtium. They vary in their edges as well as their shapes. A leaf like the forget-me-not with its smooth edge is called entire, those with jagged edges like lemon balm are toothed, and the wavy dusty miller leaf is lobed. Leaves offer a tremendous variety of color, too. It's true that most leaves are green, but there are also the blue-gray of lavender and wormwood. Coleus is available in many brilliantly

This hybrid columbine flower will bring great pleasure to a gardener. But the real reason for its unusual beauty is attracting bees to pollinate it, so it will develop fruit, then seeds, and ultimately, new plants.

colored cultivars, with streaks of orange, red, green, and yellow. Leaves that are striped or blotched with different colors, like those of some geraniums, are called variegated. They also add color and interest to any planting.

Flowers, Fruits, and Seeds

Most plants possess flowers, and those of annuals and perennials bloom in every imaginable color, fragrance, size, and shape. They range from the funnel-like petunia to the radiating coneflowers and daisies, the cup-shaped tulips and peonies to the snapdragons with their protruding lips. But this visual and olfactory feast is not designed for our benefit, but to attract bees, butterflies, and other pollinators to transfer pollen from the anther (the male part) of one flower to the stigma (the female part) of another flower of the same species. If the pollen fertilizes the egg inside the second flower's ovary, the result will be seeds.

The ovary ripens into a fruit, which contains the seeds. Plant fruits vary enormously, just like the flowers they come from. They can be fleshy, like

apples, strawberries, and tomatoes; they can be dry fruits that open when they are finally ripe, such as stock, poppies, and lupines; or they can be dry fruits that don't open, such as sunflowers, corn, and all the nuts. When the fruits finally mature, and not or dry, the seeds are released from the original plant; they can be spread by wind, birds, animals, and humans. If and when conditions are right, the seed will germinate and a new plant will begin to grow.

Plant Growth

A plant depends on light, moisture, temperature, oxygen and other gases, and nutrients, to germinate, grow, and thrive.

Start with the Seed

The first two things a seed needs to grow into a new plant are warmth and water. If the soil is too cold or too dry, the seed remains dormant. Warmth is usually more reliable than water. Soil temperatures don't change as rapidly as air temperatures, so once the soil is warm enough for growth to begin, it usually stays warm enough for growth to continue.

From petunias and flowering tobacco to showy stonecrop and sunflowers, a garden full of annuals and perennials offers a rich diversity of flower color, shape, texture, and smell.

Chapter heading indicates the subject being discussed within a main section.

Gardening tips and detailed suggestions about problems you may encounter and how they can be dealt with.

Photographs of individual plants, showing what they look like when grown in the right conditions.

Botanical name

Family name

Common name

Information about plant

Gardening with Annuals and Perennials

From the first dainty crocuses in early spring to fall's display of brightly colored asters or ornamental cabbages, annuals and perennials provide an endless variety of flowers and forms in an ever-changing display throughout the growing season. Some evergreen perennials even provide interest in the coldest months, and you can bring certain annuals and bulbs indoors in containers for winter bloom. This chapter introduces you to the basics about annuals and perennials—the fun and easy way to add color and beauty to your landscape.

Some Basic Botany

You will probably choose the annuals and perennials for your garden on the basis of the color and fragrance of their flowers. But don't forget to also consider their attractive leaves for those times when they aren't in bloom, and the many decorative seedpods or useful fruits that appear when flowering time is over.

Knowing a little basic botany will not only help you to identify and select the plants that are best suited for your garden. It will also help you to understand how your garden grows, so you can maintain your plants most effectively.

Root System

A plant's root system is vitally important, and certain root systems may be better suited to your soil than others. Roots help to hold the plant firm and stable in the soil and provide it with a system for absorbing water and nutrients. They may also act as storage organs (root vegetables do this), holding nutrients for use during times of vigorous growth or flowering.

Most annuals have a fibrous root system (made up of many fine and branching roots), which does not penetrate deep into the soil. Rather, it tends to remain quite shallow. Because this type of root system does not penetrate particularly deeply, you will need to pay special attention to the water requirements of such plants when rain is scarce.

Some plants, including many of the perennials, have strong central roots, called taproots, that travel straight down in search of water and nutrients. The taproot is a single, thick, tapering organ (a carrot, for example, is actually an

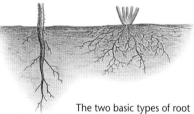

The two basic types of root system: the taproot (left) and fibrous roots (right).

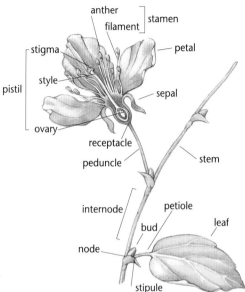

Knowing some of the common plant parts, identified here, will help you understand the descriptions you read in books and catalogs.

enlarged taproot) with thin branch roots at the side. Taprooted plants can more easily withstand fluctuating soil moisture conditions, but many are more difficult to transplant because their roots tend to penetrate more deeply into the ground and can be very sensitive.

Plant Stems

The stems of your annuals and perennials support the leaves, flowers, and seedpods, and also serve as pathways for movement of nutrients and water between roots and leaves. Just like roots, stems are storage organs, too. Bulbs and corms, from which tulips and gladioli grow, for example, are actually specialized storage stems.

Some plant stems are specially adapted for vegetative reproduction. Stolons (also known as rhizomes) are stems that travel horizontally along the soil surface. At certain intervals along the stolon, new shoots and roots will form, and these give rise to new plants. Sweet woodruff and sweet violets are examples of plants that produce stolons. Plants such as irises form new plants from underground stems, which are called rhizomes.

From petunias and flowering tobacco to showy stonecrop and sunflowers, a garden full of annuals and perennials offers a rich diversity of flower color, shape, texture, and smell.

Simple leaf

Compound leaf

Lobed

Toothed

Entire

Ovate

Linear

Many perennials and some annuals can be propagated by stem cuttings. Swollen buds, or nodes, located along the stems are the sites for new growth. When you take stem cuttings from your plants to make new plants, the new root systems form underground at active nodes on the cutting. See "Propagating Perennials" on page 164 for more on taking cuttings.

Foliage

Among annuals and perennials, you will find every shape, texture, and color of leaf imaginable. Leaves that are whole and undivided, like those of marigolds and coneflowers, are called simple. Leaves divided into two or more parts on the same stalk are called compound. The lacy, finely divided leaves of yarrow, cosmos, and love-in-a-mist are compound leaves. Leaf shape ranges from the long, thin, linear leaves of irises to the eye-shaped, elliptical leaves of petunias and the almost circular nasturtium. They vary in their edges as well as their shapes. A leaf like forget-me-not with its smooth edge is called entire, those with jagged edges like lemon balm are toothed, and the wavy dusty miller leaf is lobed. Leaves offer a tremendous variety of color, too. It's true that most leaves are green, but there are also the blue-grays of lavender and wormwood. Coleus is available in many brilliantly colored cultivars, with streaks of orange, red, green, and yellow. Leaves that are striped or blotched with different colors, like those of some geraniums, are called variegated. They also add color and interest to any planting.

This hybrid columbine flower will bring great pleasure to a gardener. But the real reason for its unusual beauty is attracting bees to pollinate it, so it will develop fruit, then seeds, and ultimately, new plants.

Flowers, Fruits, and Seeds

Most plants possess flowers, and those of annuals and perennials bloom in every imaginable color, fragrance, size, and shape. They range from the funnel-like petunia to the radiating coneflowers and daisies, the cup-shaped tulips and peonies to the snapdragons with their protruding lips. But this visual and olfactory feast is not designed for our benefit, but to attract bees, butterflies, and other pollinators to transfer pollen from the anther (the male part) of one flower to the stigma (the female part) of another flower of the same species. If the pollen fertilizes the egg inside the second flower's ovary, the result will be seeds.

The ovary ripens into a fruit, which contains the seeds. Plant fruits vary enormously, just like the flowers they come from. They can be fleshy, like apples, strawberries, and tomatoes; they can be dry fruits that open when they are finally ripe, such as stock, poppies, and lupines; or they can be dry fruits that don't open, such as sunflowers, corn, and all the nuts. When the fruits finally mature, and rot or dry, the seeds are released from the original plant; they can be spread by wind, water, birds, animals, and humans. If and when conditions are right, the seed will germinate and a new plant will begin to grow.

Plant Growth

A plant depends on light, moisture, temperature, oxygen and other gases, and nutrients, to germinate, grow, and thrive.

Start with the Seed

The first two things a seed needs to grow into a new plant are warmth and water. If the soil is too cold or too dry, the seed remains dormant. Warmth is usually more reliable than water. Soil temperatures don't change as rapidly as air temperatures, so once the soil is warm enough for growth to begin, it usually stays warm enough for growth to continue.

These coneflowers grow exuberantly until they are ready to bloom from midsummer onward. Such strong growth depletes the nutrients in the soil, so the edges of the clumps tend to be most vigorous.

roots expand to counterbalance the aboveground parts of the plant. In many cases, the root mass is larger than that of the stems and leaves.

As roots grow, they produce chemical compounds that help make nutrients more soluble and therefore more available to the plant. Throughout their life, roots absorb water and dissolved nutrients from the soil. When they die, the roots add organic matter and nutrients to the soil.

The chemicals that roots produce and the dead cells they shed create an environment that soil microorganisms find attractive. They multiply more rapidly in the root zone than they do in the surrounding soil. As a result, organic matter breaks down faster, making nutrients more available in the soil that the roots touch. More roots encourage more organisms, which release more nutrients into the soil and promote more roots—a productive natural cycle.

Growth and Flowering

As plants grow, the water and nutrients the roots absorb flow up through the plant to the leaves and stems. During a process known as photosynthesis, the leaves and stems convert the water and nutrients to sugars; the sugars then flow down to the

Young seedlings thrive in warm, well-drained soil. By growing them indoors, you control moisture and heat and make sure conditions are just right.

Water is less dependable than warmth. If the soil dries out after germination begins, the young seedling soon dies. Soils with good structure increase the odds that the seed will germinate; the soil particles are fine enough to closely surround the seed, holding moisture against it.

Shoots and Roots

When the seed germinates, it puts out a temporary root, called the primary root, or radicle. The radicle stores some of the food that provides the energy the first aboveground shoot needs to push up

through the soil (the rest of its food is in the seed leaves, which are the leaf-like parts attached to the shoot). The radicle also anchors the plant, so the shoot won't blow or wash away.

About the time the first shoot reaches the soil surface, lateral roots begin to grow from the radicle. Like the radicle, the lateral roots anchor the plant in the soil. Throughout most of the plant's life, the

This geranium has variegated leaves, which do not photosynthesize as effectively as all-green leaves.

roots to be stored as carbohydrates—food energy. Before it flowers and sets seed, the plant uses this energy for growth. While the stems and leaves are growing, the roots rapidly expand through the soil to reach water and nutrients. Once the plant flowers and the seed ripens, root growth slows as more energy is channeled to these demanding processes.

If the plant is an annual, it grows old and dies after the seed ripens. Its decaying roots, leaves, and stems return nutrients to the soil. If the plant is a perennial, it stores carbohydrates in its roots to use to start growing in the spring. Its leaves and stems die back and decay, adding nutrients to the soil to start the cycle over.

There are more than 250 species in the *Aster* genus; the New England aster, or *Aster novae-angliae*, is just one. Knowing the common and botanical names will help you obtain the plants you really want.

What's in a Name?

Botanical names can often tell you something about the plants they identify, such as the flower color or the growth habit. Listed below are some words that you may notice again and again in botanical names, along with their definitions.

Albus: white
Argenteus: silver
Aureus: golden yellow
Caeruleus: blue
Luteus: yellow
Nanus: dwarf
Palustris: swampy, marshy
Perennis: perennial
Prostratus: trailing
Purpureus: purple
Reptans: creeping
Roseus: rosy
Ruber: red
Sempervirens: evergreen
Speciosus: showy
Spinosus: spiny
Variegatus: variegated
Viridis: green
Vulgaris: common

Ajuga

Know Your Plant Names

One of the tricks to growing plants successfully is to learn their names. Members of your neighborhood plant society may understand common names, like bee balm for instance. But if you go to an out-of-town nursery and ask for bee balm, you may only get puzzled stares. Perhaps they call the plant Oswego tea, based on the fact that American pioneers used it as herbal tea. Alternatively, if you are looking for bee balm in a catalog, you may only find it listed under its botanical name, *Monarda didyma*.

You can see from this example that one plant can have a number of common names. Likewise, one common name can apply to several different plants. By getting to know botanical names, you will know exactly which plant you are talking about, planting, or ordering.

Scientists name plants with a system that gives each plant two names. Every naturally occurring plant that is able to reproduce is called a species, and each species is given a two-part name, for example, *Aster novae-angliae*, or New England aster. The word *Aster* indicates the genus (plural "genera") that includes all types of asters;

novae-angliae refers to the particular type of aster called New England aster.

Species may be divided further into subspecies, varieties, and forms. These terms refer to variants of a species that occur in nature. Cultivars, on the other hand, are distinct horticultural types that are selected or produced by breeding under cultivation. For example, the plant *Lavandula angustifolia* 'Munstead' is a cultivar of English lavender. Cultivar names are always placed between single quotation marks. Cultivars are often mistakenly called varieties.

Sometimes plants from different species or genera will cross-pollinate, producing offspring that share the characteristics of both parents. These "new" plants are called hybrids. Hybrids may occur naturally or be man-made. An "x" in a plant's name (as in *Iris* x *germanica* var. *florentina*) usually indicates that the plant is a hybrid.

Botanical names can be easier to remember if you determine what they tell about the plant. Some refer to the person who discovered the plant or to what part of the world it was discovered in; others are descriptive. For instance, *Viola odorata* is the botanical name of sweet violet, which bears an especially fragrant flower.

All About Annuals

One of the great joys of gardening comes from experimenting with different plants. Annuals offer some particularly exciting opportunities. If you're a beginner, you'll be gratified by the success you'll have with many of these easy-to-grow plants. As you gain more experience in flower gardening, you'll enjoy mixing all kinds of annuals with perennials, groundcovers, and other plants to create eye-catching combinations.

Part of the pleasure of growing annuals lies in their versatile natures. No matter where you live or what growing conditions you have to offer, you can find annuals that will thrive where you plant them.

Of course, annuals aren't just grown because they're practical and adaptable: They're beautiful, too! Their flowers come in a rich palette of colors that will suit every gardener's fancy. Some also offer handsome foliage. Others are treasured for their distinctive fragrance, their nostalgic associations, or their charm as cut flowers. And they are the greatest bargains in the gardening world: For the price of one container-grown perennial, you can buy

A restful corner has been lightened and brightened by the addition of annuals—cosmos and alyssum in the foreground, a dense row of larkspur encircling the stone bench in the background. Flowers in containers can be changed according to the season, and ever-popular daylilies give a vivid final note.

enough annual seeds to fill an entire garden bed (and then save the seeds from those plants to grow more each season!). It's difficult to imagine a garden that wouldn't benefit from the addition of a few more annuals.

Understanding Annuals

True annuals germinate, grow, flower, set seed, and then die all in one season. Their goal is to reproduce themselves. This is good news for the gardener, since it means that most annual plants will flower like mad to achieve their goal. Some of the best-known annuals—including petunias and marigolds, poppies and annual phlox—have achieved their great popularity because of their free-flowering

nature. Even better news, if you use tricks such as deadheading (removing the spent flowers) to prevent seed formation, many annuals will step up flower production and continue to bloom well over an extended period until cold weather arrives.

The first hard frost usually kills the plants and signals the end of the bloom season for that year. Although you'll need to replant most annuals the following spring to get another show, some will sprout from seed dropped by this year's plants. See "Reseeding Annuals and Biennials" on page 21 for species that can return for years after just one planting.

Besides these true annuals, there are a number of perennial plants that are often thought of as annuals. These include tropical perennials, such as the many zonal geraniums, or perennials that will flower the first season from seed, such as four o'clocks (*Mirabilis jalapa*). These plants can live for years in frost-free climates, but, like true annuals, they meet their death at the hands of freezing temperatures in cold-winter climates. "Perennial Annuals" on page 18 lists some of the perennial plants that are normally grown as annuals.

Create beautiful seasonal scenes by combining annuals with bulbs that bloom at the same time of the year, like these pansies and tulips.

Forget-me-nots (*Myosotis* spp.) are hardy annuals. You can sow them in early spring, or even in the preceding fall in mild areas.

Kinds of Annuals

Annuals are sometimes further separated into three groups—hardy, half-hardy, and tender—based on their cold tolerance. Some can withstand frost and freezing temperatures; some are quite delicate, and are quickly killed off by being planted out in such conditions. It's useful to know what kind of annuals you're growing because then you'll know how soon you can get away with planting your annuals in the spring. The catalog, seed packet, or plant tag should tell you if your plant is hardy, half-hardy, or tender.

Hardy Annuals Hardy annuals include forget-me-nots (*Myosotis* spp.), pansies, snapdragons, and other plants that can withstand several degrees of freezing temperatures. Almost all of these plants perform best during cool weather. They are often planted out in early spring by gardeners in cold-winter areas or in winter by gardeners in the South and West. Some hardy annuals, such as ornamental kale, are associated with cool fall weather.

Half-hardy Annuals Half-hardy annuals fit somewhere in the middle of hardy and tender. They will often withstand a touch of frost near the beginning or end of the gardening season. Many of the commonly grown annuals fit in this category.

A half-hardy designation is like yellow on a traffic signal: You need to use your judgment to decide when you can plant safely. If your spring has been a bit on the warm side and you're itching to plant—even though your average frost-free day has not yet arrived—you might just get away with planting half-hardy annuals. If you do, though, be prepared to cover them if cold night temperatures are

Marigolds are generally classified as half-hardy annuals. They prefer warm weather but are able to survive a light frost in the fall.

predicted. Consider hedging your bets by planting out only part of your half-hardy seeds or transplants at one time; then wait a week or two to plant the rest.

Tender Annuals Tender annuals, originally from tropical or subtropical climates, can't stand any degree of frost. More than that, they often grow poorly during cold weather and may be stunted by prolonged exposure to temperatures below 50°F (10°C). For best results, wait until late spring to plant tender annuals, such as celosia (*Celosia* spp.) and Joseph's coat (*Amaranthus tricolor*).

Biennials

Biennials have much in common with annuals, but they differ in one major respect: They take 2 years to complete their life cycle rather than the annuals' 1 year. The first year after sowing, they produce a leaf structure, building energy for the next year. The second year they flower, set seed, and die. Common garden biennials include sweet William (*Dianthus barbatus*), honesty (*Lunaria annua*), and foxglove (*Digitalis purpurea*).

Showy petunias bloom from early summer until fall and the first frost. No wonder they are so popular with gardeners, whether massed in beds and borders as here, or used as fillers in established plantings.

Annuals in Your Garden

You could spend a lifetime exploring the rich diversity of annuals. With their range of colors, heights, habits, and bloom times, there are annuals for every purpose and every garden. If you're looking for exciting ways to enjoy these plants in your yard, here are some ideas to get started.

Many beginning gardeners draw their inspiration from public parks and gardens. Few American parks go without the summertime institution of brilliantly colored annuals laid out in formal blocks, rows, or patterns. These eye-catching displays tempt the first-timer to experiment with a few plants at home, almost inevitably lining up their annuals in rows.

Unfortunately, this mimicking of large public plantings is rarely satisfactory in a home garden, since the scale and budget are inevitably much reduced. When you have to pay for the plants, prepare the soil, and maintain the garden, large plantings usually aren't a realistic option. And the formal row arrangements that look fine in a public garden may look awkward and overly formal in a backyard setting.

Rows can be satisfactory for some purposes: along sidewalks leading to the front entrance, as a crisp edging to delineate paths and beds, or for formal displays to match a particular architectural theme. But many of us line things up simply because we don't trust our own design skills. A straight line seems like a safe bet, so we stop there and don't take it any further. But if you're willing to be a little more creative, you'll be amazed at all the fun ways you can add annuals to your landscape.

Annuals Alone

In some places, you may choose to go with a basic bed of annuals only. Plants that have been specially bred or exclusively selected for a certain height or color are ideal for this kind of design. These compact, uniform annuals, which inclue zinnias, dwarf marigolds, and scarlet sage (*Salvia splendens*), readily lend themselves to lines as well as to mass plantings of geometric shapes.

A single color of one annual—massed together—can make an eye-catching landscape accent. This kind of planting is useful for long-distance viewing (such as from the street), for marking

Purple verbenas interweave with red geraniums, while yellow marigolds are grouped behind. The shifting masses of color look effective because plants of similar height have been chosen.

Perennial Annuals

You may be surprised to discover that some of the most popular annuals are actually perennials! The plants listed below are grown as annuals in most climates, but they can live for years in mild or frost-free areas.

Argyranthemum frutescens (marguerite)
Begonia Semperflorens-cultorum hybrid
 (wax begonia)
Bellis perennis (English daisy)
Catharanthus roseus (Madagascar periwinkle)
Dianthus chinensis (China pink)
Erysimum cheiri (wallflower)
Eustoma grandiflorum (prairie gentian)
Gazania hybrids (treasure flower)
Heliotropium arborescens (heliotrope)
Impatiens wallerana (impatiens)
Mirabilis jalapa (four o'clock)
Pelargonium x *hortorum* (zonal geranium)
Rudbeckia hirta (gloriosa daisy)
Salvia farinacea (mealy-cup sage)
Salvia splendens (scarlet sage)
Senecio cineraria (dusty miller)
Solenostemon scutellarioides
 (coleus)
Torenia fournieri
 (wishbone flower)
Verbena x *hybrida*
 (garden verbena)
Viola x *wittrockiana* (pansy)

Pansies

drives or entry gates, or for drawing attention to a door or entryway. But keep in mind that color doesn't have to be shocking to attract attention. The standard American attention-getter—sheets of red geraniums or scarlet sage—definitely has a lot of room for improvement. Expanses of startling color may be exciting for a few weeks, but they aren't particularly easy on the nerves when you have to look at them for month after month. By varying the main color (such as different shades of red and pink) or by adding accents of complementary or contrasting tones (like very pale yellow marigolds with deep purple petunias), the picture becomes more pleasurable throughout the season. "Creating a Color-theme Garden" on page 56 has lots of great ideas you will be able to use to plan your bed and border plantings around your favorite flower colors.

Annuals as Accents

Being fast-growing and relatively inexpensive, annuals are invaluable for providing quick color to new gardens. But don't forget that these yearly visitors can enhance an existing landscape as well. Repeated plantings of a particular type of annual or a certain color can give a note of continuity to the framework of shrubs and trees already established.

Experimenting with new colors and combinations allows a new twist on the theme each year, without the expense of changing the framework itself. Annual additions also enliven established borders of perennials. Purists may object to the inclusion of annuals in their herbaceous plantings (perennial-only plantings). But there's no law against it so why limit your options? While compact bedding plants may look awkward alongside larger perennials, many annuals have an airy grace that earns them a place among the most beautiful border plants. Foxgloves (*Digitalis purpurea*), hollyhocks (*Alcea rosea*), and black-eyed Susans (*Rudbeckia hirta*) are a few of the many annuals and biennials that make fine partners for perennials. As a bonus, long-blooming

Toadflax (*Linaria* spp.) is a fast-growing, bushy annual. It gives a long and colorful display, making it very useful as a bedding plant.

annuals can provide a steady supply of color to fill in as perennial companions come into and go out of flower.

When deciding what to grow with your annuals, though, don't just stop with perennials. In an "everything goes" cottage garden, you can combine annuals with all kinds of other plants—bulbs, shrubs, grasses, herbs, trees, and whatever else looks good to you. There are no rules here; simply put each plant where it will thrive and complement its neighbors. Annual flowers are also a fun addition to a traditional vegetable garden, adding a bit of color or filling in after early-season crops are harvested. Some annuals, such as nasturtiums, sunflowers, and scarlet runner beans (*Phaseolus coccineus*), even have good flavor to match their good looks. For more fun ideas on incorporating annuals into your garden, see "Beds and Borders, Screens and Fillers" on page 62.

Combining different colors of the same plant adds variety and excitement to this mass planting of nemesia, a tender annual grown for its beautiful flowers.

This patio garden with arch and pond has pots full of annuals scattered amongst shrubs, ornamental grasses, and vines. They work as brief, seasonal highlights, adding interest to the established design.

Annuals, such as the petunias and licorice plant (*Helichrysum petiolatum*) here, combine well with evergreen shrubs planted in containers.

your garden, or change the plantings to set a new mood. Instead of combining several different plants in one container, group several smaller pots of individual plants. This is a good way to group colors, pick up predominant colors from nearby beds, or try out new color combinations. For more ideas, see "Growing a Container Garden" on page 72.

Annuals for Scented Gardens

For many gardeners, fragrance is an important consideration when deciding which annuals to grow and where to put

If you enjoy fragrant flowers, tuck sweet peas and other scented annuals in your beds and borders. They make lovely fresh cut flowers, too.

Annuals in Containers

One of the easiest and most popular ways to bring excitement to any garden is with containers. These plantings may vary from year to year and even season to season. Pansies can dominate in cool weather, for instance, while ageratums or geraniums take over during the heat of summer.

A large pot or tub, overflowing with a carefully selected variety of flowering and foliage plants, is a classic way to show off annuals. Even with small containers, you can make hundreds of different combinations to liven up decks, patios, and balconies. You can have multiple pots that repeat the same theme throughout

Need a screen to block a view until you can put in a hedge or fence? Try tall annuals or biennials such as foxgloves (*Digitalis purpurea*).

them. Sweet alyssum (*Lobularia maritima*) smells of honey on a hot afternoon, while night-scented stock (*Matthiola longipetala* subsp. *bicornis*) wafts a sweet scent on an evening breeze. Scented blooms are also delightful in containers or beds sited near windows or outdoor sitting areas. If you usually spend your summer evenings outdoors, you might want to concentrate on evening-scented blooms; if you're only outdoors during the day, flowers that are fragrant during the evening may not be useful to you. "Flowers for Fragrance" on page 86 offers more tips on choosing scented flowers and foliage that are right for your needs and your garden.

Annuals for Cut Flowers

If you enjoy bringing your garden flowers indoors, consider starting a separate cutting garden. That way, you can have a generous supply of flowers for cutting without raiding your more visible displays. Annuals that are good for cutting produce lots of flowers and last well indoors; these include zinnias, snapdragons, cosmos, pot marigolds (*Calendula officinalis*), China aster (*Callistephus chinensis*), and rocket larkspur (*Consolida ambigua*). Scented flowers also make a delightful inclusion in any arrangement. So-called everlasting flowers—such as statice (*Limonium sinuatum*), globe amaranth (*Gomphrena globosa*), and strawflowers (*Bracteantha bracteata*)—are an important part of many cutting gardens, since their beauty lives on into the winter in dried arrangements. For more information on growing and harvesting annuals for arrangements, see "Creating a Cutting Garden" on page 76.

Annuals for Garden Challenges

Annuals are adaptable and quite easy to grow, making them the ideal solution for all kinds of challenges that your garden may throw at you. If you have just moved into a house, for example, you could fill the garden with annuals for a year or two while you decide on your long-term plans for the landscape. Or if you rent a home with a plot of ground, growing annuals will allow you to enjoy flower gardening without the more permanent investment in perennials. Annuals are great for city gardens, since they can make the most of compact spaces and give quick results in less-than-ideal growing sites. Tall annuals or biennials such as foxgloves and hollyhocks and annual vines such as morning glory are also excellent as temporary screens to hide unsightly views, objectionable fences, stumps, or neighbors' yards; see "Screens and Fillers" on page 66 for more ideas on using these plants effectively.

Reseeding Annuals and Biennials

Many gardeners count on self-sowing annuals and biennials for perennial pleasures. Far from being a nuisance, these reliable repeaters delight many gardeners with their perseverance and their ability to pop up in the most unexpected places. Exactly which plants will self-sow depends on your region, but the ones listed below are some of the most dependable reseeders.

Four-o'-clocks

Alcea rosea (hollyhock)
Amaranthus caudatus (love lies bleeding)
Calendula officinalis (pot marigold)
Centaurea cyanus (cornflower)
Cleome hasslerana (cleome)
Consolida ambigua (rocket larkspur)
Coreopsis tinctoria (calliopsis)
Cosmos bipinnatus (cosmos)
Digitalis purpurea (foxglove)
Eschscholzia californica (California poppy)
Helianthus annuus (common sunflower)
Iberis umbellata (annual candytuft)
Impatiens balsamina (garden balsam)
Ipomoea tricolor (morning glory)

Lobularia maritima (sweet alyssum)
Lunaria annua (honesty)
Mirabilis jalapa (four o'clock)
Myosotis sylvatica (forget-me-not)
Nicotiana alata (flowering tobacco)
Nigella damascena (love-in-a-mist)
Papaver rhoeas (corn poppy)
Portulaca grandiflora (rose moss)
Sanvitalia procumbens (creeping zinnia)
Tanacetum parthenium (feverfew)
Tithonia rotundifolia (Mexican sunflower)
Tropaeolum majus (nasturtium)
Verbascum bombyciferum (mullein)
Zinnia angustifolia (narrow-leaved zinnia)
Zinnia elegans (zinnia)

Perennial Favorites

A spring border of perennials, which includes polyanthus primroses and paper daisies, makes an eye-catching display under the blossoms of an established magnolia tree.

Gardening with perennials is a joy that everyone can share. Whether your garden is large or small, sunny or shady, wet or dry, a wide variety of perennials will thrive there and provide you with beauty for years to come.

Hollyhocks are short-lived perennials. However, they make up for a brief life span by self-sowing so prolifically they are often grown as annuals.

Understanding Perennials

Let's begin by establishing just what we mean by "perennial." Perennial plants live and bloom for more than two growing seasons. Many will survive a decade or longer if planted in the right location; hardy perennials come back year after year, so you don't have to buy and replant them each spring. But even the short-lived plants are worth growing. For instance, blanket flowers (*Gaillardia* x *grandiflora*) bloom vigorously for a long portion of the summer, although they seldom return more than two years. Other perennials, such as columbines (*Aquilegia* spp.) and hollyhocks (*Alcea rosea*), have a short natural life span, but set seed that replaces the parent plant; the latter may be grown as an annual because of this. Occasionally, a biennial plant like foxglove (*Digitalis purpurea*) or sweet William (*Dianthus barbatus*), which normally grows foliage the first year and flowers the second, will live on for the third year. Despite their different life spans, you can call all these plants perennials. Most bulbs—including tulips, daffodils, hyacinths, and crocuses—are also perennials; they are discussed in greater detail in "Bountiful Bulbs" on page 28. Bulbs go dormant after flowering, freeing up space for annuals or maturing perennial plants to thrive.

Identifying perennials by their two-year life span may seem reasonably tidy, but the definition gets more complicated. This is because trees and shrubs are also perennials. However, they are exempted from our definition because they develop woody stems and limbs. With the exception of tree peonies (*Paeonia suffruticosa*) and a few other plants, perennial garden plants are herbaceous, which means they lack woody stems. In most cases, the foliage of perennials dies back down to the underground roots each dormant season. A few perennials, like rock cresses (*Arabis* spp.) and coral bells (*Heuchera* spp.), have evergreen foliage that persists through the winter.

Unlike annuals, most perennials only flower for a short while (days or weeks) each season. But many do offer attractive forms and foliage, so they look almost as good out of bloom as they do in bloom. Nor do they have to be replanted every year; these beauties come back on their

The arresting blues and architectural stature of delphiniums make them a fine accent when planted amidst red and white rose bushes.

own. They are cheaper than most trees and shrubs, and they're relatively simple to move or dig up and replace if you want to change the look and layout of your yard. Perennials are dependable and easy choices for beginners, and they come in enough variety to satisfy even the most experienced gardener.

Perennials in Your Garden

Now that you know what a perennial is, you can start to explore the many possibilities of incorporating them into your garden. With thousands of species and cultivars to choose from, there's a good chance that you'll find plenty of plant forms, leaf textures, and flower colors and shapes to fit the garden you have in mind. Any yard—large or small, sunny or shady—can be accented with perennials. A few clusters of perennial flowers will bring colorful highlights to drab corners; a garden full of perennials will become a landscape highlight. You can use perennials as accents, focal points, masses of color, or scenes of change.

Don't make the mistake of thinking that your flowering perennials should be separate from the rest of the landscape. To get the most enjoyment and the greatest effect from these plants, you first need to establish a garden size and shape that looks natural in your landscape and also fits in well with the existing elements, like buildings and trees. Then choose perennials with colors, textures, and forms that enhance your entire landscape. By combining your perennials with annuals, biennials, shrubs, and trees in the one glorious garden, you will be able to enjoy the benefits of each kind of plant while minimizing any of their drawbacks. For example, plant early-blooming perennials like irises and peonies with annuals like cleomes (*Cleome* spp.) and cosmos, which start blooming in

Of the very many different types of perennials, dahlias are but one. These bulbs bloom from midsummer through fall in almost every color of the rainbow except blue. The bright yellow sunflowers are annuals.

early summer and carry on until frost. Use large sweeps of bold perennials in beds and borders beside the lawn, beneath openings in trees, and in front of hedges and shrub plantings. Put smaller clumps of dramatic perennials in strategic locations to highlight the entrance to walks, the location of a door, or the view from a

window. Consider nesting a trio of three gold-centered, broad-leaved hostas (such as *Hosta* 'Gold Standard') at either side of the entrance of a woodland path. Or use a clump of common torch lilies (*Kniphofia uvaria*) to frame the top of a drive. A stand of irises is an attractive feature near a Japanese bridge in a water garden.

A clump of Siberian iris provides an elegant contrast to the bright green foliage of the trees behind and the splash of orange in front.

Seasonal Change

One of the most delightful features of perennials is their ability to change throughout the season—growing and spreading, passing into and out of bloom, and sometimes even coloring up nicely in fall or producing seed heads to stand over winter. The changeable quality of perennials can add life to an otherwise boring planting, such as a row of evergreens or a mass of annuals.

Succession of bloom is one reason the changeable nature of perennials is so appealing. By mapping out a garden plan and selecting the plants you will use carefully, you can have perennials blooming throughout the growing season, from early spring to late fall. You can arrange your garden so that there are some flowers, seed heads, or foliage of interest

A mixture of pink and white perennials—lilies, common rose mallow, and bellflowers—come into bloom in summer, amidst a background of purple and green foliage, to create a lovely show.

at any time during the growing season. Let the beauty of the flowers create a shifting sequence of harmonies and contrasts. Spring might be rich with purple violets and yellow primroses. In early summer, the garden could be ripe with red peonies and violet-blue Siberian iris (*Iris sibirica*). In late summer this might change to purple coneflowers (*Echinacea purpurea*), ivory chrysanthemums, and pink Japanese anemones (*Anemone* x *hybrida*).

Before and after the flowers, let the show continue with the beauty of foliage and form alone. Enjoy the excitement of watching the plants grow and thrive, from the first shoots to the much-anticipated blooms. Note how the flower stalks rise gracefully over the foliage or peep from between the stems. Watch the leaves late in the season, as they ripen to bronze or lemon, then disappear.

Perennial Style

Perennials look lovely when grouped into individual beds and borders, but they also make wonderfully flexible tools for

Geometry and symmetry are the hallmarks of a formal garden where clipped borders of English lavender are planted under standard roses.

decorating all parts of your landscape. Small perennials can enliven a deck or patio; others are large enough to screen your unsightly objects such as trash cans, which you don't want to see from the patio. Depending on where you place your perennials, you can make a small yard seem bigger or divide a large yard into intimate, comfortable spaces, or rooms. A winding path lined with foliage plants or flowers can create a little bit of mystery and lead people to a seat in the shade, a small sculpture, or a wonderful view.

Perennials can be used to create flower gardens of many different moods, whether traditional or nontraditional in design style. This can include formal gardens, cottage gardens, herbaceous borders, island beds, and cutting gardens. They can also be used to make the most of the conditions your site has to offer with special gardens for meadows, woodlands, and rocky areas. Whether your site is dry or wet, sunny or shady, there's a garden style that's just right for you.

Formal Gardens

Historically, formal gardens were only found on large estates, where there was plenty of space to lay out vast geometric patternings of neatly clipped plants. But today, this style of garden is spreading into smaller yards. Formal beds mimic the

A spring bed of pink tulips and yellow primroses gives a display of vivid contrasting colors. The use of perennials or annuals under bulbs looks much more attractive than leaving the soil bare or mulched.

prevailing angles of houses and patios, blending in where space is too limited to soften the scene with curving lines.

Formal gardens are usually laid out in squares or rectangles with low hedges of clipped boxwood, hollies, or other evergreens. Plant the beds symmetrically, using the same sequence of perennials and edging plants on either side of a central axis. Make your own patterns with lines, angles, and curving rows. Choose plants carefully—limit your selection to those perennials that will stay in place and keep a uniform height and neat appearance. Try new cultivars developed for their uniformity, such as 'Moonbeam' thread-leaved coreopsis (*Coreopsis verticillata* 'Moonbeam'), 'Stella de Oro' daylily, and 'Blue Clips' tussock bellflower.

If the classic formal garden is too rigid for your taste, you can always take a more modern approach. Plant sections of the garden with a touch of informality by maintaining the basic geometric shapes of the formal section but softening the angles with creeping and trailing edgers.

Daylilies are hardy plants that produce showy, colorful blooms in a range of different climates.

Cottage Gardens

The classic cottage garden is an eclectic collection of plants, including perennials, annuals, herbs, and roses, allowed to ramble and intertwine. Cottage gardens usually are at least partially enclosed within walls, hedges, or fences, making them a natural choice for a small suburban house or a modern townhouse with an enclosed yard. You might allow the plants to spread unchecked or to self-sow, letting the seedlings arise where they may. For this to work well, though, you must be willing to do some pulling up and rearranging if the new arrivals pop up where they're not wanted. Unify the scene with a permanent focal point, such as a path that marches through the garden's center to a door, patio, or bench.

Perennial Borders

Borders are the most popular and versatile of all the ways to grow perennials. A border is a planting area that edges or frames another feature of the garden. It may separate the

lawn from a hedge, fence, steps, deck, or wooded area; set off a path from the lawn or the driveway; or divide the vegetable garden from the lawn. Be sure to look at the transition areas in your property to find potential areas for borders.

Most perennial borders are designed to be viewed primarily from the front. It's best if you set the shorter plants in the foreground and the taller plants in the back. You can plant a border exclusively with perennials to produce what is known as an herbaceous border. Or add structure, excitement, and four-season interest by creating a mixed border of woody plants, bulbs, and annuals as well as perennials.

A cottage garden gives a loose, casual effect by the careful selection and positioning of plants.

This border has an informal feel, with common thrift hanging over the pathway while lupines stand tall at the rear.

Island beds will be viewed from all sides. When planting them, it's a good idea to set the tallest annuals and perennials toward the center of the bed and the shorter ones along the outside.

Island Beds

Unlike borders, which are usually seen from one side, island beds are designed for you to walk around them and see them from all different angles. Because they are located away from structures like houses and fences, island beds are exposed to maximum sun and air penetration. As a result, plant stems are stockier and need less staking, and the garden tends to be healthier and easier to maintain.

Locate your island bed in some open situation, but don't just plunk the bed down in the middle of the lawn. Like a border, you must tie it in with existing permanent structures to make it look good. Use an island bed to create an oasis of color in the back corner of the yard, to echo the shape of shrub groupings elsewhere in the lawn, or as a "welcome garden" at the foot of the drive.

The Cutting Garden

Many perennials produce flowers and foliage that are ideal for indoor use in arrangements. You can snip a few flowers from your perennial borders, but if you take too many the garden will look bare. To have lots of flowers for picking, grow a utilitarian garden just for cutting. You don't need a fancy design or a particular shape—pick a suitable spot and line up your plants in rows, just as you would for vegetables. Cage the stems of floppy perennials like delphiniums and dahlias with a wire grid or stake to keep them supported and straight. Add annuals and bulbs to your cutting garden to round out your choice of materials for arrangements.

Meadow Gardens

Natural gardens combine the beauty of local wildflowers with an informal, often low-maintenance, design. The most popular of these are meadow gardens that feature durable, sun-loving flowers. If you don't have room for a whole meadow, you can easily create a meadow look in a smaller garden by using plenty of reliable cultivated perennials and then mixing in meadow flowers and grasses among them. Common perennials that are natural choices for most meadow gardens include butterfly weed (*Asclepias tuberosa*), New England aster (*Aster novae-angliae*), purple coneflower (*Echinacea purpurea*), and bee balm (*Monarda didyma*). Look in wildflower gardening books or check with local wildflower societies to find out which plants grow best in your area.

Once you've chosen the plants that will be in your meadow, you'll need to help them gain a roothold by preparing a good seedbed. You can't just scatter seed in a lawn or an open piece of ground and

ABOVE: Versatile, easy-to-grow clumps of orange coneflower can be used in formal or informal beds or borders, cottage gardens, and even meadows.
BELOW: A meadow of wildflowers is an excellent option for brightening up out-of-the-way corners.

expect good results. You'll also need to keep the soil moist at the time when the seeds are germinating, and weed regularly for the first few years. Once the meadow is established, a yearly mowing in late winter will help control those woody plants that would otherwise overwhelm the perennial flowers. Beyond that, you can let these perennials grow and mingle as they will.

Container Gardens

Take a break from petunias and grow perennials in containers instead. Potted perennials are great as accents for steps, decks, and patios, especially in small gardens. Compact, long-blooming, and drought-tolerant perennials make natural choices for containers. Some perennials for containers include 'Stella de Oro' daylily and the Galaxy series of yarrow (*Achillea* 'Galaxy Series'). Or try spring-blooming bleeding heart (*Dicentra spectabilis*); when it goes dormant in the heat of summer, cover it with annuals. Containers dry out more quickly than gardens, so you may need to water daily during the hot, dry parts of the summer.

A bog garden is a great site for many kinds of irises. The flowers are beautiful in early summer, and the spiky leaves look good all season.

Rock Gardens

Some perennials are particularly attractive grouped among rocks in a wall or rock garden. These are the plants that have evolved to grow best in full sun and soils that have exceptionally good drainage and low fertility. Some, such as perennial candytuft (*Iberis sempervirens*), wall rock cress (*Arabis caucasica*), and basket of gold (*Aurinia saxatilis*), cascade gracefully over the rock surface. Others, like the more petite Labrador violets (*Viola labradorica*) and primroses (*Primula* spp.), as well as a host of unusual alpine plants, nestle in between the rocks. All of these plants are delightful choices for planting on rocky slopes, in raised beds, or in the crevices of drystone retaining walls.

Bog Gardens

Some perennials have an affinity for wet ground and will thrive at the edge of a pond or in boggy or marshy areas. Perennials for low, moist areas include Japanese iris (*Iris ensata*), goat's beard (*Aruncus dioicus*), turtlehead (*Chelone* spp.), marsh marigold (*Caltha palustris*), and cardinal flower (*Lobelia cardinalis*).

If you already have a pond or wet spot, a bog garden is the solution. If you don't have a naturally wet area but enjoy bog plants, you can create your own bog. Dig a trench at least 12 inches (30 cm) deep and line it with a heavy plastic pond liner. Put

a soaker hose on the top of the plastic and refill the trench with humus-rich soil. The open end of the hose should protrude slightly so that you can attach it to your garden hose and fill the "bog" with water. Repeat as necessary to keep the soil moist.

Woodland Gardens

If you have a wooded lot with lots of lovely, large trees, take advantage of their shade to create a woodland garden. To brighten the area in early spring (before the trees leaf out and shade the area), try early-blooming woodland wildflowers like wood anemone (*Anemone nemorosa*), wild columbine (*Aquilegia canadensis*), Virginia bluebell (*Mertensia virginica*), and common bleeding heart (*Dicentra spectabilis*). To extend the season of interest, add ferns and shade-tolerant perennials that retain their foliage all season. These include hostas, Lenten rose (*Helleborus orientalis*), Siberian bugloss (*Brunnera macrophylla*), Solomon's seal (*Polygonatum odoratum*), and lungwort (*Pulmonaria saccharata*).

Start the spring season early with a container full of cold-tolerant primroses and daffodils, with a few pansies added to the mix as well.

Shady nooks provide a cool, peaceful refuge that hellebores like. Water them regularly for the first few years; after that, they'll tolerate dry shade.

Bountiful Bulbs

Beautiful and versatile, bulbs are one type of perennial that belong in every landscape. Many of the popular bulbs—including daffodils, crocus, hyacinths, and tulips—are traditionally associated with spring gardens. But with a little planning, you can have bulbs in bloom in your garden from late winter through midfall. And to fill the few months that bulbs aren't blooming outdoors, you can bring some types indoors and enjoy their vividly colored flowers all winter long.

Understanding Bulbs

There's a time and place in the garden for nearly every bulb. The dainty blooms of early bulbs such as crocus and snowdrops (*Galanthus* spp.) signal the beginning of the gardening season with their arrival. Daffodils, tulips, and other larger bulbs are the epitome of the spring garden, while gladioli, lilies, and others strut their stuff in the summer. Some, including fall crocus (*Colchicum autumnale*) and hardy cyclamen (*Cyclamen hederifolium*), flower very late, marking the transition to winter temperatures despite their fragile, spring-like appearance. If you choose carefully, you can have bulbs blooming in your garden nearly the whole year round!

Bulbs flower at different times because they are naturally adapted to different growing conditions. Learning a little about how bulbs grow and the various kinds of bulbs will help you to understand more about growing these colorful and versatile plants in your garden.

How Bulbs Grow

Over time, bulbs have developed in their own unique way to cope with particular environments. A bulbous plant stores energy and water below ground in an enlarged root or stem. This storage area allows the plant to grow and flower when the growing conditions are favorable and to ride out unfavorable weather in a dormant state.

Tulips, for example, evolved on the high plains of western Asia. Between the hot, dry summers and freezing winters, a tulip takes advantage of the two mildest seasons. It roots in fall, relying on late rains to pump moisture into the bulb.

There are thousands of tulip cultivars, here planted with daffodils. They bloom at different times, so you can enjoy them all through spring.

Aboveground growth begins in early spring, often before cold weather has completely retreated. Melting snow waters the emerging buds, and bright sunshine stimulates the leaves to store energy

A dense planting of grape hyacinths creates a path of purple, broken only by groupings of multicolored tulips, yellow crown imperials, and white spring daisies.

Tulips rise above a carpet of red wallflowers. Make the most of your space by underplanting tall bulb flowers with low-growing annuals.

depleted by the flowering process. As hot, dry weather arrives, the bulb goes back into a dormant state.

Of course, bulbous plants come from environments all around the globe, so they don't all behave in the same manner. Some may be stimulated to grow by the return of the rainy season; others respond to the warmth of spring or summer. While you don't need to know exactly which conditions encourage a particular bulb to bloom, it's helpful to realize that all your bulbs will go through some kind of seasonal cycle of growth and dormancy. The individual entries in the "Guide to Popular Perennials," starting on page 202, will explain the cycle for each bulb, so you'll know when to plant, when to expect flowers, and when to divide or move the bulbs you've chosen.

Kinds of Bulbs

The many different plants that have underground storage structures are grouped together under the general term "bulbs." But technically speaking, these underground structures take on several forms, which include true bulbs, corms, tubers, and rhizomes.

True Bulbs True bulbs, such as tulips, daffodils, lilies, and hyacinths, must reach a particular size before they can flower. A full-size bulb contains layers of food-storing scales

bulb

surrounding a tiny flower, formed during the previous growing season. If it has sufficient water, nutrients, and light, the bulb will blossom reliably the first year; this makes true bulbs a good choice for beginning gardeners. Encouraging true bulbs—especially some tulips—to bloom in subsequent years can sometimes be a little trickier. The growing requirements are quite specific, and vary for different species, but most true bulbs are easy to grow and maintain for years.

True bulbs reproduce by two methods: by seed and by bulblets produced at the base of the mother bulb (or, in the case of some lilies, in the leaf axils of the stem).

Corms Corms, such as those of crocus or gladioli, resemble true bulbs on the outside. Cut one open, however, and you'll discover a major difference. The corm is solid—a reservoir full of energy without an embryonic flower inside. Under favorable conditions, a corm draws on its stockpile of food to produce leaves and flowers from growth buds on the top of the corm. As it grows, a corm exhausts its resources and often, but not always, grows a new corm to replace the old one. Corms also reproduce by forming small new corms, called cormlets or cormels, around the main corm.

corm

Tubers Like corms, tubers are solid storage structures. But unlike corms, which form roots only at the bottom, tubers can sprout roots from "eyes" (buds) scattered over their surface. The one tuber everyone knows is the potato. Most other tubers bear a resemblance to it, although some may be flatter or thinner. Caladiums and tuberous begonias grow from tubers. Dahlias grow from similar structures, which are called tuberous roots.

Most tubers originated in areas where summer

tuber

Lilies grow from scaly bulbs. You may notice that the bulbs have fleshy roots when you buy them; other bulbs shouldn't have roots.

temperatures are fairly warm and rainfall is plentiful. They can adapt to a whole range of conditions as long as they have warmth and sufficient moisture. Many will not survive in frozen ground, however, so it's important to remember to dig them up in fall and store them indoors over winter. Most tubers can be cut or broken into pieces to increase your stock of a plant; just make sure each piece has one or more eyes so it can produce new shoots.

Rhizomes A rhizome is a fleshy, creeping stem that is sometimes visible at ground level but is often hidden underground. Roots are produced on the undersides of each rhizome. Perhaps the most easily recognized rhizome belongs to the old-fashioned bearded iris; other examples include the tender cannas and calla lilies (*Zantedeschia aethiopica*).

To plant most rhizomes, place them horizontally just below the soil surface, so the roots can easily grow down into the soil. You can increase rhizomes very easily by simply cutting them into pieces and then replanting them.

rhizome

Daffodils are traditional favorites for adding color to spring gardens. Pair them with a carpet of forget-me-nots to add sparkle to beds and borders.

Later-blooming bulbs such as lilies and dahlias add height and color to mid- and late-season borders. "Beds and Borders, Screens and Fillers" on page 62 lists more ideas on using bulbs in flower gardens.

Bulbs for Flower Arrangements and for Fragrance

Madonna lilies (*Lilium candidum*), tuberoses (*Polianthes tuberosa*), hyacinths, along with some other bulbs, are renowned for the sweet fragrances that they offer. Their scents are delightful both outdoors and indoors. But be sure to use moderation when cutting these flowers for arrangements; a single bloom can pleasantly scent a room, but a mass of them can be overpowering.

Even without fragrance, many hardy and tender bulbs can be enjoyed indoors in arrangements, so make sure you include them in your cutting garden. Start the season with tulips and daffodils, followed by summer snowflake (*Leucojum aestivum*) and lilies, as well as gladioli and dahlias. In the South, you can even grow amaryllis (*Hippeastrum* hybrids) outdoors for cut flowers. "Creating a Cutting Garden" on page 76 offers more details for growing and handling bulbs for cutting.

Bulb Magic

Like annuals, bulbs are often used in masses in large-scale landscapes. While it's difficult to re-create those grand displays found in public parks when you have limited space and money, well-chosen bulbs can create equally stunning effects in many parts of the home garden.

Bulbs in Beds and Borders

It's hard to beat bulbs for early color. What could be more welcome to a winter-weary gardener than a patch of brightly colored crocus by the back door? While bulb flowers are pretty on their own, you can also combine them with other early-blooming perennials or shrubs to create stunning effects, such as a golden flood of daffodils beneath a blooming forsythia. Many spring-blooming bulbs enliven planted areas beneath trees before the trees have leafed out. The bulbs finish just as the shade-loving ferns, hostas, or annuals come into their own.

Bulbs are especially useful when tucked into perennial plantings, because they will get the bloom season off to an early start. And summer beds make a great place for showcasing tender bulbs, such as cannas and gladioli, among annuals or perennials.

TOP LEFT: Create a pretty spring picture by combining snowdrops with the lovely foliage of Italian arum.
BOTTOM LEFT: Mix bulbs with annuals and perennials to create beautiful color-theme plantings. White tulips stand out in the midst of a silver-and-white garden, which looks crisp and clean all day long.
TOP RIGHT: Purple hyacinths have a rich, sweet scent that will waft through your garden and linger in your house when used in arrangements. Tulips, though unscented, make a lovely cut flower, too.

Large pots can hold an entire garden. This shallow planter supports daffodils and hyacinths, as well as some primroses.

Bulbs in Containers

Bulbs are perfect for pots, either alone to give a touch of spring color or combined with annuals or perennials for a longer season of interest. They can also be potted up in fall for later indoor pleasure. Tender bulbs, such as amaryllis and paperwhite narcissus, are very easy to grow and flower on the windowsill with little fussing. Hardy bulbs, such as tulips and hyacinths, need to be potted and chilled for several months to give them a condensed form of winter before bringing them inside. This process is known as "forcing," although the bulbs aren't forced to do anything except bloom a bit ahead of schedule, either in the house or on the patio. Depending on where you live, there are different methods of forcing bulbs; you'll find details in "Forcing Bulbs" on page 74.

Bulbs in Lawns and Woodlands

Naturalizing—planting bulbs in random, natural-looking drifts under trees, lawns, meadows, or unmanicured woodsy areas—is another fun way to add bulbs to your yard. Look for species and selections that are described as good for naturalizing; almost all daffodils and crocuses qualify, as do grape hyacinths (*Muscari* spp.), Siberian squill (*Scilla sibirica*), and Spanish bluebells (*Hyacinthoides hispanicus*). It's easy and low maintenance to do, and the results look better and better every year as the bulbs multiply to produce even more blooms.

Naturalized bulbs are often best in less high-visibility areas, where you can enjoy the blooms but not be bothered by the sight of the ripening leaves. Space bulbs in irregular patterns for the most natural look, and plant lots of them so you'll see them from a distance. More information on this process is in "Making a Meadow Garden" on page 78. Very early bulbs, such as spring crocus, are sometimes naturalized in lawns to provide color. You may have to put off the first spring mowing for a week or two to let the bulb foliage turn yellow, but after that you can mow as usual. Fall-blooming bulbs can also look good in grassy areas, but you'll have to stop mowing in late summer, as soon as you see the flower buds beginning to sprout from the soil.

Create a sea of spring color by planting some crocus in your lawn. They will spread and naturalize as the years pass, but be sure not to mow until the crocus leaves have yellowed.

Blooming Bulbs through the Year

With some planning, you can have bulbs blooming with your perennials from spring through fall. Below is an approximate bloom schedule for gardens in Zone 6. Zone 3 gardens are usually a good 2 weeks later; gardens in Zone 8 and warmer parts of Zone 7 are about 1 week earlier. (If you're not sure which zone you live in, check on the USDA Plant Hardiness Zone Map on page 276.)

Species crocus (including *Crocus tommasinianus*): early March
Snowdrops (*Galanthus* spp.): early March
Reticulated iris (*Iris reticulata*): early March
Dutch crocus (*Crocus vernus* hybrids): late March
Early daffodils: late March to early April
Species tulips: April
Grape hyacinths (*Muscari* spp.): mid-April
Siberian squill (*Scilla sibirica*): mid-April
Daffodils and narcissus: late April
Hyacinths: late April
Crown imperial (*Fritillaria imperialis*): late April
Hybrid tulips: late April to May
Giant onion (*Allium giganteum*): early summer
Lilies: early to late summer
Autumn crocuses (*Colchicum* and *Crocus* spp.): early fall to midfall
Hardy cyclamen (*Cyclamen* spp.): fall or early spring

Crown imperials

Understanding Your Garden

You may have some idea of what you want from plants, but do you know what kind of growing conditions you have to give them? A new garden will get off to a successful start if you take stock of your growing conditions, including the soil, topography, and exposure of your garden, and your local climate. These factors will have a great effect in determining which annuals and perennials will grow well in your garden, as well as how and where you plant them.

Study the Soil

Gardening can be a breeze if you have deep, fertile soil that is rich in organic matter. But even if you don't (and very few gardeners do), you can still have a beautiful garden. Developing and then maintaining healthy garden soil is a critical part of establishing thriving annuals and perennials. You must balance the mineral and organic components of your soil to provide the air, water reserves, and nutrients needed by plants and other living organisms. You can improve the soil you have—by adding organic matter or building raised beds, for instance—and you can also look for plants that are adapted to your conditions. Either way, you'll need to know a few basic things about the soil you're starting with.

The soil in this lush spring garden obviously provides the right conditions for bluebells, forget-me-nots, and rhododendrons.

Soil Composition

Sand, silt, and clay—all the mineral elements that make up your soil—are categorized by size. Sands are the largest mineral particles. A coarse grain of sand can be as big as 1 millimeter in diameter; finer sand may dwindle down to one-tenth that size. Sand particles are found irregularly in the soil. They leave loose, air-rich pockets, called pore spaces, that allow water and dissolved nutrients to drain away. Consequently, sandy soils tend to be dry and infertile. Clay particles, the ultrafine elements, are about 1,000 times smaller than sand. They can pack together to make a tight, water- and nutrient-rich but poorly oxygenated soil. Between sand and clay are the medium-sized silt particles, from 0.05 to 0.002 millimeters in diameter. They are intermediate in their effects on water retention and aeration.

Soil Texture

Most soils are a mix of the three different particle groups. The ideal soil texture for most annuals and perennials is a loam, with a ratio of 40 percent sand, 40 percent silt, and 20 percent clay. Loam drains quickly, but not so quickly that plant roots cannot absorb water and nutrients. And the pores between the soil particles hold enough air for roots to be able to get enough oxygen for their needs.

As the percentages shift in any direction, gardening becomes more challenging. Loose sandy soils, which have at least 35 percent sand, don't hold water and nutrients well and so they'll need more frequent watering

Sandy soil loses nutrients and water quickly.

Clayey soil drains slowly but holds nutrients well.

Silty soil can become packed and drain poorly.

and fertilizing. You can pick plants that are adapted to drier, infertile soil. And remember, too, that these soils are good for slowing the growth rate of vigorous plants and reducing root or crown rots on susceptible plants. Tight, clayey soils hold water too well, becoming soggy, water-logged, and hard to work. They can be ideal for heavy feeding, moisture-loving perennials like astilbes, or for perennials grown in warm, dry climates; otherwise, you'll probably want to loosen the soil with organic matter or build raised beds

Loamy soil, with its balance of sand, silt, and clay particles, is the most desirable soil type. It is usually well drained and often quite fertile.

to improve drainage. Silty soils have some characteristics of both extremes, but tend to be more like clay than like sand. If and how you want to amend silty soil will depend on what plants you'd like to grow.

Soil Structure

Another important characteristic of your soil is its structure. Soil structure refers to the way in which the sand, silt, and clay particles join together to form clumps (known as aggregates). A soil with high amounts of sand or clay will usually be too loose or too dense to support good plant growth. A well-balanced soil tends to form crumbly, granular clumps. Unlike soil texture, which is very difficult to change, soil structure can be improved by adding organic matter on a regular basis.

Organic Matter

Organic matter—basically the decaying remains of plant material such as leaves and grass, manure, and other animal products—is a critical component of all soils. Healthy soils usually have 5 percent organic matter or more. Soils that are high in organic matter tend to be dark brown or black and have a loose, crumbly feel and a nice earthy smell.

No matter what kind of soil you have, adding organic matter—in the form of compost, aged manure, chopped leaves, or other nutrient-rich materials—is the number-one way to make it suitable for a wide range of plants. Organic matter improves garden soil by loosening up heavy clays, improving water retention, promoting better drainage, and increasing fertility by retaining nutrients. Organic matter can hold up to twice its weight in moisture, slowly releasing water to plant roots and improving moisture retention in sandy soils (so you'll be able to water and fertilize less frequently). It encourages fine clay particles to clump together into larger soil aggregates, and this will improve soil aeration. It also encourages healthy populations of earthworms and other soil organisms, which in turn contribute nutrients and encourage root growth. All of these factors lead to vigorous, healthier plants that look great and are naturally more resistant to pest and disease problems. Organic matter is decomposing all the time, so you must add more to help replace the decaying particles and keep nutrient levels high.

If you have a soil that is clayey and tends to hold lots of water, the perfect solution is to grow moisture-loving plants such as astilbes.

The Ribbon Test

You can make a rough estimate of your soil's texture by making a ball of just-moist soil in your fist, then squeezing out a ribbon of earth between your thumb and index finger. Sandy soils will break up immediately. Clayey soils hold together, forming a ribbon 1 inch (2.5 cm) long or more. Loamy soils fall somewhere in between.

Soil Depth

The actual depth of your soil has an impact on root growth and this in turn affects what plants—deep- or shallow-rooting—will thrive in your garden. In some regions, the soil is a thin dust over bedrock. In others, thousands of years' worth of decayed prairie grasses have formed soils 6 feet (1.8 m) deep.

Compost is an invaluable source of organic matter and nutrients. Work it into the soil (top) or spread it on the surface as a mulch (bottom).

Perennials tend to have deeper roots than annuals, so if your soil is shallow, you could build raised beds to ensure good growth.

It's easy to tell which conditions you have—just dig down into the soil in your yard with a shovel. If you can go 2 feet (60 cm) without hitting a sheet of rock or a band of dense, tightly compacted soil, you'll be able to grow a wide range of annuals and perennials as well as vegetables, herbs, and other shallow-rooted plants with little trouble. Larger plants, like shrubs and trees, generally need soil that's at least 3 feet (90 cm) deep to have vigorous growth. Soils less than 2 feet (60 cm) deep are not as hospitable to root growth; they may also be prone to water-logging, and often have

Soil forms as solid bedrock weathers into smaller and smaller mineral pieces. Organic matter gives the soil surface a darker color.

fewer nutrients than deeper soils. If your soil is shallow, you may decide to build raised beds and fill them with a good soil to provide more area for root growth. A 6-inch (15-cm) high bed should accommodate most annual flowers; you'll need an 18- to 24-inch (45- to 60-cm) bed for perennials. (Raised beds can dry out quickly, though, so you may have to water them more often.) Or you could stick with more shallow-rooted plantings that are adapted to limited root zones.

Soil Organisms

There is abundant life in a healthy soil. Among the beneficial organisms are fungal mycelia, strands of fungus that run through the soil. They bind small soil particles into larger ones and improve soil structure. Beneficial bacteria can decompose organic and mineral elements, freeing nutrients for plants to use. Earthworms tunnel through the soil, consuming and breaking down organic matter, and leaving behind nutrient-rich castings. All of these organisms thrive in the same conditions that the roots of most plants prefer: a loose, moist, but well-drained soil with plenty of organic matter. Soil that is compacted, low in organic matter, or excessively wet is generally low in soil organisms, and your plants probably won't flourish there either.

Earthworms (left) and millipedes (above) are two soil organisms that play an important role in breaking down dead plant matter in the garden.

Soil Fertility

Fertility is the availability, not just the presence, of nutrients in the soil. In order to grow, plants draw large amounts of nitrogen, phosphorus, potassium, magnesium, calcium, and sulfur from the soil. They also require traces of iron, manganese, molybdenum, boron, chlorine, copper, zinc, and nickel. Many of these nutrients are released naturally for plants to use through mineral-rich rocks breaking down into soil.

Most plants grow best when the soil contains an ample supply of balanced nutrients, but some actually grow better if soil nutrients are low. Nitrogen-rich soils, for instance, will cause plants like yarrow and coreopsis to form lush, floppy growth that requires yearly staking. In the same conditions, nasturtiums will grow leaves at the expense of flowers. Grown in less fertile soil, the same plants do much better. Knowing the nutrient content

Coreopsis grows best in soil that isn't very fertile; too much nitrogen can cause weak stems.

of your soil will help you select the most appropriate plants for the conditions.

A soil test can tell you if your land has the right nutrients in the right balance for normal plant growth. If the results show that the pH is extreme or your soil is low in available nutrients, use an organic fertilizer to correct the problem. (This is discussed in greater detail in "Fertilizing for Good Growth" on page 134.) Use restraint when correcting a deficiency, though; too much fertilizer can easily be as bad as not enough. Follow the application rates given on the product label.

Soil pH

Soil pH—the measurement of your soil's acidity or alkalinity—is another factor that can determine which plants will grow well because pH affects the availability of nutrients in your soil. Chemically, pH is the measure of hydrogen ions in the soil. It is measured on a scale of 1 to 14, with 7 as neutral. Soils that have pH ratings below 7 are acidic, and as the pH drops, the soil becomes increasingly more acidic. Soils with pH ratings above 7 grow

increasingly more alkaline. An acidic pH—5.5 to 6.5—is ideal for most of the flowering plants. But a few, such as pinks (*Dianthus* spp.) and baby's breath, need a soil that is more alkaline, or rich in limestone. Their ideal pH is slightly higher than neutral, at around 7.5.

You can determine your soil pH yourself with a simple home test available at your local garden center, or you can send a sample to a soil-testing laboratory for analysis. If the soil test shows you need to adjust the pH level, begin by adding extra compost when you are preparing the

bed or applying a top-dressing. If that is not sufficient to moderate excess acidity, add some calcitic limestone (calcium carbonate) or dolomitic limestone (which contains both calcium and magnesium) for magnesium-deficient soils. Organic matter also helps lower the pH of overly alkaline soils. If it is not enough, you can also add powdered sulfur. The quantity of pH amendments you use will vary with how far you need to adjust the pH and what type of soil you have. For more on preparing soils for planting, see "Getting the Soil Ready" on page 106.

In most cases, it's best to choose annuals and perennials that will thrive in your soil conditions rather than to change the soil to fit the plants. If you really want to try to grow plants that need different conditions, consider grouping them in one bed, where you can more easily adjust the soil to fit their needs.

Flowers for Acid Soil

Here are just a few of the plants that tolerate or even appreciate acidic soil, which has a pH below 6.5.

Chrysanthemum spp.
  (chrysanthemums)
Convallaria majalis (lily-of-the-valley)
Lilium spp. (lilies)
Tagetes spp. (marigolds)

Flowers for Alkaline Soil

If your soil's pH is on the high side (7.5 or higher), consider some of the following plants, which are naturally adapted to alkaline soil.

Ageratum houstonianum (ageratum)
Anemone x *hybrida*
  (Japanese anemone)
Antirrhinum majus (snapdragon)
Bergenia spp. (bergenias)
Cosmos spp. (cosmos)
Dianthus spp. (pinks)
Gypsophila paniculata
  (baby's breath)
Heuchera spp.
  (coral bells)
Paeonia spp.
  (peonies)
Verbascum spp.
  (mulleins)
Zinnia spp.
  (zinnias)

Peonies

This garden bed of mostly annuals needs fertile, nutrient-rich soil. Annuals are the tourists of the flower garden; their short stay means they don't have much time to extract the nutrients they need to bloom.

Your Local Climate

To have healthy, vigorous perennials that will grow and thrive year after year with minimal care, you need to choose plants that are well adapted to your climate.

Understanding Hardiness Zones

Find out what hardiness zone you live in so you can choose the right plants for your area. You'll find a copy of the USDA Plant Hardiness Zone Map, which divides the continent into many different zones based on average minimum yearly temperatures, on page 276. If you choose plants that are reportedly hardy in your zone, you can be fairly confident that those plants will survive an average winter in your area. To really be on the safe side, you may want to stick with plants that are hardy to at least one zone colder than yours. If you live in Zone 6, for instance, you can depend on perennials that are hardy to Zones 4 or 5.

Tulips, daffodils, grape hyacinths, and many other bulbs are ideally suited to Zones 4 to 8. They are a fast and easy way to add spring color.

town or city, for instance, your local area may be significantly warmer than the hardiness map would predict. Elevated and open, exposed areas may get colder than other properties in the same zone. In cold areas, consistent snow cover provides fabulous insulation and may allow you to grow plants from warmer zones. For annuals and bulbs in particular, you will need to know the dates of the average first and last frosts in your area, to determine when it's safe to sow or transplant.

Knowing when and how much it rains in your area is very important if you want to choose plants that won't need regular watering. As a broad rule of thumb, most annuals and perennials need about 1 inch (25 mm) of rain each week during the growing season (spring and autumn). If your area doesn't get enough rain during the crucial growing months, you'll have to provide water for your plants or switch to water-wise landscaping.

Wind is another factor to consider. It can make your climate more severe than

You'll find that the plant entries in this book and in many other books and catalogs give a range of hardiness zones—such as "Zones 5 to 8"—for a particular plant. That's because cold temperatures aren't the only factor that determines if a plant will grow well in an area; heat can have a great effect, too. The upper limit of a plant's hardiness range will give you an idea of what kind of summer temperatures that plant can tolerate. If a plant is listed as hardy in Zones 5 to 8, for example, you could grow it in Zones 5, 6, 7, and 8; Zones 4 and lower would probably be too cold, and Zones 9 and 10 could be too hot.

Learning about Local Weather

Hardiness zones are helpful for narrowing down your plant choices, but they aren't foolproof guidelines. If you live in a large

A garden in a cold climate will suit low-growing, hardy perennials adapted to alpine conditions.

A garden in the Southwest uses combinations of stone, cactus, and agave with flowering verbena.

Consider Your Climate

Understanding your climate will help you choose the annuals and perennials that are best adapted to the conditions available in your garden. This list of temperate and subtropical climates explains how your climate will influence the plants you can grow.

Cool summer and cold winter (Southern Canada and New England): You'll need to look for cold-hardy annuals and perennials that emerge after spring freezes subside and that bloom early enough to escape fall freezes.

Hot summer and cold winter (Midwest and Northeast): You can grow a wide range of annuals and perennials that are hardy and moderately heat-tolerant.

Cool summer but mild winter (Northwest coast): Many annuals and perennials will thrive and bloom here, flowering longer than they would in warmer areas.

Mild winter and hot summer (South Central and Southeast): These areas have enough cold for a dormant period, but their long, hot summers may stress annuals and perennials. If summer is humid,

fungal diseases are more likely to plague susceptible plants, so look for disease-resistant cultivars. Winter rains may leave the soil wet for long periods, increasing the potential for rotting; consider growing plants in raised beds.

Arid climates (Southwest): Periods of drought can stress plant growth, so grow drought-tolerant plants in sunken beds with good irrigation. Salt buildup may damage plant roots; look for salt-tolerant species like sea lavenders (*Limonium* spp.).

Subtropical (Southern Florida and Texas): If a cold dormancy period is limited or lacking altogether, select suitable tropical and subtropical plants. Or if you want to grow more common annuals and perennials, you can take special measures, like planting in fall or giving plants a rest period by cutting foliage back.

California poppies, drought-tolerant and easy to grow, work well in Midwest wildflower gardens.

cold, winds can draw water out of exposed plant tops and roots faster than it can be replaced, leading to severe damage or death. Yet wind can actually be an asset in very humid climates, where good air circulation becomes more important in preventing the development of plant diseases.

Where winds are strong or frequent, protect your gardens by locating them on the sheltered side of walls, solid fences, or hedges. In exposed areas with cold winter winds and no consistent snow cover, choose plants that are rated for at least one zone colder than yours to be on the safe side. Or, if you're willing to go to the extra trouble, you could cover plants that are normally adapted to your zone with a generous layer of branches (or chopped leaves) for winter protection.

you think. As you spend time in your yard, observe which direction the wind usually comes from. Is your yard exposed to strong winds, or is it fairly sheltered by trees, hills, or buildings? Strong winds may quickly dry out plants and erode bare soil. When it's

With its climate of mild winters and cool summers, the Northwest coast provides good conditions for gardening. Roses, rose campions, and spike speedwell will flower longer here than in warmer regions.

Sea lavender is a tough perennial that is quite adapted to sites with sandy or salty soil.

The Lay of the Land

The topography of your yard—whether it slopes or is uniformly flat—will influence how plants grow, when they bloom, how long the display lasts, and how you'll design your garden. Each kind of topography has its own advantages and disadvantages for gardening.

Gardening on a Flat Area

If your yard is as flat as a cornfield, you are faced with your own particular design opportunities and growing considerations. Actually preparing the site is usually fairly easy, since you don't have to worry much about soil erosion, although you may have

A wall covered with wisteria and golden chain tree provides a lovely, protective enclosure that will keep out harsh winds and wild weather.

drainage problems if your soil is high in clay. A major design challenge is often the lack of a background for your garden. As part of your landscape design, think about installing fences or planting shrubs and trees to "frame" your flower gardens. Another option is to regrade the site, creating gentle, natural-looking rises that will add visual interest.

If only part of your property is flat, be sure to reserve it for recreation—perhaps a barbecue area or a play area for children.

Gardening on a Hilltop

A garden on a hilltop will face different conditions from gardens just down the slope. The soil on a hilltop may be thin due to erosion, and is often very well drained. Hilltop sites are often windswept as well. Strong winds can topple tall plants, so you'll either need to stake your annuals and perennials or stick with shorter plants. Winds can also dry out plants quickly, so you may have to water more often. The stunning views available from many hilltop sites turn all of these problems into minor inconveniences, however. When planning a landscape for a hilltop site, you may want to design your flower gardens to frame a particularly nice view of the surrounding countryside. If excessive wind is a problem, you can decrease the velocity by setting a fence, hedge, or vine-covered trellis between the prevailing wind direction and your garden.

Make the most of a flat section on an otherwise undulating or hilly site—use it for an entertaining area.

Terraced beds of stone or timber will allow you to create a garden on a sloping site. Then plant the beds out with petunias and salvias.

Gardening on a Slope

A hilly yard has great potential for interesting settings for your annuals and perennials. It also has more microclimates—the slight variations in growing conditions that will affect plant displays. In general, soils on slopes tend to be well drained, but the topsoil may be thin because of erosion. Flowering gardens on slopes are less prone to late-spring and early-fall frosts, as the cold air tends to settle down in the valley and the warm air rises up over the slope.

Slopes are ideal sites for rock gardens. If the slope isn't naturally rocky, you can add groupings of large boulders or layers of flat rock that resemble natural outcroppings. Leave pockets of soil between the rocks in which to grow small perennials like candytuft (*Iberis sempervirens*), sweet violets (*Viola odorata*), and primroses (*Primula* spp.), along with small bulbs and dwarf conifers.

If your site has a very steep slope, though, think twice before stripping

the existing vegetation to plant a flower garden. The soil might wash away before most of the annuals and perennials can root and stabilize the slope. One way to handle slopes is by planting them with those plants that take root and spread aggressively, such as daylilies, ajuga (*Ajuga reptans*), and geraniums (*Geranium* spp.). Space the plants closely for more rapid stabilization of the bank, and use burlap or straw to hold the soil in place until the roots do their job.

If you don't want to rely on plants alone to control erosion, you can terrace the hill or install a retaining wall to moderate the slope. A beautiful rock or timber retaining wall will give your landscape interesting structure and let you grow plants that do not root strongly enough to survive on a slope.

Gardening in a Valley

At the base of a slope, flower gardens are more prone to late-spring and early-fall

Use any rocks you find on your property as the framework for a raised rock garden or as a pathway of flagstones.

If you live in a valley, you may have a pond or even just a spot that always seems wet. This is where primroses, hostas, and irises will thrive.

frosts. Frost and cold air will inevitably concentrate in low-lying areas, known as frost pockets, slowing or damaging spring growth and fall flowers. The same frost may miss plants growing in warmer areas slightly uphill. Gardeners in low-lying areas may want to wait a little later than others to remove protective winter mulches. And moisture will collect at the base of the slope too, just like frost. Valleys are rich in rainfall runoff and often have natural water features such as ponds and streams. Topsoil eroded from surrounding slopes tends to collect here, but if the soil is clayey, it may not drain well. A common way to deal with this drainage problem is to plant perennials in raised beds. If poor drainage is really a problem, you could install drainage tiles to channel the excess water into another area.

In valleys and flat terrain, the best solution if you have poor drainage is to actually use the moisture around any creeks, ponds, and lakes to your advantage. Let a bubbling brook or the reflective surface of a pond become the focus around which you plant water-loving plants. Clothe the banks with the flashiest of the moisture-lovers like red-spiked cardinal flowers (*Lobelia cardinalis*), Japanese primroses (*Primula japonica*), golden-flowered big-leaved ligularia (*Ligularia dentata*), or the plume-like, rose-red rodgersia (*Rodgersia pinnata*).

Examine Your Exposure

Exposure refers to the amount of sun and shade that your yard receives in the course of the day. The exposure of different places on your property can vary widely, depending on where each garden bed is in relation to the house and also to other shade-casting features such as sheds, trees, and fences.

South-facing Sites

Locating a garden on the south side of your house (or a wall or fence) provides the maximum amount of light in the Northern Hemisphere. In cool Northern summers, many sun-loving annuals and perennials thrive against a south wall. But where summers are hot, all but the most heat- and drought-tolerant perennials may bake against south walls because of the high temperatures there.

Eastern Exposures

Many flowering plants thrive with an eastern exposure, such as that along the eastern edge of woods, on the east side of a steep hill, or against an east-facing wall. Plants on these sites receive up to a half day of direct light, and they're sheltered from the hot afternoon sun. This protection from strong afternoon rays prolongs bloom time where summers are hot. When you read a description that suggests afternoon shade for a particular plant—such as lady's mantle (*Alchemilla mollis*), cranesbills (*Geranium* spp.), or Japanese anemone (*Anemone* x *hybrida*)—try an eastern exposure.

Foamflowers favor north-facing sites. Cranesbills thrive in east-facing sites. Yarrows prefer southern exposures. Coneflowers tolerate west-facing sites.

West-facing Sites

Western exposures are a challenge for most plants. The site is generally cool and shady in the morning, but the temperature can change dramatically when strong sun hits it during the warmest part of the day. Shade-loving plants generally don't handle such extremes well; their leaves may turn brown or go off-color.

In the North of the continent, the temperature differences between morning and afternoon may be moderate enough not to harm plants, especially if a tree, fence, or outbuilding casts a little shade there in the afternoon.

In Southern gardens, try tough, drought-tolerant perennials that can take sun or partial shade, including blue false indigo (*Baptisia australis*), boltonia (*Boltonia asteroides*), patrinia (*Patrinia scabiosifolia*), Cupid's dart (*Catananche caerulea*), cushion spurge (*Euphorbia epithymoides*), daylilies (*Hemerocallis* spp.), common sundrops (*Oenothera tetragona*), violet sage (*Salvia* x *superba*), and coneflowers.

Each side of your house offers different growing conditions, called microclimates. The south side of the house will provide the maximum amount of light for your annuals and perennials, no matter the season.

Coneflowers thrive in full sun but will also grow in light shade. They are tough and long-lived.

Northern Exposures

A garden set against a north-facing wall or fence or on the north side of a steep hill receives much less light and remains cool throughout the day. If the site is open (without large trees or buildings to the east or west), it will probably still be bright. A bright, evenly cool spot is ideal for most shade-loving plants; even those preferring full shade should grow well here. Try flowering and foliage annuals and perennials such as hostas, ferns, and lungworts (*Pulmonaria* spp.).

Understanding Sun and Shade

Identifying the direction that your property faces will give you a general idea of the growing conditions that you have to offer. But unless you have a totally flat, featureless lot, you'll also have to consider the shade cast by trees, shrubs, fences, hedges, trellises, sheds, the house next door, and any other structures.

How do you tell if a particular spot has full sun, partial shade, or full shade? Watch the spot regularly over the course of a day (check on it every hour or so), and note each time you check whether the spot is sunny or shady. Any site with less than 6 hours of direct sunlight throughout the day is shady. Annuals and perennials that prefer full sun need 6 hours or more of direct sunlight to grow well. A site that receives a few hours of morning or late afternoon sun but no direct midday sun is described as having partial shade. Many perennials that prefer full sun will tolerate partial shade.

A generally bright site that receives little direct sun but lots of filtered or reflected light is said to have light or dappled shade. Typically, this kind of shade occurs beneath high-branched deciduous trees (such as honey locusts [*Robinia pseudoacacia*]) that don't cast solid shadows. Full, dense, or deep shade is darker, and fewer plants grow well in it. The area under hemlocks or other such evergreens is in deep shade all year long. Plants growing under maples, beeches, and other densely branched deciduous trees are in full shade most of the summer.

Keep in mind that shade changes during the year, both because the angle of the sun changes in the sky and because deciduous trees grow and then shed their leaves. You may find that a site that is in full sun on July 1 is shaded by a nearby

A maple tree provides deep shade during the heat of summer. In fall, its leaves color and drop, and it remains bare until the spring, providing temporary sunlight for wildflowers and bulbs.

tree or building in April or October when the sun is much lower in the sky.

The deep shade under a maple or oak disappears when the tree loses its leaves, and the ground below stays bright until mid- to late spring. Many of the spring wildflowers, including bluebells (*Mertensia virginica*) and foamflowers (*Tiarella* spp.), have adapted to readily take advantage of this temporary sun and bloom before the overhead trees leaf out. Spring-blooming bulbs that go dormant by the time the trees are fully leafed out are also good. Even if your yard is deeply shaded the rest of the season, you can probably enjoy masses of color in the spring and beautiful green and patterned foliage the rest of the year. For more specific advice on landscaping shady sites, turn to "Succeeding in the Shade" on page 98.

There's no need to despair if you have shade. Many colorful annuals and perennials, including cosmos, irises, hostas, and primroses, thrive in full or at least partial shade.

Living with Your Garden

The trick to gardening with annuals and perennials is finding and combining plants that will thrive in your particular conditions.

To have a beautiful, healthy garden, you don't have to be born with a "green thumb." The real secret to creating a great-looking garden is a keen sense of observation. To determine what kind of growing conditions you have available—how much light, what kind of climate and topography, and what kind of soil—you need to live with your yard so you can choose the annuals and perennials that will grow and thrive there.

Starting from Scratch

If you've just built a new house, moved into a new development, or inherited a particularly uninspired all-lawn landscape, you may be staring at bare soil or a large expanse of grass where you want a garden to be located.

The best way to start a new landscape may be not to start it—at least for a year or so. If you can stand it, live with the landscape through one year. See where water puddles after storms or where it runs off quickly, taking valuable topsoil with it. Note where structures and trees cast shadows on your property, and how the shadows change throughout the seasons. See how traffic patterns develop: Where do you always walk to reach the car? Where do visitors and utility people tend to tread on their way to the door? Take note of these patterns, and incorporate them into your landscape plan.

As you install your new landscape, it's wise to start on the "hard" elements—like walls, fences, and paths—first. These give overall structure. This is also the best time to plan and install an automatic irrigation system if you need one. Once permanent elements are in place, then you can start planting. You may choose to plant a few beds of annuals for quick color during the first few seasons or just wait for the perennials to develop. Don't forget that annuals are great for filling in gaps in young perennial gardens!

Adapting an Existing Garden

In some ways, adapting an existing garden is more challenging than starting from scratch. Although your garden may have

Enliven an established garden of trees and ivy with bergenia rather than pulling everything out.

Work on one project at a time, establishing different features gradually, such as a pergola that you can underplant with different perennials.

pleasant features like large trees or an established lawn to work with, you also have someone else's tastes to contend with and their mistakes to undo.

If you've lived with the garden for at least a year, you are probably very aware of its troublesome points. But don't try to convert the whole garden all at once. Instead, identify the elements you want to change, then work slowly, choosing a few (or one major one) to work on each year.

Annuals and perennials, being fast-growing and adaptable plants, can provide masses of seasonal color and beautiful foliage with just some basic care. If the existing plants are overgrown, dig them out, divide them, and replant the vigorous outer parts into enriched soil. If they are in the wrong spot, dig them up and move them in the spring.

Plant petunias for quick and easy color during the first few growing seasons in your garden.

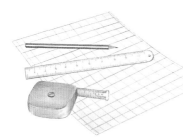

Creating a Site Map

The easiest way to record everything you've learned about your site—the soil conditions, drainage, exposure, slope, and microclimates—is by making a site plan. It will show you the factors you'll need to consider when planning which plants you can grow and where you can put them. The more accurate your plan, the more useful it will be.

You'll need just a few simple tools: a 50- or 100-foot (15- or 30-m) tape

Make the Most of Microclimates

Each garden might have several unique growing areas, normally called microclimates. Shady nooks fit into this category. So do hot spots, like beds that get extra heat from walls or paving.

As you plan your plantings, look for these special spots where particular annuals and perennials may thrive. A sunny, south-facing bed along a brick terrace, for instance, could hold extra warmth for a great show of crocus and pansies in early spring. The same site, though, would probably be too hot for the pansies in summer, so you'd need to replace them with heat-tolerant annuals or perennials, such as the many types of daylily (*Hemerocallis* spp.), treasure flowers (*Gazania* hybrids), or sun-drops (*Oenothera tetragona*).

Your site map can be plain or fancy—the important thing is that it's clear enough for you to follow. The more details you include, the more useful it will be for planning.

borrowed view (neighbor's trees)

badly drained area (suitable for pond)

large trees

large trees

dappled shade

full sun

sunny area suited to vegetables and herbs

hedge

paved courtyard

vine over pergola

garage

garbage & recycling

clothesline

compost bin

back door

neighbor's trees

paling fence

measure, graph paper, a pencil, and a ruler. A second person is a big help. If you're by yourself, you may find measuring easier if you use a long (100 foot [30 m]) piece of string that is tied to a short, pointed stake at each end.

It's good to start with a survey map of your property. If you don't have one, draw a rough outline of the yard to scale: 1 inch (2.5 cm) on paper for each foot (30 cm) of garden space is a good scale for gardens shorter than 10 feet (3 m). Locate north with a compass or a local street map, and indicate it on your map. Draw outlines of your house, driveway, paths, and patios. Also sketch in sheds or garages, plus fences, hedges, and existing gardens.

Don't forget to mark any significant topographical features on your map, too. Include low areas (and whether or not they are wet), hilltops, and large boulders. Note which direction slopes face and

whether slopes are gentle (easy to walk up or mow) or steep (hard to walk up).

Include trees and large shrubs on your map. If an area contains many trees and shrubs, outline it and mark it as woods. Note any other areas that get less than 6 hours of direct sun and whether they have light, partial, or dense shade. Also note areas that may be sunny in spring and shady once the trees leaf out.

Finally, look for good views that you'd like to preserve and bad views that you might want to screen out. Mark nice views with an arrow so you'll remember not to block them with tall perennials. Also indicate which windows you look out of to see your yard. Mark anything you'd like to screen, such as trash cans, and areas you don't want to mow, such as around posts and trees.

Make several photocopies of your finished map, so you'll be able to sketch in different landscaping ideas and test how they look before you start digging.

Creating a Flower Garden

This chapter summarizes some basic landscape design principles, so you know how to combine different plants and design a garden that looks good the whole year round.

The Planning Stage

For a garden to be effective, it has to match your site conditions, your style, the amount of time you can set aside for gardening, and the results you want from the garden. Ideally, it should also blend in with the topography and complement your house so everything looks like it belongs right where it is. A little thinking and planning will ensure you end up with a beautiful, healthy, easy-care garden. And knowing your personal goals will guide you through the planning process and ensure that you end up with the garden you want. Don't jump into creating a flower garden without sufficient planning.

Deciding Where to Plant

You may have your heart set on growing particular plants, in which case you'll have to choose a site on your property that's suitable. Your site choices are probably limited; you will need a spot that can provide the right amount of light and the right soil conditions for your plants. Alternatively, you may have decided where you want to have a garden and then pick the plants that are adapted to those growing conditions. Either way, the key is to match the plants to the place they're growing. Use the information you

An underplanting of pink and white annuals perfectly complements a flowering cherry tree.

gathered for your site map (as explained in "Living with Your Garden" on page 45) to decide where that is. If you have a fairly flat site with moist but well-drained soil, you can plant a wide variety of annuals and perennials. But chances are good that you'll have at least one area in the yard with more challenging conditions, such as slopes or wet spots.

If you have a very difficult spot, you might decide to ignore it and limit your plantings to the most hospitable areas of the yard. Or you may choose to take up the challenge and plan a garden of annuals and perennials that are naturally adapted to those tough conditions. You may be pleasantly surprised to see how well-chosen plantings can turn a problem site into a pleasing garden area. You'll find specific suggestions for dealing with slopes, wet spots, and other difficult sites in "Problem-solving with Annuals and Perennials" starting on page 88.

If you don't have particular plants in mind, you have a lot more freedom in site selection. Here are some points to consider when deciding on a planting area.

- How much sun does it get? Many annuals and perennials thrive in full sun, but some adapt to or even need at least partial shade.
- What is the soil like? Is it loose and sandy, hard and clayey, very wet, very dry, or very rocky? There's an annual or perennial for just about every site, but fairly loose, well-drained soil that isn't too dry or rocky is ideal. If you're stuck with miserable, compacted clay soil, you could excavate the area and refill it with good topsoil. For very clayey, rocky, or wet sites, raised beds are another alternative.
- Is it easy to reach? A flower bed at the end of your driveway or by your mailbox may seem like a nice idea, but it could be a hassle to maintain— especially if you have to lug water out to it regularly. Try to keep plantings closer to the house, where you can reach them easily for any watering, grooming, and general maintenance.
- What's growing there now? Neglected areas will have to be cleared of weeds. If the area is currently a lawn, you'll need to remove the turf. Clearing out overgrown shrub plantings can be an even bigger task. However, just about any site can be prepared for planting if you're willing to put the time and effort into it.

Creating the garden that you want will take planning, patience, and imagination—and it should be fun.

Combine plants with similar needs so it's easier to keep them in top condition. Yarrow and torch lilies, for example, don't need regular watering.

How Big Should Your Garden Be?

A key part of planning a great-looking landscape is being realistic about how much time you have to spend on it. Digging up and planting the area is the most obvious chunk of time you'll spend in the garden. But you may be surprised at how much time you'll need to allow for the aftercare—the mulching, weeding, watering, fertilizing, staking, and pest and disease control that your chosen plants will need every year to look their best.

For example, you'll probably need to spend at least a few hours each month out in the yard to maintain a 200-square-foot (18.6 sq m) flower garden once it's been established. And that doesn't include any planning or preparation time. It also assumes you keep it mulched to discourage weeds and reduce the need for watering.

Your own garden may take more or less time, depending on the plants you choose, how immaculate you want them to look, and how carefully you've planned for your site. It's safest to start small, so plan your first garden a bit smaller than you think you want. Live with your first garden for a few years, and see how comfortable you are with the time you spend on it. As the plants become established, you'll have less watering and weeding to do, and you'll get a good idea of how much maintenance your garden really needs. Then, if you decide you want to expand, you'll have a more realistic feel for how much garden you can actually handle.

What's Your Style?

Deciding where and how big you want your perennial plantings to be are two

A clipped hedge is a common feature of formal gardens. But a slight curve, and the loose clumps of mealy-cup sage, adds a touch of informality.

important aspects of planning a practical garden. But not all gardening has to be practical; choosing a style for your garden is a chance to add a fun and personal touch to your yard.

Informal gardens tend to have curved lines and a variety of casual plantings.

Formal gardens are laid out with straight lines and symmetrical plantings.

One thing you'll want to consider is whether your landscape will have a formal or an informal feel. Formal landscaping uses straight lines, sharp angles, and symmetrical plantings with only a limited number of different plants. These kinds of landscapes often include features such as clipped hedges or brick walls to define different spaces in the garden. Formal designs tend to have a restful feel. But they may not be as restful for the gardener, since you will need to clip, stake, and weed on a regular basis to keep your plants and design looking perfect.

Zinnias

Informal landscapes use curving lines to create a more natural feeling. They tend to have few permanent features such as walls, although elements such as rustic split-rail fences and wood-chip paths add to the informal feel. These kinds of gardens generally include many different kinds of plants—trees, shrubs, herbs, and vines as well as annuals and perennials. They are relaxed and lively. Since the plants are free to spread, they tend to need less regular maintenance. You won't need to keep sharp edges on the beds, and a few weeds won't immediately be obvious and ruin the look of the garden.

Plan Your Plant List

You probably already have some idea of what you want to grow in your garden. As you flip through books, magazines, and catalogs for more ideas, it's fun to make a wish list of plants you'd like to try. Along with the names, you'll also want to note the characteristics of each plant, including its light and soil needs, height, color, and bloom time.

If you have already chosen a site for your garden, the next step is to go through your list and select the plants that are adapted to the site. "Creating Great Combinations" on page 52 offers some tips on grouping your selections based on height, color, and bloom time; jot down a list of about 5 to 10 different plants. If you'd rather grow your annuals and bulbs for a particular purpose—for cutting, perhaps, or fragrance—you'll have to consider the needs of each plant you want to grow and then find a spot in your yard where it will thrive.

Your list will remind you what you're looking for as you browse through catalogs and shop at your local nursery. Check off the plants as you buy or order them, so that you won't forget and purchase the same plant twice by mistake!

Whether you choose a formal or informal landscape may depend on your personal style or the style of your house. It can be hard to mix informal and formal areas effectively; a simple solution is to choose one for harmonious landscaping.

Putting It All Together

By now you probably have lots of ideas and thoughts swirling around in your head. You know where and how big you want the garden to be and which plants you want to grow. In this section, you'll learn about the different techniques and steps you can use to organize your gardening ideas.

Try Out Your Ideas

Now head outside with a copy of your plant list and your site plan (the one you drew up with the help of "Creating a Site Map" on page 45). Outline the shape of the planting area with flexible hose or rope. Step back and walk around the yard to see how the dimensions look from several viewpoints (including the view through your windows). If you have trouble visualizing how the filled bed will look, use trash cans, filled leaf bags, or boxes to give the area some height and mass. Adjust the outline of the area until it looks balanced from all viewpoints.

Put Your Plan on Paper

Sketching garden designs will allow you to try out many different ideas, however unrealistic, without the hassle of physically digging up and moving existing plants. Your plan may simply be the outline of the bed with scrawled notes as to roughly where the plants will go. Or you may want to invest the time in drawing up a formal scale plan of the bed so you can make sure the garden will have just the right blend of colors, heights, and textures and so you'll know just what you need to buy.

To make a scale plan, measure the final outline of the bed decided on in "Try Out Your Ideas," and transfer the dimensions to paper. If your garden is small, you could

Limiting your choices to a color theme can make shopping easier, and it creates an elegant look.

Check your garden layout with tools, buckets, and other items to represent the various plants.

Planning is a fun wintertime activity that allows you to try out different design options. It can also help you spot possible problems before digging.

draw the area right onto your site map. In most cases, though, it's easier to draw each planting area on a separate piece of graph paper; that will give you more room to write. Choose the largest scale that allows your design to fit on one sheet: 1 inch (2.5 cm) on paper to 1 foot (30 cm) of planting area works well for gardens shorter than 10 feet (3 m). Mark the scale you are using on the page for future reference. Make several copies of this plan so you can try out different ideas.

Draw rough outlines on your base plan to show where each plant will go. Check heights to make sure you don't have tall plants at the front blocking short ones at the back, unless the short plants bloom before the tall plants fill out. If you have room, allow space for 3 or 5 plants of each type—a few different plants in large masses can have a more dramatic effect than many single plants. Mark dots (or small xs) within outlines to show locations of individual plants.

As you plan the layout, check the spread of each plant, which is listed in the individual plant entries starting on page 172. Leave enough room between plants so that each can mature to its full spread and overlap by no more than a few

inches. If your budget is tight, space the perennials farther apart; you can increase them by division the following year, or fill the gaps with annuals and bulbs. Allow for some unplanted (mulched) space at the front of the bed so the plants can sprawl out a bit without flopping onto the lawn and creating a mowing headache.

Fine-tune Your Plan

If you really want to make sure your design is just right, you can make colored maps or overlays to help you visualize color combinations and different seasons. Make several copies of your scale plan, or use several sheets of tracing paper as overlays.

Use a different copy or overlay sheet for early spring, late spring/early summer, late summer, and fall; you may also want one for winter interest. Color the plants that bloom at each time. If you have old plant catalogs with color pictures, clip swatches of particular flowers and glue them inside the outline instead of just coloring. If foliage color is important, add the color as a thick outline surrounding the area of flower color. When you're satisfied that your design meets your needs, make a clean copy that includes plant names.

When doing your plan, add elements to liven up your plants with a focal point, such as a trellis.

The time you spend planning what to grow will be worth it when your careful groupings of plants bloom.

Great Design Ideas

With so many wonderful annuals and perennials to choose from, it's hard to resist planting one of each. But if you buy them one by one and plop them in the ground wherever there's room, your garden will look like a plant collection—interesting, perhaps, but not beautiful. You'll need to figure out what you want to grow and where you want to grow it. Garden design is basically the process of refining your plant choices, placement, and combinations to get the best effect. This is what transforms a collection of individual plants into a pleasing composition, a good landscape design.

Part of the fun of landscaping with annuals and perennials is creating an ever-changing display. Working with living material, material that changes from week to week and season to season, makes designing a garden different from redecorating a room, even though it builds on the same principles of contrast, balance, texture, and color.

Design Rules

While designing a garden is a very personal and creative activity, it is a good idea to follow some basic design rules. These rules will give your finished garden a very polished or natural look. The key rules are to create balance and rhythm and to add a dominant feature to tie the garden together.

First, keep the garden in balance. Include plants with a mix of heights and sizes throughout your plantings. Don't plant all of the tall or massive flowers on one side, with a group of low, delicate plants at the other end. In formal gardens, you may balance one side of the garden by planting the same design on the other, making a mirror image. For an informal garden, you can vary the plantings, perhaps matching a large blue-flowered annual on one side with a lower-growing plant that has bright red flowers. In this case, you are balancing brighter color with larger size.

Second, create a rhythm, or a sense of continuity, throughout the entire garden. You can repeat groupings of the same plant or use other plants with identical colors or similar flower shapes. Let a middle-of-the-border plant drift from the foreground to the background, giving a sense of movement and uniting the different layers of the garden.

Third, establish a dominant feature. This focal point can be as simple as a spectacular long-blooming perennial. But since perennials come in and out of bloom fairly quickly, you will have to establish a new focus when the first bloom ends. For a more permanent accent, you can feature a path, sculpture, birdbath, or tree as your center of interest, and build the garden around it. This brings you back to the concept of making the annual and perennial garden part of the overall landscape. The annuals and perennials can brighten existing permanent structures, and the structures can bring stability and focus to the continually changing display of foliage and flowers.

Creating Great Combinations

When it comes to garden aesthetics, there are no hard-and-fast rules that can be applied. After all, our tastes in flowers are as individual as our taste in clothing. However, there are a number of general guidelines that will help you create good plant combinations. Great-looking gardens are basically sequences of many individual plant combinations. The best aren't just based on flower color and season of bloom; they consider the quality, color, and texture of each plant's leaves as well. Good combinations also feature different plant heights and forms: short, medium, or tall; mat-like, spiky, or rounded. Equally important is the overall texture—whether a plant is fine and delicate in appearance, like baby's breath (*Gypsophila* spp.), or coarse and dramatic, like peonies and ligularias (*Ligularia* spp.). You should also remember sunlight and soil requirements.

A lovely ceramic jar, nestled among hostas and nasturtiums, draws the attention of people strolling by.

The lines created by gravel footpaths, weaving among beds of feverfew and lavender, create a sense of movement, inviting you to venture further into the garden. The plants form similarly rounded shapes and are of a similar height; this, along with the repetition of color, works to give rhythm and continuity.

Lilies, yellow loosestrife, butterfly bush, and bee balm like full sun but can tolerate light shade, too.

Contrasts and Complements

Well-planned gardens balance contrast and similarity. Contrasting colors, sizes, or other design elements give a bold and stimulating effect. Use contrast to draw attention to a particular location and to add a lively feel. But overusing contrast—too many different textures or too many strong colors—can give your garden a jumbled, chaotic look.

Similarity—the absence of contrasts—increases the sense of harmony. Use subtle variations of related colors and gradual height transitions to create a soothing garden design. Too much similarity risks being uninteresting, so add a touch of contrast—a few perennials of different height, color, or texture—for balance.

Repetition acts as a bridge between similarity and contrast. Repeating similar elements will unify even the boldest designs. Exact, evenly spaced repetitions of particular plants or combinations create a formal look. Combine different plants with similar flower colors or leaf shapes to give an informal garden a cohesive but casual look.

Choose Compatible Plants

The first step to any good combination is choosing plants that prefer the same growing conditions. You might think that cornflowers (*Centaurea cyanus*) would look charming with impatiens, for instance, but they probably won't grow well together; one needs full sun and the other prefers shade. Know the site conditions you have available, and stick with plants you know can thrive there.

To begin, group species that have similar light requirements. If your garden includes both lightly shaded and sunny areas, you have greater design freedom because you can pick from a wide range of suitable plants. Or if you want to blend some annuals and perennials that need partial shade in a sunny bed, you can plant them on the shaded north side of taller plants or in the filtered sunlight that reaches near the base of lanky plants. For instance, you could put Siberian bugloss (*Brunnera macrophylla*) in the northern shadow of a daylily. Or grow clumps of sweet violet (*Viola odorata*) below a tall purple coneflower (*Echinacea purpurea*).

You also need to consider the plants' preferred soil conditions and group those

with similar needs. For instance, you can combine prairie-type plants, like thread-leaved coreopsis (*Coreopsis verticillata*), New York aster (*Aster novi-belgii*), and common sneezeweed (*Helenium autumnale*), in a well-drained soil that is not excessively fertile. Similarly, group plants that take a more moist, more fertile soil, like sun-loving delphiniums and garden phlox, or plants that prefer to grow in light shade, like astilbes, bleeding hearts (*Dicentra* spp.), and coral bells (*Heuchera* spp.).

Think about Bloom Time

A plant's bloom season is another important thing to consider. Annuals make great companions for bulbs, since the annuals can fill in the garden space left when the bulbs go dormant. But if you want plants to be in flower at the same time, look for annuals and perennials with similar bloom seasons.

The yellow of coneflowers makes a great contrast with the purple of mealy-cup sage. Both plants like the same conditions, too.

Large masses of plants in single colors add unity to this garden of pot marigolds, borage, rose campions, and poppies. The repetition of yellow and orange stands out most vividly amid the other colors.

Color Combinations

Colors have different qualities. Warm colors—those related to red, orange, or yellow—are bold. They are stimulating and stand out, grabbing your attention in a landscape. Cool colors—those related to violet, blue, or green—are more tranquil and appear to recede from the viewer. Pure hues—like true yellow, blue, and red—are more vibrant than lighter or darker versions of the same color. Mixing warm and cool colors will add depth and interest to your plantings.

Color combinations are very personal creations. While certain combinations and types of colors tend to create specific effects, only you can decide whether you like that particular effect. Some gardeners enjoy the lively result of mixing orange and yellow with purple or blue; others prefer the crisp look of whites or the restful feel of pale yellows, soft pinks, soothing blues, and silvers.

Combining similar flower colors in the garden creates a harmonious, balanced effect. Try grouping reds with oranges and yellows, yellows with greens and blues, or blues with purples and reds. Colors that share the same intensity of lightness or darkness are also similar; for instance, several different pastels—like pale blues, yellows, apricots, and pinks—blend more harmoniously than several pure hues. Place pale blues, soft pinks, lavender, and dark violet up close where the colors won't fade into the background.

If contrast and excitement are what you're after, choose complementary hues like yellow and violet, red and green, or blue and orange. Or place a light tint next to a very bright or dark shade of the same hue (try pale blue with intense blue or dark blue or pale pink next to fuchsia or a deep burgundy).

White and gray don't appear on the color wheel, but they play an important role in the garden. White has a split personality: It can be exciting or soothing. Bright white is surprisingly bold; it stands out starkly among bright and dark colors, and even holds its own in a group of soft pastels. A dash of pure white in a spread of harmonious colors is as dramatic as a dash of a bright complementary color. Cream and similar muted whites are softer; they blend well with everything.

Gray is the great unifier. Silvery or gray foliage works even better than green to soften the transition between two bold or complementary colors. Gray adds a certain drama of its own by contrasting with neighboring green foliage.

When you're deciding on colors for your garden, limit yourself to two main colors and possibly a third for accent. Also add some minor colors for small touches of diversity. If possible, match flower or foliage colors with the other elements in the landscape, like walkways, shutters, or flowers or berries on nearby shrubs. But keep the color scheme simple. If you use too many colors, the garden will look fragmented and chaotic.

Be especially careful about color compatibility. Colors have many different hues, and they don't all look good together. You will find that, typically, the following rules hold true:

- Warm and cool colors are a surefire combination when mixed together. Try blue and pink, green and red, blue and orange, or purple and yellow.

Red and white tulips are even more striking when partnered with the strong blue of forget-me-nots.

- Take advantage of foliage color—add plants that have silver, blue, gold, or variegated leaves if they work well with surrounding flowers.
- Magenta is hard to mix, but it works with cream or pale yellow.
- Muted colors can look washed out against strong, clear tones. Stick with one or the other.
- Reddish blues may not work beside yellowish blues.
- Orange-pink flowers will clash next to purple-pink flowers.
- White flowers do not look good next to cream.
- Mix orange-red with scarlet, salmon with yellow, or pure pink with lavender only in cool climates or partially shady sites where the colors will stay vivid. In heat or full sun, these colors can fade to less compatible combinations.

As well as offering harmonious color, this group of chives and euphorbia has interesting texture.

Texture and Form Factors

Texture and form are as important as color in creating interesting combinations and landscapes. Masses of even-textured foliage can often tone down bold colors; dramatic leaf shapes can add extra zip to a pastel planting. Here are some other tips you can try to plan effective plantings:

- Balance rounded clump-formers, such as shasta daisies (*Leucanthemum* x *superbum*) and coreopsis, with spiky plants such as mulleins (*Verbascum* spp.), foxgloves (*Digitalis* spp.), and spike gayfeather (*Liatris spicata*).

Don't Forget Foliage

Flowers aren't the only source of color. Foliage comes in a surprising array of different greens, from the blue-green of California poppy (*Eschscholzia californica*) to the yellow-green of summer cypress (*Kochia scoparia*) or the deep green of geraniums. Fortunately, nearly all greens go well together and set off almost all flowers. As a background, it blends and harmonizes strong colors—such as reds, yellows, and oranges—that you probably wouldn't think to combine in an outfit. Pastel colors like soft pinks, blues, and yellows may look washed out against a light-colored shirt, but they never get lost against dark-green leaves.

Foliage can come in other colors, too. Silver-leaved plants such as dusty miller look great in almost any kind of garden. Yellowish leaves, such as those of golden feverfew or some coleus, can be pleasing with pinks and blues. You can add a bold spire of color with the blazing red leaves of Joseph's coat (*Amaranthus tricolor*) or a subtle accent with the bronzy leaves of wax begonias.

The muted shades of this mossy green garden are lifted by a blaze of purple at the entranceway.

- Contrast shiny leaves—like those of European ginger (*Asarum europaeum*) and bear's breech (*Acanthus mollis*)—with velvety or fuzzy leaves, such as those of lamb's ears (*Stachys byzantina*) or lungworts (*Pulmonaria* spp.).
- Contrast fine foliage, such as lacy fern fronds, with the smooth, broad leaves of hostas and similar plants.
- Include spiky leaves, like those of irises, gladioli, and blackberry lilies (*Belamcanda chinensis*); they'll stand out from mat-like or mounded plants long after their flowers fade.
- If you have a small garden that you'll see from a distance, use bold colors, bold textures, or bold shapes to make it appear larger and closer to the viewer.

Coordinating Heights and Habits

Mix annuals and perennials of varying heights to add visual interest to your garden design. Organize heights to progress from short to tall so no flowers will be hidden behind taller plants. If you view a garden from the front, put the tallest plants toward the back of the garden. Or with a bed that you see from

Flowers can have intriguing shapes and textures. Bells of Ireland has an unusual flower color, too.

A Combination Case Study

Once you start grouping plants with an eye for compatible heights, habits, and colors, you'll develop a feeling for which ones could look good together. But when you're a beginner, the idea of planning pleasing combinations may be a little intimidating.

To see how easy it can be, let's look at one simple combination and figure out why it works. We'll start with a patch of Madagascar periwinkle (*Catharanthus roseus*), with its flat, five-petaled, deep-pink blossoms. Behind that, we'll add a group of mealy-cup sage (*Salvia farinacea*) for its spikes of small, blue flowers. And to enhance this duo, let's tuck in a few plants of airy yellow cosmos (*Cosmos sulphureus*) toward the back.

Why does this trio work? First, all three annuals share the need for a sunny spot and perform best in the summer heat. The shape, texture, and height of each plant is different but compatible; the flower sizes and shapes also vary. Finally, the colors—pink, blue, and yellow—work well together; each contrasts with the other, but none is so strong that it overwhelms the others.

If you really like this combination, you could create a whole bed of just these three kinds of plants. Or you could expand it by adding other compatible plants— perhaps the blue-flowered, low-growing annual lobelia or a dramatic yellow Asiatic hybrid lily to serve as a focal point. Once you start trying out new flower and foliage combinations, the fun never ends!

all sides, cluster the tall plants near the center, and let the lower plants taper down in height toward the edges.

Many plants have shapes or growth habits that make them particularly useful for certain purposes. Low-growing plants like common thrift (*Armeria maritima*), pinks (*Dianthus* spp.), and coral bells (*Heuchera sanguinea*) have neat foliage and make attractive edgings. Try full or

Fleeceflowers (*Polygonum* spp.) and other spiky plants look good with mounded plants like hostas.

tall types like goldenrod (*Solidago* spp.), boltonia (*Boltonia asteroides*), or black snakeroot (*Cimicifuga racemosa*) to hide unattractive views or to serve as a background for large beds and borders.

Some annuals and perennials are excellent groundcovers. They can squeeze out weeds, provide attractive foliage, and give you a more interesting alternative to English ivy. Use groundcovers by themselves, one species per bed, or blend several with different foliage textures and colors but similar growth rates. Try creeping phlox (*Phlox stolonifera*), ajuga (*Ajuga reptans*), spotted lamium (*Lamium maculatum*), forget-me-nots (*Myosotis sylvatica*), and sweet alyssum (*Lobularia maritima*), among others.

For visual interest, make the most of the graduating heights and varying forms of annuals and perennials.

Creating a Color-theme Garden

You can design beautiful gardens around a theme as simple as a single color. This may sound plain, but it's anything but that—color-theme gardens are attractive and dramatic additions to any landscape. Even gardens that are based on green leaves contain varying tints and shades, as well as textures and patterns, from the frosty blue-greens of some hostas to the deep glossy green of European wild ginger (*Asarum europaeum*). When you start including flower colors against the greens, you add an extra level of interest. Even if the flowers you choose are all in the same color group, the many different shades and tints create a mosaic of changing colors throughout the season.

Planning a color-theme garden starts by picking the color you want to work with. Try a monochrome (based on one flower color) border if you have a favorite color or love collecting flowers of a particular color. Or make a small monochromatic section part of a long mixed-color border, perhaps using silver foliage to separate it from flowers of other colors.

If you have a couple of unconnected small beds, you might want to try using a different color in each. Or choose a single color for the whole garden in each season: perhaps pink for spring, white for summer, and yellow for fall, or whatever colors appeal to you.

Gardens with lots of yellow flowers and foliage look cheerful and sunny, even on dreary days.

Gardens based on purple and blue flowers are soothing—a perfect place to relax after a rough day.

White gardens are especially charming at night, when the pale blooms reflect any available light.

Another option to consider is a two-color border. Blue and white is a classic combination. Or perhaps pinks and yellows are more to your liking. Yellow or chartreuse with maroon or burgundy is another popular color combination.

The key to creating a beautiful and effective color-theme garden is to pick the colors that you like and those that blend well with your house. White flowers, for instance, can look dirty against cream-colored siding, while bright pinks can clash with rusty orange brick.

If you're not sure how certain colors will look in a given setting, try growing the plants there in a container for a year. If the colors look good to you, go ahead and plan a full-scale garden; if they don't fit the bill, move the pot elsewhere, and try a different combination in that spot next year. You'll save yourself a lot of time and money this way, and you'll be more confident about the results.

In the sections below, you'll find more tips for planning gardens around some of the most popular colors.

Beautiful Blue Gardens

Blue is a popular color theme for annual and perennial plantings. Many beloved summer-blooming plants have blue flowers, including delphiniums, Siberian iris (*Iris sibirica*), bellflowers (*Campanula* spp.), and pincushion flower (*Scabiosa caucasica*). To extend the season, add blue-flowered shrubs, such as caryopteris (*Caryopteris* x *clandonensis*), and annuals such as ageratum and the intensely blue lobelia (*Lobelia erinus*).

For spring color, plant bulbs such as Spanish bluebells (*Hyacinthoides hispanicus*) and Siberian squills (*Scilla sibirica*). For even more choices, expand your list to include the many flowers in the blue-violet range.

Several plants offer bluish foliage; amethyst sea holly (*Eryngium amethystinum*) and blue false indigo (*Baptisia australis*) offer blue flowers as well. Many of the finest hosta cultivars—including 'Krossa Regal', 'Blue Giant', and 'Hadspen Blue'—have cool blue leaves that look super in shady gardens. Rue (*Ruta graveolens*) and blue fescue (*Festuca cinerea*) produce their best blues in full sun. Also include silver foliage, which is stunning in blue borders.

Pretty Pink Gardens

Pink is an easy choice for a color theme, since so many annuals, perennials, hardy bulbs, and flowering shrubs come in this color. Use pink flowers alone, or try a two-color combination of pink and red, pink and white, or pink and pale yellows. Pink foliage is hard to find, but purples—like purple garden sage (*Salvia officinalis* 'Purpurascens')—and silvers—such as lamb's ears (*Stachys byzantina*)—are perfect additions to pink borders.

Wonderful White Gardens

Elegant white theme gardens offer perhaps the widest range of flower choice, as so many annuals, perennials, hardy bulbs, and flowering shrubs and trees come in bright white, off-white, or cream.

All-white designs are sometimes known as "moon gardens" because the flowers almost glow under the light of a full moon. This effect can also be achieved under street lights in urban gardens or at the edge of a well-lit patio. Moon gardens include many plants with silver or gray foliage; they may also include flowers in the palest pastels, as these reflect moonlight almost as well as white. For gardens near the house, include fragrant types of white roses, lilies, and peonies, along with fragrant annuals such as sweet alyssum (*Lobularia maritima*) and flowering tobacco (*Nicotiana alata*).

Rousing Reds, Oranges, and Yellows

Hot-color borders are exciting and vibrant. Yellow gardens have a sunny, cheerful look and are fairly easy to arrange without fear of clashing colors. Reds and oranges make the loudest statements of the various color themes, but red flowers also have the greatest potential to clash with each other. Before planting a whole border of these bright colors, consider trying a small bed or part of a border first to see if you like the effect.

TOP: Red flowers look marvelous against green leaves. The contrast between the two is dynamic.
BOTTOM: Mixing a variety of reds, yellows, and oranges can produce exciting combinations, too.

Attractive purple and silver foliage will remain long after the showy rose and clematis blooms are over.

Orchestrating All-Year Interest

You see your yard every day of the year, so make sure it's worth looking at. A good selection of spring-, summer-, and fall-blooming annuals and perennials, plus a few plants with evergreen leaves for winter interest, will give you a landscape that is truly attractive all year long. All-season interest starts with flower displays that spread beyond one season. Choosing plants for different seasons is easy: Look under "Flowering Time" in the individual plant entries starting on page 172.

Foliage and plant form are other features you can use to keep your garden looking beautiful as flowers come and go. From spring through fall, many annuals and perennials have leaves in attractive colors—like the maroon leaves of 'Palace Purple' heuchera (*Heuchera* 'Palace Purple')—or interesting shapes, such as the starry leaves of blood-red cranesbill (*Geranium sanguineum*). Unusual plant forms—such as the spiky leaves and flowers of hollyhock (*Alcea rosea*), foxgloves (*Digitalis* spp.), blackberry lily (*Belamcanda chinensis*), yuccas, and spike

gayfeather (*Liatris spicata*)—add drama, especially next to mounds such as cushion spurge (*Euphorbia epithymoides*). Use different types of foliage and forms to add contrast, or repeat similar leaves and shapes to unify a planting scheme.

Your Spring Landscape

After a long, dreary winter, few things are more welcome than colorful spring flowers. In spring, Lenten rose (*Helleborus orientalis*) and crocuses bloom before most of the garden shrugs off winter. Plant early bulbs where you'll see them from windows or as you enter the house so you can enjoy their bright colors when it's cold outside. Many wildflowers and shade-loving plants bloom as trees leaf out, so spring is a good season to draw attention to areas that will be shady and green later on. Supplement early-blooming annuals and perennials with flowering shrubs and trees such as forsythias, azaleas, magnolias, dogwoods, flowering cherries, and crab apples.

A Wealth of Summer Color

As spring turns into summer, many old-fashioned annuals and perennials—including cornflowers, peonies, irises, and columbines (*Aquilegia* spp.)—reach their peak, making it an easy time to feature flowers. Supplement these with early summer shrubs and vines such as rhododendrons, roses, clematis, wisteria, and honeysuckle (*Lonicera* spp.).

Bulbs such as bluebells (*Hyacinthoides* spp.) blend beautifully with spring-flowering shrubs.

Cornflowers and corn poppies are easy-care, hardy annuals that will provide masses of color all summer.

sundrops (*Oenothera tetragona*) turn beautiful shades of red, balloon flower (*Platycodon grandiflorus*) and amsonia (*Amsonia* spp.) leaves turn bright yellow, and many ornamental grasses bleach to gold. Jack-in-the-pulpit (*Arisaema triphyllum*) and white baneberry (*Actaea pachypoda*) are perennials with dramatic berries that may last into fall.

Perennials for Winter Interest

After the leaves drop, attention turns to evergreen plants and those with seedpods or fruits. Perennials with showy winter seedpods include coneflowers, blue false indigo (*Baptisia australis*), blackberry lily (*Belamcanda chinensis*), and astilbes.

Many crab apples and shrubs such as viburnums, cotoneasters, and deciduous and evergreen hollies (*Ilex* spp.) display fruits well into winter. Ornamental grasses remain attractive for months; cut them to the ground when they look tattered to make way for spring's new growth.

As summer progresses, daisy-like annuals and perennials—including blanket flower (*Gaillardia* x *grandiflora*) and coreopsis (*Coreopsis* spp.)—take center stage. Good-looking foliage keeps up appearances where early perennials have finished blooming. Silver leaves make dramatic partners for hot- or cool-hued flowers; yellow, purple, or variegated foliage also attracts attention. Flowering shrubs for July and August include abelia (*Abelia* x *grandiflora*), butterfly bush (*Buddleia davidii*), and hydrangeas. Sourwood (*Oxydendrum arboreum*) and Japanese pagoda tree (*Sophora japonica*) are large trees that bloom prolifically in late summer, as does the large trumpet creeper vine (*Campsis* spp.).

Combinations for Fall

Asters, boltonia, and Joe-Pye weeds (*Eupatorium* spp.) keep blooming after fall frosts nip most annuals. As flowers fade, foliage brightens—and not just on trees or shrubs such as burning bush (*Euonymus alata*). Leaves of peonies and common

Plants such as this ornamental thistle can add a bold, architectural statement amid your plantings.

Beds and Borders, Screens and Fillers

Two of the most common ways to group annual and perennial plantings are as beds and borders. They also have another widely used function, to screen out ugly views or hide the old garden shed or the back fence that's seen better days. And annuals are the perfect solution for filling in empty spaces. When you're starting a new garden, one of the hardest parts of the process is waiting for all those empty patches of soil to fill in, and that's when annuals will come to the rescue.

This delightful lavender border combines the structure of a double border with the casual feeling from the lavender's sprawling growth.

Borders and Beds

Borders typically are long, rectangular areas that create a visual edge to a lawn or other part of the landscape. You can also design them with gentle curves for a more informal look. They are usually sited to be viewed from a distance and because they're usually seen from one side, borders generally have a distinct front and back, with taller plants located to the rear.

Generally, the longer a border is, the wider it should be—to a point. This will keep you from making awkward-looking squares. A rectangle extends the garden and maintains enough depth for varying plant heights. In a small suburban yard, you could make a border that is 4 feet (1.2 m) wide by 14 feet (4.2 m) long. Or in a larger yard, extend the border to 5 feet (1.5 m) wide by 21 feet (6.3 m) long. However, there is no reason why you can't make a border any length and width that you want, as long as it complements the existing structures.

If you want a really wide border, it's a good idea to put an access path of a couple of stepping stones through the middle so you can maintain all sections of the border without walking on the garden soil. If you want a border more than 3 feet (90 cm) wide in front of a hedge or wall, leave space behind it for a mulched or grassy access path so you can get to all parts of your border.

If a border must be small to fit a small yard, give it more power by placing it close to the house and using small but

Multiple purple blooms on the stems of clustered bellflowers make this an excellent border plant.

effective groupings of flowers. Especially in a small garden, every plant must be attractive for as long as possible, so look for plants that have a long bloom season and attractive foliage.

Borders of hybrid tulips interplanted with blue phlox mark a pathway through a woodland garden.

Beds come in many shapes and sizes. Try to choose a shape and style (formal or informal) that matches or balances nearby features in your yard. The front of the bed can curve even if the side up against the house must be straight. Keep the bed narrow enough to allow you to reach all the plants from outside the bed, or place stepping stones in it for easy access.

Beds surrounded by lawn are called islands; often these are oval or kidney shaped. They are a great way to add color and height to new property while you're waiting for the trees and shrubs to mature. Island beds are also useful for replacing the grass under trees, reducing the need for trimming and making mowing easier.

Like borders, beds are usually designed to be seen from a distance. And because island beds are often viewed from all sides, the design needs to look attractive all around, like a table centerpiece. Since there's no "back," put your tallest plants toward the middle and surround them with the lower plants.

As a general rule, make island beds three times as long as they are wide for the most natural effect. You also make one end wider than the other so you can grow taller flowers there. But be sure to balance the extra bed width by putting an appropriate group of bold plants in or near

Flower beds of spring annuals, all of a similar height, are an easy and popular way to make a display.

the narrower side. Since you can view an island bed from all sides, put the tallest plants in the center. If, on the other hand, you will view it primarily from one angle, perhaps from the house or patio, make the highest point in the back. Then you can add extra tiers of midborder plants and still have some low-growing annuals and perennials on the far side.

Perennial Plantings

Perennial borders may stretch along a driveway, walkway, fence, or the edge of woods, although they don't really have to "border" anything; borders may merely create the illusion of a boundary to a "room" within the landscape.

Perennial borders are sometimes just that—only perennials. But more and more gardeners are enjoying the benefits of mixing their perennials with other plants, including shrubs, small trees, hardy bulbs, annuals, and ornamental grasses. These plants complement perennials by adding extra height, texture, and color to the border. Shrubs,

trees, grasses, and bulbs add year-round interest; annuals are brief but brilliant.

Perennial beds are often located closer to the house than borders, perhaps along the foundation or edging a patio. If you're going to put a bed where you'll see it all the time, choose your plants carefully for all-season interest. High-visibility beds will also need either some extra work or carefully chosen, low-maintenance plants to look their best all the time.

Annuals Alone

Flower beds are traditionally one of the most popular ways to display annuals. Setting aside separate beds for annual flowers is an easy way to go. Since you start with an empty area each year, spring

Asiatic lilies, with their lovely large blooms, are good for adding height to beds and borders.

An island bed may become a feature, especially if filled with spring bulbs.

Bed and Border Planning Pointers

Borders and beds can be designed to feature one big seasonal show or to showcase long, overlapping seasons of bloom. If you have the room for several different beds or borders, it can be fun to arrange each one with a different bloom season. That way you will always have at least one bed that is loaded with lovely flowers.

In small gardens or in plantings that you see every day, it's worth planning for long bloom times, attractive foliage, and year-round interest. Here are some planning tips you can try:

- Include some spring-, summer-, and fall-flowering annuals and perennials in each planting area.
- Look for plants that have great-looking foliage all season, such as hostas, artemisias, and lady's mantle (*Alchemilla* spp.).
- Choose long-blooming species and cultivars, like wild bleeding heart (*Dicentra eximia*) and 'Moonbeam' coreopsis (*Coreopsis verticillata* 'Moonbeam'); they can bloom for 8 weeks or longer.
- Include a few plants with good-looking evergreen foliage to give interest during the colder months. Bergenias and some alumroots (*Heuchera americana*) often turn a lovely reddish color in the cool temperatures of fall and winter.

soil preparation is a snap—you simply clean up any debris left in the bed, scatter some compost over the top to add nutrients and organic matter, and dig or till to loosen the top layer of soil.

Formal Gardens Formal flower beds tend to have a simple, geometric shape—such as a square, rectangle, or circle—and a limited number of different plants. The simplest may contain a mass of just one annual, such as marigolds or geraniums. For a little more variety, you could combine two or three different annuals, planted in straight rows or patterns.

If you grow different annuals together, pick those with varying heights. Select one that's low and spreading—such as edging lobelia (*Lobelia erinus*) or sweet alyssum (*Lobularia maritima*)—for the outer edge. The plants for the inside of the bed should be taller, usually no more than about 2 feet (60 cm). If the bed is in a spot where you can see it from all sides, you might want to include a taller "focal point" annual, such as castor bean (*Ricinus communis*) or love lies bleeding (*Amaranthus caudatus*), as a dramatic accent in the center.

The key to success with a formal bed is uniformity: You want the plants to be evenly spaced and evenly developed. If you're growing a bed of just one kind of annual—all marigolds, let's say—you could sow seed over the prepared bed, thin the seedlings to an even spacing, and expect fairly uniform results. In most cases, though, you'll get the best results by starting with transplants. All of the plants will be at the same stage, so they'll start blooming at the same time, and you can set them out at the proper spacing to get a nice, even look.

Low-growing plants can soften the edges of paths and steps; just trim them back as needed.

Informal Gardens If you enjoy a more casual-looking garden, then an informal planting may be more your style. Informal gardens can be any shape you like, though they often have a flowing outline that curves around the base of shrubs or other structures. Informal plantings usually include at least three or four different annuals. As with formal plantings, the plants you choose for informal beds should have varying heights for visual interest. But you aren't limited to having to plant informal beds in masses or rows. You can set plants out in whatever drifts, masses, or groupings look good to you.

Starting an informal flower bed from transplants is a good idea if you have

For a formal look, try a classic single border. An edging strip and gravel path make for easy maintenance.

specific plant groupings in mind. Placing transplants just where you want them gives you the most control over which colors and plant heights are next to each other. If you plan to plant different annuals in separate drifts, you could also start from seed sown directly in the garden. Or if you want a really casual, meadow-like effect, you could mix all the seeds together and scatter them over the soil; for more tips on starting a meadow garden, see "Making a Meadow Garden" on page 78.

Annuals with Other Plants

Although they look wonderful by themselves, annuals also have a lot to offer in groupings with other plants. In borders predominantly planted with perennials, bulbs, and shrubs, you can use annuals as a formal or informal edging, suggesting a flowering necklace around the border. While the other plants come in and out of bloom, the annual edging adds consistent color through most of the season. Repeating the same annual edging in different flower beds is a good way to link the separate beds in a garden picture.

Of course, you can also add annuals to the inside of borders as well. While

A border planted with vines and shrubs is enlivened with an edging of annuals like pansies.

the compact, uniform annuals that are excellent for formal bedding can look stiff and awkward next to perennials, many other annuals have a looser, more graceful habit. In fact, annuals and biennials such as larkspur (*Consolida ambigua*), foxgloves (*Digitalis purpurea*), and Canterbury bells (*Campanula medium*) are so charming when mixed with perennials that they are often considered traditional parts of a perennial border. Tall annuals and biennials such as cosmos,

A garden bed can be practical as well as pretty. Why not consider planting a bed of herbs?

For a Foundation

A foundation planting is similar to a bed; it's that small strip of soil that surrounds the house, and it may be the most misunderstood area in the garden. Evergreen shrubs are typically chosen for a foundation planting because they grow quickly and are "interesting" all year. But the plants that look just right in 5 years often take over the house in 15 or 20. Shrubs may need frequent pruning, and in cold areas they may be damaged by heavy, wet snow sliding off of the roof above.

Perennials, alone or with hardy bulbs and annuals, grasses, trees, vines, and shrubs, offer attractive and more colorful alternatives to a boring row of clipped evergreens. Well-chosen perennials won't drastically outgrow their location, and they're dormant when snow falls off the roof. Mixing perennials that have evergreen leaves—such as heart-leaved bergenia (*Bergenia cordifolia*) and perennial candytuft (*Iberis sempervirens*)—with hardy bulbs and ornamental grasses can create year-round appeal. Plus, perennials change continually through the season.

Foundation sites may have extreme growing conditions. Light levels and microclimates can vary dramatically on different sides of your house. Eaves may create a constant drought by blocking rainfall. At the drip line, the soil may be totally compacted by the impact of falling or dripping water. To cope with this, plan to cover the strip from the house to just past the roof edge with mulch. If this strip is too wide to be hidden behind a row of plants, plant drought-tolerant species that can take these tough conditions.

Choose the plants that can take the conditions and that look good to you. Include some fragrant flowers for a welcoming touch. Many herbs offer fragrant flowers or leaves, and are handy for cooking.

For a formal look, keep the lines straight with a pathway of bricks or square or rectangular flagstones and straight edges to plantings. For a less formal design, curve the edge of the bed to create a gentle, casual feel and to allow a few of the plants in front to sprawl a bit onto the path.

cleome, hollyhocks, and mulleins (*Verbascum* spp.) are ideal for adding height to the back of a mixed border. And shorter, airy annuals blend easily into border edgings; try plants like pot marigolds (*Calendula officinalis*), annual candytuft (*Iberis umbellata*), and annual baby's breath (*Gypsophila elegans*) with low-growing perennials and bulbs.

Screens

While the word "annual" commonly brings to mind compact, small plants like petunias and marigolds, there are a number of fast-growing annuals that can reach amazing heights of 6 feet (180 cm) or more in a single season. Tall-growing biennials and perennials may take a little longer, but they are just as effective at screening out an unpleasant view. Then there are the annual vines, with their twining stems that quickly cover trellises or fences for welcome shade and privacy. With these great plants to choose from, why spend another season staring at your neighbor's yard?

A row of sunflowers will make a cheerful cover-up.

Common foxgloves are real showstoppers. Plant them thickly to make a lovely temporary fence.

Tall Annuals and Perennials

Grow tall annuals and perennials in your yard to block out or cover up unattractive features, such as dog runs, trash cans or clothesline poles. Or plant a row or mass of tall annuals to create a "neighbor-friendly" temporary fence that delineates your property line or separates different areas of your garden. Some top-notch tall plants include hollyhocks (*Alcea rosea*), sunflowers (*Helianthus annuus*), Mexican sunflower (*Tithonia rotundifolia*), the wide variety of foxgloves (*Digitalis* spp.), castor bean (*Ricinus communis*), delphiniums, and cardinal flowers (*Lobelia cardinalis*), and the spreading masses of goldenrod (*Solidago* spp.), spotted Joe-Pye weed (*Eupatorium maculatum*) and Queen-of-the-prairie (*Filipendula rubra*).

Annual Vines

A leafy curtain of annual vines is an ideal way to ensure privacy on a porch or patio without appearing to be unneighborly. Flowering vines also add a quaint, old-fashioned touch to the most ordinary, unsightly support. A cloak of morning glories can convert a ho-hum garden shed into a charming garden feature, while a

mass of scarlet runner bean will accent an arch or liven up a lamppost.

Most annual vines cover territory in a hurry. You can easily train them to climb a wooden or wire trellis, chain-link fences, lattice work, or even strong twine. Tall wooden or bamboo stakes also make effective supports. While annual vines are usually lighter than woody vines (such as wisteria or trumpet creeper), they can put on a lot of growth in one season, so supply a sturdy support. Unlike clinging vines such as ivy, annual vines mostly climb with tendrils or twining stems, so don't expect them to scamper up a bare wall without assistance.

Morning glories (*Ipomoea tricolor*) have long been loved for their heart-shaped leaves and beautiful, trumpet-shaped flowers. The closely related moonflower (*Ipomoea alba*) is another popular vine; it offers large, white, heavily fragrant flowers that open in the evening. Besides being covered with clusters of colorful blooms, scarlet runner bean (*Phaseolus coccineus*) has the added bonus of edible beans. Other popular annual vines include cup-

Cup-and-saucer vine quickly covers fences or trellises, its blooms changing color with age.

The area under trees doesn't have to be dull. Plant annuals like pot marigolds and violas for season-long show and variety.

you need to allow ample space for these plants to fill in as they mature, the bare soil in between is boring and empty, and it provides an open invitation for weeds to get started. And while mulch can suppress weeds, it doesn't add a great deal of excitement to a new planting. That's where filler annuals come in handy.

Fillers for Flower Beds

If you're looking for annuals to fill in around your new perennial plantings, choose those with a similar range of heights and colors as the perennials. Select a few short or trailing annuals for the front of the border, a few medium-sized plants for the middle of the border, and a few tall annuals for the back. While you could sow annual seed directly into the ground around the perennials, it's often easier to start with transplants of the annuals you want. Good filler annuals such as cleome (*Cleome hasslerana*) and cornflower (*Centaurea cyanus*) will drop seed and come back year after year. If your annuals do reseed, thin the seedlings to allow the expanding perennials room to develop.

Fillers for Groundcovers

Low-growing annuals such as rose moss (*Portulaca grandiflora*), baby blue-eyes (*Nemophila menziesii*), and sweet alyssum (*Lobularia maritima*) can be excellent fillers for young groundcover plantings. Use one kind of annual for a uniform effect. It's just as easy to scatter seed around the groundcover plants, although you could also set out annual transplants in the available spaces instead. While

Try a colorful planting of low-growing annuals to fill in the bare spots around new shrub plantings.

many low-growing annuals will self-sow, you may want to scatter some fresh annual seed over the planting for the first few springs until the groundcovers fill in.

Low-growing pansies mix well with groundcovers such as ajuga and Japanese primrose.

and-saucer vine (*Cobaea scandens*), black-eyed Susan vine (*Thunbergia alata*), sweet pea (*Lathyrus odoratus*), and hyacinth bean (*Lablab purpureus*).

Fillers

When you start any new garden, one of the hardest parts of the process is waiting for plants to fill in. This is especially true of perennial and shrub beds, since these plants can take 3 or 4 years to really get established and look like anything. New groundcover plantings can appear pretty sparse for the first few years, too. While

Incorporating Herbs

Versatile, colorful, flavorful, and often fragrant, herbs have a place in any landscape. Mix them with other annuals and perennials in beds and borders, or group them together in a formal herb garden. Either way, you can also enjoy their delightful scents and colors in crafts and in the kitchen as well as in the garden. They're easy to grow, and they'll produce generous quantities of tasty leaves or seeds to spice up your favorite dishes.

Creating a Herb Garden

Regardless of the size, shape, or location of your garden, its style is a reflection of your own tastes. At one extreme are the formal herb gardens with their angular knots and pruned hedges, and at the other are random groupings of whatever suits the season. The number of possible styles

Herbs look great any way you use them—grouped separately or mixed with other annuals and perennials.

for a herb garden is limited only by your imagination and creativity. You can plan one or more theme gardens to concentrate on a particular aspect.

Some gardeners prefer to group their collection of herbs into a special herb garden. This makes it easier to find the particular ones you want so you can enjoy their various scents or harvest them for cooking or crafts.

Plan your herb garden as a regular bed or border, or give it a more formal look with paths, edgings, and separate growing beds. A basic herb garden could consist of several square raised beds edged with wooden sides and separated by paths. For even more formality, you could lay out the garden beds in geometric shapes, wheel spokes, or intricate knots.

Garden Shape

The simplest herb gardens to set out and manage are square or rectangular. Laying out your garden with square or rectangular beds not only may be the most practical way, but can give the garden a formal look that appeals to many gardeners.

Alternatively, you may choose to lay your garden beds following the curve of a

hill, stream, fence, or stone wall, or design them to accent the shape of a building. If you want to be especially creative, garden within unusual boundaries like circles or ovals. You can make a garden in the shape of a spiral, with one continuous bed beginning in the center and spiraling out in circles. A book or magazine on garden landscaping will offer you examples to follow in shaping your garden beds.

Elaborate knot gardens of interwoven herbs first became popular in the 15th century in Europe.

Start annual and biennial herbs from seed and use them to fill in between longer-lived perennials.

Growing herbs and flowers in your vegetable garden will help to attract beneficial, pest-eating insects.

Chicory is a surprisingly hardy herb, given its delicate appearance, that thrives in full sun.

If you choose to garden in several small patches, position plants that need daily attention or frequent picking close to the house. If space is limited, take advantage of borders along paths and fences. At the least, you can dress your windows outdoors with boxes of luscious herbs close at hand.

Garden Design

Paths are a necessity for work in your herb garden, and a garden stroll can also follow the paths you've planned. Once you've located your paths, beds, or rows, it's time to begin selecting and arranging your plants. Prepare a list of the plants you want to grow, along with their growth habits, size at maturity, and special soil, space, or environmental requirements. Remember that because single plants tend to become lost in the crowd, it's more effective to plant in clumps. It's generally best to plant the tallest herbs at the back, the shortest in the front.

Define the edges of formal beds with low, clipped hedges of bluish rue, green hyssop, or silvery santolina—or even a combination of all three. Or be more casual and allow the herbs that are growing along the edge to sprawl a little onto the paved or gravel paths. For a traditional touch, plan a small round bed in the center of the garden, and accent it with a sundial, statue, domed straw bee skep, or large potted bay (*Laurus nobilis*) or rosemary as a special focal point.

Locate culinary herb gardens as close to the kitchen as possible so that they're easy to access. Grow what you'll use fresh in cooking plus extra to dry or freeze for winter. Remember to include attractive, edible herbs such as silver thyme and variegated sages for color contrast. Add annual herbs and edible flowers such as purple basil, nasturtium, and borage for even more color.

Keep the following in mind when you plan the design of your herb garden:
- Use your site's limitations to your advantage. If you're confined to gardening in the shade, use the opportunity to grow as many shade-loving herbs as possible. Include angelica, chervil, lemon balm, and sweet cicely. In wet areas, select from the wide assortment of plants in the mint family. Among so many herbs, you'll find plants to fill just about every niche.
- Divide a large garden, or create several small gardens, by grouping herbs that serve particular purposes. Medicinal, dye, fragrance, and culinary gardens are some examples.

Herb gardens can be beautiful and useful. Mix in a variety of herbs with colorful leaves and flowers.

- Select herbs that flower at the same time or whose blooms share the same color. Lavender and blue themes in particular are easy to create with herbs. Or focus on foliage, and plant blue-green or silvery herbs mixed with darker greens for contrast.
- Group the perennials together, since they tend to have similar requirements, and this will help you avoid mistakes. If you're planning to grow some invasive perennials like mint in among other herbs, plant them in buried containers like clay drainage pipes or bottomless large pots that are at least 1 foot (30 cm) deep.

Easy Annuals and Biennials

Annual and biennial herbs are among the easiest herbs to grow; they germinate and grow quickly from seed. There are a few short-lived perennial herbs, such as fennel, that also grow quickly from seed, so you can treat them as annuals.

Annuals: Anise, basil (sweet), borage, calendula, cayenne pepper, chervil, coriander, dill, fennel, fenugreek, mustard, nasturtium, plantain, safflower, vervain.
Biennials: Burdock, caraway, curly- and flat-leaved parsley.

Dill

and white spring flowers, but it spreads too much to work well in herb beds; grow it as a groundcover under shrubs instead. Mints are also notorious for spreading rampantly. To keep them from taking over the rest of the yard, be sure to constrain them with some type of barrier, as discussed before. Many invasive herbs also adapt well to growing in pots.

Perennial Herbs

There are even more perennial herbs that you can include in your garden. Deciding which ones to grow and where you'll grow them is really no different from choosing other perennial plants for your garden. You either need to make a list of the herbs that you want to grow and then find a place for them or, alternatively, pick a site and look for herbs that will thrive there.

Annual Herbs

As with other annuals, annual herbs are quite useful for filling the gaps around new perennial plantings. If you have a formal herb garden with traditional

Adding Herbs to Other Plantings

If you don't have room for a separate herb garden, tuck your favorite herbs into other perennial beds and borders. Most herbs look good in formal designs; many also make a natural addition to casual cottage gardens as well.

Versatile, aromatic, and pretty, chamomile is ideal in a cottage garden and in beds and borders.

A number of herbs are also well suited to container gardening, so you can move them around to add fragrance and color wherever you need it.

Herb Gardening Basics

If you meet the simple needs that herbs have, you'll find them to be among the least demanding plants to grow. Sunny sites will suit the widest range of herbs. It is possible to grow some herbs in partial to full shade, but your choices will be limited. (Mints, lemon balm, and sweet woodruff are your most likely subjects for success in shade.)

Make sure the soil is well drained, ideally with a pH near neutral to slightly alkaline. Build raised beds to improve drainage if your soil tends to be wet all season. Work in some compost as you prepare the soil. The compost will supply the nutrients your herb plants need, so don't add extra fertilizer before planting.

Allow ample room for ornamental herbs to grow without crowding. Space culinary herbs closer together, since the frequent trimming for harvest will also keep the plants smaller.

Some herbs will spread so quickly that they need special controlling measures. Sweet woodruff may be a charming, low-growing perennial with whorled leaves

Some herbs, like pennyroyal, help protect other plants by deterring insects from settling on them.

Sage is useful in the garden for its attractive foliage and in the kitchen for its tasty flavor.

perennial herbs, such as sage, thyme, and mint, scatter the seed of annual herbs among the young plants. Or use annual herbs throughout your yard as you would any other filler annual and you'll find you have flower beds that are productive as well as beautiful.

If you enjoy cooking with herbs, annuals provide lots of scope for experimentation. Some commonly grown annual herbs include anise, basil, borage, chervil, coriander, dill, and parsley. Here are some details on a few of the most popular ones.

Basil What would a cook's garden be without basil? This peppery herb is a traditional part of pestos and tomato dishes; finely sliced basil on fresh tomatoes is simply delicious. It's also a snappy addition to salads, poultry, pasta, rice, eggs, and vegetable dishes. For the best growth, give basil a site with full sun and rich, well-drained soil. Sow seeds of this heat-loving herb directly into the garden in late spring, or set out transplants after all danger of frost has passed. Snip the leaves as needed. For extra interest, look for purple-leaved basil cultivars; they are ornamental as well as edible.

Coriander Actually, coriander is the name commonly used for the seeds of *Coriandrum sativum*, while the leaves are often referred to as cilantro. The leaves have a powerful odor and a flavor that combines sage and citrus. The fresh leaves and roots are popular in many cuisines for use in salads, sauces, and relishes. The citrus-flavored seeds are a nice addition to herbal teas or desserts. Sow the seed outdoors in spring in a spot with sun to light shade and rich, well-drained soil. Sow again every 2 to 3 weeks until late summer for a continuous supply of fresh leaves. Pick the leaves as needed; harvest the seeds when they begin to fall from the flower heads.

Dill Grow dill for its lacy green leaves and flavorful seeds. The fresh leaves (often called "dill weed") are a popular addition to fish dishes, as well as vegetable dishes, sauces, and salads. Dill seed is most commonly used as a pickling spice. Sow the seed outdoors in spring in full sun and rich, well-drained soil. Snip the leaves as

Containing herbs in wooden retainers is one way of preventing them from becoming invasive.

Popular Perennial Herbs

Perennial herbs form the backbone of most herb plantings. These hardy plants return year after year, giving structure and continuity to your herb garden. Among the best known are:

Agrimony, aloe, angelica, anise hyssop, arnica, bergamot, betony, burdock, catmint, chamomile (Roman), chicory, chives, clary, comfrey, costmary, dandelion, dock, elecampane, feverfew, garlic, germander, ginger, goldenrod, hop, horehound, horseradish, horsetail, hyssop, lady's bedstraw, lavender (English), lemon balm, lemongrass, lovage, madder, marjoram, marsh mallow, mint, mugwort, nettle, oregano, orris, pennyroyal, red clover, rosemary, saffron, sage, santolina, savory (winter), soapwort, sorrel, southernwood, sweet cicely, sweet woodruff, tansy, tarragon (French), thyme (garden), valerian, violet, wormwood, and yarrow.   Clary

needed; collect the seeds when they turn brown and begin to drop.

Parsley Both the curly-leaved and flat-leaved types of parsley are edible, but the flat-leaved type has the best flavor. Parsley goes with just about any kind of food except desserts. Mix minced parsley into butter or margarine for a flavorful spread, or add chopped parsley to salsa. In the garden, parsley forms attractive clumps that make a nice edging for a flower garden. Sow seed directly into the garden in early spring, or set out transplants. Snip the outer leaves as needed. Parsley is a biennial; it will flower and produce seeds (but few leaves) during the second year.

Growing a Container Garden

Using plants in containers gives you the freedom to change your displays with the season while finding creative solutions to garden challenges. Here, the bare steps leading to a house are brightened.

No matter what size or style of garden you have, growing flowering plants in pots can greatly expand your planting options. Try a few combinations of annuals or perennials in containers and discover how fun, practical, and versatile these movable gardens can be.

Solving Challenges with Containers

With a little creativity, you'll find many different ways to use containers to solve problem spots. If you can't kneel or if you garden from a wheelchair, you can grow plants at a convenient height in raised planters. If your soil is too hard or rocky to dig, grow flowers in half-barrel planters instead of in the ground.

If you've got a shady spot that's crying out for color, try using potted annuals or perennials to create a rotating display: As flowers fade, move the shady pot to a sunnier spot and replace it with one that's robust from sunshine. Or tuck a few pots into a dull planting to add quick color. If space is really limited, create your own garden paradise on a rooftop or porch or in a window box.

Don't limit your container gardens to just practical uses, though. Growing annuals and perennials in pots is a great way to experiment with different plant combinations before you commit to putting them in the ground. If you don't like a combination, just separate the pots and group them with other possibilities.

Containers can also make great garden accents. Choose bold, sculptural perennials such as Adam's needle (*Yucca filamentosa*) for formal designs; mix lots of different colors and cascading plants for a cottage look.

Be as imaginative as possible when choosing a container, but try to use annuals that are the same height or shorter than the height of the container.

Choosing a Container

Pot possibilities are endless. You may buy commercially made plastic or clay containers or make your own out of old barrels, washtubs, or even buckets. Large pots tend to provide the best conditions for growth, since they hold more soil, nutrients, and water, but they are also quite heavy if you need to move or hang them.

Geraniums in a container add a spot of mobile color to a garden bed and provide an accent, too.

A large planter cascading with annuals and perennials is a great garden accent on a patio.

Perennials for Containers

Just about any perennial will grow well in a pot, as long as you give it the growing conditions and routine care that it needs. Plant several perennials in one pot or group several in individual containers. Good choices include those with a long season of bloom, such as golden orange 'Stella d'Oro' daylily. Other perennials that look especially nice are those with attractive foliage, such as lady's mantle (*Alchemilla mollis*), spotted lamium (*Lamium maculatum*), heart-leaved bergenia (*Bergenia cordifolia*), hostas, and ornamental grasses. Foliage plants will extend the period of interest.

Plants that are bushy and trailing, such as ivy geranium, look good filling a hanging basket.

Pots or baskets that are about 8 inches (20 cm) deep are usually able to hold enough soil for good growth without getting too heavy. If you don't plan to move the planter, it can be as big as you want. Be creative; almost anything you can put drainage holes in—from clay drainage tiles to old leather work boots—can be pressed into service.

Solid-sided containers, such as plastic pots, hold water longer than porous clay. Plastics are great if your summers tend to be hot and dry, since you'll have to water less often. But if you live in a wet climate, or if you tend to overwater, porous containers are probably best. Plastic pots are lighter, making them easier to move, but they are more prone to blowing over. Clay pots are heavy and less likely to blow over, but they often crack when they do tip.

In windy areas or for tall plants, place rocks in the bottom of any pot to increase stability. Empty clay pots or bring them indoors before freezing weather; wet soil expands as it freezes and will crack the pot. Dark pots heat up in bright sun and dry out quickly; avoid black plastic pots for container gardens that are growing in full sun.

Planting Bulbs in Pots

Fill the bottom of the container with a well-drained commercial potting mix. Adjust the thickness of this layer to match the needs of the bulbs you're planting. Lily bulbs should sit deep enough to have 5 to 6 inches (12.5 to 15 cm) of potting mix over their tops; set smaller bulbs so they're covered with 3 to 4 inches (7.5 to 10 cm) of mix. Fill the container with potting mix to within 1 to 2 inches (2.5 to 5 cm) of the rim. If you plan to include annuals, now is the time to plant the young plants in the container as you normally would, firming them in well and watering thoroughly.

STEP 1: Add potting mix to the container, then set in the bulbs.
STEP 2: Cover the bulbs with more mix, then water them thoroughly.

Annuals for Containers

Annuals make perfect container plants. They grow quickly, flower profusely, and provide a long season of good looks. Some offer distinctive foliage, while others perfume the air with their sweet scents. Groups of small- and medium-sized containers create charming spots of movable color; large planters can showcase a stunning mix of colorful annuals in a relatively small space. Window boxes and hanging baskets are other options for displaying a wide range of flowering and foliage annuals, especially when space is limited.

As with any kind of garden, the first step to planning successful container plantings is choosing plants that have similar growth needs. If you have a shady area, impatiens, monkey flower (*Mimulus* x *hybridus*), and other shade-lovers are your best bets. Sunny spots can support a wider range of colorful annuals, including treasure flower (*Gazania* hybrids), mealy-cup sage (*Salvia farinacea*), marigolds, and narrow-leaved zinnia (*Zinnia angustifolia*).

Single-annual containers can be pleasing, but mixed plantings of 3 or 4 different annuals are even more exciting. The exact plants that you decide to grow together are up to you; however, there are some basic guidelines you can follow to create a successful, balanced container planting. First, select a "star" plant. That is, base your container planting around a single centerpiece plant—perhaps a bushy marguerite daisy (*Argyranthemum frutescens*), a free-flowering tuberous begonia, or a bold ornamental cabbage. Then choose a "supporting cast" of other annuals to complement the star plant and fill out the pot. Try one or two with bold leaves or an upright habit—such as dusty miller (*Senecio cineraria*) or coleus—and one or two that sprawl or trail—such as edging lobelia (*Lobelia erinus*) or creeping zinnia (*Sanvitalia procumbens*).

Bulbs for Containers

Bulbs make excellent companions for annuals in pots, since the annuals usually root in the upper soil layer while the bulbs are planted much deeper. The bulbs also benefit from the covering of annuals, which shade

Bulb Forcing Made Easy

There's nothing more heartwarming to a gardener than a pot of flowering bulbs on the windowsill in the depths of winter. Happily, it's relatively easy to convince most spring bulbs to rush the season a bit. The process is called "forcing," although there's not much force involved. You simply provide a condensed version of the winter the bulbs would otherwise get when growing in the ground outdoors.

STEP 1: Plant your bulbs in pots, with the tips of the bulbs just visible over the soil.
STEP 2: Set the pots in a cool, dark place (temperature between 33° and 45°F [1° and 7°C]) until shoots appear; then give them light.

look especially good with a cascade of annual blooms beneath them. Other great summer bulbs for containers include small gladioli, calla lilies (*Zantedeschia aethiopica*), and Peruvian daffodil (*Hymenocallis narcissiflora*). Clumps of cannas or dahlias make a dramatic impact in large pots, tubs, and planters.

Tuberous begonias are one of the most wonderful potted bulbs for partially shady spots. They bloom over a long period in a wide range of colors and flower forms.

The cascading varieties look charming tumbling out of hanging baskets or over the sides of large pots. For extra excitement, grow tuberous begonias with shade-loving annual companions, such as coleus, fibrous begonias, wishbone flower (*Torenia fournieri*) and browallia (*Browallia speciosa*). Still other good bulbs for shady pots and planters are Italian arum (*Arum italicum*) and caladium (*Caladium x hortulanum*). The latter's intricately veined leaves come in many shades, including pink, rose, red, green, and white.

the soil and pot to some extent, keeping the bulbs cool. Almost all bulbs provide beautiful blooms; some provide eye-catching foliage. And there's a bulb for almost every exposure, from bright sunshine to dappled shade.

Pots of traditional spring-blooming bulbs—including hyacinths, tulips, and daffodils—are especially welcome early in the growing season. To coax them into bloom in pots, you need to give them a chilling period, as explained in "Spring Bulbs and Winter Chilling" on page 121. These spring bloomers work beautifully with cool-season annuals, such as pansies, common stock (*Matthiola incana*), and English daisy (*Bellis perennis*).

When warm weather sets in, summer bulbs come into their glory. Asiatic lilies make a lovely show in early summer and

Potted bulbs are wonderful in spring. Then you can replace them with annuals for later color.

Container-grown plants will need more water as the weather gets warmer and as they grow larger.

Consider the size of the container and the material it's made from. Use the best-quality potting mix you can find—and fertilize!

Caring for Container Gardens

Keeping the right water balance is a key part of successful container gardening. To help in this, you need to choose a growing medium that will hold some water but not too much. Straight garden soil isn't a good choice; improve it by mixing 2 parts soil with 1 part finished compost (or peat moss) and 1 part perlite. Or use sterilized, premixed "soil-less" potting mixes. These are free of soilborne diseases and they weigh much less, which is an important consideration for rooftop gardeners or if you're using large pots.

Regular watering is another way you'll balance each container's water supply. Some containers may need watering every day; others will only need water once a week. A good general rule is to wait until the top 1 inch (2.5 cm) of soil is dry; then water thoroughly, until some comes out of the bottom. If the water seems to run right through the container, put a tray or saucer underneath; empty any water that remains the next day.

Since their rooting space is limited, plants in pots need fertilizer much more often than plants growing in the ground. After they've been growing for a month or so, give plants diluted liquid fertilizer every couple of weeks. Use fish emulsion, liquid seaweed, or a balanced organic fertilizer; follow the instructions on the package to find out how often and how much fertilizer you should apply.

Special Care for Container Bulbs

Bulbs need a little extra attention. At the end of the season, dig out the bulbs or tubers of tender bulbs for winter storage. Shake off the soil and let the bulbs air-dry for several days. Store them carefully in labeled paper or mesh bags, or bury them in wood shavings, Styrofoam packing material, or peat moss to prevent the bulbs from drying out too much. Check the bulbs once a month and sprinkle them lightly with water if they look shriveled. Or simply leave the bulbs in their pot and bring the whole pot indoors for winter storage if you have a cool basement. For more information on storing bulbs over winter, see "Lifting and Storing Tender Bulbs" on page 153.

Hanging pots look best with low, bushy plants filling the top and trailing plants spilling over.

Wonderful Window Boxes

Nothing adds charm to a house like lush window boxes filled with cascades of colorful flowers and foliage. While the general principles of container planting apply here, there are a few special tips to keep in mind to plan and maintain great-looking window boxes.

- Consider the site. Before you put up any window boxes, make sure you can reach them easily for watering and maintenance. Because window boxes are so visible, it's especially important to keep them well groomed; that means regularly removing spent flowers and yellowing leaves.
- Stick with short plants. Window boxes are usually planted to be seen from the outside, but you also need to consider the view from the inside. It's generally best to use plants that grow no taller than about 8 inches (20 cm); those much taller than that can block your view.
- Choose compatible colors. Look for flower and foliage colors that complement those of the house and trim. Silvers and whites look crisp and cool against warm-toned brick, for instance, while blues and purples look pretty against cream colors, and pinks and yellows add life to somber gray siding.

Creating a Cutting Garden

If you enjoy having armloads of flowers to bring indoors for fresh arrangements, consider adding a cutting garden to your landscape. A cutting garden is simply one or more beds where you grow flowers to be used just for arrangements. You can collect beautiful blooms from your cutting garden without raiding your carefully planned displays in the rest of the yard.

Cutting Garden Basics

Few people have enough space to put a cutting garden truly out of sight, but the more removed it is, the less you'll worry about making it look nice. Some gardeners turn over a corner of their vegetable garden to cut flowers; others create separate cutting beds along a garage, in a sunny side yard, or in a sheltered corner of the backyard.

Wherever you put your cutting beds, you want them to be easy to reach and maintain. Be sure to prepare the soil well. Sow seeds or set out transplants just as you would for any garden, but there's no need to worry about too much planning or grouping specific heights and colors; just plant them in rows. With bulbs, plant hardy bulbs in fall and tender ones in spring after the soil has warmed enough.

Best Bulbs for Cutting

Listed below are some bulbs that make colorful, long-lasting cut flowers, arranged by bloom season; choose the ones you like best.

Spring Bloom
Allium spp. (ornamental onions)
Hyacinthus orientalis (hyacinth)
Leucojum aestivum
    (summer snowflake)
Muscari armeniacum
    (grape hyacinth)
Narcissus hybrids (daffodils)
Tulipa hybrids (tulips)
Summer Bloom
Canna x *generalis* (canna)
Gladiolus x *hortulanus* (gladiolus)
Lilium Asiatic hybrids
    (Asiatic lilies)
Lilium Trumpet hybrids
    (trumpet lilies)
Fall Bloom
Dahlia hybrids (dahlias)
Gladiolus x *hortulanus* (gladiolus)
Lilium Oriental hybrids
    (Oriental lilies)
Lycoris squamigera (magic lily)

Trumpet lily

Beds full of perennials grown for cutting don't need lots of planning, but they still require all the care you would lavish on any other plants.

Mulch between the rows with a loose organic material (such as straw). Water as needed to keep the soil evenly moist for best growth and fertilize annuals that like extra nutrients. Stake floppy or long-stemmed flowers such as delphiniums, peonies, and baby's breath to keep the stems upright and the flowers clean.

Snipping tulips from regular beds is fine if you only do a few arrangements each season.

Foliage is a crucial part of many arrangements.

Japanese irises, with their gorgeous purple and yellow flowers atop elegant stems, make a lovely arrangement.

Choosing Plants for Cutting

Selecting plants for your cutting garden is much the same as choosing plants for any planting. Most importantly, you need to choose plants that will thrive in your growing conditions; if they aren't growing well, they won't produce many flowers. Here are some other things you'll want to consider when you're deciding what to include:

- If space is limited, concentrate on growing annuals and perennials in your favorite flower colors; if you have lots of room, plant a variety of colors to have lots of options.

- Grow plants with different shapes to keep your arrangements from looking monotonous. Include spiky flowers and foliage for height, flat or round flowers and leaves for mass, and small, airy flowers and leaves for fillers.

- Look for annuals and perennials with long stems. Dwarf or compact cultivars are great for ornamental plantings, but their stems are usually too short for easy arranging.

- Don't forget to include foliage—it adds body and filler to arrangements. Use

Best Annuals for Cutting

Plan to sow some each of early-, mid-, and late-summer flowers to have a steady supply of blooms throughout the season. This list of suitable annuals for cut flowers shows their normal peak bloom season to help with your planning and planting.

Stocks

Antirrhinum majus (snapdragon; midsummer)
Calendula officinalis (pot marigold; early summer)
Callistephus chinensis (China aster; midsummer)
Centaurea cyanus (cornflower; midsummer)
Consolida ambigua (rocket larkspur; midsummer)
Cosmos bipinnatus (cosmos; late summer to fall)
Cosmos sulphureus (yellow cosmos; midsummer)
Dianthus barbatus (sweet William; early summer)
Gaillardia pulchella (blanket flower; midsummer)
Gypsophila elegans (annual baby's-breath; early summer)
Helianthus annuus (common sunflower; late summer)
Iberis umbellata (annual candytuft; early summer)
Lathyrus odoratus (sweet pea; early summer)

Tulips

Matthiola incana (stock; early summer)
Rudbeckia hirta (black-eyed Susan; midsummer)
Tithonia rotundifolia (Mexican sunflower; late summer)
Viola x *wittrockiana* (pansy; early summer)
Zinnia elegans (zinnia; midsummer)

The bright flowers and ferny foliage of cosmos are fine additions to arrangements in late summer.

leaves in subtle greens and silvers to emphasize individual flowers or colors; variegated leaves make striking accents.

There are so many annuals, perennials, and hardy bulbs to choose from when arranging flowers. To add something extra to your arrangements, include ornamental grasses in your cutting garden. They look great with both flowers and foliage. Spray their delicate flowers with lacquer or cheap hairspray to make them last longer.

Gathering Cut Flowers

The best time to collect cut flowers is when the buds are just opening, not when they are in full bloom. Collect them during a cool part of the day; morning is usually best. Take a bucket of lukewarm water and a sharp pair of clippers or a knife with you. If picking bulb flowers, choose those flowers with as few leaves as possible, so the bulbs can store enough energy for the next bloom season. As you snip the stem from the rest of the plant, make a sloping, rather than straight, cut; this opens up a little more room for the stems to absorb water. Plunge the cut flowers into the bucket immediately, so they are in water up to the base of the flower. (If you are cutting dahlias, sear the bottom of the stem with the flame from a match before putting it in the water.)

As you arrange the flowers, cut the stems to their final lengths under water so no air bubbles enter. Remove leaves that will be below the waterline in the finished arrangement. After arranging, fill the vase to the top with water; refill as soon as the level drops. You can also buy commercial preservatives to help extend the life of your blooms, or add a shot of lemon-lime soda, although the easiest method is simply to change the water every few days. Flowers will last longest in a cool room out of direct light.

Making a Meadow Garden

Meadows are informal blends of flowers and grasses growing in a sunny, open spot. They provide food and shelter for birds, beneficial insects, and butterflies. They also add a casual, country touch to any yard. Best of all, established meadows require little upkeep. But do bear in mind that what you see as a meadow garden may look like a patch of weeds to your neighbors. Discuss your plans with them and check local mowing ordinances in your area before you begin, to avoid any misunderstandings and complaints as you convert your lawn into a meadow.

Steps to a Great-looking Meadow

Creating a vigorous, beautiful meadow involves more than simply shaking seeds out of a packet or can onto a grassy or dusty spot. For best results, you'll need to give your meadow the same care you'd use to start any garden. Prepare the soil well, choose the best-adapted annuals and perennials, and plant them properly. Just follow these simple steps:

1. Pick a site with well-drained soil and at least 6 hours of sun a day.

Cut down on mowing time by replacing some lawn with a field full of California poppies and goldfields.

Fill in out-of-the-way places in your yard with prolific wildflowers to create a meadow garden.

2. In spring, summer, or fall, remove existing grasses and aggressive weeds; lawn grasses can spread vigorously and smother small, new plants. Skim off slices of turf with a spade. Compost the pieces of sod or use to fill holes in the remaining lawn.

3. Spread 1 to 2 inches (2.5 to 5 cm) of compost over the area, and dig or till it into the top 4 to 6 inches (10 to 15 cm) of soil. Use a rake to remove any rocks and smooth the soil.

4. Kill all weeds and reduce the bank of weed seeds in the soil to obtain a clean weed-free site.

5. In fall, set out your perennials, bulbs, and grasses and mulch them well. Their roots will be well established by spring, and your plants will be ready to put on great growth.

6. In spring, if you wish, rake away some mulch to sow annual wildflower seeds between the perennial meadow plants. Annuals will provide quick color the first year while the perennials are growing new roots and getting established.

7. Through the first growing season, water your meadow when the soil is dry to 1 to 2 inches (2.5 to 5 cm) deep to help the growing young plants establish.

Routine Meadow Maintenance

Mow your meadow once a year to keep it looking good and to keep weeds, shrubs, and trees from invading. Late fall to early winter, after plants have formed seeds, is the best time. If you want to feed the birds, leave seed heads standing until late winter or early spring; just be aware that they'll be harder to mow after winter rain and snow have beaten them down.

Cut the whole meadow to a height of about 6 inches (15 cm). Use a sickle-bar

Meadows are beautiful and low-maintenance, and they're ideal habitats for bees and butterflies.

Kill Weeds Before You Plant

To make a clean, weed-free site for your meadow garden, remove any perennial weeds, dig or till to loosen the soil, and rake the seedbed smooth. Then try one of the methods below:

Let exposed weed seeds germinate, then hoe or till the soil shallowly to remove the weeds that pop up.

Cover the soil with a sheet of thick, clear plastic during summer. The heat generated will kill any weed seeds.

mower for large areas; a string trimmer or hand clippers can handle small patches. A regular lawn mower won't work; it cuts too low. Leave trimmings in place so plants can self-sow, or collect them for your compost pile.

Aside from the yearly trim, your only maintenance is to dig out tree seedlings and aggressive weeds such as quack grass, poison ivy, bindweed, and burdock as soon as they appear. Established meadows don't require water, fertilizer, or mulch. As the plants get more established, your meadow garden will look different each year, but it will always be beautiful.

Wonderful Wildflower Meadows

Wildflower meadows are fairly easy and inexpensive to grow from seed, and their beautiful spread will provide a welcome visiting spot for the native butterflies, bees, and birds of your region. Evenly scatter a mixture of native wildflower and native grass seeds on the soil surface and rake them in. It's well worth the trouble to track down a mix of true natives; if you buy a "one-size-fits-all" mix, you'll be paying for some seed that won't grow where you live. Ask your Cooperative Extension Service or local botanical garden to recommend plants that will grow well in your area. It will take about 3 seasons for your wildflower meadow to completely fill in, though you should have some pleasing results in the first year.

Marvelous Annual Meadows

If you enjoy the easy, informal appearance of meadow gardens but don't want to wait a few years for perennial plants to get established, try planting an annual meadow. Many catalogs are now selling seed mixes of meadow annuals, containing colorful, easy-care plants like corn poppy (*Papaver rhoeas*), cornflower (*Centaurea cyanus*), California poppy (*Eschscholzia californica*), and calliopsis (*Coreopsis tinctoria*).

Most meadow annuals thrive in full sun and average soil, so choose a site with as much sun as possible. Prepare the soil as you would for any other annual garden. It's smart to prepare the site in fall so it will be ready for planting the following spring. When you are ready to plant, hoe the surface to clear off any weeds that have sprouted, then scatter the seed

A mixture of annuals, perennials, bulbs, and grasses creates an ever-changing scene.

evenly over the surface. Rake the bed lightly to scratch the seed into the soil, then water the area well using a light spray. Keep the soil moist for 2 or 3 weeks, until the seedlings start growing.

Established annual meadows don't need a great deal of care; just hand pull any weeds you see. At the end of the

Black-eyed Susan cultivars in vivid red are a natural choice for inclusion in an annual meadow.

Grasses in the Flower Garden

As well as having a place in any meadow garden, ornamental grasses blend beautifully into many traditional flower borders. Annuals and perennials add vibrant colors to the more subtle, muted tones of many grasses. The grasses, in turn, supply all-season interest and soothing backgrounds for delicate flowers.

Choose companions for your grasses based on the growing conditions you have available. In sunny areas, good choices include garden mums, delphiniums, peonies, the many different types of poppy, shasta daisies (*Leucanthemum* x *superbum*), gas plant (*Dictamnus purpureus*), and lupines (*Lupinus* spp.). Under trees, plants like ferns, hostas, and lily-of-the-valley (*Convallaria majalis*) combine well with shade-loving sedges. In dry locations, colorful rock garden plants—including maiden pinks (*Dianthus deltoides*), wall rock cress (*Arabis caucasica*), and woolly yarrow (*Achillea tomentosa*)—are ideal with low-growing grasses. And in wet places, rushes (*Juncus* spp.) form naturally beautiful combinations with water-loving perennials such as blue flag (*Iris versicolor*) and Siberian iris (*Iris sibirica*).

Grasses look great with flowers in all parts of the garden. Spring bulbs such as daffodils, crocus, grape hyacinths, snowdrops, and tulips make a colorful display early in the season; as they fade, the fast-growing grasses neatly camouflage the dying bulb foliage. In semiwild areas, wildflowers combine beautifully with the less showy grasses, including broomsedge (*Andropogon virginicus*), tufted hairgrass (*Deschampsia caespitosa*), switch grass (*Panicum virgatum*), and prairie cord grass (*Spartina pectinata*).

season, mow or cut the plants to the ground as outlined above. While many meadow annuals will reseed themselves, the second and subsequent years seldom rival the beauty of the first; sowing a fresh mix of seed each year will provide the best results.

Naturalizing with Bulbs

The bulb equivalent of a meadow garden is known as naturalizing. Bulbs are planted in random, natural-looking drifts in grassy areas, under trees, or in woodlands. It's easy to do, and the results look better and better every year as the bulbs multiply to produce even more blooms. The result will be flowers that you plant once and enjoy forever, with no need for yearly fussing.

Deciding Where to Plant

Naturalized bulbs are often best in low-maintenance areas, where you can enjoy the blooms but not be bothered by the sight of the ripening leaves. Very early bulbs, such as spring crocus, are sometimes naturalized in lawns to provide color. You may have to put off the first spring mowing for a week or two to let the bulb foliage turn yellow, but after that you can mow as usual. Fall-blooming bulbs can also look good in grassy areas, but you'll have to stop mowing in late summer, as soon as you see the flower buds sprouting from the soil.

Thick grass may be too competitive for some bulbs, but a sparse lawn—especially under deciduous trees—is just the right environment to help bulbs take hold. The bulbs get plenty of spring sun and moisture before the trees leaf out, and the flowers add cheerful spring and/or fall color to otherwise drab areas. If you have many trees, you can combine sweeps of naturalized bulbs with shade-loving annuals, perennials, and shrubs to create a charming woodland garden with four-season interest.

To grow masses of wildflowers, find a native seed mix of plants that are sure to grow in your area.

Groundcovers make another great companion for naturalized bulbs. The leaves and stems of the groundcovers support the bulb flowers, provide an attractive backdrop, help to keep soil from splashing onto the blooms, and mask the ripening bulb leaves. In turn, the bulbs provide a pretty seasonal show of flowers to make the groundcovers more exciting.

Purple coneflowers, phlox, and thin-leaved sunflowers form a lovely, easy-care combination.

Start your meadow off in spring with naturalized bulbs, such as crocuses. The best planting technique for so many crocuses is to lift up large sections of sod, loosen the soil, plant the bulbs, then replace the sod.

Daffodils planted in grass will multiply over the years to provide a thick carpet of yellow.

Planting Naturalized Bulbs

The key to successful naturalizing is to plant your bulbs in natural-looking arrangements rather than in straight rows or patterns. It's usually best to place them randomly over the planting area by hand until the arrangement looks right to you. Don't just toss out handfuls of bulbs from a standing position; the bulbs may get bruised or damaged as they fall and be prone to pest and disease problems.

Many gardeners find that a narrow trowel is the easiest tool to use for planting small bulbs. You simply insert the trowel into the ground at an angle, lift up a flap of sod, tuck the bulb into the soil, and replace the flap. Or you can plant bulbs in groups by lifting up larger sections of sod, loosening the exposed soil, pressing the bulbs into the soil, and replacing the sod. (This technique works best with small bulbs such as crocus.) If you have lots of bulbs to plant, you may want to try using an auger attachment that connects to a power drill to dig many holes quickly and easily. (These attachments are usually sold in garden centers and through garden-supply catalogs.) For more information on bulb-planting techniques, see "Planting Bulbs" on page 119.

Marvelous Meadow Plants

The recipe for a magnificent meadow includes a blend of tough perennial flowers and noninvasive perennial grasses, with a scattering of annuals and a dash of daffodils and other naturalized spring bulbs for early color. Below you'll find some suggested flowers you can consider for your moist or dry site, along with some great meadow grasses.

Sneezeweed

Perennials for Dry Meadows
Achillea filipendulina
   (fern-leaved yarrow)
Asclepias tuberosa (butterfly weed)
Baptisia australis (blue false indigo)
Echinacea purpurea
   (purple coneflower)
Gaillardia x *grandiflora*
   (blanket flower)
Helianthus x *multiflorus*
   (perennial sunflower)
Liatris spicata (spike gayfeather)
Oenothera tetragona
   (common sundrops)
Rudbeckia fulgida
   (orange coneflower)
Solidago rigida (stiff goldenrod)

Perennials for Moist Meadows
Aster novae-angliae
   (New England aster)
Chelone glabra (white turtlehead)
Eupatorium maculatum
   (spotted Joe-Pye weed)
Eupatorium rugosum
   (white snakeroot)
Filipendula rubra (queen of the prairie)
Helenium autumnale
   (common sneezeweed)
Lobelia cardinalis (cardinal flower)
Physostegia virginiana
   (obedient plant)
Thermopsis caroliniana
   (Carolina lupine)

Great Grasses for Meadows
Andropogon virginicus (broomsedge)
Bouteloua curtipendula
   (side oats grammagrass)
Festuca spp. (fescues)
Schizachyrium scoparium
   (little bluestem)
Sporobolus heterolepis
   (prairie dropseed)

Blue grass

Creating a Cottage Garden

Perennials, annuals, shrubs, and trees combine in a charming cottage garden of purple and pink hues.

The tall, spiky flowers of foxgloves and the brilliant red of oriental poppies add a dramatic touch as feature flowers in a cottage garden.

The ultimate in informality, cottage gardens display a glorious riot of colors, textures, heights, and fragrances. Cottage gardens defy many gardening "rules": Plants are planted so they are packed closely together, with standard spacing ignored. Colors aren't organized into large drifts. Tall plants pop up in front of shorter ones. Flowers are allowed to flop over and grow through each other to create a delightful, casual mixture.

While cottage gardens may appear effortless and unorganized, they need to be planned, planted, and maintained just like any other flower garden. In this section, you'll learn the tricks to capturing the informal cottage garden effect without creating a messy-looking mixture.

Choosing a Site

Locate cottage gardens next to the house, especially by a door. If your front or side yard is small, you may want to devote the whole space to the garden. In this case, a gravel, brick, stone, or even cement path is essential; make it wide (at least 3 feet [90 cm]) to allow room for plants to spill out onto it.

Picking the Plants

To create a pleasing jumble rather than a chaotic mess, combine a variety of different flower shapes and sizes. Thinking of flowers in terms of their visual impact will help you get the right balance.

"Feature" flowers are the ones that first catch your eye; they have strong shapes—like spiky lupines (*Lupinus polyphyllus*) and massive peonies—or bright colors.

"Filler" flowers tend to be smaller and less obvious than feature plants. Baby's breath (*Gypsophila paniculata*) is a classic.

"Edgers" are low plants used in the fronts of beds or spilling over onto paths; think of thymes and catmint (*Nepeta* x *faassenii*).

These categories aren't rigid: Lavender and the flowers of lady's mantle (*Alchemilla mollis*) make nice fillers, but both are often used to edge paths as well. Rose campion (*Lychnis coronaria*) works as a filler, but if set among flowers with contrasting colors,

A mixed cottage border includes milky bellflowers, lamb's ears, and a feature planting of giant sea holly.

Delphiniums are traditional favorites, ranging from white through all shades of blue and purple.

its bright magenta flowers may stand out as a feature. The key is to use some flowers that serve each purpose, so you don't have all bright (and probably clashing) feature flowers, all small filler flowers, or all low edging plants.

As you choose plants for the garden, include some that have scented foliage or flowers (choosing fragrant plants is discussed in more detail below). It's also important to choose flowers that bloom at different times for a continuous display.

Perennials aren't the only plants you can grow in your cottage garden: Annuals, herbs, shrubs, vines, and bulbs all can

Shasta daisies, loosestrife, and rose mallow offer a harmonious variety of color, texture, and height.

have a place in your cottage garden, too. Old-fashioned roses, either shrub types or climbers, are a classic ingredient and an important source of fragrant flowers. Climbing roses or honeysuckles look great trained over a door or archway; let clematis climb up lampposts or railings.

Including unusual and unlikely plants is a cottage garden tradition of long standing. Accent yours with dwarf fruit trees, and tuck in some other edibles for surprise: Try colorful lettuces, curly parsley, red-stemmed 'Ruby' chard, and maroon-podded 'Burgundy' okra.

Pretty Perennials for Cottage Gardens

These great cottage garden flowers have been favorites for years. Use feature flowers for bold colors and textures, edging plants to line the front, and filler flowers to tie the whole design together. You can discover more about the specific plants listed below by referring to the "Guide to Popular Perennials," starting on page 202.

Purple rock cress

Feature Flowers
Alcea rosea (hollyhock)
Campanula persicifolia
  (peach-leaved bellflower)
Delphinium x *belladonna*
  (Belladonna delphinium)
Dictamnus albus (gas plant)
Iris bearded hybrids (bearded iris)
Lilium hybrids (lilies)
Lupinus polyphyllus (garden lupine)
Paeonia lactiflora
  (common garden peony)
Papaver orientale (oriental poppy)
Phlox paniculata (garden phlox)
Verbascum chaixii
  (nettle-leaved mullein)

Edging Plants
Aubrieta deltoidea (purple rock cress)
Aurinia saxatilis (basket of gold)

Campanula portenschlagiana
  (Dalmatian bellflower)
Cerastium tomentosum
  (snow-in-summer)
Dianthus gratianopolitanus
  (cheddar pinks)
Euphorbia epithymoides
  (cushion spurge)
Heuchera sanguinea (coral bells)
Nepeta x *faassenii* (catmint)
Primula vulgaris (English primrose)
Pulmonaria saccharata
  (Bethlehem sage)

Filler Flowers
Alchemilla mollis (lady's mantle)
Aquilegia x *hybrida*
  (hybrid columbine)
Aster novae-angliae
  (New England aster)
Astrantia major (masterwort)
Centaurea hypoleuca (knapweed)
Centranthus ruber (red valerian)
Coreopsis verticillata
  (thread-leaved coreopsis)
Geranium sanguineum
  (blood-red cranesbill)
Gypsophila paniculata (baby's breath)
Leucanthemum x *superbum*
  (shasta daisy)
Lychnis coronaria (rose campion)
Patrinia scabiosifolia (patrinia)

The delicate blooms of peach-leaved bellflowers have long been a favorite in the cottage garden.

Gardening for Butterflies

A cottage garden is a mass of flowers, and that means that it can be a very attractive place for butterflies. Planting a landscape for butterflies is a great way to add an exciting element of moving color to your yard. Choosing and growing the right annuals and perennials will supply the food butterflies need throughout their lives. You'll also want to provide water and shelter to encourage the butterflies that arrive to stay.

Growing Food for Butterflies

To find out what plants the butterflies in your area like, look for them in nearby gardens, old fields, and at the edges of woods. Observe which flowers they prefer and where they stop to sun themselves. If you see a pretty butterfly sipping nectar from a particular flower, consider growing that plant. Imitating nature is the secret to successful butterfly gardening.

To have a great butterfly garden, you must get used to a few holes in the

Encourage thirsty butterflies with a water source.

leaves of your plants. You need to let the caterpillars feed in order to keep the adult butterflies around. Many "flowers" listed for butterfly gardens—including violets, parsley, hollyhocks (*Alcea rosea*), and milkweeds (*Asclepias* spp.)—are really food sources (leaves) for the caterpillars.

Adult butterflies that are ready to lay eggs are attracted by the plants that will feed their developing larvae. Some adults also feed on flower nectar. Plants that have clusters of short, tubular, brightly colored flowers are especially popular. Many shrubs—including butterfly bush (*Buddleia davidii*) and abelia (*Abelia* x *grandiflora*)—are also natural choices.

Growing local wildflowers will provide a food source for the butterfly species native to your area.

Orange coneflowers offer nectar for fritillaries and crescentspots, while the flowers of showy stonecrop are a magnet for tortoiseshells.

A variety of different plants in a sheltered, sunny spot is sure to attract the local butterflies. This walled garden is a fine example.

Just Add Water Butterflies are attracted to shallow puddles and muddy soil. Dig a small, shallow basin, line it with plastic, and cover it with sandy soil and gravel to form a butterfly-luring water source.

Diversify Your Yard Adding diversity to your landscape means creating different mini-environments as well as increasing the number of different plants you grow. Edge habitats—where woods meet lawn or meadows and lawn meets garden or shrub plantings—provide great environments for butterflies

Most butterflies are fussy eaters, feeding on just one or a few plant types. To be sure your garden has what they want, grow a range of plants.

Arranging Your Butterfly Plantings

If you have an informal landscape, consider planting a meadow garden (as explained in "Making a Meadow Garden" on page 78). If you don't have room for a meadow, grow some of the many wildflowers that double as garden perennials, such as asters and coneflowers (*Echinacea* and *Rudbeckia* spp.). Scatter these plants throughout your landscape, or put several of them together in a special butterfly garden. Large splashes of color are easier for butterflies to find than a single plant, so group several plants of the same color together.

Providing a Safe Haven for Butterflies

Along with growing their favorite food and nectar plants, you can take a number of steps to encourage butterflies to stay in your yard.

Make a Spot for Sunbathing All

butterflies like sun and dislike wind, so plant flowers in sunny spots with walls or shrubs as windbreaks. Set flat stones in a sheltered, sunny spot for butterflies to bask on.

Best Bets for Butterflies

Here are some beautiful perennials that are especially popular with butterflies. To learn more, look up the individual entries in "A Guide to Popular Perennials," starting on page 202.

Achillea filipendulina (fern-leaved yarrow)
Asclepias tuberosa (butterfly weed)
Aster novae-angliae (New England aster)
Astilbe x *arendsii* (astilbe)
Baptisia australis (blue false indigo)
Boltonia asteroides (boltonia)
Centranthus ruber (red valerian)
Dianthus gratianopolitanus (cheddar pinks)
Echinacea purpurea (purple coneflower)
Erigeron speciosus (daisy fleabane)
Eupatorium maculatum
   (spotted Joe-Pye weed)
Eupatorium rugosum (white snakeroot)
Gaillardia x *grandiflora* (blanket flowers)
Leucanthemum x *superbum* (shasta daisy)
Lupinus polyphyllus
   (garden lupine)
Monarda didyma (bee balm)
Phlox paniculata (garden phlox)
Rudbeckia fulgida
   (orange coneflower)
Scabiosa caucasica (pincushion flower)
Sedum spectabile (showy stonecrop)

because they offer protection from predators. If you can, allow a corner of your yard to go wild; a tangle of brush offers perfect protection.

Most butterflies have very specific tastes. By increasing the variety of plants to provide a smorgasbord of food and nectar sources, you will attract many different species from early spring through fall.

Avoid Using Pesticides One of the most important steps in having a butterfly haven is ensuring that you are creating a safe, pesticide-free habitat. Even organically acceptable pesticides such as rotenone and pyrethrin kill butterflies and their eggs and larvae. BT, a biological control used against many garden pests, is also fatal to the larvae of desirable butterflies. Use safer techniques such as handpicking and water sprays to remove pests from plants. If you don't want butterfly larvae to munch on your vegetable garden (carrots, celery, cabbage, broccoli, and parsley are a few of the preferred butterfly targets), protect those crops with floating row covers.

Gardening with Fragrance

Annuals and perennials with fragrant leaves and flowers have a place in any landscape, not just the cottage garden. There's nothing like the fresh scent of mint to perk you up after a long day. And who could resist resting on a cozy garden bench near a patch of peonies in full, fragrant bloom? In beds, borders, cottage gardens, and foundation plantings, mixing in some scented perennials will add an extra-special touch to your yard.

Fragrance in Flowers

When you mention fragrance in the garden, most people automatically think of flowers. Peonies and lilies are probably the most well known perennials, and among annuals, consider sweet William (*Dianthus barbatus*) or China pinks (*D. chinensis*), two carnation relatives noted for their spicy scents. Sweet alyssum (*Lobularia maritima*) is a common and easy-to-grow annual that's beloved for its fresh, honey-like fragrance. Mignonette (*Reseda odorata*) is an old-fashioned favorite with small, insignificant flowers but a powerful and delightful fragrance. There are many other plants that have pleasing scents as well; see "Favorite Fragrances" for more ideas.

Traditionally, scented flowers were grown close to the house so the fragrance could be appreciated through open doors and windows. But they're equally nice

Heady, scented roses are a classic part of any fragrance garden. Whether in miniature, bush, or climbing form, they combine beautifully with annuals and perennials for extra color and even additional scents.

near outdoor eating areas and porches— any place where people linger. Raised planters are great for short, fragrant flowers so you don't have to get down on your hands and knees to enjoy the scents.

Many fragrant flowers are also visually beautiful, so you can enjoy looking at them and sniffing them as you walk around or work in the yard. Cutting these flowers for arrangements brings this pleasure indoors. A few annuals withhold their scents until the sun sets, then release their sweet perfume on the evening breeze. Night-scented stock (*Matthiola longipetala* subsp. *bicornis*), sweet rocket (*Hesperis matronalis*), and flowering tobacco (*Nicotiana sylvestris*) carry remarkably potent night scents.

Fragrance in Foliage

A number of plants have fragrant foliage, but you need to touch these to smell them. Plant lavender and bee balm (*Monarda didyma*) where you'll brush against them as you walk by. Grow lemon balm (*Melissa officinalis*) near a garden seat or in a raised container so you can easily rub the leaves to release their delicious lemony odor. Wormwood (*Artemisia absinthium*) and rue (*Ruta graveolens*) leaves have pungent scents that some

Scented foliage and vivid flowers make bee balm an attractive inclusion in the garden. Plant it along a path to enjoy its scent when brushing past.

people find pleasing and others find disagreeable; try sniffing these plants before you buy them. Some annuals have fragrant leaves as well. Scented geraniums (including *Pelargonium tomentosum*, *P. crispum*, and *P. graveolens*) are noted for their aromatic leaves. When you rub them, they release scents resembling those of peppermint, lemons, roses, and many other plants. Annual herbs such as basil, anise, and dill also offer fragrant foliage.

Flowering tobacco dazzles by day, then fills the night with a wonderfully sweet fragrance.

Stock has a rich, spicy fragrance that is noticeable in the garden or in fresh arrangements indoors. One species even has a potent scent at night.

Fragrant Plants

The real key to having a scented garden that you enjoy is smelling plants before you buy them. The fragrance that a friend raves about may be undetectable or even unpleasant to you. Visit nurseries or public gardens when the plants you want are blooming, and sniff the flowers or foliage to see what you think. Different cultivars of the same plant may vary widely in their scents, so smell them all before you choose. "Favorite Fragrances" gives you some ideas of specific annuals and perennials that most gardeners agree are great additions to any scented garden.

To get the most pleasure from your fragrant plants, grow them where you

Catmint has gray-green leaves that give off a pungent, minty smell—it's irresistible to cats.

Favorite Fragrances

Here is a list of a few easy annuals, biennials, and perennials that are commonly grown for their fragrance. Keep in mind that scents are subjective; what's pleasing to one person may be undetectable or offensive to another. If possible, try to sniff plants before you buy them to see if you like the fragrance. For complete growing information, see the individual entries starting on page 172.

Sweetpeas

Annuals and Biennials
Dianthus barbatus (sweet William)
Dianthus chinensis (China pink)
Erysimum cheiri (wallflower)
Heliotropium arborescens (common heliotrope)
Ipomoea alba (moonflower)
Lathyrus odoratus (sweet pea)
Lobularia maritima (sweet alyssum)
Matthiola incana (stock)
Mirabilis jalapa (four o'clock)
Nicotiana alata (flowering tobacco)
Petunia x *hybrida* (petunia)
Perennials for Fragrance
Centranthus ruber (red valerian)
Convallaria majalis (lily-of-the-valley)
Dianthus gratianopolitanus (cheddar pinks)
Hemerocallis hybrids (daylilies), mainly yellow types
Hyacinthus orientalis (hyacinth)
Iris bearded hybrids (bearded iris)
Lavandula angustifolia (lavender)
Lilium hybrids (lilies), especially regal lilies, trumpet hybrids, and oriental hybrids
Narcissus hybrids (daffodils)
Nepeta x *faassenii* (catmint)
Paeonia lactiflora (common garden peony)
Phlox paniculata (garden phlox)
Polygonatum odoratum (fragrant Solomon's seal)

will walk, sit, or brush by them often. Try them along the path to your front door, around a deck or patio, or in a foundation planting near open windows for your indoor enjoyment. Raised beds and container gardens are especially good spots for scented plants, since they'll be closer to your nose and easier to sniff.

Just as a bed of many different flower colors can look jumbled, a mixture of many strong fragrances can be distracting or even downright repulsive. As you plan your garden, try to arrange it with just a couple of scented plants in bloom at any given time. That way, you can enjoy different fragrances all through the season without being overwhelmed by too many at once.

The flowers and leaves of lavender are scented, and they retain their spicy fragrance after drying.

Problem-solving with Annuals and Perennials

It's a rare property that doesn't have at least one difficult spot. Maybe it's a steep, hard-to-mow slope between the yard and the street. Or a dry, shady area under mature maple trees on the side of the house. Or a low, soggy spot that never really dries out, even in the heat of summer. Whatever the problem, some careful thought and plant selection can turn a difficult site into a beautiful landscape feature. This section gives you some ideas about how to solve your garden problems with annuals and perennials.

Time-saving Gardening Tips

No matter what kind of site you have, you probably have a problem that is common to most gardeners: a lack of time. With today's busy lifestyles, it is hard for many gardeners to find the time they'd like to spend keeping their yard looking great all year long. Even if you do have plenty of time to work in the garden, there are probably a number of chores—such as weeding or edging—that you tend to put off while you spend your time doing fun things, like planting.

The solution is good planning, so your garden doesn't become just another series of chores that must be done and it doesn't take more time than you have. No matter what kind of garden you want, you can tailor your landscape plans and plant choices to focus on maximum return for minimum effort. A few hours of careful planning and site preparation will cut down amazingly on maintenance. You'll spend less time working on your yard and have more time to enjoy it!

If you're going to plant under trees, make sure you choose shade-loving annuals and perennials.

Picking plants that are adapted to the growing conditions you have to offer is a key part of creating a healthy, beautiful, easy-care garden. Many annuals and perennials can adjust to a wide range of different light and soil conditions; others are particularly well suited to certain challenging growing conditions.

What's the Most Work?

The key to low-maintenance landscaping is identifying your most bothersome gardening tasks. Which chores take the most time? Which do you like least? Landscape your yard to minimize the unpleasant chores so you can focus on the things you like most, whether it's fussing over a formal herb garden or sipping lemonade in the shade. Below are easy-care solutions to some of the most time-consuming landscape tasks.

Hand Trimming

Reduce hand trimming around tree trunks, fences, posts, and bird baths by replacing the grass there with hostas, daylilies, or other groundcovers.

Edging

If you hate doing the edges on the flower beds and loathe digging out the grass that invades from the lawn, install edging strips. Make sure the strips are level with or slightly below the top of the grass so you can mow over them.

Eliminate mowing and trimming under trees by replacing grass with groundcovers and stepping stones.

Weeding

Minimizing weeding starts at planting time. First, be sure not to skimp on site preparation. Every weed you remove before you start means a whole bucketful of weeds you won't have to remove later. After planting, apply and maintain a good mulch cover. Check the mulch depth 3 or 4 times a year and add more if needed. You might have to remove a few weeds that sprout in the mulch occasionally, but they'll be easy to pull.

One of the best things you can do to cut down on weeding is to get in the habit of pulling weeds as soon as you see them. Otherwise, you give them a chance to spread or set seed and you'll end up with more work. Carry a basket, bag, or bucket with you every time you walk around the yard to collect pulled weeds. (They may reroot if you leave them on the soil.)

Watering

If hauling hoses around the yard isn't your idea of fun, planning a water-wise garden will cut down on your watering chores. First, look for plants that thrive in your area without extra water. Fields, roadsides, graveyards, and abandoned lots are good places to get ideas of tough plants that can survive without supplemental watering.

The mulch that you use on finished plantings to keep weeds down will also

Mowing is just one of the many tasks involved in maintaining a lawn area. But there are alternatives.

help to keep the soil moist and reduce watering chores. If you must water, consider laying soaker hoses or drip irrigation systems; then you'll only have to hook up the hose or turn on the system when you need to water, instead of standing there watering by hand.

Reducing the Lawn Area

Lawn maintenance is probably the most routine and time-consuming part of caring for a traditional landscape. The obvious but surefire way to save on mowing time is to grow less grass. There are plenty of ways to cut down on mowing areas. Build a deck or patio. Line the area below the swing set with landscape fabric and cover it with bark nuggets. Eliminate grass from hard-to-mow areas and replace it with an easy-to-maintain mulch. In small gardens, urban areas, or dry climates, consider eliminating the lawn altogether. Annuals and perennials look great next to paving stones, bricks, cement pavers, or gravel.

All of these solutions have their place. But they don't cool things off the way a big area covered with plants can, and they just aren't as soothing to the eye. If you like growing things but want to mow less,

a meadow garden, especially one of hardy local wildflowers, could be the answer; you'll find more information at "Making a Meadow Garden" on page 78. Or you could try groundcovers.

Great Groundcovers

Groundcovers are a fine alternative to lawns. They are also great for reducing trimming chores along walls and fences and under tree and shrub plantings.

Choosing hardy, drought-tolerant perennials like purple coneflowers will reduce watering chores.

Make mowing easier with edgings or pathways to prevent plants from sprawling onto the lawn.

For loads of color, it's hard to beat maiden pinks blooming all summer long in sunny spots.

Getting Started Just like lawns and meadows, groundcover plantings grow best in well-prepared soil. Remove any sod and weeds, and then loosen the soil thoroughly, working in a ½- to 1-inch (12- to 25-mm) layer of compost or other organic matter. Rake the surface smooth, and you're ready to plant.

A general rule of thumb for spacing is to set plants 1 to 3 feet (30 to 90 cm) apart; use the closer spacing for small or slow-growing species, and the farther one for larger plants or fast growers. At these

A mixture of different thymes makes a beautiful, fragrant, and useful groundcover for a sunny site.

You can find a groundcover that is ideally suited to just about any site and taste. They can come in the form of creeping vines, low-growing perennials, or clumpy shrubs. As well as having attractive deciduous or evergreen foliage, they may offer showy flowers and fruits. Some prefer shade, some like sun; others can take a bit of both. One thing most groundcovers can't take is foot traffic. Mulch or lawn is the best choice for heavily trampled areas.

Choosing Good Groundcovers
Because there are so many terrific groundcovers to choose from, it can be hard to know where to start. Begin by identifying the conditions where you want the plants to grow: Is the site sunny or shady? Is the soil moist or dry? Then think about how tall the groundcover can grow; their heights can range from a few inches (centimeters) up to a few feet (a meter). If you're planting on a slope, you need to plant a fast-spreading, dense groundcover to prevent erosion. You will find growing information for some of the most popular ground-covers in "A Guide to Popular Perennials" starting on page 202.

Lily-of-the-valley

Got It Covered

Many creeping vines and perennials make excellent groundcovers. Some are well adapted to life in spots that get plenty of filtered light but no direct sun, while others will take full sun.

Ajuga reptans (ajuga)
Antennaria dioica (pussy toes)
Asarum europaeum (European wild ginger)
Calluna vulgaris (heather)
Campanula portenschlagiana
  (Dalmatian bellflower)
Chamaemelum nobile (Roman chamomile)
Convallaria majalis (lily-of-the-valley)
Dianthus deltoides (maiden pink)
Galium odoratum (sweet woodruff)
Geranium sanguineum (blood-red cranesbill)
Hemerocallis hybrids (daylilies)
Hosta hybrids (hostas)
Lamium maculatum (spotted lamium)
Liriope spicata (creeping lilyturf)
Oenothera speciosa (showy sundrops)
Pachysandra procumbens
  (Allegheny pachysandra)
  Pachysandra terminalis
  (Japanese pachysandra)
  Phlox stolonifera (creeping phlox)
  Saxifraga stolonifera
  (strawberry geranium)
  Stachys byzantina (lamb's ears)
  Thymus serpyllum (mother of thyme)
  Tiarella cordifolia (foamflower)
  Vancouveria hexandra
  (American barrenwort)
Waldsteinia fragarioides (barren strawberry)

spacings, most groundcovers will take about 2 years to form a solid carpet. If you want faster results, use closer spacings, but keep in mind that the project will then cost more, since you'll need to buy more plants.

Caring for Groundcovers Because some groundcovers can take a few years to completely cover the soil, mulch with straw, chopped leaves, or a similar light material to prevent erosion and suppress weeds. Or plant annuals in the bare spots. Water and weed regularly until the plants are established (usually by the end of the first season). For extra interest, try interplanting your groundcovers with spring bulbs like crocus and daffodils. The groundcovers will help to hide the ripening bulb foliage.

Quick and Easy Flowers
To some people, just the mention of low-maintenance landscaping conjures up images of gravel-covered front yards or expanses of boring green groundcovers. But there's no reason why low care has to mean no flowers. With a little planning, you can have "knock-your-socks-off" color and spend a minimum of time on routine maintenance.

The lifespan characteristics of the different groups of flowering plants (annuals, biennials, and perennials) will influence how much and what

Flower meadows are ideal for sunny spots. Fairly easy and inexpensive to grow from seed, they also attract a wide range of butterflies and bees to your garden.

kind of maintenance you'll need to put into the flowers you choose to grow.

Annuals live only one growing season. Since the parent plants die off at the end of the season, you need to replace them every year with seeds or transplants. Their strong points are that they're very easy to grow (even if you get a late start in spring planning and planting), they bloom for a long time, and they come in just about any color and height you want.

Hardy perennials come back year after year, so you don't have to buy and replant them each spring. But unlike annuals, most perennials only flower for a short while (days or weeks) each season. Many do offer attractive forms and foliage, however, so they look almost as good out of bloom as they do in bloom. Most bulbs go dormant after flowering, freeing up space for annuals or maturing perennial plants.

Biennials flower in the second year. Some, like pansies, are commonly grown as annuals. Some that reseed easily, like hollyhock (*Alcea rosea*), are as dependable as perennials. It takes some planning and patience to get a good show from most biennials, so they tend to be grown less frequently than annuals and perennials.

Combining them into one glorious garden lets you enjoy the benefits of each group while minimizing the drawbacks. Early-blooming perennials (like irises and peonies) combine well with annuals like cosmos and cleomes (*Cleome* spp.), which start blooming in early summer and carry on until frost.

Within each group you can find low-maintenance plants. The trick is to choose those that don't need special attention such as staking, indoor winter storage, or frequent pruning. Do look for plants that shrug off heat, scoff at drought, and laugh in the face of pests. And while adopting the low-maintenance option eliminates some touchy species, you'll still have more to choose from than you could ever hope to grow.

Hostas, the easy-care solution for shade, can be green, yellow, blue, or variegated in gold or white.

Easy Annuals

Annual flowers are great for low-maintenance gardens. They're easy to grow, as long as they get the light and water they need. They come in just about every color and height you'd want. They're cheap, so you get a big effect for a little money, and if one isn't healthy, you can toss it out without much anguish. In addition, you can plant most annuals as late as early summer if you don't get around to spring gardening as soon as you'd like.

You can grow your annuals from seed or buy transplants. Growing them from seed is less expensive and gives you a greater choice of cultivars. But you have to sow most annuals indoors 6 weeks before you move them outside, which means you have to worry about soil mixes, moisture, temperature, light, and all the other factors that influence success with seeds. Starting your own annuals indoors from seed can be fun and rewarding, but it's not the route to go if you really want minimal maintenance. Fortunately, many colorful, low-care annuals, such as marigolds and zinnias, are easy to start by sowing seeds directly where you want them to grow. Follow the information on the seed packets for sowing times and depths.

Buying transplants is much easier than starting seeds indoors, and it is still relatively inexpensive. Just figure out how many plants you need and head to the garden center around planting time. (For most annuals, this is around the average date of the last frost for your area. If you're not sure of your last frost date, ask your gardening neighbors or the local Cooperative Extension Service.)

As you pick through the stock, try to avoid buying plants that are

Dependable, Easy-care Perennials

Here's a list of some of the most trouble-free perennials you can grow. All of the plants below thrive in sun and average, well-drained soil with little fuss. You'll find complete information about growing all these plants in the individual plant entries starting on page 202.

Achillea filipendulina (fern-leaved yarrow)
Alchemilla mollis (lady's mantle)
Anemone x *hybrida* (Japanese anemone)
Armeria maritima (common thrift)
Asclepias tuberosa (butterfly weed)
Aster novae-angliae
   (New England aster)
Baptisia australis (blue false indigo)
Boltonia asteroides (boltonia)
Centranthus ruber (red valerian)
Coreopsis verticillata
   (thread-leaved
   coreopsis)
Echinacea purpurea
   (purple coneflower)
Echinops ritro
   (globe thistle)
Gaillardia x
   grandiflora
   (blanket flower)
Geranium sanguineum
   (blood-red
   cranesbill)
Hemerocallis hybrids
   (daylilies)
Iris sibirica (Siberian iris)
Leucanthemum x *superbum* (shasta daisy)
Liatris spicata (spike gayfeather)
Lilium hybrids (lilies)
Narcissus hybrids (daffodils)
Nepeta x *faassenii* (catmint)
Paeonia lactiflora (common garden peony),
   single-flowered cultivars
Physostegia virginiana (obedient plant)
Platycodon grandiflorus (balloon flower)
Rudbeckia fulgida (orange coneflower)
Sedum spp. (sedums)
Salvia x *superba* (violet sage)
Veronica spicata (spike speedwell)
Yucca filamentosa (Adam's needle)

Blanket flower

already blooming—they'll only take longer to make new roots. Put back any that have discolored stems or leaves, holes in the leaves, or any other sign of either disease or insect damage. Don't buy annuals that are spindly or pale; look for compact, leafy, deep green plants. When possible, set transplants out on a cloudy day, so they'll be less prone to transplant shock.

Low-maintenance Perennials and Bulbs

Adding perennial plants to a low-maintenance landscape requires some thought. Compared to most annuals, perennials flower for a shorter period, so you have to figure out what will be blooming when and whether it will look good with its neighbors. They're more expensive, so you'll want to provide them with ideal conditions to keep them healthy and vigorous. And you have to plant early—sometimes the preceding fall—to get good color during the season.

Why take the trouble? Because well-chosen perennials, once established, come back year after year with little or no help from you. Some give a splash of color in the early spring, just when your late-winter depression verges on true dementia. Their successive bloom seasons give you an incentive to get outside and walk around the yard to see what's flowering. For some, perennials bring back fond memories of favorite people or places from the past.

Below are some tips for choosing perennials for your yard. "Caring for Annuals and Perennials" starting on page 122 will give you the details on maintaining your flowers.

Picking Easy-care Perennials If you really want to avoid lots of laboring, shun tall or floppy perennials, such

California poppy is an easy-to-grow annual for sunny gardens: just scatter the seed in a well-drained soil.

Balloon flowers have saucer-shaped flowers. To avoid having to stake them, use short cultivars.

The list goes on. For more ideas, look at gardens that bloom even though you know no one bothers with them. And before you plant any perennial, research its growth requirements to be sure it suits your conditions.

as hybrid delphinium (*Delphinium* x *elatum*) and baby's breath (*Gypsophila paniculata*), which will need staking. Also steer clear of tender perennials, such as

The delicate blooms and ferny foliage of bleeding heart are a lovely and hardy addition to a garden.

canna (*Canna* x *generalis*) and dahlia (*Dahlia* spp.), that you will have to dig up and store over the winter. Unless you want to cover a large area, avoid those that spread, like lamb's ears (*Stachys byzantina*) and goutweed (*Aegopodium podagraria*). Pass up those that die out after a few years, like many perennial asters. And don't plant those that have a serious pest in your area, unless you can get a resistant cultivar.

What's left? A lot, starting with dependable spring bulbs like crocus and daffodils; irises, if iris borer isn't a severe problem in your area; daylilies (there are thousands to choose from); and hostas, for shady areas. Try short cultivars of balloon flower (*Platycodon grandiflorus*) and bellflowers (*Campanula* spp.). Choose coreopsis (*Coreopsis* spp.) and other native wildflowers, especially in a natural garden. Be sure to include old-time favorites like bleeding heart (*Dicentra* spp.). And don't forget ornamental grasses like fountain grass (*Pennisetum alopecuroides*) and blue fescue (*Festuca cinerea*), great for their foliage and interesting seed heads.

Easy Annuals from Seed

Save the step of transplanting by sowing seeds of these tough annuals directly in the garden.

Calendula officinalis (pot marigold)
Centaurea cyanus (cornflower)
Cleome hasslerana (cleome)
Consolida ambigua (rocket larkspur)
Eschscholzia californica
    (California poppy)
Helianthus annuus
    (common sunflower)
Lathyrus odoratus (sweet pea)
Lobularia maritima
    (sweet alyssum)
Nigella damascena
    (love-in-a-mist)
Papaver rhoeas
    (corn poppy)
Portulaca grandiflora
    (rose moss)
Tagetes spp. (marigolds)

Oriental poppy

Handling Hillsides

Terraces or low walls can turn a troublesome slope into an eye-catching landscape feature.

With a little imagination and work, you can transform a sloping site from a maintenance headache into a landscape asset. Hillsides are awkward to mow and weed, so the best strategy is to cover them with plants that take care of themselves. Or, if you're willing to invest some time and money, you can build retaining walls or terraced beds that will safely and attractively support a wide range of beautiful annuals and perennials.

Super Plants for Slopes

Grass is probably the most common groundcover used to hold the soil on slopes, but it isn't especially interesting, and it can be a real pain to mow every week. For an attractive and easy-care solution, replace the turf grass with tough, low-maintenance plants that look great and protect the soil, too. To get you started, "Great Groundcovers for Slopes" lists some of the most reliable options for sunny and shady sites.

Sunny Slopes

One good option where you have a sunny slope is planting a mixture of sun-loving groundcovers, taller spreading perennials (such as daylilies), and spreading shrubs, such as creeping juniper (*Juniperus horizontalis*). Or, if you like a casual look and you're willing to mow the slope once a year, consider turning it into a wildflower meadow. You'll find more information on planning and planting a meadow garden in "Making a Meadow Garden" on page 78.

"Making a Meadow Garden" on page 78.

Simple Planting on Steep Slopes

If you're turning a steep, grassy slope over to groundcovers, try this tip: Cover the area with black plastic for several weeks to kill the grass. Then remove the plastic and plant your groundcovers right into the dead sod. The sod will keep the soil from washing away while the groundcovers are establishing. Finish off the planting with a layer of mulch for good looks.

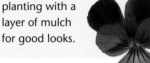

Building a rock garden is another great solution for a sunny, well-drained slope. Place large rocks at irregular intervals throughout the area. Bury each so that more than half is underground to keep it from rolling or washing away. Large, secure stones will give you a steady foothold so you can get

Plantings along walls (and even in the wall if possible) will soften the look of any hard edges.

Slopes tend to be well drained and are natural sites for rock gardens. Choose drought-tolerant annuals and perennials with a low-growing, spreading habit, so they will cascade over the rocks and onto steps.

Thrift is adapted to harsh conditions, so its dense spread of flowers from late spring to summer offers great color for rock and wall gardens.

into the garden for occasional weeding. Between the stones, plant sprawling, sun-loving annuals and perennials, such as wall rock cress (*Arabis caucasica*), snow-in-summer (*Cerastium tomentosum*), and basket of gold (*Aurinia saxatilis*), with small hardy bulbs, such as crocus and reticulated iris (*Iris reticulata*).

Shady Slopes

On shady slopes, spreading species and hosta cultivars make great groundcovers, alone or combined with other annuals and perennials. Other good companions include lily-of-the-valley (*Convallaria majalis*), pachysandra (*Pachysandra terminalis*), and common periwinkle (*Vinca minor*). For extra interest, add spring-flowering bulbs to get early color from groundcover plantings.

If the slope is shaded by deciduous trees, create a woodland garden by combining groundcovers such as ajuga and European wild ginger (*Asarum europaeum*) with early-blooming wildflowers. Creeping phlox (*Phlox stolonifera*), wild bleeding heart (*Dicentra eximia*), and Allegheny foamflower (*Tiarella cordifolia*) are a few species that will bloom in spring before the trees leaf out fully and shade the area.

Establishing Plantings

Good soil preparation is a key part of successful slope landscaping. Remove the existing grass and weeds, and dig the soil

to loosen it. If the slope is steep, you'll need to build temporary terraces before you plant. Long, flat boards anchored behind 2-foot (60-cm) spikes driven partly into the ground hold the soil in place for a year or two. Once plants have gotten established and filled in, you can remove the boards and spikes.

Set the plants into the ground as you would for any garden; see "Planting Time" on page 114 for details. Water well and add a thick mulch layer. Weed and water regularly for the first year to get the plants off to a good start; after that, they should need little care.

Terraces for Slopes

Constructing permanent terraces requires more time, effort, and money up front, but the terraces last for years and they will dramatically increase the variety of perennials you will be able to grow.

Low retaining walls (up to 2 feet [60 cm] high) are reasonably easy to construct from flat stones or lumber. But do consult a professional landscaper or builder for any wall that must be taller than 2 feet (60 cm): Large retaining walls must be well anchored on the slope and properly designed to take the weight of the soil they will hold. This keeps them from washing out, cracking, or tumbling down later. It's easier to make walls correctly than to repair them.

Fill finished terraces with good topsoil. After the soil settles for a few weeks, add a bit more if needed to level the top of the beds. Then plant your perennials. Keep in mind that terraces may dry out more quickly than regular in-ground beds, so you're better off looking for plants that can take dry conditions.

On gentle slopes, make shallow basins to trap moisture and minimize erosion. Terraces are a better option if you have to handle steep slopes.

Great Groundcovers for Slopes

Here are some tough and trouble-free perennials that adapt well to life on a sloping site. To learn more about specific plants, look them up in the individual plant entries starting on page 202.

Groundcovers for Sun
Cerastium tomentosum (snow-in-summer)
Dianthus gratianopolitanus (cheddar pinks)
Phlox subulata (moss phlox)
Sedum spurium (two-row sedum)
Stachys byzantina (lamb's ears)
Groundcovers for Shade
Ajuga reptans (ajuga)
Asarum europaeum (European wild ginger)
Epimedium x *rubrum* (red epimedium)
Galium odoratum (sweet woodruff)
Hosta hybrids (hostas, spreading types)
Lamium maculatum (spotted lamium)

Succeeding in the Shade

Shady nooks provide a cool, peaceful refuge for plants and people who can't take the hot summer sun. Shade-loving plants may not always glow with the vibrant colors of poppies and peonies, but they offer many wonderful possibilities to the open-minded gardener who wants to experiment with subtle shades and textures. Success in shady sites, as in any kind of garden, depends on careful planning and on choosing plants that grow happily in such conditions.

Picking Your Plants

The two main factors that will determine which plants can grow well in your shade garden are how much light the garden gets and how much water is available.

Sites that get a few hours of direct sun or a full day of filtered light can support a wider range of plants than a spot that's in deep shade all day. Gardens under deciduous trees may get lots of sun until early summer, when the developing tree leaves begin to block the light. "Examine Your Exposure" on page 42 can help you figure out what type of shade you have. The individual plant entries starting on

Single or double, white, pink, red, orange, or lavender—impatiens add vivid color to the shady garden.

page 172 will tell you which kind of conditions each plant prefers.

Shady gardens can also vary widely in the amount of moisture that's available. Plants that grow well in moist woodland soils usually aren't happy in the dry shade under roof overhangs or shallow-rooted trees such as maples and beeches. In moist shade, you may need to seek out slug- and snail-resistant plants; some hostas that are

less prone than others to slug damage include 'Blue Angel', 'Sum & Substance', 'Krossa Regal', *Hosta sieboldiana*, and *H. fortunei* 'Aureomarginata'.

As with planning any garden, look for perennials that are attractive as well as adaptable. Spring tends to be the primary bloom season in a shade garden, but you'll be seeing the plants all season long, so choose ones that also look good when they're not flowering. Along with all the varying shades of green, leaves come in many colors, including silvery blue, blue-green, yellow-green, and purple. Plants with multicolored (variegated) leaves are also good choices for adding sparkle to a shady corner. Hostas are available in many leaf colors and variegations, and they flower as well. Several species of lungwort (*Pulmonaria* spp.) offer silver-speckled leaves, along with pink-and-blue spring flowers. Ferns, lamiums (*Lamium* spp.), and hellebores (*Helleborus* spp.) are other natural choices for foliage interest. If you're gardening under shallow-rooted trees like maples and beeches, look for drought-tolerant shade-lovers like barrenworts (*Epimedium* spp.) and yellow archangel (*Lamiastrum galeobdolon* 'Herman's Pride'). And for extra color in summer, remember annuals such as impatiens and begonias and the colorful foliage of coleus and caladiums.

To give your shade garden a strong start, thin out branches to admit more light, enrich and mulch the soil, and plant close to tree trunks, where there are few feeder roots to compete with your plantings.

Make the most of early spring, before trees leaf out, with spring bulbs like Siberian squill.

Planning and Planting Tips

Take advantage of several strategies for succeeding in shade. First, direct traffic away from shallow-rooted trees and areas you wish to keep as deep shade so you can replace scraggly lawn with groundcovers. Use stepping stones or heavily mulched paths to guide visitors around planted areas. A bench on an informal stone patio makes an inviting destination and works well in the deepest shade or beneath the most shallow-rooted trees.

Second, enrich the soil with lots of organic matter. A good supply of organic matter may mean the difference between death and survival in shade, especially dry shade. If you are gardening under trees, you can't just till in the organic matter

The colorful foliage of coleus adds a bright touch.

or dump a thick layer on the surface; either way, you'll harm the tree roots. Instead, try digging and then enriching individual planting pockets close to the tree trunk, where there are few feeder roots. Dig a hole about 8 inches (20 cm) in diameter for each plant and mix in a handful or two of compost; then plant as usual.

After planting, water the area thoroughly and apply a layer of mulch. In dry shade, water regularly until the plants are established, and plan on watering even mature plants during dry spells.

Shade gardens need less water because the drying sun doesn't beat down on them. But they also are perfect for fungal diseases that like humid, cool, dark conditions. For that reason, it's important to space shade plants at the distance recommended—or even wider—to get good air movement. When you do water, irrigate so you wet the soil rather than the leaves.

Slugs and snails, being very fond of moist areas, can be troublesome in shade gardens. If you're finding holes in your leaves (hostas are a favorite target), encircle the bed with a strip of copper edging to keep the pests out. Catch slugs that are already inside the bed by trapping them in fruit rinds set upside down on the soil surface; check traps and remove pests daily until the problem decreases. If they become a real problem, you may want to remove some or all of the mulch; despite all of its benefits, mulch also provides shelter for these troublesome pests.

Super Plants for Shade

Here's a list of just some annuals and perennials that will thrive in a shady garden. You'll find more information in the individual entries starting on page 172.

Annuals
Begonia Semperflorens-Cultorum hybrid
  (wax begonia)
Celosia cristata (celosia)
Impatiens wallerana (impatiens)
Lobelia erinus (edging lobelia)
Lunaria annua (honesty)
Myosotis sylvatica (forget-me-not)
Nicotiana alata (flowering tobacco)

Perennials
Actaea pachypoda (white baneberry)
Ajuga reptans (ajuga)
Aquilegia spp. (columbines)
Arisaema triphyllum (Jack-in-the-pulpit)
Asarum europaeum (European wild ginger)
Astilbe x *arendsii* (astilbe)
Bergenia spp. (bergenias)
Brunnera macrophylla (Siberian bugloss)
Cimicifuga racemosa (black snakeroot)
Dicentra eximia (fringed bleeding heart)
Epimedium x *rubrum* (red epimedium)
Helleborus orientalis (Lenten rose) (see below)
Hosta hybrids (hostas)
Iris cristata (crested iris)
Lamium maculatum (spotted lamium)
Polygonatum odoratum (fragrant Solomon's seal)
Pulmonaria saccharata (Bethlehem sage)
Smilacina racemosa (Solomon's plume)
Tiarella cordifolia (Allegheny foamflower)
Uvularia grandiflora (great merrybells)

Turning Bogs into Beds

Don't let a wet yard or soggy spot deter you from gardening in that area. Even a year-round spring or bog can be attractively landscaped with beautiful, easy-care annuals and perennials. You may decide to approach the area as you would any other garden, with a formal planting plan in mind. Or you may choose to go for an informal feel and create a casual-looking natural area.

Options for Organized Plantings

If your problem site is under water most of the year, go with the flow—leave it as a wetland or convert it into a small pond and plant annuals and perennials to cascade over its edges. Some of the most beautiful native plants, including cardinal flower (*Lobelia cardinalis*), white or pink turtleheads (*Chelone* spp.), queen of the prairie (*Filipendula rubra*), and some ferns, prefer to grow where their feet are wet. They look equally good in perennial beds and wild settings.

If you would like a more traditional flower bed or border where soil is constantly soggy, raise the level of the soil in the planting area at least 4 inches (10 cm). Adding a healthy dose of organic matter and bringing in additional soil to make raised beds can often transform a constantly wet site into an evenly moist site—the ideal condition for many classic garden flowers. If the bed is still soggy, even in summer—that is, the soil never gets dry enough to crumble when you squeeze some—and you don't want to raise the bed any higher, stick with the plants listed in "Plants That Like Wet Feet."

Building Raised Beds

One solution for poor drainage is to raise the plants above the existing soil. If you're planting trees and shrubs, build low, wide mounds of soil called berms and plant in those. If growing vegetables and flowers, construct raised beds that are about 6 inches (15 cm) high in cool climates or no more than 4 inches (10 cm) in warm climates (where raised beds can dry out quickly). If you make the beds 3 to 4 feet (90 to 120 cm) wide and leave a walkway between them, you can work the bed from either side without having to step on the soil (which can lead to compaction).

Create temporary raised beds in the vegetable garden by raking soil into broad,

Plants That Like Wet Feet

Here are some super perennials that will thrive in consistently moist soil. For more information, see the individual entries starting on page 202.

Arisaema triphyllum (Jack-in-the-pulpit)
Aruncus dioicus (goat's beard)
Asarum europaeum (European wild ginger)
Astrantia major (masterwort)
Brunnera macrophylla (Siberian bugloss)
Chelone spp. (turtleheads)
Eupatorium maculatum (spotted Joe-Pye weed)
Filipendula rubra (queen of the prairie)
Galium odoratum (sweet woodruff)
Iris sibirica (Siberian iris)
Ligularia dentata (big-leaved ligularia)
Lobelia cardinalis (cardinal flower)
Lysimachia punctata (yellow loosestrife)
Monarda didyma (bee balm)
Physostegia virginiana (obedient plant)
Polygonum affine (Himalayan fleeceflower)
Primula denticulata (drumstick primrose)
Smilacina racemosa (Solomon's plume)
Tradescantia x *andersoniana* (common spiderwort)
Trollius x *cultorum* (hybrid globeflower)

A bog garden is a great site for many kinds of iris, with their spiky leaves and beautiful flowers.

Diverting excess water into a pond or retaining basin can add an attractive feature to a garden.

Build raised beds with timber frames and good soil to turn a wet site into a well-drained garden.

flattened mounds. For more permanent beds in any part of the landscape, frame the beds with landscape timbers or wide boards secured with braces and anchored with metal stakes. Stone or brick can give beds a particularly attractive appearance for ornamental plantings. Fill the frame with organically enriched soil. When you add soil to build a berm or raised bed, be sure you're not covering the roots of existing trees or shrubs.

A Natural Solution for Soggy Sites

If you enjoy the informal feel of naturalistic landscaping, wet spots are a perfect place to "go wild." Healthy wetlands serve important ecological roles by purifying groundwater, replenishing the water table, and supporting a wide variety of plants and wildlife that would not normally be attracted to a garden.

A mixed planting of moisture-loving perennials can provide season-long interest in a wet spot. It's not really necessary to carefully plan out your plantings to ensure there are different heights, textures, and colors—just set your plants out in random order. Great blue lobelia (*Lobelia siphilitica*), swamp milkweed (*Asclepias incarnata*), marsh marigold (*Caltha palustris*), yellow flag (*Iris pseudacorus*), and blue flag (*Iris versicolor*) are a few colorful perennials that grow happily in constantly soggy soil. Angelica (*Angelica atropurpurea*), a native perennial

herb, forms lush, leafy clumps and tall flower clusters in wet soil. Native cattails (*Typha latifolia*) thrive in standing water, but they may choke out everything else (which isn't a problem if you like them). Royal ferns (*Osmunda* spp.) and beech ferns (*Thelypteris* spp.) are also great additions for foliage interest.

If your soil is constantly moist but not saturated, your planting options expand dramatically. Most woodland plants and wildflowers prefer moist soil to dry soil. Many sun-loving wildflowers also grow happily in moist soil. If the area dries out enough to support grass, try a wet meadow, with rugged perennials like spotted Joe-Pye weed (*Eupatorium maculatum*) and New England asters (*Aster novae-angliae*). Cut the meadow with a string trimmer once a year (wear boots to keep your feet dry!) in late fall or early spring. You'll learn more about planning, planting, and also maintaining such areas in "Making a Meadow Garden" on page 78.

For more ideas, take a look at natural marsh, streamside, or pond habitats in your area to see what is thriving there and how it looks. You'll get lots of ideas about other plants that will grow well in your particular area and how you can arrange them. (Just remember to gather ideas and inspiration only from these wild, natural areas, not the plants themselves. In any case, many garden centers are expanding

Accent a small wet spot with a clump of moisture-loving plants like these bright yellow primroses.

their selections to include water-garden plants, so you should have no trouble buying the plants you've decided upon.)

Turtleheads take their name from their unusual flower shape, like a turtle with its mouth open. And like their namesakes, they prefer moisture.

Growing a Water-wise Landscape

If you live where rainfall is scant or undependable or if your soil is so sandy that water runs right through, it makes sense to plan your landscape accordingly. You'll spend less time tinkering with your sunny garden if you choose plants that can take the heat. Consider the wide variety of fabulous flowers that thrive in full sun and can withstand dry spells. Using water-wise gardening techniques will also save you more than just water—it can save you time and money, too! Plus, you'll be spared the disappointment of watching poorly chosen plants wither and die as the heat and drought take their toll. Instead, you'll have a landscape that not only looks great but can weather tough conditions with little extra help from you.

Water-saving Basics

Water-wise gardening involves a two-part approach. One is keeping the rainfall that you do get in the soil or in storage, so it's available to plants when they need it. The other part is reducing the total amount of water that your garden needs to thrive.

Keeping Water Where You Need It

Good soil care is a key step in ensuring that moisture stays where plant roots can get it. Loose, crumbly soil can easily soak up rainfall that would just run off of beds that were compacted. Digging the soil thoroughly at planting time and keeping it loose by not walking on the beds will keep the soil in good shape.

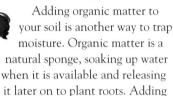

Adding organic matter to your soil is another way to trap moisture. Organic matter is a natural sponge, soaking up water when it is available and releasing it later on to plant roots. Adding ample quantities of organic matter when preparing your soil before planting time will help plants withstand dry spells. Also use liberal quantities of mulch to replenish the supply of organic matter and to prevent moisture that is already in the soil from evaporating.

Channeling and storing rainfall are two other ways to reduce the need for supplemental watering. Regrading areas of your yard may help to keep rainfall from running off into the street, or at

Brilliant pot marigolds bloom from summer to fall, thriving in full sun and dry, average soils.

least slow down the water so that it has more chance to soak in. Building terraces (as explained in "Handling Hillsides" on page 96) is a great way to slow or stop runoff on sloping sites. Place a large plastic trash can (cut a hole in the lid to let water in) or commercially available rain barrel under a downspout to collect rainwater for later use.

At planting, set plants out in shallow depressions, so the crowns and the soil immediately around them are slightly below the normal soil level. Or use extra soil to form a shallow basin around each

A water-wise landscape could include lamb's ears, yarrow, torch lilies, sedum, Russian sage, and grasses.

Plants for Hot, Dry Places

These plants don't mind heat and are happiest in soils that are very well drained and even sandy. Once established, they withstand extended dry spells. For more information on specific plants, check out the individual entries in starting on page 172.

Turkestan onion

Annuals

Amaranthus caudatus
  (love lies bleeding)
Calendula officinalis (pot marigold)
Catharanthus roseus
  (Madagascar periwinkle)
Centaurea cyanus (cornflower)
Gaillarda pulchella (blanket flower)
Gomphrena globosa (globe amaranth)
Helianthus annuus
  (common sunflower)
Nicotiana alata (flowering tobacco)
Rudbeckia hirta (black-eyed Susan)
Sanvitalia procumbens
  (creeping zinnia)
Verbena x *hybrida* (garden verbena)

Perennials

Achillea filipendulina
  (fern-leaved yarrow)
Allium giganteum (giant onion)
Artemisia absinthium
  (common wormwood)
Asclepias tuberosa (butterfly weed)
Aubrieta deltoides (purple rock cress)
Aurinia saxatilis (basket of gold)
Baptisia australis (blue false indigo)
Catananche caerulea (Cupid's dart)
Centranthus ruber (red valerian)

Cerastium tomentosum
  (snow-in-summer)
Coreopsis verticillata
  (thread-leaved coreopsis)
Dianthus gratianopolitanus
  (cheddar pinks)
Echinacea purpurea
  (purple coneflower)
Echinops ritro (globe thistle)
Eryngium amethystinum
  (amethyst sea holly)
Euphorbia epithymoides
  (cushion spurge)
Gaillardia x *grandiflora*
  (blanket flower)
Helianthus x *multiflorus*
  (perennial sunflower)
Oenothera tetragona
  (common sundrops)
Perovskia atriplicifolia (Russian sage)
Rudbeckia fulgida (orange coneflower)
Salvia officinalis (garden sage)
Salvia x *superba* (violet sage)
Sedum spectabile (showy stonecrop)
Sedum spurium (two-row sedum)
Stachys byzantina (lamb's ears)
Verbascum chaixii
  (nettle-leaved mullein)
Yucca filamentosa (Adam's needle)

If dry spells are common in your area, consider replacing lawn pathways with mulch or gravel.

- When planting, leave a little extra space between all plants so their roots can reach farther for water without competing with each other. (Mulch the bare soil between plants.)
- Block or moderate drying winds with a hedge or a windbreak. Or locate your garden on the sheltered side of an existing structure.
- If you must water, do it early or late in the day, preferably using drip systems or soaker hoses. "Mulching and Watering" on page 130 will tell you how to judge when your plants really need to be watered.

plant (new or already established) to collect and hold available water.

Reducing Overall Water Needs

Cutting down on the amount of water your yard actually needs is another important part of planning a water-wise landscape. Here are some ideas to try:

- Mulch, then mulch more! A thick layer of organic mulch will help hold moisture in the soil for plant roots.
- Reduce the size of your lawn. Lush lawns just aren't compatible with arid climates. Prairie and meadow gardens are adapted to drier conditions; once established, they don't need watering (see "Making a Meadow Garden" on page 78 for details).
- Group plants together in garden beds according to their water requirements. Locate thirsty plants closest to the house, rain barrel, or water faucet, where you can reach them easily. Landscape outlying areas with species that need little if any supplemental water; see "Plants for Hot, Dry Places."

A generous layer of mulch will help moderate soil temperatures as well as conserve moisture.

Preparation and Planting

Careful planning and plant selection will take you a long way toward a great-looking landscape. The next step is to follow through with good soil preparation, informed plant purchasing, and the right planting techniques to get those plants off and growing. This chapter will guide you through the process of preparing the site, acquiring your plants, and planting them, so that your annuals and perennials stay healthy and beautiful all season long.

Getting the Soil Ready

Along with proper plant selection, preparing a planting bed so that it contains good, granular soil is critical to the success of your flower garden. If you do a thorough job at this stage, you will be rewarded by quicker plant establishment and less weeding later.

Timing

If possible, start digging your new garden a season or a year before you intend to do any planting. That way, you can do a really thorough job of preparing the soil, and the soil will have a chance to settle before you plant. If spring typically is too wet to work the soil in your area, dig the garden in fall instead. If you can't prepare the soil ahead of time, you can usually get the bed ready and start planting in the same season. See "Planting Time" on page 114 for suggestions on the best time to actually plant.

Making New Beds

When you're digging a garden bed in a lawn, begin by marking the bed outline with rope, a garden hose, or string and stakes. Strip off the sod with a flat spade by cutting long, spade-width strips across the width of the bed. Slide your spade under the strips to sever them from the soil. Roll up the turf as you go or remove it in rectangles, and take the bundles to the compost pile. As an alternative, you can kill the grass by covering it with black plastic. However, this can take several weeks or more than a month depending on the weather—the hotter it is outside, the faster the plastic works. Till in the turf when it has decayed.

Working the Soil

Once you've cleared the beds, it's time to break up the soil. Consider your choice of tools carefully. Decades ago, gardeners turned the soil with garden spades, forks, and other hand tools. In recent years, many have turned to rotary tillers. These machines can churn the top 5 to 6 inches (12.5 to 15 cm) of soil with much less effort on your part. But tillers aren't always the best choice. Excessive tilling, or tilling when the soil is too wet or too dry will break up the good, granular soil

Careful digging and regular additions of organic matter will help maintain a good, granular soil.

structure into tiny particles and lead to soil compaction. If you choose to use a rotary tiller, make sure you work the soil when it's evenly moist. For details on determining soil moisture, see "Squeeze Your Soil to Test Moisture."

Use a broadfork to prepare previously worked beds or to aerate compacted soil before planting.

Preparing a Bed

1. Set out stakes and string to mark the area you're going to dig.

2. Remove the sod by stripping it off the soil with a spade.

3. If a soil test indicates the site is too acid, apply lime to the soil.

4. Spread a layer of compost over the area and dig it into the bed.

Double-digging will provide ideal conditions for good root growth. Your plants will thrive, particularly your deep-rooted perennials.

Loose, well-drained soil is the secret to success with cranesbills, yarrow, and yellow loosestrife.

If you have a small garden and are willing to dig with hand tools, you can usually loosen the soil to a depth of up to 6 to 8 inches (15 to 20 cm), which is deep enough for annuals. Or you can make the bed 12 inches (30 cm) deep, which is better for the longer roots of perennials, if you double dig. Complete instructions on double-digging can be found below.

Add compost before planting so you can work it in throughout the bed. For a heavy clay or light sandy loam that is low in organic matter, lay a 4-inch (10-cm)

Work compost into the soil before planting to provide nutrients for healthy, steady growth.

thick layer over the entire area and work it into the top 8 inches (20 cm) of soil. Use less compost if you want to plant yarrows, artemisias, and other perennials that grow best in dry, sunny sites. Add more compost in warm climates—where organic matter seems to "burn up" in a few weeks—to compensate for the fast rate of decomposition. After working the soil, rake the surface to smooth it and break up any large clods. Then let the bed soil settle for several weeks before planting.

Double-digging

Double-digging is hard work, but it can be worthwhile if you are gardening in heavy clayey soil or if you're growing perennials and want to encourage them to root extra deeply in drought-prone areas. Remove the sod and weed roots first. Starting at one end of the bed, dig a trench 12 inches (30 cm) wide and as deep as your spade across the width of the bed. Put all the topsoil you unearth into a wheelbarrow and move it to the far end of the garden. Now loosen up the exposed subsoil with a garden fork or your spade. Then back up to dig the next 12-inch (30-cm) wide strip. Shift that topsoil, with some added compost or other organic matter, into the first trench and then loosen the new area of subsoil. Continue in this fashion until you reach the far end of the bed. Finish the last strip with the topsoil from your wheelbarrow and rake the bed smooth. Once you've prepared the bed, avoid stepping on it; otherwise, you'll compact the soil and undo all your hard work. If you can't reach in from the sides to plant, lay a board across the soil and step on that. Remove it when you're done.

Squeeze Your Soil to Test Moisture

Walking on or working wet soil can quickly destroy the porous, open structure you're trying so hard to build. So before you break out your shovel and work boots, try this simple test: Take a handful of soil and squeeze it. If moisture runs out between your fingers, the soil is too wet to work. If it does not, open your hand. The soil should be in a ball in your palm. If it will not cling together, it is too dry to work. In that case, water the bed thoroughly, let it sit for 24 hours, and evaluate again. If the soil stays in a ball, tap it lightly with a finger. If the soil breaks apart easily, it is ready to work. If it stays tight, it is still too wet. Wait a few more dry days and try again.

Adding Nutrients

As you prepare your new garden for planting, you should also think about adding any nutrients your plants may need. The right nutrients in the right balance will help ensure that your annuals and perennials get off to a good start.

Understanding Plant Nutrients

The availability of soil nutrients is as important to plant health and vigor as vitamins and minerals are to people. The nutrients that plants require to grow are called essential elements. Three of the essential elements plants need—carbon, hydrogen, and oxygen—come from the air. The other essential elements come from the soil.

The essential elements supplied by the soil are divided into two groups—macronutrients and micronutrients (also known as trace elements). Three macronutrients are especially critical—nitrogen, potassium, and phosphorus. These are the primary nutrients, represented on fertilizer bags in ratios tagged by their elemental initials: N, P, and K. Nitrogen (N) powers growth and protein formation; phosphorus (P) is essential for root and fruit development and for photosynthesis; and potassium (K) is crucial to root and flower development as well as water and sugar flow. All three of these nutrients must be present in the right balance for your annuals and perennials to grow and thrive. The secondary macronutrients—sulfur, calcium, and magnesium—are used in smaller amounts. Micronutrients include iron, molybdenum, manganese, zinc, chlorine, boron, copper, and nickel.

Plants use relatively large amounts of the macronutrients, much as humans use a lot of carbohydrates, proteins, and fats. They use smaller quantities of the micronutrients, much as humans need

Annuals as well as vegetables and herbs are heavy feeders, so if you're planning an edible garden, be sure to give your plants a nutrient boost.

small amounts of vitamins and minerals. The difference in the amount plants use doesn't indicate a difference in how important the element is. All of them are essential, and a lack of just one affects how effectively plants can use the others. That's why balancing soil fertility is so important for good plant growth.

Fertilizers or Amendments?

The first step to choosing the right organic material is knowing the difference between a true fertilizer and a soil amendment. Fertilizer is a material that contains significant amounts of the chemical elements that plants need to grow, like nitrogen, phosphorus, and potassium. It may also contain material that improves the soil, such as organic matter. But its primary function is to add

nutrients. Bloodmeal, bat guano, and greensand are examples of organic fertilizers.

An amendment is a material that physically improves the soil —usually its structure or its drainage—or enhances microbial activity. It may contain some nutrients, but not enough to be called a fertilizer. Compost, grass clippings, lime, and peat moss are examples of soil amendments.

The material you use really depends on what effect you want. Fertilizers are useful for correcting specific nutrient deficiencies and for providing a general nutrient boost during the growing season. Amendments are important for long-term soil health, since they add organic matter and humus. Using a balance of fertilizers and amendments will help ensure your plants have all the nutrients they need and help build soil humus as well.

Start with a Soil Test

Before you invest in a big bag of fertilizer, find out what's in your soil to start with. It may already contain everything your plants need to grow beautifully. You can use home test kits or you can send soil samples to a lab for testing before you plant. To have your

Lupines belong to the same family as peas and beans. These plants seldom need extra nitrogen.

Flowering plants can have very different nutrient needs. Group those with similar needs together, as in this border that includes verbena, sage, and sedum.

soil analyzed by a lab, contact your local Cooperative Extension agent, land-grant university, or professional soil-analysis laboratory for information or directions.

Applying Nutrients

How you actually apply organic nutrients to your garden depends on several factors. If you're starting a new bed, for instance, mix in potassium, phosphorus, and any other fertilizers or amendments (like lime or sulfur) recommended in the soil test results at the same time that you dig. Or better yet, add them to your compost pile, then add the compost to the soil—the abundant microorganisms in the compost help break down rock powders and other low-solubility fertilizers faster than the smaller, less-active populations in the soil do. Potassium and phosphorus are very important to encourage healthy roots that will keep perennials returning each year.

With that said, be aware that flowering plants can differ widely in their soil needs.

Some, like California poppy (*Eschscholzia californica*), are well adapted to shallow, dry, infertile soil and may not flower well in deep, fertile conditions. Others, like astilbes (*Astilbe* x *arendsii*), will turn brown and crispy unless they have rich, evenly moist soil. Either buy plants that are adapted to the conditions your garden

Adding gypsum will supply your soil with calcium and sulfur, but it won't change the soil pH.

has to offer or be willing to put some work into creating the right conditions to fit the plants you want to grow. You can find out the soil and moisture needs of flowering plants by looking in gardening books and magazines or by referring to the individual entries for specific annuals and perennials starting on page 172.

Remember that annuals only last for a season, which means they don't have a great deal of time to extract slow-release fertilizers from the soil. Before planting them, mix a balanced fertilizer or compost into the soil to feed the microorganisms and provide a small, steady supply of nutrients to the annuals.

Once your annuals and perennials are established, you can supply them with nutrients by working fertilizer materials into the soil around the base of each plant and by mulching with organic materials like chopped leaves or compost. For more on fertilizer materials, see "Fertilizing for Good Growth" on page 134.

Choosing the Right Plants

Starting with healthy plants is a key step in having a naturally healthy garden. It's crucial, after all those hours spent planning your design, carefully deciding what to grow, and getting the soil ready, that you buy strong, problem-free plants and bulbs.

Buying from Local Retailers

A good local nursery or garden center—one that offers a variety of plants and takes good care of them—is a real treasure. Usually its staff members are good sources of information specific to your area, such as which plants grow well there. The nursery may even have a demonstration garden where you can see how plants look when fully grown and compare different cultivars.

Advantages and Disadvantages

One advantage of buying locally is that you can inspect plants and bulbs before buying them. Also, your plants won't have to suffer through shipping. Most nurseries and garden centers offer container-grown plants, which are easiest to handle. On the down side, the selection they have on sale may be limited, and the plants may be more expensive.

If you want a particular cultivar of a plant, you're most likely to find it via a mail-order source.

Buying by Mail

If you want unusual plants, don't have access to a local nursery, or want to get the best possible prices, mail-order sources provide limitless possibilities. Write for catalogs several months before you want to plant so you'll have time to compare selections and prices. Some catalogs have information on the virtues of specific plants and useful growing information.

Advantages and Disadvantages

Catalog shopping is a fun way to while away dreary winter evenings, and it's convenient, too. You can learn about exciting new plants and often find good prices when you compare several catalogs. On the down side, you don't really know what you're paying for until you get it. Shipping stress can weaken even the strongest plants. If you get bareroot perennials (with roots that are wrapped in packing material), they'll need to be planted or potted up almost immediately.

Buying Tips

The best approach to ordering by mail is to ask gardening friends which catalogs they've ordered from and which they would buy from again. If you don't know anyone who gets annual or perennial catalogs, visit a library and get addresses and phone numbers from advertisements in recent gardening magazines.

When you order from a source for the first time, just buy a few plants and see how they look when they arrive. If you're happy with the quality for the price, order more; otherwise, shop elsewhere. Remember, if an offer sounds too good to be true, it probably is!

Inspect mail-order plants as soon as they arrive. If they are damaged, you should return them; contact the source right away to find out how to do so. Mail-order perennials are often shipped when they are dormant (not actively growing) and may look dead. Plant them anyway and water them well. If they don't produce any buds or new growth in a few weeks, contact the source.

If your plants were shipped in pots, water them as needed and keep them out of bright sunlight for the first few days. Mail-order plants may also arrive bareroot—without any pot or soil. If they're bulbs, they're happy that way; keep them cool and in the dark until you're ready to plant. Other bareroot plants need more attention; for best results, plant them within a couple days of their arrival.

A favorite pastime for the keen gardener is a trip to the local nursery to find new plants for the garden.

Don't be swept away by the enormous choice of plants. Check they are healthy before buying.

To plant out a cottage garden, especially one on this scale, it's most cost-effective to buy by mail order.

Healthy Plant Checklist

A stressed, diseased, or pest-infested plant is a recipe for disappointing results. So before you pay for your purchases, take a minute to check them over carefully—following the points here—to make sure you're getting the best plants possible.

1. Look to see if the plant is tagged with its botanical and cultivar name. If not, or if it's labeled only by common name or color, chances are that it's not an improved type and you may not want it.

2. Test for root-bound plants, which may have been sitting around for a long time in a small pot. Give the plant a soft tug and see if the root ball pops out of the pot readily. If the roots are packed into a solid mass or circle around the inside of the pot, the plant is root-bound and may be slow to adapt to garden conditions.

3. Look at the roots. Firm, white roots are a sign of good health. If you can't pull the plant out of its pot to see the roots, check where the shoots emerge from the soil. Emerging stems should not be brown, soft, blemished, or wilted—these are symptoms of rots and other diseases.

4. Give the same thorough inspection to the stems and foliage. Look for signs of diseases such as brown or black leaf spots, white powdery mildew, or tiny orange spots of rust. You don't want to bring these problems home to infect plants in your garden.

5. Check the color of the foliage. If it is a deep and uniform color, the plant is most likely healthy and well fed.

6. Be on the lookout for weed shoots emerging through or near the crown (base) of the annual or perennial. Grasses and perennial weeds will reemerge and can invade your newly planted garden.

7. Last, check for insect pests. Look beneath the leaves, along the stems, in the shoot tips, and on the flower buds for soft-bodied aphids, cottony mealybugs, and hard-shelled scale insects. Spider mites, another common pest, will make leaves stippled or turn them yellow or bronze. If there are pests on one plant,

Different Ways to Buy Perennials

Perennials that are container grown may cost a bit more but they will give an instant effect in the garden.

Field-dug perennials are often quite mature and usually adapt quickly once planted in a new site.

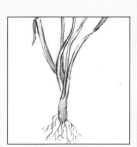

Bareroot perennials take a bit of care because their roots are exposed, but they are often less expensive.

Gently slide a plant from its pot to check the roots. Avoid plants with massed or circling roots.

Good-quality plants will have healthy white roots that are still growing through the soil ball.

they may be on every single plant in that greenhouse or garden center. Consider shopping elsewhere.

Buying Annual Transplants

Look for annuals that are fairly uniform and seem healthy. Avoid those that are wilted, as well as those with visible problems. (Review the "Healthy Plant Checklist" to get a good idea of the signs and symptoms to look for.) While wilted plants usually recover when watered, repeated wilting can stunt their growth and make them less likely to perform well in your garden over the season.

Another thing to consider is whether or not the plants are in bloom. If you're looking for specific flower colors, you may want to buy plants that already have some blooms. In most cases, though, you'll get the best growth from plants that aren't yet blooming. If you can only buy transplants that are already flowering, pinch off the

flowers at planting time. It seems hard to do, but it will help your plants in the long run. They'll put their energy into making new roots and then quickly start producing bushy new growth and dozens of new flower buds.

Buying Perennials

There are several ways to sell the same perennial plant—in a container, bareroot, or field-dug. What follows are some specifications that will help you evaluate how to use your plant budget most wisely.

Container-grown Perennials

Perennials are most commonly sold in containers. Container-grown perennials are convenient and easy to handle. You can keep the pots in a warm, well-lit location until you are ready to plant. Then you can slide the root ball out and plant the perennials in the garden with minimal disturbance.

However, there is a catch. Horticultural researchers are finding that the roots tend to stay in the light, fluffy "soil" of synthetic potting mixes, rather than branching out into the surrounding garden soil. But you can avoid this problem by loosening roots on the outside of the ball and spreading them out into the soil as you plant. (For more information on planting, see "Planting Perennials" on page 116.)

Container-grown perennials come in different sizes, so their prices vary widely. Larger-sized pots, usually 1- and 2-gallon (4.5- to 9-liter) containers, are generally more expensive. The cost may be worthwhile if you need immediate garden impact. On the other hand, you can buy younger plants inexpensively in

Plants that look strong and healthy are likely to grow well. Weak, sickly plants may introduce pests and diseases into your garden.

multicell packs or small pots. These sizes work fine if you don't mind waiting a year or more for them to fill out and bloom with abandon. In fact, young plants tend to become established in the garden faster than older ones, catching up to the bigger plants in a short time.

Garden mums, or chrysanthemums, are usually sold as container-grown perennials. Unless you want a particular flower color, it's best to buy perennials that aren't in bloom.

Bareroot Perennials

You will come across many species of dormant bareroot plants for sale early in the growing season. In late summer or early fall, you can also find bareroot items such as bearded irises, peonies, common bleeding heart (*Dicentra spectabilis*), and oriental poppies (*Papaver orientale*). You may choose to buy bareroot plants to save money—they are usually less expensive than large container-grown plants—or you may receive them unexpectedly. Mail-order companies often send plants bareroot to save on shipping and space. You open the box to find long spidery roots and—at best—a small tuft of foliage. These plants look more dead than alive, but looks can be deceiving. If you keep the roots moist and cool and plant them quickly and properly, most bareroot plants will recover and thrive.

When the plants arrive, tend to them promptly. Open the box to let some air in. The plants' roots should be wrapped in a protective medium like shredded newspaper, excelsior, or sphagnum moss. Be sure to keep this medium moist but not soggy.

Field-dug Perennials

You may be able to find a plant collector, hobbyist plant breeder,

Avoiding Wild-collected Bulbs

Part of being a good shopper is knowing where the bulbs you buy are coming from. While much progress has been made in limiting the collection of species bulbs from the wild, some disreputable sources still gather the bulbs they sell from native habitats. You'll want to buy only from dealers that sell cultivated bulbs.

Dutch companies now label all of their bulbs with their source, and they supply that information in their catalog. American dealers are not required to inform their customers whether their bulbs were grown in production fields or collected from wild sources. However, most American sources actually do provide that information and are against taking plants from the wild.

Wild collection is not an issue with hybrids and cultivars, since these plants don't grow in the wild. But it can be a concern when you're buying species bulbs, including Grecian windflower (*Anemone blanda*), hardy cyclamen (*Cyclamen* spp.), winter aconite (*Eranthis hyemalis* and *E. cilicicus*), snowdrops (*Galanthus* spp.), snowflakes (*Leucojum* spp.), species daffodils (such as *Narcissus asturiensis*, *N. bulbocodium*, and *N. triandrus*), and sternbergia (*Sternbergia* spp.). Make sure you purchase only those bulbs you're sure are from cultivated stock. If you can't tell, ask the supplier or find another source.

Daffodils

and labor it takes to produce them, but you can rely on them for truly spectacular results. A higher price, however, doesn't always mean that one tulip or daffodil cultivar is better than another. New cultivars tend to be much more expensive than older ones that have been around for a while. New cultivars are fun to try, but the old standbys that have proven to be good performers through the years are usually both economical and dependable.

A top-quality bulb is firm to the touch (not mushy or squishy) and free of large blemishes or scars. Some bulbs, such as tulips and hyacinths, may have a trace of blue mold on them. A few small mold spots will not harm the bulb, but a noticeable layer may indicate that the bulb was stored improperly before being offered for sale, and is best avoided. Look for bulbs that show little or no root or shoot growth except for a pale growth bud at the top. (Lilies are an exception, since they often have fleshy roots attached.) It's wise to shop early in the season so you can get the bulbs before they dry out from sitting in a store for weeks.

farmer, or nursery owner who will sell you mature plants dug from the field. If you handle the root ball carefully, you can move field-dug perennials much later in the summer than bareroot plants because the roots are protected by soil. Set the root ball, surrounded by soil, in a firm wooden flat or sturdy bucket. Cover it with a moist towel, damp peat moss, or compost to keep the roots and soil moist. Replant it as soon as you get home.

Buying Bulbs

High-quality, full-sized bulbs command top dollar, based on the amount of time

Bulbs come in many shapes and sizes. Buy those that are plump and firm; avoid shriveled ones.

Buy generous quantities of bulbs and plant them in drifts or large clumps for a dramatic spring show.

Planting Time

You have your plants, and you have a place to put them. Now you're ready to turn your dream garden into a reality. Although you may have been anticipating the moment of planting for months, don't rush when it arrives. Planting properly takes time and a lot of bending. Work slowly and deliberately to save wear and tear on your body and to get each plant settled as well as possible. Try not to compact the soil. Lay boards across the bed when you need to step in it. This spreads your weight across a broad area instead of concentrating it in one spot.

Planting Annuals

Planting time for annuals varies. In cold areas, it is around the average date of the last frost for your area. In tropical and subtropical areas, you can plant many annuals virtually all year round. But before you set them out in the garden, make sure your transplants, or seedlings, are "hardened off"—adjusted to outdoor conditions. For details on this important step, see "Handling Hardening Off."

Transplants that are in flower will take a little longer to get established and put on new growth.

If you want to tuck transplants in around existing plants, dig individual holes for each transplant.

When actually planting your annuals, check back to the instructions on the seed packets, plant labels, or entries in the "Guide to Popular Annuals," starting on page 172, for suggested information on spacing. If you live in a hot, dry climate or a very cool area that only has a short growing season, you may want to set the plants a little closer together so they'll shade the soil and fill in faster. In humid climates, use the suggested spacings or slightly wider spacings to allow good air circulation between plants; this will help minimize disease problems.

Plants that like average, well-drained soil and full sun will be easy to care for if planted together.

Step-by-Step Guide to Transplanting

1. Dig a hole, then carefully remove the plant from its container.

2. Set the plant in the hole so the base of the stem is level with the soil surface.

3. Gently firm down the soil around the base of the plant so it is stable.

4. Water the plant thoroughly with a fine spray to wet the soil around the roots.

When possible, set transplants out on a cloudy day so they'll be less prone to transplant shock. Use a trowel to dig a hole twice as big as the root mass. Tip the pot or cell pack on its side and gently slide the plant out of its container. Or, if the plant is growing in a peat pot, just tear off the upper rim of the pot and place the whole pot in the hole. Set each plant so the stem base is at the same level as it was in the pot. Fill around the roots with soil, firm the soil gently, and water thoroughly.

Protecting Young Plants

If temperatures are unseasonably warm, your transplants may like a few days of sun protection, especially during the afternoon. Use the lath fencing you used for hardening them off (see "Handling Hardening Off" for details), or shelter them with sheets of newspaper clipped to stakes or cages. Mist seedlings occasionally if they wilt, but don't add a lot of extra water to the soil; swampy soil is as bad as dry soil for tender roots.

If late frosts threaten, protect plants through the night with overturned cans, buckets, or clay flower pots. Floating row covers (weigh down the edges with rocks or boards) can provide a few degrees of frost protection and also protect young plants from birds and animal pests.

Sometimes, soil-dwelling caterpillars called cutworms will feed on seedlings at

Row covers can be handy for protecting tender seeds from frosts.

Handling Hardening Off

If you buy greenhouse-grown seedlings or raise your own indoors, they will need to be hardened off before they are ready for transplanting. This involves gradually exposing them to the harsher outdoor conditions: more sunlight, drying winds, and varying temperatures.

Start by moving seedlings outdoors on a nice day. Set shade-loving annuals in a sheltered, shady spot for 2 or 3 days before planting. Give sun-loving annuals about 1 hour of full sun, then move them into the shade of a fence or covered porch. (Take them in at night if frost threatens.) Lengthen the sun time each day, over a period of at least 3 days, until plants can take a full day of sun. Then you can plant them in the garden.

If you don't have a shady spot or if you work during the day and can't run home to shift flats of annuals, make a simple shelter with a section of lath fencing (sometimes called snow fencing). Support the section with bricks or blocks and slide your seedlings underneath. The laths will give a continuously shifting pattern of sun and shade. After 3 or 4 days, your seedlings should be in ideal condition for transplanting.

night, eating them off right at ground level. To protect young plants, you can surround them with a metal or cardboard collar. Slip sections of paper towel rolls over seedlings or open-ended soup or juice cans over transplants. Press the collar into the soil, so at least 1 inch (2.5 cm) is below the soil and several inches are left above. Remove after 2 to 3 weeks, or mulch over them and remove at the end of the season; paper collars will break down on their own.

Sowing Seed in the Garden

Many popular annuals grow just as well from seed sown outdoors as they do from transplants, which have grown from seed sown indoors. Some even grow better from direct-sown

seed because they like cool outdoor temperatures or because they don't respond well to transplanting. A few annuals in this easy-to-grow group include morning glories (*Ipomoea* spp.), California poppy (*Eschscholzia californica*), and rocket larkspur (*Consolida ambigua*). To find out if the annuals you want to grow can be direct-sown, check the seed packet or the entries in the "Guide to Popular Annuals," starting on page 172. These sources will also tell you the best time for sowing.

Direct-sowing is simple. First, get the soil ready for planting (as explained in "Getting the Soil Ready" on page 106). Sow medium-sized and large seeds individually or scatter them evenly over the surface. Try to space them ½ to 1 inch (12 to 25 mm) apart. If you have very small seeds, mix them with a handful of dry sand and distribute them over the seedbed.

Cover most seeds with a thin layer of fine soil or sand. If you're dealing with fine seeds, just pat them into the soil or tamp down the area with a board. After sowing, make sure the seedbed stays moist until the

Start your garden by setting out indoor-grown transplants, then direct-sow seeds around them.

Planting a Container-grown Perennial

1. Dig a planting hole that is larger than the root ball.

2. If desired, add a handful or two of compost to the hole.

3. Add enough water to just moisten the soil before planting.

4. Gently slide the perennial plant out of its container.

5. Use your fingers to loosen the soil mix around the roots.

6. Set the plant in the hole. Backfill with soil, then firm lightly.

Planting Perennials

Planting your perennials at the right time of year is an important factor in giving them a good start. Time your planting efforts so your new perennials will start growing in a period of abundant rainfall and moderate temperatures—usually spring or fall. In cool climates, like Zone 5 and colder, concentrate your planting efforts in spring. (If you aren't sure what zone you live in, see the USDA Plant Hardiness Zone Map on page 276.) Planting in spring allows the new plants enough time to establish strong root systems before winter arrives. You can take a chance with late-summer planting for very hardy or seasonally available perennials. In warmer climates with mild winters, such as Zones 9 and 10, plant in fall so perennials will be well established before the long, hot summer. In areas where summer isn't too hot and winter isn't too cold—Zones 6 through 8—you can plant perennials in fall or spring. If your climate has periods of drought, plant whenever there is abundant natural rainfall and temperatures are between about 40° and 70°F (4.4° and 21.2°C).

Plant Spacing

Before you actually plant the perennials, set them in place to see how they look.

seedlings are visible. If there isn't enough rainfall, water gently with a watering can, sprinkler, or fine hose spray. Covering the seedbed with a layer of floating row cover helps to keep the soil moist and protects the seed from drying winds, heavy rain, and birds. (Remove the cover once the seedlings emerge.)

If seedlings are crowded, you'll need to thin them out for good growth. Dig up and carefully transplant extra seedlings, or use scissors to cut off the stems of unwanted seedlings at ground level.

Planting Biennials

If you decide to grow biennial plants, such as foxgloves (*Digitalis purpurea*) and forget-me-nots (*Myosotis sylvatica*), you need a slightly different growing approach than if you were planting annuals. Most biennials will sprout well when sown outdoors. But if you sow them directly into the garden, their leafy, first-year growth will take up room without adding much interest to your flower display.

The easiest and most effective method is to set aside a temporary growing area (called a nursery bed) where your biennials can grow through the summer. Prepare your nursery bed just as you would any garden area, but site it in an out-of-the-way spot. Sow the biennial seeds directly into the bed in spring or summer and thin them as needed. Dig the plants up and move them to their final garden spots in late summer or early fall; they will be ready for bloom in the following spring or summer.

Large, double types of marigold are best grown from transplants.

A newly planted garden may look a little sparse at first, but don't despair—it will fill in surprisingly fast.

If you are grouping several of the same kind of plant, mark the outside edge of the mass on the soil surface with a hoe, a trickle of limestone, or a row of pegs. Then set the plants, still in pots, inside the markers. Move them into a natural-looking arrangement—clustered unevenly rather than lined out in geometrical rows. Be certain each plant has enough space. If you crowd plants, they will grow weakly and be more susceptible to disease.

Double-check spacings with a tape measure—measuring distances by eye is not always effective. Check lines and masses of a single species of perennial to be sure the spacing is even. Leave more space between the faster growers. Let difficult-to-move plants like peonies, blue false indigo (*Baptisia australis*), and gas plant (*Dictamnus albus*) have enough elbow room to mature to their full size. You can use tighter spacings for smaller, more slow-spreading plants like coral bells (*Heuchera* spp.), since they are easy to move when the plants need more room.

As you work out the spacings, decide if you want to leave some open areas here and there within the garden to let air circulate and sun penetrate. A more open garden lets you enjoy the attractive silhouettes of plants. However, a tightly packed garden will be an ocean of color and texture—a more intense display. Stand back and study the appearance of the bed from different angles to get some idea of how the finished garden will look. Readjust as needed. When you are satisfied, start planting.

Planting

In most cases you'll set new plants in the ground at the same depth at which they are growing presently. Replanting at the

Planting a Bareroot Perennial

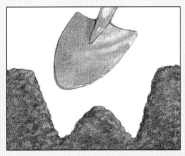

1. Dig a hole large enough to hold the roots without bending them.

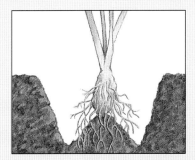

2. Set the crown in the hole. Spread the roots over the mound.

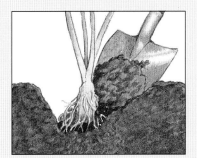

3. Backfill the hole with soil, firm gently, and water well.

same depth keeps the crown—the point from which shoots emerge—from being buried in damp soil, where it is likely to rot. However, if you have just prepared the soil, it will settle 1 to 2 inches (2.5 to 5 cm) over the coming months. In a new bed, plant the perennials slightly deeper so their roots and crowns do not stick up above the soil once it has settled. Exactly how you plant perennials depends on whether you are using container-grown, bareroot, or field-dug stock.

Container Plants If you are planting a potted perennial, you can easily see how low in the ground to plant it. Dig deeply enough so the surface of the container soil will be at the top of the hole (adjusting as necessary for new beds). Fill the hole with water to moisten the soil.

Now, get the plant ready for planting. Slip it out of the pot—most larger plants are root-bound enough to slide out quite easily. If not, you can gently squeeze the base of the plastic pot to loosen the root ball. Then break up the edges of the root

Some plants, like blue false indigo, can be tricky to move because of their deep root system.

ball so the roots will have more contact with the soil. Place in the hole and cover with soil to the crown.

If the roots are wrapped around themselves, they may not break free and root into the soil. You will have to work them loose. You can quarter the roots of fibrous-rooted perennials like garden mums. Although the process may seem harsh, it will encourage new root growth. Make four deep slices, one on each side of the root ball, or make a single cut two-thirds up the center to divide the ball in half. Mound some soil in the center of the planting hole. Open the root quarters out from the cuts and spread them out over the mound. Cover the rest of the roots up to the crown. Don't try this technique on perennials with taproots like monkshoods (*Aconitum* spp.).

After planting, firm the soil gently around the plant, water

it well, and mulch. Mulching your bed with organic materials like compost, straw, or shredded leaves will conserve moisture and reduce weed competition. (New beds are especially weed-prone, since turning the soil exposes weed seeds.) For more information on choosing and using mulches, see "Make the Most of Mulch" on page 130.

Field-dug Plants Plant your field-dug perennials that have a lot of soil still around the roots in a hole the same size as the root ball. If much of the soil has fallen off the roots, make the hole slightly larger so you can move the roots into the best position. Drench the hole with water and set in the perennial at the same depth it was growing. Work any exposed roots into the surrounding soil as you refill the hole, then firm the soil gently.

Bareroot Plants When you start with bareroot plants, you will have to take more time settling the plants into the

Best Bulbs for Naturalizing

Small bulbs tend to be the best choices for naturalizing: They bloom dependably, they're easy to plant, and they're usually relatively inexpensive. Daffodil bulbs tend to be large, but even they are often sold in bargain mixtures for naturalizing. Listed below are some of the bulbs that adapt well to naturalizing.

Allium moly (lily leek)
Anemone blanda (Grecian windflower)
Colchicum speciosum (showy autumn crocus)
Crocus spp. (crocus)
Galanthus nivalis (common snowdrops)
Hyacinthoides hispanicus
    (Spanish bluebells)
Leucojum aestivum
    (summer snowflake)
Muscari armeniacum
    (grape hyacinth)
Narcissus hybrids (daffodils)
Scilla sibirica (Siberian squill)

Siberian squill

Good soil preparation of beds and careful planting will give your plants every chance of success.

ground. This process can be tricky the first few times, but be patient and don't be afraid to work with the roots. You'll soon get it right.

First, soak the roots in a bucket of lukewarm water for a few hours to prepare them for planting. If you don't have time to plant straight after obtaining your bareroot plants, keep the roots moist and store them, in their original package, in a cool location for a day or two. If you need to wait longer than that to plant, pot up the plants or set them into a nursery bed until you are ready. When you are ready to plant, identify how deeply the plants have been growing in the nursery. The aboveground portions—green foliage tufts, leaf buds, or dormant stems—usually emerge from the root system above the former soil line. Plant so these structures will stay slightly above the surface of the soil in your garden once it has settled. (Peonies are an exception, since their

shoots will emerge through the soil from about 1 inch [2.5 cm] underground.)

Next, make a hole that is deep and wide enough to set the plant crown at the soil surface and stretch out the roots. Form a small mound of soil in the bottom of the hole. Set the root clump on it with the crown resting on top of the mound. Spread the roots gently in every direction and fill in around them with soil. Then firm the soil gently, water well, and apply a layer of mulch. Keep the soil evenly moist for the next few weeks.

Planting Bulbs

Planting bulbs requires some imagination on your part. After all, when you buy bulbs, you get a bunch of brown-wrapped packets of plant energy that have the potential to transform themselves into brilliantly colored crocus or daffodils. With proper planting and good care, your bulbs will be able to fulfill that potential.

Plant drifts of polyanthus primroses with spring bulbs like daffodils, tulips, and Spanish bluebells.

When You Get Them Home

It's usually best to plant bulbs within a few days of buying them, so they'll have plenty of time to adapt to their new home and send out a good crop of roots. If you can't plant right away, store your bulbs in a cool, dark, and relatively dry place until you're ready for them.

Planting in Beds and Borders

Once you've prepared the soil, planting is easy—just dig the hole to the proper depth, pop in the bulb, and cover it with soil. The proper hole depth will vary, depending on what bulbs you're growing. A general rule of thumb is that the base of a bulb or corm should be planted 3 to 4 times as deep as the height of the bulb. For example, a crocus corm that measures 1 inch (2.5 cm) high should be planted 3 to 4 inches (7.5 to 10 cm) deep; a 2-inch (5-cm) high tulip bulb needs a hole 6 to 8 inches (15 to 20 cm) deep. If your soil is on the sandy side, plant a bit deeper. To find out the best planting depth for your bulbs, check the catalog description or packet label or refer to the individual entries in the "Guide to Popular Perennials," starting on page 202.

Set the bulb in the hole with the pointed growth bud facing upward. If you can't tell which side should be up—and it's often difficult with small bulbs such as Grecian windflowers (*Anemone blanda*)—set the bulb on its side or just drop it into the hole and hope for the

To get your perennials off to a good start, plant when temperatures are moderate and rainfall abundant.

Naturalize grape hyacinths and daffodils under a spring-flowering tree. To plant bulbs in grass, especially large bulbs like daffodils, use a hand-held bulb planter or trowel to make individual holes.

make a small hole. Insert the bulb, firm the soil and sod over it, and water in well.

For larger bulbs, it's often easier to use a shovel or spade to remove a larger patch of turf, about 1 foot (30 cm) square. Loosen the soil to the proper depth, plant the bulbs, replace the turf, and water. You can also buy special bulb planting tools to make individual holes for your large bulbs. Hand-held planters look like deep cookie cutters and work pretty much the same way. They are fairly inexpensive but can be very tiring to use. A similar type of planter that's mounted on a handle is a little easier to use, since you can push the cutting edge into the ground with your foot instead of your hand.

For easier planting, try an auger attachment that connects to a regular hand-held power drill. These tools can be hard to use around rocks and tree roots, but they will allow you to make many holes quickly and easily under most conditions.

Hand-held bulb planting tools

Special Care

Different bulbs have adapted to survive in very different conditions. Although most bulbs flower at spring time, that is not the case for all bulbs. So the time of year that you plant your bulbs is crucial if you want them to perform to their best.

best. Most bulbs have a strong will to grow, and they'll find a way to send up their shoots.

Space the bulbs so each one has ample room to grow. As a general rule when planting in beds and borders, you should leave 5 to 6 inches (12.5 to 15 cm) between large bulbs and 1 to 3 inches (2.5 to 7.5 cm) between small bulbs. Once you've got the spacing the way you want it, carefully replace the soil around the bulbs to refill the hole. Firm the soil by patting it with your hand or the back of a rake, then water the area well.

Planting in Grassy Areas

When you "naturalize" bulbs in a lawn or meadow, you don't have the luxury of preparing a nice, loose planting area all at once. Fortunately, the bulbs that grow well in these situations are pretty tough.

The easiest bulbs to plant are the small ones, such as crocus, Siberian squill (*Scilla sibirica*), and grape hyacinth (*Muscari armeniacum*). Simply get down on your hands and knees with a narrow trowel, dandelion digger, or garden knife. Insert the tool into the soil to lift up a flap of turf, or wiggle the tool back and forth to

When planting in masses, it's usually easiest to dig a large planting area that can hold many bulbs.

Spring Bulbs It's easy to add spring bulbs to your garden, but it does take a little advance planning. Mail-order catalogs of spring bulbs often arrive in spring to early summer, so you can decide what your garden needs and place your order for delivery in fall. Late summer and fall are also the times you'll find spring bulbs for sale at local garden centers. In Northern gardens, early to midfall is the best time to plant; in Southern areas, the planting season continues through early winter.

Spring Bulbs and Winter Chilling

Winter chilling is an important step in the life of most spring-blooming bulbs. If you live in a warm climate, where winter temperatures generally stay above freezing, you may find that some spring bulbs bloom poorly or don't bloom at all in the years after planting. Hybrid tulips commonly have this problem; some daffodils and crocus (below) also grow poorly without a chilling period.

To have a great show of blooms each year, look for species and cultivars that don't need much chilling. (Ask your neighbors, local garden center, or Cooperative Extension Service to recommend the bulbs that grow best in your area.) You can also look for "precooled" bulbs, or give new bulbs an artificial cold period by storing them in the vegetable drawer of your refrigerator for 6 to 8 weeks before planting them in early to midwinter.

Water spring bulbs just after planting and again as needed if the soil dries out in winter or spring. Scatter compost or balanced organic fertilizer over the soil when the new shoots appear in spring to provide a nutrient boost for healthy growth and good flower bud formation for next year.

Most spring bulbs thrive in full or partial sun (that is, at least 6 hours of sun a day). They are ideal for planting under deciduous trees, since the bulbs can bloom and their foliage ripen before the tree leaves expand fully and block the sunlight. Unless you're planning to plant new, replacement bulbs each year (as may be necessary with hybrid tulips), always allow the bulb leaves to wither away naturally after flowering. They may look unsightly, but if you cut off, pull off, or bundle the leaves together, the bulb won't store the energy it needs and it may bloom poorly or even die by the next year.

Summer Bulbs Some summer bulbs—including lilies and ornamental onions (*Allium* spp.)—can live from year to year, so you'll plant them once and enjoy their blooms for years to come. These "hardy" bulbs are usually planted in fall for bloom the following summer, although lilies can also adapt to early-spring planting. The key is to plant them early enough so the root system can get established before warm weather promotes lush top growth.

Other summer bloomers are classified as "tender" bulbs. These cold-sensitive beauties may not be able to survive the winter in your area. Unless you live in a warm climate (roughly Zone 8 and south),

For a great show of hybrid tulips each year, pull them out after bloom and plant new tulips in fall.

you'll need to plant gladioli, cannas, dahlias, and other tender bulbs in spring to early summer and dig them up in the fall for winter storage indoors.

Fall Bulbs The trick with fall-flowering bulbs is remembering to plant them at the right time of year. Magic lilies and naked ladies are best planted in early summer, when the bulbs are dormant. Late summer or early fall, just before their bloom starts, is the best time for most other fall-flowering bulbs.

Like other bulbs, fall bloomers need to ripen their leaves fully to store enough food for good flowering. So live with their leaves until they wither away—don't cut or pull them off before they turn yellow. If you "naturalize" fall bulbs in grassy areas, you'll also need to remember to stop mowing as soon as you see the first flower buds emerging from the soil in late summer to early fall.

Caring for Annuals and Perennials

Once your annuals and perennials are planted, you need to know how to keep them looking their best. Fortunately, there are some simple but effective steps you can follow to help promote the health of your garden. And remember, maintenance is easiest if you do it regularly, as this will keep little tasks from mushrooming into overwhelming ones.

Tools and Equipment

When it comes to caring for your garden, the task will be made much simpler if you've got good tools to hand. Using the right tool makes any job easier, as you know if you've ever used a butter knife when you couldn't find the screwdriver or the heel of a shoe as a substitute for a hammer. But a shopping trip for garden tools can be so baffling that you may well decide to stick with the butter knife and shoe. When faced with a wall-long display of shovels, spades, forks, rakes, trowels, and cultivators, it can be hard to decide what tools, and which version of them, you need.

You may decide on a whole collection of garden tools, or just a few of the basics, depending on your needs and budget.

A Basic Tool Collection

Fortunately, most gardeners can get away with a half-dozen basic tools. You'll need a spade to turn the soil and a shovel for digging holes and for moving soil, sand, and amendments around. A spading fork is useful for turning the soil, working in amendments and green manures, turning compost, and dividing perennials. You'll also need a metal rake for smoothing the soil, a hoe for weeding, and a trowel for planting and transplanting. If you have a huge vegetable garden, you may want to get a rotary tiller, wheel hoe, or even a garden tractor to which you can attach various implements. Hand pruners may be necessary for pruning perennials. However, if you garden in containers, the only tools you'll need will be a trowel and hand cultivator.

Spades

A spade is used to turn soil, remove sod, or cut straight edges between lawns and beds. The square edge and flat blade also make spades handy for digging trenches.

To use, push the blade into the soil, resting your foot on the top rim of the blade and leaning your body weight onto it. Pull the handle back and down. When lifting, bend your knees before sliding one hand down the handle; if possible, brace the handle of the spade with your thigh.

Shovels

Shovels with pointed blades are handy for digging holes, whereas shovels with straight blades are the best type to use for scooping up loose materials such as sand, soil, gravel, or soil amendments. For good leverage, the handle should reach your shoulder at least; your nose is even better.

Good-quality tools can be expensive, but they are a pleasure to use and can last for many years.

When digging with a shovel, use your foot to push the blade into the soil. Use your legs and arms, not your back, to lift the load. Before tossing the load, turn your whole body, not just your upper torso, in the direction of the toss.

Forks

Spading forks and English garden forks are useful in many areas of the garden. Use them for turning heavy or rocky earth, working cover crops and organic matter into the soil, fluffing compost, aerating soil, lifting root crops, and dividing clumps of crowded perennials. A border fork is a smaller version of the spading fork. Pitchforks are for fluffing compost and moving piles of hay or straw, but not for digging.

To turn soil or work in organic matter, use your foot to push the tines into the soil, lift the fork, then dump the load with a twist of your arms and wrists. Avoid using a fork to pry rocks out of the soil or you'll bend the tines.

To fluff compost, dig the tines into the compost at a 45-degree angle and lift it with a slight toss. To aerate a lawn, use your foot to push the fork into the soil, then push the handle back and forth.

Separate perennial clumps by inserting the fork to loosen the center, then pull the crown apart with your hands.

A shovel is good for digging holes or scooping up loose materials like sand, soil, or bark chips.

A mattock is a handy tool for wrestling with hard, rocky soil or digging out stubborn stumps.

Choose from a range of different cultivators.

Broadforks

Also called U-bars or bio-forks, broadforks are used to loosen soil down to quite sizeable depths without actually turning it over like forks and spades do. However, broadforks don't loosen or aerate the soil as much as double-digging does. They're good tools to use if you don't want to mix poor-quality lower soil layers with the good, granular topsoil. Broadforks are also useful for cultivating beds with fragile soil structure, heavy soil that needs frequent loosening, or sandy soil that you don't want to over-aerate.

Rest your foot on the crossbar to which the tines are attached. Use your body weight to push the tines into the soil. If you're loosening the soil for planting, pull the handles toward you and push down so the tines lift out of the soil. To break up a hardpan, push the tines into the soil, then push and pull the handles back and forth.

Mattocks

Mattocks, also called grub hoes, are handy for removing stumps and breaking up hard or rocky soil that gets in the way of your landscaping plans. You can also use them to dig holes.

Use a swinging motion with the pick end to sever woody plant roots and to break up stony soil. Use the blade with a chopping motion for digging a hole or for prying rocks you've loosened with the other end.

Crowbars

A crowbar—also known as a caliche bar, pry bar, or axle rod—is a handy tool for prying large rocks, stumps, or pieces of broken concrete out of the ground. You can also use it to break up tight caliche soil (a soil type found in the Southwest), make holes in hard soil for garden stakes, or roll big rocks into place when building a stone wall.

When prying out a rock, use the edge of the hole or another rock as a fulcrum: Put the bar's tip under the heavy rock, rest the center of the bar on the fulcrum, and push down on the free end.

A trowel and hand cultivator are all you need for container gardens.

Trowels

Trowels are standard equipment for on-your-knees digging. Use a trowel when digging a hole for bulbs or transplants, making a furrow for seeds, or even weeding around small plants. Transplant trowels have narrow, cupped blades that are very handy for planting or working in small spaces.

Dig holes by using the trowel as a scoop to loosen and lift the soil. Or hold the handle in your fist with the face of the blade pointing toward you and dig by stabbing the soil and pulling back and up.

Rakes

A metal garden rake is an indispensable part of any garden tool collection. Use rakes for clearing stones, leaves, sticks, and other debris from beds and making a smooth surface for planting. Rakes are also handy for forming and shaping raised beds, working fertilizer into the soil, and spreading manure, compost, mulches, and other organic matter across the soil surface. If you're smoothing the soil before planting, work when the soil is slightly moist.

Both the tines and the back of the rake are useful for pushing and pulling soil and organic matter around.

A plastic or more durable metal rake is very useful.

Hoes are handy for many tasks—laying out rows, digging furrows, and weeding around plants.

Cultivators

Depending on the type of cultivator, you can use it to loosen and aerate the soil, scratch in dry fertilizer, and pull out weeds. Hand-held cultivating tools are good for working around the base of plants and other small spaces. There are a number of different cultivators, each of which is used in a slightly different way.

Asian hand cultivators: These resemble a trowel with a pointed end. The blade curves into a scooped shape, making it useful for deep cultivating.

Cape cod weeders: This tool has an L-shaped blade; pull the blade along just below the surface for weeding and loosening the soil.

Dandelion weeders: Also called asparagus knives or fishtail weeders, these tools have a blade that resembles a forked tongue; use them to dig out weeds with long taproots and to harvest asparagus.

Hand cultivators: These very handy tools have three claw-like tines and either a short or long handle. Use them to work closely around plantings, rake weeds from the soil, or scratch in a side-dressing of dry

fertilizer. Spring-toothed weeders are similar, but a spring gives the tines some bounce, making them more flexible.

Hand forks: Hand forks resemble small garden forks and can work the top 4 inches (10 cm) of soil or make holes for transplants. They're good for tight places.

Heart hoes: These hoes, also called one-prong cultivators, have a single C-shaped tine with a heart-shaped end. They let you work close to plants without doing damage. (A long-handled version may be called a biocultivator.)

Hotbed weeders: Hotbed weeders have a C-shaped blade that cuts along three of its edges, making them good for cutting small weeds in tight places.

Pavement weeders: These tools have an angled, pointed blade that you use to scrape between sections of sidewalk or driveway. (An old kitchen knife will work just as well.)

Hoes

Hoes are generally used for slicing weeds off at soil level, though they can have other uses, too. The eye hoe is designed for heavy digging and moving soil. Hoeing is easiest when the soil is slightly moist.

If you're using a standard pull or draw hoe—where the neck of the hoe curls back toward you—position your hands with your thumbs pointing up and pull the hoe toward you with a sweeping motion. If you use a push hoe—with the blade pointing away from you—hold the handle with your thumbs pointing down. Push it in front of you as you walk, with the blade just under the soil surface.

Rotary Tillers

Rotary tillers are most useful in medium to large vegetable gardens or annual flower beds. Use them for preparing bare soil for planting and for working in

A rotary tiller is most useful for cultivating bare soil in a large vegetable garden or annual flower bed.

A pair of hand pruners is invaluable for keeping your flowering plants trim, tidy, and in bloom.

amendments or green manure crops. Avoid using them to clear a sodded area; they can cause weed problems by chopping up the plants and perennial weed roots and spreading them through the soil. Till the soil only when a soil ball, made in your fist, easily falls apart when touched. Tilling when the soil is too wet or too dry can destroy soil structure.

Hand Pruners

Most gardeners of annuals and perennials will need little more than a pair of hand pruners. They are used to remove growth that's ¾ inch (18 mm) in diameter and smaller. Choose bypass pruners over anvil-type pruners: The latter tend to crush stems, while the scissor action of the former makes a cleaner cut. Ratchet-action hand pruners have also become more available and may be worthwhile for people with limited strength in their hands. However, don't be tempted to use the extra power to cut pieces larger than ¾ inch (18 mm); you may crush or tear the tissue left on the plant.

Carrying pruners in your pocket can be tough on your clothes and on you, too, if you forget they are there! A holster for your hand pruners is a wonderful accessory because it keeps them comfortably close at hand. With pruners at the ready, you're more likely to make a cut when you see the need.

If you find yourself using both hands to make a cut with your hand pruners, stop and reach for a pair of loppers. Loppers work best on cuts up to 1¾ inches (4.3 cm) in diameter. Choose wood handles (preferably ash) over metal ones for better shock absorption and pick bypass loppers over anvil loppers; the bypass version has the better cutting mechanism. Also look for models with a rubber disk that functions as a shock absorber when the tool snaps closed.

Buying Good Tools

There's nothing quite like the feel of working in your garden with a good-quality, well-constructed tool. Here are some things to consider as you shop for garden equipment, so you'll get the best tools for your money.

Cost

How much you spend on buying your tools depends on how long you want them to last. If you want to keep the tools for

Avoid open-socket tools (left) that have the top of the blade partly wrapped around the handle. Solid-socket tools (right) are much more durable.

decades, get the best you can afford—$40 for a spade or hoe isn't unreasonable. If you're on a tight budget, if you plan to move in a few years and don't want the extra baggage, or if you leave your tools outside all the time, buy the bargain basement kind for about $15. Be warned, however, that cost-cutting on materials and design makes cheap tools more difficult to use than their more expensive counterparts. And cheap tools might not even make it through a season without bending or breaking.

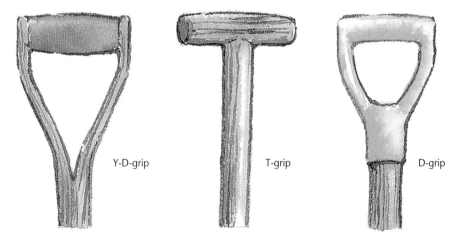

Tool handles come in several different styles of grip; choose the one that feels most comfortable to you.

If possible, choose tools with a handle length that is comfortable for you; this minimizes aches and pains.

Construction

When you go shopping for garden tools, read the labels carefully to see whether the metal part of a tool is stamped steel or forged steel. Forged steel is much stronger, but makes the tool cost 20 to 30 percent more than a stamped steel tool. If you want the item to last well, decide upon a forged steel product. If budget is an issue, consider the stamped steel tool.

Also investigate how the handle attaches to the metal part. Don't buy the tool if the metal wraps only partway around the handle; this construction, called open socket, leaves the wood exposed to water and mud, which can lead to rot. Also avoid tools where the handle is poked onto a spike at the top of the metal portion of the tool, then surrounded with a metal collar to keep the handle from splitting. Neither this type of construction, called tang and ferrule, nor open socket is durable and may only last a season or two. Instead, choose tools with metal that wraps all the way around the handle (called solid-socket construction) or has strips of metal bolted to the handle (known as solid-strap construction).

Handles

If you want a wooden handle, look for one made of white ash. Handles of spades and forks are sometimes made from hickory, but it's heavier and less flexible. The grain should run the length of the handle, without knots. Painted handles often hide low-quality wood; don't buy them.

Alternatives to wood are fiberglass or solid-core fiberglass. Both are stronger than wood; solid-core fiberglass is nearly unbreakable. Fiberglass adds about $8 to the cost of a tool, while solid-core fiberglass adds about $16. The additional cost is worth it if you want a tool that will last you for years and years.

Grips

If the end of the handle has a grip for you to hang on to, check how the grip is designed. Make sure it is fastened to the handle and not just slipped over it. Beyond that, the style you choose is a matter of preference (and availability). Try out a few to see which feels best.

Size

If you have a choice from the array of tools available, pick those with a handle length that feels most comfortable to you. Shovels should reach at least shoulder height; rakes can be even longer to give you a better reach. A hoe's handle should be long enough to let you stand upright when the blade is about 2 feet (60 cm) from your feet and just about flat on the ground. Short-handled tools, such as spades and forks, usually have 28-inch

For dependable service, brush tools and equipment off after use and clean and oil them thoroughly before storing for winter.

(70-cm) handles, but tall gardeners should look for ones with 32-inch (80-cm) handles. For hand tools such as trowels, choose the length that feels comfortable in your hand. When buying a mattock or pick, choose a weight that you can lift and swing without strain.

Caring for Tools

Once you've gone to the trouble of buying good tools, it's worth a little extra effort to keep them in shape. Without proper care, even the best built and most expensive tool can get corroded and dull after a season or two, making it as unpleasant to use as the cheapest department-store tool. When you are ready to dig, you'll be glad of the few minutes you put into keeping your tools clean and sharp.

Keep Them Clean

It's pretty easy at the end of a hot and grimy day in the garden to justify putting the tools away dirty. And you can even get away with it a few times. But eventually the moist soil clinging to your tools will make them rust. And once you finally do get around to cleaning them, the dry soil is harder to get off than the moist soil would have been.

For that reason, it's a virtue to force yourself into the habit of cleaning your tools when you're done with them. This doesn't mean just scraping the shovel off with the trowel. For one thing, then you have to scrape the trowel off with the shovel, then the shovel off with the trowel again, and so on. Also, all that scraping of metal on metal damages tools.

Better alternatives include using a stick, wooden spoon, or paint stirrer to scrape off the clinging soil. Or try a long-handled, heavy-duty scrub brush that you put in a convenient spot in your shed. Another trick is to keep a tub of sharp sand around and dip the tool up and down in it until the soil comes off.

It's especially worthwhile to clean all your tools before storing them away for the winter. Clean off any soil, then use steel wool or a wire brush to remove any rust. Coat the metal with a light oil and hang the tools someplace where you can see and admire them all winter long.

Since your skin touches the handle the most, you may want to keep wooden handles smooth by sanding any rough spots. If you wish, apply varnish or another sealer (like tung oil) to protect the wood. If a handle breaks, pick up a replacement during your next trip to the hardware store; don't just try to tape the old one back together.

Keep Them Sharp

Your spade and hoe will do a better job for you if you keep them sharpened. You'll get the best results if you sharpen them briefly and often rather than making it a big job for the end of the year.

For most gardeners, a metal file is an adequate sharpening tool. Use a file that matches the contour of the tool's surface—a flat file for a flat-bladed hoe or spade and a half-round file for a curved shovel blade. The aim is to keep the angle of the existing edge but to thin it a bit and remove any nicks. If you have many tools, a whetstone or grindstone will do the job more quickly. If you don't want to sharpen them yourself, you can take your tools to someone who does it professionally. The best time to do this is in late fall, as you prepare your tools for storage. Sharpeners are often swamped with work in spring and they may not have time to do your tools as soon as you need them if you wait.

Oil and sharpen your hand pruners to keep them in good working order, so they give a nice, clean cut rather than crushing plant stems.

Mulching and Watering

Cocoa shells make an attractive mulch, but they break down quickly and need to be reapplied.

All plants need a certain amount of moisture—some more, some less—in order to grow. Watering with hoses, sprinklers, and watering cans will be necessary at certain times of the year, but there are other ways of making sure your plants don't go thirsty.

Make the Most of Mulch

Mulch is one way as it protects the soil, slowing evaporation and keeping it moist longer after each rain or watering. In fact, it is an important part of producing healthy plants in almost any climate. It helps keep out weeds by preventing weed seedlings from getting a foothold, and organic mulches add nutrients and organic matter to the soil as they decay.

If you use mulch on frozen soil during the winter, it will keep the earth evenly frozen; this reduces the rapid freezing-and-thawing cycles that can damage plant roots and push plant crowns out of the soil (a process known as frost heaving). In hot-summer climates, mulch will slow the rapid decay of organic matter added to the soil, so each application will last longer. In any climate, mulch can work double duty as an attractive background for your annuals and perennials.

Mulching with compost is a good way to add nutrients to your garden. It may be all you need to fertilize light feeders, such as common thrift (*Armeria maritima*),

coreopsis (*Coreopsis* spp.), and yarrow (*Achillea* spp.). Compost mulch will conserve moisture, but unfortunately, it will not do much to squeeze out weeds.

As useful as mulch is in most gardens, there are situations when mulching can actually cause garden problems. If slugs and snails are your garden's major pests, an organic mulch can provide them with the cool, dark, moist conditions they prefer. If you're trying to garden in heavy, wet clay, mulch can slow evaporation even more, contributing to root rot.

However, in cold-climate areas with short growing seasons, mulch will keep the soil cool for longer in spring and give your plants a late start. In these areas, only mulch in summer after your plants have appeared and the soil has warmed up. Remove the mulch and compost it when you clean up the garden in fall.

If you mulch with uncomposted wood chips or sawdust, keep in mind that these materials can rob your plants of soil nitrogen as they decompose. If you must mulch with these woody materials, top-dress the soil with a high-nitrogen material like bloodmeal or cottonseed meal before adding the mulch.

Many organic materials are useful for mulching, including bark chips, compost, and leaves.

Choosing a Mulch

The time you take to choose the right mulch for your needs is time well spent. You want a mulch that looks good and is free of weeds. Cost and availability may also be important factors in your choice.

Newspaper is a cheap weed-suppressing mulch; cover with a decorative mulch to stop it blowing away.

Fallen leaves will provide a wealth of excellent organic material for mulching—and they're free!

Many kinds of organic mulches are available. Shredded leaves make a useful mulch and they are free, so the price is right. Grass clippings scattered around plantings are a good way to recycle your lawn waste. Cocoa bean hulls have an attractive dark color and chocolaty aroma but they are not widely available. Dark-colored, fine-textured, well-decomposed compost can act as a mulch, too; it also gives the soil a rich, healthy look as well as improving soil fertility.

Straw is a good mulch for vegetables, but it may look too utilitarian for most flower gardens. Chunks of shredded bark or wood chips may be suitable for large, bold perennials; they are hard to work without gloves, however, and will dwarf small, fine-textured annuals and creepers. Sections or shreds of newspaper are good placed under more attractive mulches. But do not use colored newspaper as some inks can be toxic.

Try to choose a mulch that won't pack down into dense layers. Dense layers of fine-textured or flat materials, like grass clippings or an extra thick coating of shredded bark, tend to shed water. Rain and irrigation water will run off the bed instead of trickling down into the soil. If you want to use these kinds of mulches,

create air pockets between the particles by mixing in coarse, fluffy material like shredded leaves, small bark chunks, or ground corncobs.

If you use a mulch that won't pack down and your garden has well-drained soil, you can lay the mulch as much as 4 to 6 inches (10 to 15 cm) deep to get maximum weed control. On soils that tend to stay wet or in gardens that do not have a big weed problem, reduce the mulch layer to 2 to 3 inches (5 to 7.5 cm) deep. Leave 4 to 6 inches (10 to 15 cm) of unmulched ground around the base of each plant; this way, the crown stays drier and is less likely to rot.

All organic mulches will gradually decompose over a period of weeks or months, so you need to replace the mulch layer frequently to keep the soil covered. You will have to reapply softer mulches like compost or grass clippings more often than harder wood chips or shredded leaves, which decompose more slowly.

Your plants will grow lushly with an organic mulch to moderate soil temperatures and conserve moisture.

Watering Wisely

A garden that is actively growing and flowering will need a source of moisture at all times. If water is in short supply, flowers and flower buds are the first to suffer damage; if water is overly abundant, plant roots rot. You will have to fine-tune your watering depending on several factors, including the type of soil you have, the amount of natural rainfall, the plants you grow, and the stage of growth the plants are in.

Consider Your Soil

If you do not already know how moisture-retentive your garden soil is, find out. For instance, will it provide reserves of water for 1 week after a good drenching or will most of the moisture drain away within a day? To answer this question, water a portion of the garden thoroughly. After 48 hours, dig a small hole 6 inches (15 cm) deep. If the soil is reasonably water-retentive, the earth at the bottom of the hole will still be moist. If it is not, you can improve its water-holding capacity by working in lots of compost. This organic matter acts like a sponge, holding extra moisture reserves that plant roots can draw on. If you do add a great deal of organic matter, you can water less frequently. But when you do irrigate, water extra thoroughly to saturate the organic matter.

Keeping Track of Rainfall

Monitor the rainfall in your garden and vary your irrigation schedule accordingly. Overwatering can be as bad as underwatering, especially in heavier soils. You can tell how much rain has fallen if you leave out a rain gauge, which is like a narrow measuring cup with inches (millimeters) of rainfall marked on the side. If you don't want to buy a rain gauge, you can set a small, clean can out in an open part of the garden and use a ruler to measure how much rain water it collects. Check your gauge once a week to keep track.

A good rule of thumb to follow is that your garden should get 1 inch (25 mm) of water a week. This amount of water will wet the soil deeply and thus encourage roots to grow down farther underground. Of course, some annuals and perennials need more moisture and some need less, so you'll have to

If natural rainfall is inadequate, water your plants regularly to promote healthy, vigorous growth.

adjust your supplemental irrigation depending on the needs of your plants.

Different Plants Have Different Needs

Some annuals and perennials thrive in moist soils. Others will grow weakly or rot where water is abundant. It's important to group plants with similar water needs together. Water more frequently if you grow plants that need evenly moist soil. These include delphiniums, astilbes, and

Unsure about your soil's moisture content? Check below the soil surface to see if the root zone is dry.

When dry spells are common in your area, consider planting drought-tolerant perennials such as asters, sedums, sages, and *Stipa* grass.

Whenever possible, avoid overhead watering. It wastes water and can encourage disease to spread.

possible, use a drip or trickle irrigation system or a soaker hose that releases droplets of water onto the soil without wetting plant leaves. Keeping the leaves and flowers dry reduces disease problems. Also, letting the water trickle into the ground is efficient because little is lost by way of evaporation.

Water conservation is even more effective if you organize your network of "leaky" tubes or soaker hoses so they irrigate only the annuals and perennials, not the weeds or open areas. But don't expect annuals and perennials to grow roots in areas of the garden that remain dry. Since the root spread of your plants may be limited to

Drip irrigation systems with individual emitters will deliver a small but steady supply of water directly to the base of each plant.

the real moisture-lovers, bog plants such as Japanese primroses (*Primula japonica*) and marsh marigolds (*Caltha palustris*).

Let the soil dry out more between waterings for drought-tolerant plants, such as lavender, coneflowers (*Rudbeckia* and *Echinacea* spp.), torch lilies (*Kniphofia* hybrids), perennial candytuft (*Iberis sempervirens*), and Cupid's dart (*Catananche caerulea*). These plants will probably need no more than ½ inch (12 mm) of water per week.

Expect to coddle newly planted plants until their roots establish and spread far enough to support the plants. If the weather is warm and dry, you may have to water daily until a drenching rain comes. If the season is cool and rainy, you can let nature handle the irrigation.

Ways to Water

When rainfall is not sufficient for plant needs, you'll have to irrigate the plants in your garden. Supply moisture gently so it will seep down instead of running off. Whenever

How to Conserve Water

The following list gives ideas on how you can conserve water in your garden.
- Designate separate parts of the garden for plants with low, medium, or high water requirements and water them individually. Annuals will need more water than deep-rooted, established perennials.
- Insulate the soil surface with a thick layer of organic mulch.
- Work in plenty of compost to maintain your soil's organic matter. Organic matter holds water in the soil like a sponge.
- Eliminate weeds as soon as they appear.
- In dry climates, select plants that are drought-tolerant.
- If paths are included in the design of your garden, use gravel or pulverized bark to pave them. A living cover like grass will compete with your plants for moisture.

irrigated zones, be sure to soak the soil deeply in those areas where you do water so the root systems can grow big enough to support the plants.

You also can apply water to individual plants with a trickling hose or watering can. To reach extra deeply into the soil or to supply additional water to a wilting plant on a hot day, sink a water reservoir into the soil. This can be a plastic drainage tube, clay pot, or leaky plastic bucket filled with water. For slower release in sandy soils, plug the largest holes on pots and tubes and let the moisture slowly seep out of small, pin-prick openings.

Overhead sprinkling, which wastes lots of water through evaporation, is not a good choice for gardens. It waters weeds, helping them grow, and it wets foliage and flowers, increasing plant disease problems. Watering by hand is also inefficient as it will probably take hours, unless you've got a very small yard. Of course, for container gardens, watering by hand—either with a hose or a watering can—is the most realistic irrigation option.

Fertilizing for Good Growth

Supplying your plants with the nutrients they need is a critical part of keeping them healthy and vigorous. How much fertilizer you should add to your garden will depend on how fertile the soil is and which plants you're growing.

The texture and natural fertility of your soil will have a great impact on how much and how often you need to add supplemental nutrients. A sandy soil will hold fewer nutrients than a clayey soil or a soil that's high in organic matter, so you'll need to fertilize a sandy soil more frequently.

Nutrient Needs

The amount and type of fertilizer you use in your garden, and how you apply it, will vary, depending on whether you're growing annuals or biennials, perennials or bulbs. Fertilizer requirements also vary depending on the type of perennial.

Annuals

Annuals grow quickly, so they need a readily available supply of nutrients for

Yarrows and sages have similarly light nutrient needs, so it's a good idea to grow them together.

good flowering. In spring, scatter a 1- to 2-inch (2.5- to 5-cm) layer of compost over the bed and dig it in as you prepare the bed for planting. Or, if you're tucking annuals around perennials and other

permanent plants, mix a handful of compost into each planting hole. If you don't have compost, you could also use a general organic garden fertilizer. Once or twice during the season, pull back the mulch and scatter some more compost or fertilizer around the base of each plant, then replace the mulch. For most annuals and biennials, this will provide all the nutrients they need.

For plants that appreciate extra fertility, such as wax begonias and sweet peas (*Lathyrus odoratus*), or for those that are looking a little tired by midsummer, a monthly dose of liquid fertilizer can provide a quick nutrient boost. Spray the leaves or water the plants with diluted fish emulsion or compost tea (made by soaking a shovelful of finished compost in a bucket of water for about a week, then straining out the soaked compost). Regular doses of liquid fertilizer (every 1 to 3 weeks) will also keep container plants healthy and vigorous.

Perennials

Perennials stay in the same place for years. Since you only have one chance (before planting) to get the soil into good shape, take time to prepare their beds well. Once they are established, most perennials—all but the heavy feeders—will grow happily with a light layer of compost applied once or twice a year.

Some perennials, such as yarrows (*Achillea* spp.), sages (*Salvia* spp.), and coreopsis (*Coreopsis* spp.), should receive no more than an annual layer of compost; otherwise, they will become leggy and topple over from too much fertilizer. But you may want to give other perennials a little fertility boost to encourage new growth or rejuvenation. Fertilize in spring as the plants begin growing, as well as after planting or dividing, and after deadheading or cutting back.

To meet the requirements of heavy feeders, or to encourage exceptional blooms from perennials such as pinks (*Dianthus* spp.), lilies, and delphiniums, use extra fertilizer. Push aside any mulch

Cosmos, like many annuals, will grow well with several applications of compost throughout the season.

Spring is a good time to fertilize spring- and fall-blooming bulbs. You may add bonemeal in fall.

or compost first. Add phosphorus and potassium, as well as any other nutrient recommended in your soil test results; see page 37. Apply them just as the plants begin setting flower buds. Scratch the fertilizer into the soil lightly with a hand cultivator, then replace the mulch.

Bulbs

Most bulbs will get along just fine without you having to add a lot of extra fertilizer. Working compost or other organic matter into the soil at planting time and using it

as a mulch will provide much of the nutrient supply your bulbs need.

For top-notch growth, you can also sprinkle commercial organic fertilizer over the soil around the bulbs, following the package directions. Use a mix blended especially for bulbs if you can find one; otherwise, a general garden fertilizer is acceptable. Fertilize spring- and fall-flowering bulbs in spring. Summer-flowering bulbs usually grow best with several small applications of fertilizer in early- to midsummer.

Tuberous begonias, lilies, and other bulbs growing in pots benefit from weekly or bimonthly doses of liquid fertilizer. Spray the leaves or water the plants with diluted fish emulsion or compost tea.

Applying Fertilizers

When you fertilize, you can eliminate deficiencies by applying either liquid or dry fertilizer or both. If you decide to use a combination of fertilizers, make sure you don't apply more total nutrients than your plants need. Remember that too much fertilizer can be as bad as not enough, leading to weak stems, rampant, sprawling growth, and disease problems.

A Sampler of Organic Fertilizers

A wide variety of organic materials is available for correcting nutrient deficiencies. Before you buy any fertilizer, check the label for information about the nitrogen, phosphorus, and potassium content. This is indicated by a series of three numbers, such as 5-10-5. This means that 100 pounds (45 kg) of a fertilizer with this formulation contains 5 pounds (2.25 kg) of nitrogen, 10 pounds (4.5 kg) of phosphorus, and 5 pounds (2.25 kg) of potassium. Use this information to compare the nutrient content of different fertilizers and to figure out how much of a given material you need to add to your garden based on your soil test results. Compost is one source of many plant nutrients. Listed below are other commonly used organic fertilizers, along with their nutrient content.

Bloodmeal: 12-0-0 to 14-0-0, contains nitrogen plus iron.

Bonemeal: 1-10-0, contains about 20 percent calcium. If processed with some meat or marrow, bonemeal can contain higher percentages of nitrogen.

Fish emulsion: 3-1-1 to 5-2-2, releases most of its nitrogen quickly. It is often sprayed onto leaves for a fast-acting nutrient boost.

Fish meal: 5-3-3, contains both immediately available nitrogen and a slow-release form of nitrogen that supplements the soil for up to 2 months.

Seaweed extract: 1-0.5-2.5, usually made from kelp, provides trace elements and natural growth hormones. Use liquid kelp as a foliar spray. Kelp meal is a concentrated form high in potassium and boron.

Perennials grow in the same place for years, so prepare the soil well and enrich it before planting.

Liquid Fertilizers

Commonly used liquid fertilizers include fish emulsion, liquid seaweed, and compost tea. Use a single dose of liquid fertilizer for a quick but temporary fix of a nutrient shortage, or apply it every 2 weeks for a general plant boost. You can spray these materials directly onto the plants, which will absorb the nutrients through their foliage.

Dry Fertilizers

Dry fertilizers are released to plants more slowly than liquid fertilizers. Scratch them into the surface of the soil in a circle around the perimeter of the plant's foliage, so the nutrients are released gradually as they dissolve in soil moisture. This encourages roots to extend outward.

Using Compost

Compost is a balanced blend of recycled garden, yard, and household wastes that have broken down into dark, crumbly organic matter. It is the key to success in any garden, being an excellent source of nutrients for your plants. The time you spend making compost and applying it to your garden will be more than returned by improved soil and plant health.

Creating Your Own Compost

Making compost is a lot like cooking—you mix together ingredients, stir them up, and let them "cook." But with a compost pile, the source of heat isn't electricity or gas—it's the activity of decomposer organisms like bacteria and fungi that live in soil and break down dead plant and animal tissues. These organisms work best when given warmth, moisture, plenty of oxygen, and a balance of carbon and nitrogen.

You can add a wide variety of materials to your compost. Vegetable scraps from the kitchen, grass clippings, fallen leaves, and soft plant trimmings are all good choices. If you have access to manure from animals such as chickens, rabbits, cows, or horses, you can add that also. There are some things you should avoid, including fats, bones, and meat scraps, which can attract scavengers to your pile. Also avoid composting manure from humans, dogs, and cats—this material can carry disease organisms.

Choose a shady, well-drained spot for your compost pile. For your convenience,

Applying Fertilizer

Scatter dry organic fertilizer evenly over the bed to slowly release nutrients.

Or apply the dry fertilizer in a ring around the base of each plant.

Spray liquid fertilizer on the leaves for an immediate nutrient boost.

Keep your compost close to the garden so you can easily add trimmings or get finished compost.

put it as close to your garden as possible. If you're concerned that a loose compost pile would be unattractive, you can contain it in a bin. Make a homemade bin from wire fencing, wood, or concrete blocks, or buy a commercially available bin.

Hot Composting

Hot composting takes some work, but it will provide you with high-quality compost in a matter of weeks. There are many different systems of hot composting, but they tend to have some elements in common. Most require building a large pile of different layers of high-nitrogen and high-carbon elements, along with some soil or finished compost to make sure the right decomposers are present. Turning or fluffing the pile every few days or weeks, to provide the decomposer organisms in the pile with oxygen, is another critical part of encouraging fast breakdown.

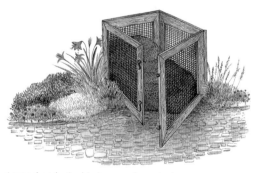

A wood-and-wire bin is a good way to keep your compost contained and easily accessible.

A yearly application of compost will supply all of the nutrients most perennials need to thrive.

To create a hot-compost pile, blend both soft and green (high-nitrogen) plant scraps, like lawn clippings, lettuce scraps, and dandelion leaves, with tough and brown (high-carbon) scraps, like fallen leaves, straw, and woody flower stalks. The moist, green items provide the decomposers with the nitrogen they consume as they break down the high-carbon materials.

Chop up the debris you plan to compost, and combine about 1 part of high-nitrogen elements with 2 parts high-carbon material in a pile about 3 feet (90 cm) high and wide. Pile up these elements in layers or just jumble them together. Add a shovelful of soil or finished compost in between each layer and enough water to keep the pile evenly moist. Turn the pile with a pitchfork every few days to add oxygen.

If all goes well, your compost should be ready in a few weeks. The material may break down more quickly in hot weather or more slowly in cold weather. When your compost is fairly cool and most of the original materials are unrecognizable, it is ready to use.

Cold Composting

Making "cold" compost is easier than making hot compost, but it takes longer. (A cold-compost pile won't really feel cold; it just doesn't get warm like a hot-compost pile.) Since the period of decomposition is extended up to a year or more, more nutrients can wash away in rainwater. You'll have to leave more space for the slower decomposing piles, and you'll have to wait much longer until it's ready. Cold compost will not heat up enough to kill seeds or disease organisms, so don't add mature weeds or diseased plant material to the pile.

To create a cold-compost pile, just choose a shady, well-drained place to drop your organic scraps. Let them build up to a pile about 3 feet (90 cm) wide by 3 feet (90 cm) high and then begin again in a new location. After a year or so, the original materials should be broken down, although the compost will probably still be fairly lumpy. Use the compost as it is, or screen out the lumps and leave them to break down for a while longer.

Using Compost

There are many different ways to add compost to your garden. If you are preparing a new bed, you can work it in as you dig. In an established garden, use compost as a mulch. As a general rule, cover the bed with 2 inches (5 cm) a year to maintain a fertile soil. Use more if you are growing moisture-loving perennials like astilbes; it will soak up and retain water. Use less around perennials such as yarrow that prefer drier, less-fertile soils. Compost breaks down gradually over the growing season—add more as needed.

If your compost supply is limited, spread a thin layer around each plant and top with a mulch.

Pests, Diseases, Weeds

A healthy, vigorous garden, with plants that are not too crowded, is less inviting to pests and diseases.

Growing annuals and perennials will offer many pleasures as well as a few challenges—such as pests, diseases, and weeds. With good soil and good care, your plants will naturally be more resistant. Gardeners often notice that after several years of building up the soil, keeping the garden clean, and encouraging natural predators, insect and disease problems diminish from a constant battle to the occasional flare-up. And weeds can be kept under control by applying mulches. But it's important to be able to identify and handle any problems that do arise.

Prevention and Control

Generally, pests and diseases are not a big problem for annuals and perennials. You may never have to spray if you seek out the most disease-resistant species and cultivars and then plant them where they will thrive. Strong, healthy plants do not make easy targets for pests or diseases. Just as we are constantly exposed to cold and flu germs, plant pests, fungi, viruses, and bacteria are all around. They will infect weaker or stressed plants before harming vigorous ones.

Pests, diseases, and weeds are easiest to control if you catch them before they get out of hand. Inspect your garden regularly to help you spot problems before they spread. If you find a pest or disease problem, you'll need to properly identify it. Insect damage on your annuals and perennials can vary widely, depending on the pest causing the problem.

You need to figure out what's causing the damage in order to be able to choose the best control. Only then can you decide how to treat it: by handpicking, trapping, or by some other organically acceptable control.

If you use a commercial organic spray, always read the label first. Labels list important information on proper storage, target pests, and effective application. Even organic sprays and dusts can irritate skin or lungs, so wear protective clothing and gloves to be on the safe side.

Identifying Some Common Pests

Knowing about the most common pests to attack annuals and perennials will help you notice any infestations on your plants

Aphids cling to leaves and buds.

Japanese beetles chew into leaves.

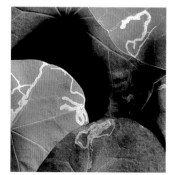

Leafminers leave trails inside leaves.

Spider mites build tiny webs.

Spittlebugs suck the sap of plants.

Slugs chew large holes in leaves.

Thrips attack leaves and flowers.

Mealybugs attack stems and fruit.

and also be able to identify them. You can identify insects by the appearance of the larvae or adults and also by the kind of damage they do to the plant.

Aphids

Aphids are tiny, soft-bodied, pear-shaped insects that feed on a wide variety of annuals and perennials. They tend to cluster near the growing tips and on the undersides of leaves. Large groups of aphids can cause the foliage, flowers, or shoots of plants to twist, pucker, or drop, and they leave a trail of sugary excrement (called honeydew), which is sticky and often harbors a black, sooty mold. Aphids also can spread viral diseases as they feed.

Japanese Beetles

These shiny, metallic blue-green beetles with bronze wing covers feed on many different annuals and perennials, including hollyhocks (*Alcea rosea*), New York asters (*Aster novi-belgii*), foxgloves (*Digitalis* spp.), and purple coneflowers (*Echinacea purpurea*). They will eat the green part of leaves, so that only the leaf veins remain, and also chew on flowers. The grubs are white with brown heads; they feed mostly on lawn grass roots.

Leafminers

Leafminers are the tiny larvae of small flies. The larvae tunnel inside perennial foliage, leaving light-colored trails that you can see from the top of the leaf. They can be a problem on columbines (*Aquilegia* spp.), delphiniums, and garden mums (*Chrysanthemum* x *morifolium*).

Spider Mites

These tiny, spider-like pests will attack many perennials, especially when the weather becomes hot and dry. The brown, red, or green mites make very fine webs over plants and suck the plant sap from the underside of a leaf, causing it to curl and its upper surface to turn speckled, pale, and dull-looking.

Plant Bugs

Tarnished plant bugs are green or brown with yellow triangles on their forewings; four-lined plant bugs are yellowish green with four black stripes down their back. Both of these insects will leave irregular holes or sunken brown spots in the middle of leaves. They also cause distorted growth on the leaves or growing tips of many annuals and perennials.

Slugs and Snails

Slugs (slimy mollusks) and snails (slimy mollusks with a coiled shell on their back) can be a problem anywhere the soil stays damp, and this is especially a problem in shady gardens. They crawl up on annuals and perennials and chew ragged holes in the leaves, stems, and flowers. They can eat the entire plant in this way. They can also ruin young seedlings or transplants.

Thrips

Thrips are minute, quick-moving insects that feed on the flowers and leaves of several different kinds of plants. They give the affected plant tissue a pale, silvery look in damaged areas. Eventually the infected plant parts can wither and die.

Other Pests

You also may find mealybugs (slow-moving, soft-bodied insects hidden beneath a white, cottony shield) under leaves and along stems; leafhoppers (which look like tiny grasshoppers) on stems and leaves; borers (fat pink caterpillars), which tunnel down the leaves of bearded irises and eat large cavities into the rhizomes; and cutworms (fat, dark-colored caterpillars), which chew through the stems of young seedlings and transplants.

Local Wildlife

Deer, rabbits, mice, and other animal pests can attack bulbs. All these animals may feast on both the flowers and the actual bulbs. You can try to discourage

Squirrels can do a lot of damage to your bulbs.

them by planting daffodil bulbs, which are poisonous and usually avoided by animals. Some people believe that the strong odor of crown imperial (*Fritillaria imperialis*) bulbs and plants repels voles, mice, and squirrels. Pet dogs and cats can be useful for discouraging local wildlife, but they may cause damage, too.

For more information on pests that attack specific annuals and perennials, check the "Guide to Popular Annuals" and "Guide to Popular Perennials" on pages 172 and 202 respectively.

Controlling Pests

Once you have figured out the identity of a problem-causing pest, you can choose the best method for controlling it.

Handpicking

If you only find a few pests among your annuals and perennials, you can pick them off the plants by hand and crush them under your heel. This is effective for large, slow-moving pests like snails and slugs, Japanese beetles, and cutworms, but not for small pests or large infestations.

Traps and Barriers

Avoid garden damage by catching pests in traps or deterring them with barricades. Sticky traps are very effective for some pests: Yellow sticky traps will attract aphids, while white traps will catch tarnished plant bugs. You can either buy pre-made sticky traps at a garden center or make your own by painting pieces of wood or cardboard the appropriate color and coating them with petroleum jelly. Hang the traps on stakes throughout your garden and clean or replace them as needed to keep them effective.

You can trap slugs and snails with a shallow container of beer set in the soil so the top rim is at ground level; they crawl in and drown. Surrounding plants with a ring of diatomaceous earth (a powdery

Paper collars protect seedlings from cutworms.

material composed of tiny, spiny-shelled algae) will also keep slugs and cutworms at bay; renew the barrier after each rain.

To protect your bulbs from the local wildlife, it is possible to take preventive measures when planting where mice, voles, shrews, and squirrels are especially troublesome. Although it takes some doing, you can fashion bulb crates—a little like lobster traps—out of sturdy wire mesh. Choose mesh with a grid size of about 1 inch (2.5 cm). Small animals can sneak through larger mesh, while your bulb shoots may not be able to poke through smaller mesh. Dig a hole large enough to hold the crate, so the top is just below the soil surface. Place the crate in the hole and backfill with some of the soil you removed. Plant your bulbs in the crate, then fill the rest of the cage with soil and close the lid. Use the remaining soil to cover the lid and fill in around the rest of the cage.

Biological Controls

You can use biological weapons like *Bacillus thuringiensis* (BT), a bacterial disease, and milky disease to eliminate pests without harming people, animals, or beneficial insects. To control damage by many different kinds of caterpillars, spray or dust foliage with BT. (Don't use this material if you want to encourage butterflies in your garden, though; it will

kill the larvae of attractive butterflies as well as those of other, unwanted insects.) Another bacterial disease, known as milky disease, attacks Japanese beetle grubs. Apply this granulated material over your lawn and water it into the soil, where it will infect the grubs.

Beneficial Insects

When you plant a number of different annuals and perennials, most of which produce nectar and pollen, you will attract many beneficial insects—such as lady beetle and lacewing larvae, praying mantids, and wasps—that eat or parasitize pests. In a healthy garden, natural populations of such insects will go a long way in keeping pests under control.

Organically Acceptable Insecticides

If, after you've tried other options, you still can't control a pest, you can try some of the less toxic insecticides that come from natural sources. These tend to break down faster than chemical pesticides and leave less environmental residue. Make sure you apply these products according to package directions and at the susceptible time in the pest's life cycle.

Insecticidal soaps, made of the potassium salts of fatty acids, will kill soft-bodied insects such as aphids, leafhoppers, mealybugs, and plant bugs. You can also

Adult lacewings feed on nectar and honeydew, but the larvae eat large numbers of insect pests.

Praying mantids devour many other insects—pests and beneficials alike. They even eat each other.

Different plants are attacked by different pests or diseases. Foxgloves are susceptible to Japanese beetles, while poppies can get downy or powdery mildew.

spray with highly refined horticultural oils to coat plant leaves and to smother insects like aphids, mealybugs, leafminers, mites, and leafhoppers. Read the label carefully and apply only when the weather is cool. Before spraying a whole plant with either soap or oil, spray just a few leaves and wait a few days. If the leaves show any sort of damage, such as discoloring or spotting, find another control method.

Among the botanical insecticides, which are derived from plants, pyrethrins are effective on some beetles, caterpillars, aphids, and bugs. Rotenone will control beetles, borers, aphids, and red spider

mites. Ryania is effective against beetles and caterpillars. Sabadilla, another botanical, is a powerful insecticide; use it as a last resort for tough pests like thrips. Botanical pesticides have broad-spectrum activity, meaning that they will harm beneficial as well as pest insects.

Identifying Some Common Diseases

Annuals and perennials that are sited in ideal growing conditions seldom suffer much from diseases. Sometimes, though, the weather or other influences beyond your control will provide the right

conditions for fungal, bacterial, or viral diseases to attack your plants. Being aware of the most common diseases will help you take the appropriate prevention and control measures for your conditions.

Stunted Growth or Discolored Foliage

Diseases usually appear on particular species while ignoring others. If several different types of plants growing together have similar symptoms, you should suspect a nutrient deficiency, not a disease. Pale or yellow leaves may indicate a lack of nitrogen or iron. Mottled leaves may need

Powdery mildew is quite common.

Downy mildew has white spots.

Rust shows as light-colored spots.

Fungal wilts affect leaves and stems.

magnesium. Dark leaves with purple or red near the veins may lack phosphorus. Distorted growth and the death of young leaves and buds may indicate various micronutrient deficiencies.

The best approach to handling nutrient deficiencies is to take a soil test so you'll know what's missing and what you need to add. Sometimes, it's just a matter of adjusting the soil pH, so the nutrients that are already in your soil can become available to your perennials; more information on the nutrients that plants need can be found in "Adding Nutrients" on page 108. For a quick but short-term solution, spray the leaves of plants with fish emulsion or liquid seaweed. Working a good amount of compost into the soil before planting and using it as a mulch should keep your soil well stocked with a balanced supply of nutrients.

Fungal Diseases

Many different fungi attack annuals and perennials, causing a variety of symptoms. Rot fungi can affect perennial roots, crowns, stems, and flowers, usually making them turn soft and mushy. You will see rot most commonly on perennial roots growing in wet, heavy soil or on crowns planted too deeply in the garden. Among the most susceptible plants are baby's breath (*Gypsophila paniculata*), balloon flowers (*Platycodon grandiflorus*), coreopsis (*Coreopsis* spp.), delphiniums, irises, and garden phlox (*Phlox paniculata*).

Botrytis blight is a common fungal disease. It attacks flowers that open during wet weather, making them blacken and curl. Peonies, irises, and dahlias are especially susceptible.

Fungal leaf spots infect plants such as peonies, asters, daylilies, and columbines (*Aquilegia* spp.). The leaf spots disfigure foliage and, if not caught, can cause widespread defoliation and plant death.

Downy mildew and powdery mildew are fungal diseases that form a furry, white coating on the leaves of annuals and perennials like the different types of phlox, bee balm (*Monarda didyma*), asters, poppies (*Papaver* spp.), delphiniums, and dahlias. These diseases are unattractive and cause severely infected leaves to drop.

Rust diseases also attack annuals and perennials, including hollyhocks (*Alcea rosea*), garden mums (*Chrysanthemum* x *morifolium*), and asters. They turn the foliage a rusty color, often stunting growth and distorting leaf development.

Bacterial Diseases

Bacteria also can cause diseases that are characterized by wilting, rotting tissues,

This leaf has signs of iron deficiency, not disease.

Thin stems and cut back flowers after they've bloomed to minimize the chances of diseases developing.

Fungal and bacterial leaf spots affect foliage.

Mosaic produces yellow or white areas or streaks.

or root or lower-stem galls. Peonies and poppies can get a bacterial blight, which causes black spots on the leaves, flowers, and stems. Dahlias and baby's breath can be infected with bacterial crown gall, which stunts growth and can kill the plants. Coral bells (*Heuchera sanguinea*) can be attacked by a bacterial stem rot.

Viral Diseases

Viruses can cause perennial leaves or flowers to turn yellow or mottled yellow and green. They cause stunted growth and poor flowering or sudden wilting and death. Viruses are carried from plant to plant by sucking insects, such as aphids and leafhoppers, or by garden tools like pruning shears. Viral mosaic can attack dahlias, delphiniums, pinks (*Dianthus* spp.), peonies, and poppies. Aster yellows, which is a similar disease, infects baby's breath, balloon flowers, bellflowers (*Campanula* spp.), coreopsis, garden mums, and delphiniums.

Controlling Diseases

Good garden hygiene and proper plant selection go a long way toward preventing and controlling diseases. If you remove faded foliage in fall and cut back flowers after they bloom, you'll remove common sites of disease attack. If soilborne disease is a particular problem in your area, grow annuals and perennials in well-drained soil to reduce the likelihood of root diseases getting a start. Also, try not to damage the plant roots when you work the soil or weed.

Careful watering can help reduce disease outbreaks. Whenever possible, avoid wetting plant leaves. If foliage stays wet overnight, fungal spores may have time to germinate and attack leaves. Overhead watering and even walking through wet foliage can transfer disease from plant to plant. Use a ground-level irrigation system, like a trickle system or drip irrigation, and don't work in the garden when plants are still wet from a recent fall of rain.

If the weather is cold and wet or hot and humid—conditions that encourage disease—and if you grow susceptible plants, you may get an outbreak of disease in the garden. When a disease does strike, remove damaged plant parts promptly, before the disease can spread, and throw them away with the household trash. This can go a long way toward controlling diseases.

If your garden has had problems with diseases in past years, you may want to make a preventive treatment with eco-logically acceptable, organic materials. Antitranspirants— leaf coatings that are ordinarily used to protect broad-leaved evergreens during winter—may reduce fungal disease problems. You can try dusting foliage with powdered sulfur to prevent mildew, rust, and leaf spots. A baking soda spray (1 teaspoon of baking soda to 1 quart [1 L] of water) can prevent and control some fungal problems. Compost tea and seaweed-based fertilizer sprays can also help prevent diseases. If a disease becomes rampant and even sprays do not help, replace the plant with something that is not susceptible—a different species or a resistant cultivar.

In most cases, diseases are not a big problem in the annual and perennial garden. Choosing the right plants for your conditions, preparing the soil thoroughly, and planting with the proper spacing all contribute to problem-free plants. Inspect new additions carefully for any signs of disease before setting them loose in the garden. If you have any doubts, consider throwing the plant away or, if that seems too drastic, plant it in an isolated spot in the yard. Move it into the garden if it seems all right at the end of the season. Dispose of it if it's diseased.

Using ecologically acceptable controls against plant disease problems means you don't destroy your garden's diversity.

A mowing strip will stop the lawn from invading your plants and keep the garden looking neat.

Weed Them Out

Like pests and diseases, weeds can pop up in even the most well-cared-for gardens. The trick is to take care of the problem early, before the weeds get large enough to compete with your plants for space, light, water, and nutrients.

Perennial Weeds

Like the perennial flowers you're growing in the garden, perennial weeds will live for many years once they are established. What separates the unwanted weeds from the desirable plants is often the speed with which the weeds can spread. Many perennial weeds, like bindweed and

Loosening the soil with a spading fork can make hand-pulling weeds a whole lot easier.

Canada thistle, have creeping underground stems, called rhizomes. These rhizomes can spread quickly in the loose, rich soil of your flower garden, quickly engulfing your desirable plants. Other perennial weeds have long, tough taproots. If you break off the top of the plant, a new one will quickly sprout from the root.

Thoroughly removing the roots of perennial weeds as you prepare the soil for planting will go a long way toward keeping these weeds at bay. Mulching and regular weeding will help prevent new perennial weeds from getting started.

If perennial weeds get out of control despite your best efforts, it's often easiest to just start the bed over. Dig up your good perennials and set them aside until you can dig through the bed and remove all the fleshy roots of the weeds. Before you replant your perennials, make sure their clumps are free of weed roots, too; otherwise, the weeds will have an easy time reinvading your garden.

One of the most common weed problems in perennial gardens is lawn grass, which will creep in along the edges of beds and borders. Block invasion of grass by cutting along the garden's edge frequently with a sharp spade or edger and remove the errant sprigs of grass. Or take preventive action when you dig the bed: Add a metal, wood, stone, brick, or plastic edging to form a barrier around the perimeter of the garden. Sink the edging at least 4 to 6 inches (10 to 15 cm) deep to block creeping grass stems in their underground movement.

Annual Weeds

Annual weeds may not have the invasive roots of their perennial counterparts, but

Dandelions have deep, tough taproots that are difficult to remove. They also have fine, floating seeds that spread easily.

they will reproduce themselves hundreds of times over from seed, often growing fast and spreading far. The key to controlling annual weeds is to remove them from the garden before they set seed. Cut them off or scrape them out of the soil with a hoe or hand weeder. If the soil is soft or damp, you can easily pull the entire weed, root and all, by hand. Snip weeds with scissors if you think pulling will damage small or newly planted annuals and perennials that are nearby. Throw the weeds, as long as they are seed-free, into your compost pile.

How to Be Weed-wise

Weed control starts while you are preparing the bed for your new garden. Removing the sod from the area and composting it will remove many of the existing weeds. As you dig, keep an eye out for the long white roots of spreading weeds. Thoroughly remove any of these

Landscape fabrics make effective weed-proof covers. Lay over prepared soil, cut slits for planting, then cover with a mulch.

roots; if you leave even little pieces, roots can quickly sprout into new plants.

Once your annuals and perennials are well established, you can control most

Hoeing flower gardens once or twice early in the season can control weeds until your plants fill in to cover the soil.

weeds if you mulch and weed conscientiously for the first year or two. By the third year, your perennial clumps should be well filled in, leaving little room for weed invasion.

Pulling and Digging Pulling gets rid of annual weeds well, especially if the soil is damp enough for the roots to come up easily. Just be sure not to toss weeds that reroot easily, such as purslane (*Portulaca oleracea*), on the ground. Always try to pull annuals before they begin to flower and set seed. If they have already started flowering, collect the pulled weeds in a bucket; don't leave them on the ground, since their seeds could still ripen, drop onto the soil, and germinate.

Digging is a slightly better choice for perennial weeds, assuming you get all of the buried portions of the plant. If you don't, these buried portions can quickly produce new weeds. Use hand tools to dig out small or shallow-rooted perennials. You may need a spading fork, spade, or shovel for tough, deep roots, like those of pokeweed (*Phytolacca americana*) and dandelion.

Hoeing and Tilling When the weeds are too numerous to pull up one by one, by hand, a sharp hoe is a good solution. In most cases, hoes are best for young or annual weeds. But you can also deal a damaging blow to some established perennials—primarily those with thin or soft stems—by forcing them to use their food reserves to replace the decapitated top growth.

There are several schools of thought about the best time to

Removing weeds when they're small or preventing them from sprouting in the first place will make the job of weed control much easier.

hoe. One says you should hoe when the soil is damp, so the roots pull out easily. Another says to hoe when the soil is dry, scraping the weeds off at the soil surface without disturbing the soil or digging up new weed seed. Most of us just hoe when we find time and inspiration. All of these approaches are reasonable. If you're trying to control perennial weeds, it's most important to hoe every 7 to 14 days to cut off the top growth before it starts sending food back down to the roots.

Mowing Mowing doesn't get the roots, but it can keep all but the lowest-growing weeds from setting seed. And if you mow often enough (every week or two), it weakens perennials by making them use up their food reserves to replace the top growth you've removed.

Mowing works on woody shrubs and vines as long as the stems aren't too thick for the machine. For tall, tough weeds and tree seedlings no more than ¾ inch (18 mm) in diameter, use a heavy-duty string trimmer with a blade attachment. If you must control brush over a large area, consider renting a walk-behind tractor with a sickle-bar attachment.

Pruning and Training

Carefully pinching the growing tip out of clumping plants will promote bushy growth.

A pinch of this and a stake for that—these and other simple steps are the recipe for a neat-looking, flower-filled garden. The tips and techniques below can be used to promote sturdier stems and bigger or more abundant blooms throughout your flower garden.

Pinching

Pinching is a quick and easy technique that is useful for many kinds of annuals and perennials. Use it to:

- Promote bushy growth. Much like a heading cut, a well-placed pinch removes the stem tip bud. This generally encourages the remaining buds lower on the stem to grow, making the plant fuller.
- Reduce staking chores. Pinching also promotes sturdier stems, considerably reducing the need for staking to keep plants upright and looking good.
- Delay flowering. The best example is the traditional practice of pinching garden mums (*Chrysanthemum* x *morifolium*) to delay flowering until fall. Begin pinching them in spring and continue about every 2 weeks until July 4 in the South and mid-July in the North. Don't pinch later than that or your plants may not bloom.
- Discourage flowering altogether. Regular pinching can put off flowering

on certain plants. This technique is commonly used to promote fresh new growth on herbs such as sweet marjoram, basil, and oregano, which otherwise can become stringy and tasteless once flowering begins. Use the same trick on coleus when you wish to promote the colorful leaves instead of the insignificant flowers.

- Extend the bloom season. Extend the bloom time of a mass planting by pinching only half of the plants or by giving half of them one less pinch than the rest. The less-pinched plants will bloom earlier, followed by the more-pinched plants.

The best time to pinch annuals is at planting time. Pinch perennials as they start their spring growth, when there are several sets of full leaves on each stem. Pinch annuals and perennials by taking tip growth away with your thumb and forefinger, normally down to the first full set of leaves below the tip; also pinch away dead or yellow stems or leaves. If the stems are too tough or wiry to break easily with your fingers, use scissors or a sharp pair of pruning shears to make a clean cut.

Pinching Precautions

There are a few situations where pinching may not be helpful. You can't, for instance, depend on pinching to make a plant shorter. Many annuals, perennials, and herbs that are pinched eventually attain the same height they would have grown to had they not been pinched—they're just fuller and sturdier.

Don't pinch plants that send up a single leafy stalk (like lilies) or leafless flowering stalks (like irises). Otherwise, you'll end up taking off the flower buds, and you'll be left with plain stalks sticking up out of the garden.

A midseason pinch works well to keep annuals such as impatiens and begonias from collapsing under their own weight— or flopping under a heavy rain—during a long growing season. Reach about one-third of the way into the plant on each

Pinch your garden mums to delay flowering until fall and to promote the largest number of blooms.

stem and pinch at a joint. The pinched plants may look slightly bedraggled initially. But after a few days, they'll be off and blooming again, only shorter now, more compact, and less likely to be damaged during a storm. Do a pinch like this in the early morning or on a cloudy day to keep the tender interior foliage from being scorched. Toss the trimmings in the compost pile or root them in potting soil to make new plants.

Disbudding

If you are growing dahlias, garden mums, or peonies, you may want to try disbudding to encourage fewer but larger flowers. This technique is easy—simply support the stem gently with one hand and rub or pinch off the unwanted side buds with your other hand. Each

The Don'ts of Deadheading

Despite the advantages of deadheading, you may have good cause to skip it on occasion. Spare the seedpods of perennials that you want to self-sow, like foxgloves (*Digitalis* spp.) and wild columbines (*Aquilegia canadensis*). You may also want to leave any attractive seedpods or cones alone; they can extend the beauty of certain perennials through the dormant season. Try this with the velvety black or orange-brown cones of coneflowers (*Rudbeckia* and *Echinacea* spp.), the glossy, dark seed clusters of blackberry lilies (*Belamcanda chinensis*), the dry, feathery plumes of astilbes, the russet pods of 'Autumn Joy' sedum (*Sedum* 'Autumn Joy'), and the papery "flowers" of Lenten roses (*Helleborus* x *orientalis*). You may also want to spare the plume-like seed heads of ornamental grasses that you grow with your annuals and perennials.

Pruning shears are handy for deadheading spent flowers that have thick or wiry stems.

disbudded stem will bear one bloom that is larger and showier than normal. Disbudding is not necessarily a technique you'll use regularly, but it's fun to try if you want to have a few special, large blooms for display or use in arrangements.

Deadheading

Deadhead your annuals, perennials, and herbs by pinching off spent flowers. This practice keeps the blooms coming by directing the plant's energy back into more flowers (or into bulb formation) rather than into seed production. Deadheading also prevents plants that self-sow readily—like morning glories (*Ipomoea* spp.)—from seeding themselves throughout your garden. Don't use this technique if you want to collect the seed or if you are growing the plant for its decorative seed heads.

To deadhead, snap off faded blooms with your fingers or snip them off with pruning shears. On plants with terminal flowers, pinch the blooms back to a set of full leaves; as a result, you're likely to get additional flowers from the side buds. On plants with flowers that arise on a single, leafless stem—including hostas, poppies (*Papaver* spp.), pincushion flower (*Scabiosa caucasica*), and most bulbs—follow that stem down to its base and pinch it there.

Cutting Back

Cutting stems back with hand pruners, grass shears, or even string trimmers is a satisfying and worthwhile pruning project that you can do almost anytime.

Fall and Winter Trimming

If you like the garden to look tidy over winter, you could cut back all remaining perennials to just above ground level after the first frost. For winter interest, though, you may choose to leave ornamental grasses, evergreen perennials and herbs, and plants with interesting seed heads, like showy stonecrop (*Sedum spectabile*) and coneflowers (*Rudbeckia* spp.). You can wait until late winter to cut these plants back to just above the ground. Make sure

Deadhead poppies for rebloom, then leave the last flowers in place to allow the plants to self-seed.

If left untrimmed, sedums' dense blooms develop into seed heads that are ideal for winter interest.

you remove the old top growth before spring, or you may end up cutting off some of the new growth as well. If the plants get ratty and unattractive, you'll do no harm by cutting them back earlier.

Spring and Summer Trimming

Consider cutting back mat-forming perennials after they bloom. Shear the stems back by about half to encourage compact growth—and sometimes you may even get a second flush of bloom—on perennial candytuft (*Iberis sempervirens*), wall rock cress (*Arabis caucasica*), moss pinks (*Phlox subulata*), catmints (*Nepeta* spp.), and snow-in-summer (*Cerastium tomentosum*).

Cutting plants back by half in early summer can promote sturdier stems on many tall-growing plants, including asters, ironweeds (*Vernonia* spp.), great blue lobelia (*Lobelia syphilitica*), and tall native sunflowers (*Helianthus* spp.). Your fall garden will be graced with the later-than-normal flowers and your plants will resist the temptation to keel over when burdened with all those blooms. But do resist the urge to trim tall stems much after early summer

or the plants may not have time to develop new flower buds before frost.

Another great use for cutting back is the old "cut and come again" trick. Shear off the top third of bushy, multistemmed plants after flowering, and you may get another flush of bloom later in the season. Try this on vigorously growing mints, coreopsis (*Coreopsis* spp.), bee balms (*Monarda* spp.), gaura (*Gaura lindheimeri*), and boltonia (*Boltonia asteroides*).

Staking

Staking takes a little effort to do properly, but the end result can be magnificent. Spend time in spring to put stakes around the plants you know tend to flop—like peonies, dahlias, and asters—and you'll save yourself the heartache of seeing their beautiful blooms sprawling in the mud after a summer storm.

Bamboo Stakes

Bamboo stakes are great for supporting upright, spiky plants such as snapdragons (*Antirrhinum majus*), foxgloves (*Digitalis*

What to Cut Back

Certain perennials benefit from cutting back. Give spring bloomers a trim after they flower to tidy them up for the rest of the season. Cut back summer bloomers after their first flush; some may bloom again later in the season. Here are some perennials that like being cut back.

Spring bloomers: rock cress (*Arabis caucasica*), creeping phlox (*Phlox stolonifera*), goat's beard (*Aruncus dioicus*).
Summer bloomers: Frikart's aster (*Aster x frikartii*), catmint (*Nepeta x faassenii*), Persian cornflower (*Centaurea dealbata*), common spiderwort (*Tradescantia x andersoniana*), common thrift (*Armeria maritima*), bellflowers (*Campanula* spp.), blanket flower (*Gaillardia x grandiflora*), sages (*Salvia* spp.), lavender cotton (*Santolina chamaecyparissus*), spotted lamium (*Lamium maculatum*), soapworts (*Saponaria* spp.), pincushion flower (*Scabiosa caucasica*).

Individual wooden stakes help support the tall, bushy growth and heavy flowers of dahlias.

spp.), and delphiniums. Use stakes that are about two-thirds of the ultimate height of the stem. Place the stakes firmly in the ground when the plants are young, being careful not to insert them through the crowns of the plants. Attach soft fabric or yarn ties to the stakes and knot the loose ends around the stems as they grow.

To support bushy plants like yarrows (*Achillea* spp.) and baby's breath (*Gypsophila paniculata*), place 3 or 4 stakes around the clump so that the outer edges of the plant will cover them as the plant grows. String twine back and forth among the stakes to support the stems as they grow.

Pea Brush

Pea brush (also called pea staking) is another, far more casual-looking, option for supporting annuals and perennials with slender, floppy stems, like larkspur (*Consolida ambigua*) and asters. It's also a great way to recycle the woody prunings from trees and shrubs. However, as a precaution, you may want to let the prunings dry out in the sun for a week or so before using them as

Careful placement of plants, followed by discreet staking, routine deadheading, and trimming back at season's end, will ensure a tidy yet bountiful garden.

Cages will help flower stems to grow straight.

stakes; if you stick fresh stems into the soil, some might actually take root!

In early spring, push the stem ends of small twiggy branches firmly into the ground around seedlings, annual transplants, or emerging perennial shoots. The tops of the twigs should be slightly shorter than the ultimate height of the plants they are supporting. As the leaves fill in and the plants approach full size, the staking becomes invisible.

Cages

Cages and other wire supports are useful for bushy annuals and perennials, like asters, peonies, and Japanese anemones (*Anemone* x *hybrida*). Set commercial ring or linking stakes either over or around emerging clumps, or make your own supports with pieces of wire-mesh fencing and wooden stakes.

Finally, if you find that you're doing entirely too much staking, check your soil's fertility. Columbines (*Aquilegia* spp.), spiderworts (*Tradescantia* spp.), and other annuals and perennials that grow well in lean to moderately fertile soils often grow tall and spindly when given too rich a diet. Hold off on the fertilizer and compost for a year or two.

Preparing for Winter

Once the flowers start to fade and you can feel a definite chill in the air, it's time for the last outdoor maintenance task of the season. By preparing your garden for winter, you will ensure that your annuals and perennials will be back again in the spring.

Fall Cleanup for Perennials

To help your perennials survive their winter ordeal, give all perennial beds a thorough watering before the ground freezes. Remove dead foliage and cut dead stems back to the ground. Compost garden debris unless it's diseased or full of seeds; if so, bury or dispose of it. After the first hard frost, give your beds a generous layer of mulch to protect plants from frost heaving and dramatic temperature changes. Use about 1 inch (2.5 cm)

of heavy materials, like bark chips, or about 3 inches (7.5 cm) of light mulches, such as pine needles or chopped leaves. In particularly cold or exposed sites without dependable snow cover, also add an extra cover of light branches (those from pines or firs work well), pine needles, or (after the holidays) boughs from a discarded Christmas tree. You will have to remove this covering and pull the mulch back from around the base of the plants in early spring to let the soil warm up.

If fall is always a busy time for you and you never quite finish your garden cleanup, don't worry. Some plants, such as ornamental grasses and plants with interesting seedpods (including astilbes and blue false indigo [*Baptisia australis*]), are beautiful well into winter. You can leave these standing until early spring.

A layer of pine needles will protect your plants from the effects of extreme temperature changes.

Most of the garden won't look so tidy if it is not cut back, but it will get through the winter just the same. Standing stems actually help hold lightweight mulches in place through winter storms. Focus your cleanup time on any plants that showed signs of disease this year or in previous years; fall cleanup reduces the chance of future recurrence.

In spring, get into the garden early (when the soil dries out and no longer squishes underfoot) to cut remaining stems back before new spring growth starts. Otherwise, it will become a much more complicated and time-consuming task as you try to trim out the old growth without damaging the new shoots. If you've had problems in the past with certain plants, like mulleins (*Verbascum* spp.) and patrinia (*Patrinia scabiosifolia*), reseeding too prolifically, cut off their seed heads in the fall.

Annuals Ready for Winter

Before the first frost, take cuttings from or dig up any special annuals that you want to grow again next year and take them inside for the winter; see "Bringing Annuals Indoors" for more information. Also collect any seeds you want to save.

After the first hard frost, tender and half-hardy annuals usually turn brown; pull these out and toss them on the compost pile. Hardy annuals such as

While many plants have finished flowering by fall, love lies bleeding and certain sages are still in bloom.

alyssum (*Lobularia maritima*) may keep blooming through several frosts; you can either pull them out in fall or wait until early spring. Foxgloves (*Digitalis* spp.), honesty (*Lunaria annua*), and other biennials usually make it through winter just fine, but a protective layer of mulch applied after the ground is frozen can help in severe-winter areas.

Handling Tender Bulbs

The final part of your gardening duties before winter sets in is to see to your tender bulbs, which seem to need more work than cold-hardy bulbs such as daffodils and crocus. With the latter, you just plant them once and enjoy them for years. With the former, you may have to dig or lift them for winter storage indoors. But when you consider the beautiful blooms you get in return, you'll probably agree that tender bulbs are worth a little extra effort.

Exactly what counts as a tender bulb? Well, it depends on what climate you live in, but bulbs that often spring to mind are those from tropical and subtropical climates. These include dahlias, tuberous begonias, gladioli, cannas, and caladiums. Some tender bulbs can take more cold than others. Cannas, for instance, may survive winters in areas as cold as Zone 7. Others, including tuberous begonias and caladiums, can survive over winter only in frost-free areas.

Astilbe seed heads can look attractive even after turning brown; consider leaving them for winter.

If you're not sure which bulbs are tender in your area, you can often figure it out by noting when you find them for sale. You'll generally find tender bulbs at local garden centers in late winter to midspring. You can also check catalog descriptions or refer to the individual plant entries in the "Guide to Popular Perennials," starting on page 202. In addition to information on each bulb's preferred climate, the plant entries also provide tips on how to handle each kind of bulb for indoor storage.

Once you learn the basics, you'll see that it's not difficult to keep your favorite tender bulbs from year to year.

Most annuals turn brown after the first frosts, but alyssum is hardy and will bloom a little longer.

Bringing Annuals Indoors

The first frost of fall doesn't have to signal the end of your annuals' bloom season. With just a little effort, you can enjoy their colorful flowers on your windowsills all winter.

Tender perennials that are usually grown as annuals usually adapt best to life indoors. These include coleus, geraniums (*Pelargonium* spp., both flowering and scented-leaf types), impatiens (including New Guinea types), wax begonias, and heliotrope (*Heliotropium arborescens*).

Overwintering these plants indoors allows you to keep them year after year, so you don't need to buy new ones each year. It's also a great way to preserve plants that have special traits, like especially good fragrance, an unusual flower form, or a striking color that you particularly like.

To overwinter annuals indoors, dig up whole plants before the first fall frost, cut them back by about one-third, and plant them in pots. Or take 3- to 5-inch (7.5- to 12.5-cm) cuttings from healthy, vigorous stems in mid- to late summer. Snip cuttings from non-flowering shoots if possible; otherwise, pinch off any flowers and flower buds. Remove the leaves from the lower half of the cutting and insert the bottom one-third of the stem into a pot of moist potting soil. Enclose the pot in a plastic bag and set it in a bright place out of direct sun. When cuttings are well rooted—usually in 3 to 4 weeks— remove the bag and move the pot to a sunny windowsill.

Whether you bring in whole plants or just cuttings, inspect them carefully first for any signs of pests or diseases. Avoid bringing in affected plants if possible. If you really want to save a special plant that has a problem, treat it as explained in "Pests, Diseases, Weeds" on page 138 or check the individual entries in the "Guide to Popular Annuals" on page 172.

During the winter, look after your annuals as you would any other houseplants. In the spring, move them back into the garden after the last frost date. Help them make the adjustment between indoors and outdoors by moving them out into the sunshine gradually; see "Handling Hardening Off" on page 115 for guidelines.

Lifting for Storage

Digging tender bulbs for indoor storage is just another part of routine fall-garden cleanup. When the bulb foliage turns yellow or brown, that's a good sign that the bulb is ready for storage. If the leaves stay green or if you don't have time to dig the bulbs when they are first ready, you can wait until just after the first frost. The cold temperatures will cause the leaves to turn black, but the bulbs are protected by the soil and should survive a light frost just fine. Don't wait any longer, though—get out and start digging, or your bulbs may get damaged by the increasingly cold temperatures.

Actually digging up the bulbs is simple. First, cut any tall stems back to about 6 inches (15 cm), so you can clearly see the base of the stem. Then carefully

Lilies can be planted in fall or you can wait until spring; at least prepare the bed in fall and mulch thickly.

Showy autumn crocuses flower in fall. The leaves die down but the corms don't need to be stored.

loosen the soil all the way around the plant. Use a trowel or hand fork to work around small bulbs and those growing in pots. (You can also turn whole pots over to dump out the soil and the bulbs at the same time.) A shovel or spading fork works better for big clumps, like dahlias and cannas.

Once the soil is loose, you can lift the bulb easily. Shake off as much soil as you can from the bulbs, label them, and set them on newspaper in a cool, shady place, such as a garage, potting shed, or porch. Dust any cuts on the bulbs or tubers with sulfur and leave them to dry for several days. Keep the bulbs out of the hot sun and away from areas where squirrels, mice, and other animals can get at them; otherwise, the local wildlife may think you're providing a buffet lunch for them.

Storing

Once your bulbs have dried for a few days, you can store them. Some gardeners keep their bulbs in mesh bags (like the kind onions come in) or paper bags with a few holes punched in them for better air circulation. Others prefer to store bulbs in boxes of slightly damp wood shavings or peat moss to keep the bulbs from drying

out too much over winter. The first year or two, try storing some bulbs each way and see what works best for you; then stick with that method. Either way, make sure you keep the bulbs labeled, since many look alike and it's easy to forget which is which.

Once the bulbs are packaged, you need to find a good storage spot. It should be dark to prevent the bulbs from sprouting and on the cool side—ideally about 50° to 60°F (10° to 16°C). Possible sites include

Gladioli are tender bulbs that must be lifted and stored over winter, to be replanted in the spring.

Lifting and Storing Tender Bulbs

1. Use a garden fork to carefully lift the bulb from the ground.

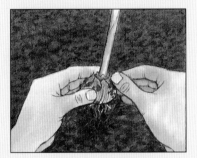

2. Brush off as much soil as you can from around the bulb and its roots.

3. Lay the bulbs out to dry in a sheltered spot for a few days.

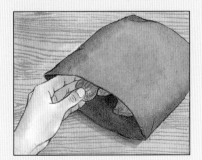

4. Store the bulbs in a bag or box and set them in a cool, dark place.

basement cupboards, insulated attics, crawl spaces, and attached garages that don't freeze. Experiment to find the best storage spot in your home.

During the storage period, check your bulbs every 3 to 4 weeks. Throw away any that are rotting. Sprinkle water on those that are starting to look shriveled. When spring arrives, retrieve your bulbs from storage and plant them in the garden or in pots as you would new store-bought bulbs. For suggested planting times, check the individual entries in the "Guide to Popular Perennials" on page 202.

When tuberous begonias are ready to grow in spring, they'll produce little green or pink shoots.

Buy new dahlia roots each year, or dig up your favorites in fall and store them indoors for the winter.

Month by Month in the Flower Garden

Like all bulbs, there is a right and a wrong time to plant ranunculus so they flower with the spring.

When is the best time to plant bulbs? When should you divide your perennials? What can you do in the garden on a cold November day? Even experienced gardeners sometimes forget what needs to be done in the garden and when to do it. In this section, you'll find a month-by-month calendar with handy reminders of the garden jobs that are appropriate for each month of the year.

This calendar is based on Zone 6, where the frost-free growing season is approximately late April to mid-October. If your garden is in a different zone, it's easy to adapt this calendar to fit your region. To find out which zone you're in, check the USDA Plant Hardiness Zone Map on page 276.

In warmer climates (Zones 7 to 9), spring comes sooner, so do the March to May chores a month or two earlier (the warmer the climate, the sooner you can start) and wait until the first frost to do your fall cleanup. In Zone 10, ignore the fall cleanup and mulching information; keep weeding, watering, and watching for pests throughout the year.

In colder zones and at high elevations (where the frost-free season is more likely to be late May or early June to late August or early September), this calendar will be about a month ahead of you for much of the year. Wait a month to do your March to May chores, finish the September chores in August, and start your fall garden cleanup after the first frost.

January

Review any notes that you made in your notebook about last year's garden; transfer important reminders (such as plants that you want to move or divide) to a list or calendar for the upcoming year. Daydream about how you want to use your yard when the warm weather returns. Start or revise your new or existing garden plans (even if you need snowshoes or an umbrella to inventory your yard).

Take stock of stored tender bulbs and any seeds that you've collected; toss out any that aren't sound. Order summer bulbs and plants from mail-order catalogs soon to avoid the rush. During thaws, check the garden beds for plant heaving; replace the soil around any exposed roots.

February

On warm days (or when the snow melts), inventory the garden to list cleanup chores for next month. Plan a weeding session; warm days in February and March are great times for getting rid of winter annual weeds, such as chickweed.

March is a good time to turn last year's compost.

March

As weather permits, clean up stray leaves, winter debris, remaining stems, and anything left undone last fall. Cut back ornamental grasses. Try not to step in beds where the soil is still wet. When the forsythias begin to show their cheerful yellow flowers, pull some of the winter mulch off of your beds so the soil can warm up. Turn last year's compost pile so it will be ready to spread when the ground warms up. Start a new pile with the debris from your spring cleanup. Take soil tests.

Nemesia needs a long, cool growing period; know your last frost date and set transplants out after then.

Perennials can be protected from frosts and extreme winter temperatures with a layer of mulch applied after the soil freezes. Start removing the mulch in March.

Thin the stems of garden phlox in May, before it blooms, to reduce the likelihood of powdery mildew.

Check out the garden shows that are held in your local area to get new garden design and planting ideas.

April

Finish your garden cleanup; pull up and discard any weeds. Dig over your annual garden beds, add plenty of compost, and include fertilizers as needed. Add any nutrients recommended by your soil test results in the general garden area, too. Start scouting for pests. In dry climates, set out drip irrigation systems for easy watering once the weather warms up.

As you enjoy your spring bulbs, jot down some notes to remind you what you want to add in the fall for next year. Top-dress bulb plantings with compost or balanced organic fertilizer for good blooms next year. Remove any spent flowers but leave the foliage until it dies back so bulbs can store enough energy to bloom next year. Side-dress clumps of emerging perennials with compost or well-rotted manure. Give annuals and any perennials that need rich soil—including phlox, delphiniums, and bee balms (*Monarda* spp.)—a little organic fertilizer. Divide summer- and fall-blooming perennials when the new shoots are about 3 inches (7.5 cm) tall.

May

Plant bareroot perennials and container-grown plants as you get them. Divide and replant spring-blooming perennials and crowded bulbs after they flower. Plant annuals, tender perennials, and tender bulbs (including dahlias and gladioli) outside once the danger of frost has passed. Add annuals to beds to hide the dying foliage of hardy bulbs. Replace and replenish mulch.

Pinch back perennials that tend to get leggy, such as New England asters (*Aster novae-angliae*) and garden mums (*Chrysanthemum* x *morifolium*). Thin out the weakest stems of clump-formers like garden phlox (*Phlox paniculata*). Pull or dig weed seedlings as soon as you spot them or they'll quickly get out of hand. Place wire ring stakes around peonies and other perennials that tend to flop; stake any tall flower stalks individually. If slugs or snails are a problem in your garden, set out shallow pans of beer to trap them; empty the traps regularly.

June

Walk through your garden regularly, both to enjoy it and to scout for problems. Remove and destroy diseased foliage. Stake annuals and perennials that need support if you didn't do it last month. Remove spent blossoms to prevent plants from self-seeding.

Watch the weather; water if rainfall is scarce. Wait until the top 1 to 2 inches (2.5 to 5 cm) of soil is dry, then water thoroughly. Container plantings may need daily watering during hot spells.

July

If you've kept up on your garden chores so far, you'll have earned a chance to relax just as the weather starts to heat up. Take some lemonade into the garden and make notes in your garden journal.

Water your perennials as needed. If the weather is very dry, consider watering the

Before you set out transplants of climbing annuals, be sure to install a support for the vines to climb on.

Foxglove penstemons should be divided every 4 to 6 years, after they have finished flowering in early fall.

compost pile, too; it will break down faster when evenly moist. Cut flowers for indoor arrangements in the morning, before the heat of the day. Remove spent flowers. Order spring bulbs this month or next to arrive in time for fall planting.

August

Now is the best time to move or divide oriental poppies (*Papaver orientale*), bearded irises, and—at the end of the month—peonies. Keep up the weeding, deadheading, pest patrol, and watering; remove all tattered or browning foliage. Cut flowers before they open fully for using in fresh arrangements, drying, or pressing. Cut leafy herbs for drying just when they start blooming.

September

September is often a dry month; monitor your soil and water as needed. Keep deadheading, weeding, and pest patrol. This is a good time to divide many perennials that have finished flowering, to dig up and rearrange plants in beds, and to plant container-grown perennials and shrubs.

Keep them well watered until winter to promote good root development.

Start new beds. Plant a cover crop—such as winter rye—to protect the soil over winter (till it under before spring planting). Or dig in chopped leaves and garden wastes; they will decompose by spring. Now is a good time to get your soil tested and to correct pH imbalances.

October

To extend your flower display a bit, cover tender plants on nights when frost is expected. Dig and store tender bulbs (such as tuberous begonias, dahlias, caladiums, and gladioli) when their foliage turns yellow and withers. Pull annuals after frost and toss them in the compost pile, or leave them if they have interesting seed heads.

Cut back the dead stems and leaves of perennials or let them stand until spring for winter interest. Remove and destroy any diseased foliage. Rake leaves for the compost pile or till them into new beds. Chop leaves with the lawn mower for good winter mulch (but don't mulch yet).

Plant spring bulbs. Record where you planted them on your site map so you won't dig into them when you plant annuals in the spring. Water perennial beds (as well as new shrub and bulb plantings) thoroughly before they go dormant to help them survive through the cold winter months.

November

Mow wildflower meadows now or wait until late winter if you want to enjoy the seed heads and leave seeds for the birds.

Retrieve stakes and replace missing plant labels. Drain and store hoses; shut off and drain outdoor water taps. Take stock of your gardening tools. Toss out what's beyond salvaging and note what needs replacing; mend, clean, and oil the rest.

If you don't have a map of your garden, make one now or next month (before snow falls) for winter planning. After the ground freezes, add a thick layer of mulch. Cover plants that need extra protection with branches.

December

Make a wish list of garden supplies for holiday presents or a shopping list for favorite gardeners. Catch up on garden reading. Look through all the books and magazines that piled up over the summer for new design ideas and new plants you'd like to try. Buy or make a new calendar for next year's garden.

Rake fallen leaves off your lawn and save them for mulching your plants after the ground freezes.

Propagating New Plants

If you enjoy planting and maintaining your garden full of annuals and perennials, then you will probably also enjoy growing your own plants from scratch. Propagation is a great way to start or expand a garden on a tight budget, to keep your favorite plants going season after season, or to simply have the satisfaction of knowing that you've grown your garden from the very beginning. It's relatively easy, and you can do it without needing a lot of special equipment.

Growing Annuals

With just a few packets of seeds, you can grow enough plants to fill an entire garden with annual color.

impatiens, need the warm conditions to get a good start in life and can then begin blooming soon after you set them out in late spring. Other annuals—including dwarf morning glory (*Convolvulus tricolor*) and strawflowers (*Bracteantha bracteata*)—grow equally well when sown indoors or out, but they'll begin blooming earlier if you start them indoors. This time saving is important in Northern gardens and especially at high elevations, where growing seasons are short.

When you're not sure if you should start a particular plant from indoor-sown seed, check the seed catalog description or seed packet. You'll also find specific growing tips in the individual entries in the "Guide to Popular Annuals," starting on page 172. When you're ready to sow, follow these guidelines.

Choosing a Container

While suitable containers come in a wide variety of shapes and sizes, they generally fall into one of two types: open trays that can hold many seedlings or pots that hold just a few seedlings each. Both types work fine, but if you're sowing small quantities of several different annual seeds, you may find it easier to keep track of them in individual pots. Buy commercially made

Growing your own annual plants from seed is great fun—and easier than you might think. A single packet of seeds can produce dozens, or even hundreds, of plants for a fraction of the cost of buying transplants. Starting from seed also gives you a much greater variety of plants to choose from, since most retail sources only grow a few cultivars of the most popular annuals. Some annuals grow best when started indoors; others are tough enough to be planted right in the garden where you want them to grow.

Sowing Seed Indoors

Starting seed indoors takes some time and space, but it also gives the best results for many annuals. Tender annuals, such as globe amaranth (*Gomphrena globosa*) and

Zinnias are adaptable annuals that can be grown successfully from seed started indoors or outdoors.

pots or trays (often called flats), or recycle milk cartons and margarine tubs. Just about any container will work, as long as it has drainage holes in the bottom.

For extra-easy transplanting, try preformed peat pots (available from most garden centers). At transplanting time, you can set the whole plant—pot and all—in the ground. The pot walls will break down, allowing the roots to spread out with no transplant shock. Peat pots are especially useful for starting seeds that are notoriously difficult to transplant, such as morning glories (*Ipomoea* spp.) and rocket larkspur (*Consolida ambigua*).

Picking a Growing Mix

For best results, buy a bag of commercial growing mix. Some gardeners select standard potting soil; others prefer mixes created specifically for seed starting. These mixes contain a balanced mixture of disease- and weed-free materials that will hold a good supply of moisture while letting excess water drain freely.

Choosing a Spot

For good growth, your seedlings will need the right temperatures and adequate light. Most annuals will sprout and grow well at average indoor temperatures (between 60°

Figuring Out Your Last Frost Date

When you're looking for guidelines on when to sow or plant annuals, you'll often find advice like "sow indoors 4 to 6 weeks before your last frost date" or "set plants out after the danger of frost has passed." That's fine, you may say, but how do I know when the last frost will be?

The answer is that you don't know exactly when your last spring frost will occur in a given year. But you can find out the average date of the last frost in your area by asking gardening friends or neighbors or calling your local Cooperative Extension Service office.

Remember that the last frost date is a guideline, not a guarantee. In any given year, frosts could end a week or two earlier than expected or—more important—sneak in a week or two later. Pay careful attention to weather forecasts around this time, and be prepared to protect tender plants if late frosts are predicted.

and 75°F [16° and 24°C]), so warmth usually isn't a problem. Finding a spot with enough light can be tricky, though. If your house is blessed with a sunroom or deep, sunny window sills, you can get good results growing seedlings there without providing extra light. Otherwise, you'll need to set up a simple light system to keep your seedlings happy and healthy. Garden centers as well as garden-supply catalogs sell lights in a variety of sizes and prices. Four-foot (1.2-m) fluorescent shop lights sold in home centers also provide excellent results, and they're generally much less expensive than grow lights.

Knowing When to Sow

You can sow most seeds indoors in early spring, about 6 to 10 weeks before your last frost date, although some need to be started earlier or later. To find out the best timing for your particular seeds, check the seed packet or the individual entries in the "Guide to Popular Annuals," starting on page 172.

Getting Started

When you're ready to sow (or, even better, the night before), dump your seed-starting mix in a large bucket or tub and add some warm water to moisten it. Start

Annuals such as celosia are difficult to transplant, so it's best to plant the seed straight in the ground.

Seedlings need plenty of light for compact, bushy growth. Near a window is a good spot.

with a few cups of water and work the mix with your hands to help it absorb the moisture. Keep adding several cups of water at a time and working it into the mix until the mix feels evenly moist but not soggy. (If you squeeze a handful of mix and water runs out, it's too wet; add some more dry mix to get the balance right.)

Once the mix is moist, you can fill your chosen containers. Scoop the mix

Step-by-Step Guide to Planting Seeds

1. Sow the seed evenly over the moistened growing medium.

2. Press the seed lightly into the surface of the medium with a wooden block.

3. Cover the seed according to the packet directions; firm the mix lightly.

4. Carefully moisten the top of the growing medium with a fine mist of water.

5. Label the container so you'll remember what you planted.

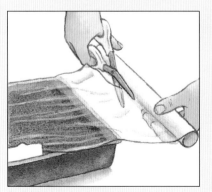

6. Cover with clear plastic until the seed begins to germinate.

Flowering tobacco has very fine seeds. Don't cover the seeds, just press them into the mix.

into each container and level it out to about ¼ inch (6 mm) below the upper edge of the container. Don't pack down the mix; just tap the filled container once or twice on your work surface to settle the mix and eliminate air pockets.

Sowing the Seed

When you're sowing large seeds, such as four o'clocks (*Mirabilis jalapa*), use a pencil to make individual holes ½ to 1 inch (12 to 25 mm) apart. For small seeds, use a pencil to make shallow rows and sow as evenly as possible into the rows. Fine seeds, such as those of petunias and begonias, can be hard to sow directly from the packet. To distribute tiny seeds more evenly, mix them with a spoonful of dry sand and scatter the mixture over the surface of the mix with a saltshaker.

If the seeds need to be buried in order to germinate (this will be indicated on the seed packet or in the individual entries in the "Guide to Popular Annuals," starting on page 172), sprinkle the needed amount of dry mix over the seed. Fine seeds are usually not covered; just press them lightly into the surface of the mix with your fingers or the back of a spoon. Mist the surface lightly to moisten it.

Set the containers in a well-lit spot where you can check them daily. Covering them with glass, plastic lids, plastic bags, or plastic food wrap will help to keep the potting mix moist with condensation and reduce or eliminate the need to water. (This is especially important for small, surface-sown seeds, since they can dry out quickly.) Most seeds sprout in 1 to 3 weeks. Remove the glass or plastic covering as soon as you see seedlings appear.

Growing Healthy Seedlings

Once your seedlings have sprouted, move them to full light (if they're not there already). Place them on a sunny windowsill or under the lights you've set up. Hang the lights so they're about 4 inches (10 cm) above the seedlings. Keep the lights on 14 to 16 hours a day. An inexpensive timer can turn the lights on and off for you automatically.

Seedling pots tend to dry out quickly indoors. Water them every few days to keep the soil evenly moist. If possible, water them from the bottom by adding about ½ inch (12 mm) of water to the tray the pots are sitting in. (Do not let the pots sit in water continuously.) Watering carefully from the top is also an option.

If your seedlings start to get crowded after the two sets of true leaves have appeared, transplant them to a larger container or to individual pots.

Saving Seeds

Collecting and saving seed is a fun and easy way to preserve some of your favorite annuals and perennials (and save a bit of money, too!). You'll get the best results if you stick with seeds of nonhybrid plants. These seeds are likely to produce plants that resemble their parents. Seeds from hybrid plants—those specially bred or selected for special traits, such as color or flower form—often produce seedlings that look quite different. (You can usually tell if a plant is a hybrid by the name or the description on the seed packet or plant tag: Look for the word "hybrid" or the symbol "F1.")

Seeds of spring-blooming annuals, biennials, and perennials usually are ready by midsummer; later-blooming annuals can mature their seeds through the first few frosts. On a dry day, gather seeds from seedpods that are dry and brittle but not yet open. Plants from the daisy family, such as marigolds (*Tagetes* hybrids), produce their seeds directly at the stem tips; simply pull or brush these off the seed head into your hand. Store harvested seed in paper envelopes in a cool, dry, mouse-proof place over the winter, until you're ready to start them in spring; then sow them as you would purchased seed.

When your seedlings have produced two sets of true leaves—the ones that appear after the first "seed" leaves—they are ready to be transplanted to individual pots or cell packs. Fill the pots with moistened potting mix. Use a knife blade or the pointed end of a plant label to dig small clumps of seedlings out of the tray. Gently separate the seedlings, holding them by their leaves (not their fragile stems or roots). Make a depression in the new pot, lower the seedling roots

into the hole, and carefully fill around the roots with the potting mix.

Set planted pots in a shallow tray of water until the soil surface looks moist. Then place the pots in a spot where they are shaded from full sun and keep them cool for a day or two before moving them back to the windowsill or their position under lights. Keep the soil evenly moist. Periodically apply a dose of liquid fertilizer (such as fish emulsion), following the manufacturer's directions for seedlings.

If you don't have the time or enough space to raise seedlings indoors, you can always try the wide variety of annuals that grow from seed planted in the garden. For more information, see "Sowing Seed in the Garden" on page 115.

A few types of zonal geranium will grow from seed sown indoors, but this is one of the few annuals that is usually propagated from cuttings.

Propagating Perennials

You can propagate perennials by a number of methods. Depending on which method you choose, you might end up with a few or a few hundred new perennials from a single plant. You will create several good-sized new plants from one large specimen by division. By taking stem or root cuttings, you can get dozens of new plants. Or start perennials from seed and you may end up with hundreds of plants from a single packet.

When you're considering a method, decide how important it is that the offspring resemble the parent plant. With vegetative methods of propagation, such as division, layering, and cuttings, you will obtain an exact clone of the parent plant in nearly every case. This is especially important when you want to propagate cultivars or hybrids, which usually produce variable offspring when grown from seed.

Seed is a good way to propagate perennials when you want species or varieties. There are also a few cultivars that come true from seed. Use seed-grown plants in informal gardens where differences in height, foliage and flower color, and bloom time don't matter or can even be considered an advantage. When uniformity matters in a formal garden, a row, or an edging, use vegetatively propagated plants to get the best results.

Delphiniums can be propagated by a variety of methods—by cuttings, seeds, or division.

When you are looking for perennial seed, you will find two types: open-pollinated and hybrid seed. There are natural hybrids, such as the Lenten rose (*Helleborus* x *orientalis*), and there are commercial hybrids, the result of controlled breeding. Hybrids tend to be more uniform than open-pollinated plants, but they are not always as consistent as vegetatively propagated plants. If you buy the seed of a hybrid and want more of that plant, you must buy more seed from the company or propagate the originals vegetatively. It will not come true from seed that you collect from your own plants.

If you want a mass of English primroses, they are easy to grow from seed sown in the garden.

Another important issue in choosing a propagation method is how long each method takes to produce flowering plants. Perennial seedlings and (to a lesser extent) cuttings will take a season or more—sometimes several years—to reach flowering size. Even when they do flower, the display may be sparse until the plants reach a substantial size. If you want quick results, use the division method or choose fast-growing perennials that may flower during their first year of life if you start them early indoors. Divisions generally recover quickly and often bloom the same season they're planted. For fast-maturing cuttings, try asters and garden mums (*Chrysanthemum* x *morifolium*). Perennials that bloom from seed the first year after a winter sowing include 'Snow Lady' shasta daisy (*Leucanthemum* x *superbum* 'Snow Lady'), columbines, delphiniums, and purple coneflowers (*Echinacea purpurea*).

Perennials from Seed

Seed is an excellent method to use when propagating certain perennials. It's a great way to stretch a tight budget if you don't mind waiting for a show. Growing your

Open-pollinated plants are likely to vary from their parent plant, which was pollinated by bees.

own seedlings allows you to select unusual species and choice varieties that you can't usually buy at greenhouses and nurseries. However, if you buy seed of a cultivar, such as 'Goldsturm' coneflower (*Rudbeckia fulgida* 'Goldsturm'), the seedlings will be variable and may not all live up to the high performance values of vegetatively propagated stock.

Always use high-quality seed, packed for the current year. Buy from a reputable seed company that offers high germination rates. You can find out the rates from the percentage of viable (live) seeds listed on the package. If you have any seed left over from last year or any home-collected seed, try sprouting a few before you sow a whole packet. Roll the seeds in a moist paper towel and enclose the rolled towel in a plastic bag. Keep the bag warm and watch for germination in the next several weeks. If only half of the seeds sprout, you will know you need to sow twice as much seed to get the number of plants you want.

Sowing Seed

Just as wild and self-sowing perennials do naturally, you can sow seed directly outdoors in a well-prepared bed. Cover the seed to the depth indicated on the package in loose soil and keep the soil moist until the seedlings begin to emerge.

Although direct sowing is certainly the easiest technique, you will probably realize that it is not the most dependable. When planted directly into your garden, your seed can be eaten by birds or insects or attacked by fungi. It may get too cold or too hot, too wet or too dry. For a better survival rate and an earlier start than direct seeding offers you, start seedlings indoors under fluorescent lights or in a sunny, south-facing window.

Depending on the size of the seed and the speed of growth, with seed that is easy to germinate, you should start it indoors 6 to 12 weeks before the last spring frost. In warm climates, start fast-germinating seed in summer to set out in the cool of fall and winter.

Other perennials will take much longer to germinate. You may need to expose the seed to a chilling period by placing the sown seed in the refrigerator for a certain number of weeks. If a perennial needs special treatment, it will be indicated

A glassed-in verandah on the sunny side of the house is a good propagating spot for the colder months.

Potting-up Seedlings

1. Put some moist potting mix in the base of the new pot.

2. Squeeze the container gently to loosen the roots.

3. Carefully slide the plant from the container with its roots intact.

4. Center the plant in the new pot and fill in with moist potting mix.

The flexible stems of bellflowers make this plant well suited to being propagated by layering.

on the seed packet or in the "Guide to Popular Perennials," starting on page 202.

Sow your perennial seed in a sterile, peat-based seedling mix that has been thoroughly moistened. This lightweight medium encourages rooting while discouraging root diseases. Start seed in small individual pots or peat pots, or save space by sowing seed in rows in flats (shallow plastic or wooden trays). Sprinkle tiny seeds lightly on top of the seedling mix and press them gently into the surface. Push larger seeds down into the soil as deep as they are wide. Cover the container with clear plastic wrap to keep the soil evenly moist until the seeds germinate, but make sure the plastic doesn't touch the soil.

After sowing, keep the medium moist and between 60° and 75°F (15.5° and 30°C). Warmth-loving perennials will come up most quickly at the higher end of the temperature range while cool-season perennials may germinate faster at the lower end. Avoid rapid temperature changes, which can stunt growth.

Caring for Seedlings

When your seedlings emerge, move them into bright light and remove the plastic. Water as often as necessary to keep the soil moist and to prevent wilting. When you water, set the container of seedlings in a tray of water so the growing medium can soak up moisture without disrupting the seedlings. If you water from overhead, you may wash the seedlings away.

If you have sown seed in flats or trays, move seedlings to their own pots when they have two sets of true leaves in addition to the bottom set of fleshy seed leaves. You can move most perennials into 4-inch (10-cm) pots if you intend to plant them outdoors in a couple of weeks. If not, you should keep moving the plants up to larger containers to prevent roots from binding. This process is known as potting up. Feed the young plants lightly with compost tea or liquid seaweed. If the weather is cold or hot, leave the transplants indoors under lights or on the windowsill. If it is relatively mild, move the plants out into a cold frame or another sheltered area for hardening off before transplanting them into your garden beds. For more details on this, see "Handling Hardening Off" on page 115.

Layering

Some plants are easy to root while still attached to the mother plant, a technique called layering. Burying a section of the stem encourages roots to form at each buried leaf node (the place where a leaf joins the stem). Layering does take up some space, since you need to bury the attached stem close to the parent plant. You won't get many new plants from this method (usually only one per stem), and it can take weeks or months for the stem to root. But layering is easy to do and the resulting plants will be exact duplicates of the parent plant.

You can use this technique with plants that have flexible stems or a creeping habit and the ability to root at the leaf axils. Good candidates for layering include pinks (*Dianthus* spp.), cranesbills (*Geranium* spp.), wall rock cress (*Arabis caucasica*), snow-in-summer (*Cerastium tomentosum*), and bellflowers (*Campanula* spp.). Layering will not work on daylilies, ornamental grasses, hostas, irises, peonies, or other bushy perennials.

Simple Layering

Layering is a quick and easy way to propagate many types of perennial, especially those that naturally tend to creep along the soil. Spring is a good time to start a layer, although it can work any time during the growing season.

1. Select a flexible stem and bend it down to the soil.

2. Use a wire pin to secure the stem, then cover it with soil.

3. Dig up the rooted layer and transplant it to another spot.

How It Works

The first step to successful layering is finding a suitable stem. If the plant is upright, look for one or several long stems that bend easily to the ground; if the plant has a creeping habit, any stem is suitable. Leave the top three sets of leaves on the stem to nourish the plant, but remove the leaves from the stem for 2 to 7 inches (5 to 17.5 cm) below the top greenery. Strip the leaves from at least two nodes (leaf joints), carefully leaving the dormant buds undamaged. Bend the stem down and see where the stripped area will contact the soil. Loosen the soil in that area to about 4 inches (10 cm) deep and water it. Bury the stem in the loosened soil, holding it in place with a bent wire pin, and firm the soil over the stem. The stem should be buried 2 to 3 inches (5 to 7.5 cm) deep with the leafy tip still exposed. If you are layering an upright shoot, encourage the tip to return to its upright position by tying it to a stake pushed into the soil if necessary.

Keep the area moist and mulched while the buried stem roots. Depending on the temperature and species, it will take several weeks to several months. The easiest way to layer is to leave the plant in place until the following season. If you want faster results, check its progress by gently uncovering the stem and looking for roots or tugging lightly to see if the shoot has become more secure in the

Division is the quick way to propagate perennials, and is especially suited to fibrous-rooted plants.

ground. Once the roots reach about 1 inch (2.5 cm) long you can cut the shoot free from the mother plant. Wait several weeks for more rooting, then dig up and transplant the new plant.

Reproduction by Division

Many perennials flower best when they're young, and their flower production drops as they mature. To keep them flowering well, you must divide them—dig them up and split the root mass into pieces. In addition to reviving older plants, division is the easiest and fastest technique for propagating perennials. It's also a good way to keep fast-spreading perennials under control, and you'll have lots of extra plants to share with friends and neighbors.

How often you need to propagate depends on why you're dividing. If you're using division to propagate, it depends on how many new plants you want and how fast the plant is growing. Divide annually to retard aggressive spreaders like bee balm (*Monarda didyma*), bigroot geranium (*Geranium macrorrhizum*), obedient plant (*Physostegia virginiana*), and yarrows. If you want to rejuvenate your perennials, you can divide them whenever flowering starts to decline. To keep performance high, you can divide asters and painted daisies (*Chrysanthemum coccineum*) every year or two. Some perennials, including peonies, daylilies, and astilbes, can go for years without division.

How to Divide

Begin dividing by digging up the root system. Shake off as much loose soil as possible and remove any dead leaves and stems. You may also want to wash most of the soil off the roots and crown so you can see the roots and buds clearly.

Perennials with fibrous roots, such as asters and garden mums (*Chrysanthemum* x *morifolium*), are the easiest to dig and divide. You can pull them apart with your hands or cut them with a spade. Others, like daylilies and astilbes, can grow woody with age. You may have to pry these roots apart with a crowbar or two garden forks

Step-by-step Division

Division is a fast and reliable way to propagate many clump-forming perennials, including daylilies and garden mums. It may not work well with more sensitive perennials, like sea hollies (*Eryngium* spp.) and gas plant (*Dictamnus albus*).

1. Use shears or your hands to divide the perennial clump into several smaller pieces.

2. Make sure each new piece has its own roots and some top growth.

3. Replant the pieces immediately, water them well, and apply a light layer of mulch.

Taking Stem Cuttings

1. Select a strong, young shoot. Use sharp pruning shears to make a clean cut just below a node.

2. Snip the leaves off the bottom half of the cutting, leaving 2 to 3 sets of leaves, with 2 to 3 leaf nodes exposed at the base.

3. Insert the bottom half of the prepared cutting into a container of moist, lightweight potting mix.

4. Cover with an upended jar or with plastic to hold in the moisture. Set in a bright place out of direct sun.

showy stonecrop (*Sedum spectabile*), and spike speedwell (*Veronica spicata*).

Taking Cuttings You should take stem cuttings when perennials are in vegetative growth, either in spring before blooming or after flowering is finished for the season. You should select a healthy medium-soft stem—one that is not soft, new growth or hard, old growth—from the lower portion of the plant, where shoots are more likely to root quickly. Cut the selected stems free with a sharp, clean knife or pair of shears.

Preparing the Cuttings Slice the stem into sections between 2 and 4 inches (5 to 10 cm) long, so that each cutting has two or three sets of leaves on the top and a couple of nodes (leaf joints) stripped of leaves on the bottom. These nodes will produce roots when you insert them into a pot of moist, sterile, peat-based growing mix.

Some stem cuttings, like those from blue false indigo (*Baptisia australis*), will root more easily if you dip their lower ends in a commercially available rooting hormone powder. However, if you find the right moisture, light, and warmth levels, most perennials will root without

held back to back or cut them with a saw or ax. Discard the woody parts, which will not reroot well.

To renew an existing planting, slice the plant into halves, thirds, or quarters. Discard the old, woody growth from the center of the clump and replant the vigorous outer portions.

When you want to build a larger stock of new plants, you can divide perennials into smaller pieces. Just make sure you keep several buds or growing shoots on the sections you will replant. Look for the buds growing along the length of the roots or clustered together in a central crown.

Work compost and other soil amendments back into the soil before replanting. Reset divisions at the same level at which the original clump was growing.

Cuttings

Cuttings—small pieces of stem or root— are another way to propagate many perennials. Cuttings take more care than other methods, like layering and division. But if you like a challenge, you can use cuttings to create many new plants from your existing perennials. Cuttings are a good way to propagate perennials that are difficult to divide and cultivars that don't come true from seed.

Stem Cuttings

Stem cuttings are effective for propagating many kinds of perennials. Try perennials such as wall rock cress (*Arabis caucasica*), garden mums, common sneezeweed (*Helenium autumnale*), garden phlox (*Phlox paniculata*), pinks (*Dianthus* spp.),

A good way to stop bee balm spreading and to produce new, healthy plants is to divide annually.

Root cuttings require a little extra care, but for delicate Japanese anemones, it will be worthwhile.

this treatment. Make a hole in the mix with a clean pencil and slide the cutting in. Firm the mix around it and water to settle the cutting into the soil.

Caring for Cuttings Cover the container with a clear plastic-wrap tent. Prop the plastic above the plant foliage to avoid rot. Keep the cuttings in a warm place and in indirect light until they root, which takes about 2 to 4 weeks. When they begin to grow, remove the plastic and move the plants into brighter light.

To determine if the cuttings have rooted, look to see if roots are emerging from the pot's drainage hole. You can also tug gently on the stem—if you meet resistance, the cuttings have rooted. Transplant the rooted cuttings into larger containers or a nursery bed to grow them to garden size.

Root Cuttings
Less common than stem cuttings, root cuttings are another way to produce new plants that are usually identical to the parent plant. Root cuttings are suitable for several kinds of perennials, including Siberian bugloss (*Anchusa azurea*), oriental poppies (*Papaver orientale*),

Japanese anemones (*Anemone* x *hybrida*), and garden phlox (*Phlox paniculata*).

Take root cuttings from fall to early spring, while the parent plant is dormant. Carefully lift the plant from the garden and wash the soil from the roots. Using a sharp, clean knife, cut off a few pencil-thick roots near the crown. Cut each root into 2- to 4-inch (5- to 10-cm) pieces; make a straight cut at the top (the end closest to the crown) and a slanted cut at the bottom. Insert the cuttings into a pot filled with moist, sterile potting mix so the flat top of each cutting is level with or slightly below the surface. Place in a cold frame until they root and then pot them individually. Once the plants reach the desired size, move them into the garden.

Taking Root Cuttings

Root cuttings are a bit trickier to take than stem cuttings, but they can work just as well with a little care. As you collect the roots, place them in a plastic bag to protect them from drying winds. Use a clean, sharp knife to minimize damage to the root tissue as you prepare the cuttings, and make a note of which end of the root was closest to the crown so you don't plant the root cuttings upside down. Don't overwater.

1. Cut a healthy, pencil-thick root piece.

2. Make a straight cut at the end that was closest to the crown.

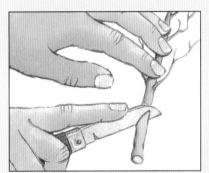

3. Make a sloping cut at the other end of the cutting.

4. Carefully insert cuttings, pointed end down, in a pot of potting mix.

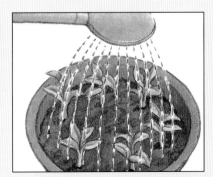

5. Keep cuttings evenly moist until they start to grow, then transplant.

Bulb Multiplication

You can also increase your bulb plantings by using division or seeds to propagate the bulbs you already have. It takes a little longer to get flowers, but you can't beat the price!

Multiplication by Division

Division is the fastest and easiest way to propagate nearly all bulbs, corms, tubers, tuberous roots, and rhizomes. Besides being quite simple to do, division has another advantage: All the new plants that you create will be identical to the parent bulb, so you can easily increase your favorite colors and flower forms.

Bulbs and Corms

Some bulbs, such as tulips and daffodils, form small "bulblets" near their base. Gladioli and other corms produce similar offsets called "cormlets." With good care, both bulblets and cormlets can grow to full flowering size in a year or two.

To divide spring bulbs, lift the clump with a spade or digging fork after the foliage has died back in late spring. To divide gladiolus corms, lift them in late summer or fall, as the foliage turns yellow. Separate the bulblets or cormlets by gently pulling them away from the mother bulb or corm. Plant the bulblets or cormlets in a nursery bed or corner of the vegetable garden, where they can grow undisturbed for a few years. Water and fertilize them regularly. When the bulbs reach flowering size, move them to their final spot in the garden.

Tubers and Tuberous Roots

Division is also an effective way to increase tuberous-rooted plants, such as dahlias and tuberous begonias. The best time to divide is in spring, just after you bring these tender plants out of winter storage. Use a sharp knife to cut begonia tubers into two or three pieces, each with at least one growth bud. On dahlias, cut tuberous roots apart at the stem end, so each root has at least one bud.

Plant each new piece in a pot and set it under grow

After the first year, tulip bulbs tend to divide into several smaller bulbs, which will not flower as well. Separate and replant them.

Growing Lilies from Bulblets

1. Remove bulblets that form below the ground along the stem.

2. Grow them in pots for a year or two before planting them out.

Unlike most bulbs, snowdrops can be divided while still in bloom in late winter and spring.

lights or in a greenhouse. Keep the temperature between 65° and 75°F (18° and 24°C). Water as needed so the potting soil stays evenly moist but not wet. (Don't fertilize newly cut bulbs—wait until they're growing in soil.) In a few weeks, you should have healthy new plants that are ready for transplanting into outdoor gardens and containers.

Rhizomes

Cannas and bearded irises are two common examples of plants that grow from rhizomes. Use a sharp knife, a spade (if the clump is really big), or your hands to pull or cut apart the rhizomes. Discard any old, woody pieces from the center of the original clump.

Divide canna clumps into pieces about 6 inches (15 cm) square, making sure that each has at least one growth bud. The best time to divide cannas is in spring, right before you plant them in pots or outdoors in the garden. Bearded irises, on the other hand, prefer to be divided just after they flower. Separate them into pieces with at least one "fan" of leaves on

each. Trim the foliage back by at least half, and replant the irises into soil that you've enriched with compost, leaf mold, or well-rotted manure.

Growing Bulbs from Seed

You can also grow your bulbs from seed if you're really patient—you'll wait a few years for flowers. When they bloom, the seedlings may not look like the parent plant, which can be

Special Tips for Lily-lovers

Lilies, like other bulbs, produce bulblets that you can separate from the parent plant and grow into new plants of full flowering size. But there are some other special propagation techniques you can try.

Bulbils: Sometimes you may notice small, dark minibulbs (called "bulbils") growing along the stems of your lilies. This is common on tiger lilies and a few other types. Gently pull or twist the bulbils off the stem in late summer and plant them in pots or a nursery bed to grow to flowering size.

Scaling: Scaling is a technique you can use on all lilies. In fall, dig up the bulb you want to propagate and remove a few of the outer scales. Dust the broken edges of these scales with sulfur. Plant the scales in pots or trays, with their base just below the soil surface, and set them under lights or in a greenhouse. New bulblets will quickly form along the base of each scale. After a few weeks, gently pull off the bulblets, put them in the refrigerator for 2 months, and then plant them in pots or an outdoor nursery bed to grow. They can reach flowering size in as little as 2 years, depending on the species or hybrid you're growing.

If you want lots of one kind of bulb, grow them from seed, but you'll wait a few years for flowers.

The rhizomes of bearded irises are easily divided with a sharp knife, a garden spade, or your hands.

fun if you like surprises but disappointing if you want the exact color of the original.

Gather seed in summer or fall, after your bulbs flower. Check the developing seedpods every few days, then collect the seeds as the seedpods begin to open. Sow the seed in well-drained seed-starting mix in pots or trays. Cover it with a thin layer of mix and set the containers in a cool, shaded place outdoors. Water as needed to keep the soil evenly moist.

When seedlings appear, move the containers to a sunny place. Continue watering until the seedlings die down. (Seedlings will go dormant for part of the year, just like their garden-grown parents.) Water sparingly until new growth appears again, then keep them evenly moist. Depending on the species you're dealing with, your baby bulbs may reach flowering size in as little as 1 year, although 3 to 5 years is more common.

A Guide to Popular Annuals

Annuals fit into any size or style of garden you wish to create, from formal beds and borders to casual cottage gardens and containers arranged on balconies and patios. Particular flower and foliage colors can be used to develop color themes in your garden, while scented annuals add an extra element of pleasure to your beautiful plantings. This guide to some of the most popular annuals will help you make your selections.

Plants are arranged alphabetically by their botanical name, with their most often-used common name displayed prominently. Each plant is illustrated with a color photograph to make identification easy. There is also a full plant description and cultivation tips. With this guide, you can begin choosing the annuals that will suit your garden and you.

Ageratum houstonianum
ASTERACEAE

AGERATUM

Ageratums need little care; just water during dry spells. If the plants stop producing new blooms, cut them back by about half; water and fertilize to promote new growth.

Description A half-hardy annual that forms tidy clumps of hairy, green leaves. From early summer until frost, the leaves are nearly covered by clusters of ¼–½-inch (6–12-mm), puffy flower heads in shades of lavender-blue, violet-blue, pink, or white.
Height and spread Height usually 6–12 inches (15–30 cm); spread 6–8 inches (15–20 cm).
Best site Full sun to partial shade; average, well-drained soil with some added organic matter. A site with morning sun and afternoon shade is best for plants in warm- to hot-summer climates.
Growing guidelines Buy transplants in spring for earliest color, or start them from seed sown indoors 6–8 weeks before your last frost date. Sow seed on the soil surface, press it in lightly, and put the pots in plastic bags until seedlings appear. Set out young plants after the last frost. Space compact cultivars 6–8 inches (15–20 cm) apart; allow 12 inches (30 cm) between plants of tall cultivars.
Landscape uses Compact cultivars are ideal for edging flower beds and adding color to containers. Tall-stemmed types are excellent for cut flowers and as accents.
Other common names Floss flower.

Alcea rosea
MALVACEAE

HOLLYHOCK

Hollyhocks are perennials usually grown as annuals or biennials. Cut down the flower stalks after the blooms have faded, or leave a few to set seed and self-sow.

Description Hollyhocks form large clumps of rounded leaves and thick bloom stalks. Plump flower buds produce bowl-shaped, single or double blooms up to 5 inches (12.5 cm) wide from midsummer until fall in white or shades of red, pink, and yellow.
Height and spread Height 3–6 feet (90–180 cm); spread about 2 feet (60 cm).
Best site Needs full sun; average, well-drained soil.
Growing guidelines For bloom the same year, sow seed indoors 8 weeks before your last frost date. Sow ¼ inch (6 mm) deep in individual pots. After risk of frost has passed, set plants out 18–24 inches (45–60 cm) apart. For earlier bloom the following year, sow outdoors in large pots or in a nursery bed in spring or early summer. Move the young plants to their garden position in fall. Stake hollyhocks growing in exposed sites to keep stems upright. Hollyhocks are prone to rust, a fungal disease that produces orange spots on leaves. If rust shows up in your garden, pull plants out after bloom.
Landscape uses Use the tall spires of hollyhocks as accents in a flower border, with shrubs, or along a wall or fence.

Amaranthus caudatus
AMARANTHACEAE

LOVE LIES BLEEDING

Love lies bleeding is lovely in fresh or dried arrangements. To preserve the flowers, stand the cut stems in a bucket so the tassels hang naturally as they dry.

Description This unusual tender annual produces thick, sturdy, branched stems with large, oval, pale green leaves. Long clusters of tightly packed, deep crimson flowers dangle from the stem tips from midsummer until frost. The ropy, tassel-like clusters can grow to 18 inches (45 cm) long.
Height and spread Height 3–5 feet (90–150 cm); spread to about 2 feet (60 cm).
Best site Full sun; average, well-drained soil. Tolerates some dryness.
Growing guidelines Sow seed indoors, ⅛ inch (3 mm) deep, 4–6 weeks before your last frost date. Set plants 18 inches (45 cm) apart when the weather is warm, 2–3 weeks after the last frost date. Seed also germinates quickly in warm soil, so you could instead sow it in the garden in late spring.
Landscape uses Makes a striking accent in flower beds and borders and in cottage gardens. Add a few plants to the cutting garden, too.
Cultivars 'Viridis' is similar but has green flower clusters. 'Pygmy Torch' has upright, crimson clusters above purplish leaves on 18–24-inch (45–60-cm) tall stems.

Antirrhinum majus
SCROPHULARIACEAE

SNAPDRAGON

A mass planting of snapdragons makes an eye-catching landscape accent. Pinch the stem tips of dwarf types once after transplanting to promote branching and bushiness.

Description These tender perennials are usually grown as hardy or half-hardy annuals. The plants may be low and mound-forming or tall and spiky. The slender stems carry narrow, bright green leaves and are topped with spikes of tubular flowers. The velvety flowers bloom through summer in nearly every color but true blue; some have two colors in one flower.

Height and spread Height ranges from 1–4 feet (30–120 cm). Spread ranges from 8–18 inches (20–45 cm).

Best site Full sun to light shade; average, well-drained soil with compost added.

Growing guidelines Buy transplants in spring, or start your own by planting seed indoors 6–8 weeks before your last frost date. Sow seed directly into prepared garden soil after the last frost date. Water during dry spells. Snapdragons are prone to rust, a fungal disease that shows up as brownish spots on leaves. The best prevention is to grow them as annuals.

Landscape uses Use the low-growing cultivars in masses or as edging plants for annual beds. Tall-stemmed snapdragons are a must in the cutting garden for fresh arrangements, and in cottage gardens.

Argyranthemum frutescens
ASTERACEAE

MARGUERITE

Marguerites offer ferny foliage covered with dainty, daisy-type blooms practically all summer. They are perennial in warm climates; grow them as annuals north of Zone 9.

Description This shallow-rooted, shrubby plant has bright green or bluish leaves. The abundant, daisy-type, 2-inch (5-cm) blooms flower from spring to fall in white, pink, or yellow.

Height and spread Height usually to about 3 feet (90 cm); spread to 3 feet (90 cm).

Best site Full sun; well-drained, moist soil with compost added.

Growing guidelines Marguerites are propagated from seed or cuttings, which can be taken at any time. Plant in a well-drained soil after the last frost. Fertilize regularly during the growing season and keep the soil evenly moist. Prune plants lightly every month or two for best flowering. Large-flowered types are not as prolific as those with small blooms. You can bring marguerites indoors for the winter and move them back outdoors the following spring.

Landscape uses Marguerites make a lovely display in flower beds or cottage gardens. They also make a good cut flower.

Other common names Paris daisy.

Bassia scoparia f. trichophylla
CHENOPODIACEAE

SUMMER CYPRESS

Cut summer cypress plants to the ground in fall before the seed matures to keep plants from self-sowing; otherwise, you may have hundreds of seedlings next year!

Description This half-hardy annual is grown for its compact, shrubby clumps of foliage and attractive fall color. Plants form feathery, oval or rounded mounds of narrow, spring green leaves that take on purplish red tints when cool weather arrives. Tiny flowers bloom along the stems in early fall.

Height and spread Height 3–4 feet (90–120 cm); spread to 2 feet (60 cm).

Best site Full sun; average, well-drained soil.

Growing guidelines Sow seed indoors 4–6 weeks before your last frost date. Don't cover the seed; just press it lightly into the soil and enclose the pot in a plastic bag until seedlings appear. Set plants out after the last frost date. Or sow seed directly into the garden after the last frost date. Set transplants or thin seedlings to stand 24 inches (60 cm) apart. Plants will look spindly at first but fill in quickly. In windy or exposed areas, support the stems.

Landscape uses Group several plants as a filler for the back of beds or borders, or use single plants as shrubby accents. It also looks great as a temporary hedge.

Other common names Burning bush, fire bush.

Begonia Semperflorens-cultorum hybrid
BEGONIACEAE

WAX BEGONIA

Wax begonias require little or no care during the season. Pull them out after frost, or cut them back by one-third after frost and pot them up for indoor bloom in winter.

Description These tender perennials are grown as tender annuals. The succulent stems bear shiny, rounded, green or reddish brown leaves. The mounded plants are covered with single or double, ¾-inch (18-mm) flowers in red, pink, or white from June until frost.

Height and spread Height and spread 6–8 inches (15–20 cm).

Best site Partial shade to sun; evenly moist soil with added organic matter. Morning sun and afternoon shade is ideal in hot-summer areas. Brown-leaved types tend to be more sun- and heat-tolerant.

Growing guidelines Wax begonias are easiest to grow from purchased transplants in spring. If you want to try raising them yourself, sow the dust-like seed at least 12 weeks before your last frost date. Don't cover the seed; just press it lightly into the soil and place the pot in a plastic bag until seedlings appear. Set transplants out 6–8 inches (15–20 cm) apart after the last frost date, when temperatures stay above 50°F (10°C) at night.

Landscape uses Wax begonias are ideal as edging plants for flower beds. They also look great in pots, window boxes, and hanging baskets.

Bellis perennis
ASTERACEAE

ENGLISH DAISY

Pinch off the spent flower stems of English daisies at the base to prolong bloom and prevent reseeding. Pull out plants after bloom and start new ones for next year.

Description These easy-to-grow, short-lived perennials are usually grown as hardy annuals or biennials. Plants form rosettes of oval, green leaves. Short, thick stems are topped with 1–2-inch (2.5–5-cm) flowers from April to June. The daisy- or pompon-type blooms may be white, pink, or red.

Height and spread Height to 6 inches (15 cm); spread 6–8 inches (15–20 cm).

Best site Full sun to partial shade; average, well-drained soil with added organic matter.

Growing guidelines If your area has cool summers, you can start seed indoors in midwinter and set plants out in midspring for bloom the same year. In hot-summer areas, or to achieve earliest spring bloom elsewhere, grow as biennials. Sow seed in pots indoors or outdoors in June or July; cover lightly. Grow seedlings in pots or in a nursery bed until fall, then transplant them to the garden. Space plants 6 inches (15 cm) apart. Protect large-flowered types with a light mulch, such as straw or pine needles, over winter.

Landscape uses English daisies are super for spring color in flower beds and window boxes. They look wonderful edging a walk, and the blooms make charming cut flowers.

Brachyscome iberidifolia
ASTERACEAE

SWAN RIVER DAISY

If Swan River daisy plants get floppy after the first flush of bloom, shear them back by half and water well to promote compact growth and more flowers until frost arrives.

Description This half-hardy annual forms bushy mounds of thin stems and lacy, finely cut leaves. From midsummer until frost, plants bear many 1-inch (2.5-cm), rounded, daisy-type flowers in shades of blue, purple, pink, and white. The delicately scented blooms may have a black or yellow center.

Height and spread Height to 12 inches (30 cm); spread to 18 inches (45 cm).

Best site Full sun; average, well-drained soil with added organic matter.

Growing guidelines For earliest bloom, buy flowering plants and set them out after your last frost date. You can also start Swan River daisy from seed planted indoors or outdoors. Sow indoors 6–8 weeks before your last frost date. Scatter the seed over the surface, lightly press it into the soil, and enclose the pot in a plastic bag until seedlings appear. Set plants out after the last frost date, or sow directly into the garden in late spring. Space plants 6–8 inches (15–20 cm) apart to form a solid, even carpet of flowers.

Landscape uses Swan River daisy makes an unusual edging for beds and borders. Its trailing habit is ideal for window boxes and hanging baskets.

Bracteantha bracteata
ASTERACEAE

STRAWFLOWER

Cutting strawflowers for fresh arrangements or drying will promote branching and prolong the bloom season. The flowers dry quickly when hung upside down in a dark, airy place.

Description This half-hardy annual is grown for its colorful, long-lasting blooms. The bushy plants have long, narrow, green leaves and daisy-type flowers with stiff, papery, petal-like rays. The flowers bloom from midsummer until frost in white, pink, rose, red, orange, or yellow. Fully open flowers are 1–2 inches (2.5–5 cm) wide and have yellow centers.

Height and spread Height 2–4 feet (60–120 cm); spread to 12 inches (30 cm).

Best site Needs full sun; average, well-drained soil.

Growing guidelines For earliest blooms, buy transplants or start your own by sowing seed indoors 6–8 weeks before your last frost date. Just press the seed lightly into the soil surface and enclose the pot in a plastic bag until seedlings appear. Set plants out 2 weeks after the last frost date, or sow seed directly into the garden after the last frost date.

Landscape uses Strawflowers add long-lasting color to flower beds and borders. Grow an ample supply in the cutting garden for drying, as well. Harvest flowers when they are about one-quarter open; they'll open more as they dry.

Brassica oleracea
CRUCIFERAE

ORNAMENTAL CABBAGE

Ornamental cabbages add a surprising and showy accent to late-season gardens. They withstand frost and can look good until late fall or even survive through winter until early spring.

Description This biennial is grown as an annual for its rosettes of colorful fall foliage. The smooth, glossy, blue-green leaves are marked with pink, purple, cream, or white. As temperatures get cooler in fall, the leaves in the center of the rosette become more colorful, until they are only green around the edge. Ornamental kale is very similar, but its leaves are more frilly.

Height and spread Height 12–18 inches (30–45 cm); spread to 18 inches (45 cm).

Best site Full sun to light shade; average, well-drained soil.

Growing guidelines In hot-summer areas, sow seed indoors; elsewhere, sow outdoors in pots or a nursery bed. Plant seed ¼ inch (6 mm) deep in midsummer. Move plants to the garden in fall. Set them in holes 1 foot (30 cm) apart and deep enough to cover the stem up to the lowest set of leaves. If caterpillars damage the leaves, pick them off by hand or spray with BT.

Landscape uses Ornamental cabbage and kale add color to fall flower beds and borders as other annuals are finishing for the season. They are also showy in containers or large window boxes.

Other common names Flowering cabbage.

Browallia speciosa
SOLANACEAE

BROWALLIA

Browallia combines beautifully with other shade-lovers, such as wax begonias, hostas, and ferns. For best growth, mulch to keep the soil moist and water during dry spells.

Description This tender perennial is usually grown as a tender annual. The bushy plants have lance-shaped, green leaves and 2-inch (5-cm) wide, starry flowers. The purple, blue, or white flowers bloom from summer until frost.

Height and spread Height and spread usually 8–18 inches (20–45 cm), depending on the cultivar.

Best site Partial shade; average to moist soil with added organic matter.

Growing guidelines Buy plants in spring, or start your own by planting seed indoors 8 weeks before your last frost date. Lightly press the seed into the soil. Enclose the pot in a plastic bag until seedlings appear. Set plants out after the last frost. Space tall cultivars 18 inches (45 cm) apart; allow only 10–12 inches (25–30 cm) between compact types. Pinch off the stem tips of young plants once or twice to promote compact, branching growth. For winter bloom, dig up plants before frost, pot them up, and bring them indoors.

Landscape uses Browallia's star-shaped flowers brighten up shady beds and borders, hanging baskets, window boxes, and container gardens.

Other common names Sapphire flower.

Calendula officinalis
ASTERACEAE

POT MARIGOLD

Pot marigolds make a brilliant display in the garden. After the first flush of blooms, shear off the spent flowers to promote later rebloom, or deadhead individual flowers regularly.

Description Easy-to-grow hardy annual. The clumps of lance-shaped aromatic leaves are topped with single or double, daisy-type flowers in orange or yellow. The yellow- or brown-centered, 2–4-inch (5–10-cm) wide flowers tend to close during cloudy weather and at night. Pot marigolds bloom from summer to fall in most areas. In hot-summer areas, grow them for late-winter to late-spring color.
Height and spread Height 12–24 inches (30–60 cm); spread to 12 inches (30 cm).
Best site Full sun; average, well-drained soil.
Growing guidelines For summer and fall bloom, sow seed indoors 6–8 weeks before your last frost date or outdoors in early to late spring. Set plants out around the last frost date. In hot-summer areas, sow seed directly into the garden in midfall for late-winter bloom. Plant seed ¼ inch (6 mm) deep. Space plants to stand 8–12 inches (20–30 cm) apart. Pot marigolds may self-sow if you let some seeds form.
Landscape uses Pot marigolds are sunny accents for flower beds, borders, and containers. The strong-stemmed blooms are excellent as cut flowers.
Other common names Calendula.

Callistephus chinensis
ASTERACEAE

CHINA ASTER

China asters bloom from late summer to frost in white, cream, pink, red, purple, or blue. To minimize disease problems, plant them in a different spot each year.

Description This tender annual is grown for its showy blooms. The stems carry toothed, green leaves and are topped with daisy-type or puffy, single or double flowers up to 5 inches (12.5 cm) wide.
Height and spread Height 12–24 inches (30–60 cm); spread 12–18 inches (30–45 cm).
Best site Full sun; average, well-drained soil with added organic matter.
Growing guidelines For late-summer bloom, buy transplants in spring or sow seed indoors, ⅛ inch (3 mm) deep, 6 weeks before your last frost date. Set plants out 12 weeks after the last frost date, when the weather is warm. For fall bloom, sow seed directly into the garden after the last frost date. Pinch off stem tips once in early summer to promote branching. Stake tall cultivars. Control aphids with soap sprays to prevent the spread of aster yellows, which causes yellowed, stunted growth; destroy infected plants. Aster wilt is a soilborne disease that causes plants to droop; destroy infected plants.
Landscape uses Grow in masses or mix with other plants in beds, borders, and planters for late-season color. Grow a few in the cutting garden, too.

Campanula medium
CAMPANULACEAE

CANTERBURY BELLS

Plan ahead for next year's flowers by starting seed during the summer, or buy overwintered container-grown plants in spring for blooms the same year.

Description Canterbury bells form leafy rosettes of toothed, lance-shaped leaves during their first year. In the second year, they send up slender stalks topped with loose spikes of bell-shaped blooms in white, pink, or purple-blue. The spring to early-summer flowers may be single or surrounded by a larger, colored cup.
Height and spread Height 18–36 inches (45–90 cm); spread 12 inches (30 cm).
Best site Full sun; average, well-drained soil.
Growing guidelines Sow seed outdoors in summer in pots or a nursery bed. Cover the seed lightly and keep the soil moist until seedlings appear. Move plants to their flowering positions in fall or early spring. Space out plants 12 inches (30 cm) apart. Pinch off spent blooms to extend the flowering time. Pull out plants that have finished blooming.
Landscape uses Canterbury bells are naturals for cottage gardens. In beds and borders, grow them in small clumps with later-blooming annuals and perennials that can fill in the space left when you remove spent plants in midsummer. Try them in containers and cutting gardens, too.

Catharanthus roseus
APOCYNACEAE

MADAGASCAR PERIWINKLE

In most areas, Madagascar periwinkle blooms from early summer until frost; it can flower nearly any time of the year in frost-free climates. Try it in pots and planters.

Description A tender perennial that is commonly grown as a tender annual, Madagascar periwinkle forms compact, bushy clumps of glossy, dark green leaves with white central veins. Stems are topped with flat, five-petaled, white, rose, or pink flowers up to 2 inches (5 cm) wide.
Height and spread Height and spread usually 12–18 inches (30–45 cm); larger in frost-free areas.
Best site Full sun; average, well-drained soil. Tolerates heat, pollution, and drought.
Growing guidelines For best results, buy transplants in spring; it grows slowly from seed. If you want to try raising your own, sow seed ¼ inch (6 mm) deep indoors 10–12 weeks before your last frost date. Keep pots in an especially warm place (75–80°F [24–27°C]) until seedlings appear, then move pots to regular room temperature. Set transplants out 12 weeks after the last frost date, when the soil is warm. Pinch off stem tips in early summer for compact growth and more flowers.
Landscape uses This is a beautiful, easy-care annual for edging flower beds, borders, and walkways.
Other common names Rosy periwinkle, vinca.

Celosia cristata
AMARANTHACEAE

CELOSIA

Celosia has showy, feathery flower spikes. Pinching off the stem tips in early summer will promote branching and encourage more numerous, smaller flower plumes.

Description These tender perennials are grown as tender annuals. Their sturdy stems carry oval to narrow, pointed leaves that are green or tinted with bronze. The flowers can bloom all summer until frost in shades of fiery red, pink, orange, or yellow.
Height and spread Height 12–24 inches (30–60 cm); spread to 12 inches (30 cm). Height and spread can vary widely, depending on the cultivar.
Best site Full sun; average, well-drained soil with added organic matter.
Growing guidelines Celosias can be tricky to get started but are easy once established. If plants are disturbed during transplanting, later growth may be slow and stunted. Sow seed directly into the garden after the last frost date or buy small transplants. Or sow seed indoors 4 weeks before your last frost date in individual pots. Set transplants out 12 weeks after the last frost date, when the soil is warm.
Landscape uses Grow in groups or masses to best show off the unusual flowers. Use compact types to edge beds and walkways and to accent container gardens and window boxes.
Other common names Cockscomb, plumed celosia.

Centaurea cyanus
ASTERACEAE

CORNFLOWER

Stick brushy prunings into the ground around young cornflower plants to support the stems as they grow. Pinching off spent blooms can prolong the flowering season.

Description This is a dependable, easy-care, hardy annual. The bushy plants have narrow, lance-shaped, silvery green leaves and thin stems topped with fluffy flower heads. The 1–2-inch (2.5–5-cm) flowers bloom through the summer in white or shades of blue, purple, pink, or red.
Height and spread Height 12–30 inches (30–75 cm); spread to 12 inches (30 cm).
Best site Full sun, but tolerates partial shade; average, well-drained soil.
Growing guidelines Grows easily from seed sown directly into the garden in early fall (in mild-winter areas) or early spring. Plant seed ⅛ inch (3 mm) deep. To extend the flowering season from an early-spring planting, sow again every 2–4 weeks until midsummer. Other ways to establish cornflowers include buying transplants in spring or starting the seed indoors about 8 weeks before your last frost date. Set plants outdoors about 2 weeks before the last frost date. Cornflowers will self-sow if you leave a few flowers to set seed.
Landscape uses Cornflowers are charming in meadow gardens and flower beds. They are also excellent cut flowers.
Other common names Bachelor's buttons.

Cleome hasslerana
CAPPARIDACEAE

CLEOME

Cleome is a must for butterfly-attracting gardens; it's also popular with bees. Plant it in large groupings to show off the spidery white, pink, or rosy lavender flowers.

Description Cleome is a fast-growing half-hardy annual. Its tall, sturdy stems and palm-like leaves are slightly sticky and have a musky (some say skunk-like) odor. Small spines form on the stems and on the undersides of the leaves. From midsummer until midfall, the stems are topped with globes of white, pink, or rosy lavender flowers. Long stamens protrude from the flowers, giving a spidery look. The blooms are followed by long, narrow seedpods.
Height and spread Height 3–4 feet (90–120 cm); spread 18 inches (45 cm).
Best site Full sun to light shade; average, well-drained soil with added compost.
Growing guidelines Easy to grow from seed sown directly in the garden in mid- to late spring. For earlier bloom, buy transplants or start your own by sowing seed indoors about 4 weeks before your last frost date. Lightly press the seed into the surface, then enclose the pot in a plastic bag until seedlings appear. Set plants out around the last frost date.
Landscape uses Try cleome in the back of flower beds and borders. Its pretty, delicate blooms look particularly nice in cottage gardens.
Other common names Spider flower.

Cobaea scandens
POLEMONIACEAE

CUP AND SAUCER VINE

The bell-shaped flowers of cup and saucer vine are light green when they first open, and then they age to purple or white. The mature flowers have a sweet, honey-like fragrance.

Description This vigorous, tender perennial climber is grown as a half-hardy annual. It has compound leaves, as well as tendrils that help the stems climb. From late summer until frost, inflated buds on long stalks open to 2-inch (5-cm) long, bell-shaped flowers. Short, green, petal-like bracts surround the base of each bell.
Height and spread Vines can grow to 10 feet (3 m) or more; ultimate height and width depends on the size of the support.
Best site Full sun (or afternoon shade in hot-summer areas); average to moist, well-drained soil with added organic matter.
Growing guidelines Make sure you have a sturdy support for the vines to climb on. Sow seed indoors 8–10 weeks before your last frost date. Soak the flat seeds in warm water overnight, then plant them on their edge in peat pots. Sow two or three seeds ¼ inch (6 mm) deep in each pot. Once seedlings emerge, clip off extras to leave one per pot. Set plants out 12 inches (30 cm) apart after the last frost date.
Landscape uses This is a super screening plant for quick shade or privacy and a wonderful background for cottage gardens.
Other common names Cathedral bells, Mexican ivy.

Consolida ambigua
RANUNCULACEAE

ROCKET LARKSPUR

Tall cultivars of rocket larkspur may need support to stay upright. Push pieces of twiggy brush into the ground around young plants to hold them up as they grow.

Description This hardy annual is grown for its showy flowers. The plants produce tall stems with finely divided, bright green leaves. Spikes of purple-blue, rose, pink, or white flowers bloom atop the stems from late spring through summer. There is a curving spur on the back of each flower.
Height and spread Height to 1 foot (30 cm) for dwarf types, up to 4 feet (1.2 m) for tall cultivars; spread to 1 foot (30 cm).
Best site Full sun; average, well-drained soil with added organic matter.
Growing guidelines Grows best from seed sown directly into the garden. Plant seed ¼ inch (6 mm) deep in fall or early spring. If you choose to start seedlings indoors, sow seed in individual peat pots 6–8 weeks before your last frost date. Set seedlings out in mid- to late spring. Thin or space plants to stand 8–12 inches (20–30 cm) apart.
Landscape uses Use the spiky flowers to add height and color to flower beds, borders, and cottage gardens. They mix well with perennials and also make great cut flowers.
Other common names Larkspur. It is also listed in seed catalogs as C. *ajacis*, *Delphinium ajacis*, and D. *consolida*.

Convolvulus tricolor
CONVOLVULACEAE

DWARF MORNING GLORY

This compact, easy-to-grow, hardy annual blooms from midsummer through early fall. The cultivar 'Royal Ensign' has rich blue flowers with a white-and-yellow center.

Description Plants form bushy, spreading mounds of oval to narrow green leaves that are topped with showy, trumpet-shaped blooms. The 1½-inch (3.7-cm) wide flowers are deep purple-blue on the outside, with a starry white center and a bright yellow throat.

Height and spread Height to 12 inches (30 cm); spread 8–18 inches (20–45 cm).

Best site Full sun is best, although these plants can take some shade; average, well-drained soil.

Growing guidelines For earliest flowering, sow seed indoors 6 weeks before your last frost date. Soak seed overnight, then plant it ¼ inch (6 mm) deep in individual peat pots. Dwarf morning glory also grows easily from seed sown directly into the garden after the last frost date. Set transplants or thin seedlings to stand 8 inches (20 cm) apart. Stick short pieces of twiggy brush around the young plants to support the stems. Water during dry spells. Pinch off spent flowers to prolong the bloom season.

Landscape uses Grow near the front of flower beds and borders or in container gardens. It looks especially charming cascading out of window boxes and hanging baskets.

Coreopsis tinctoria
ASTERACEAE

CALLIOPSIS

Calliopsis grows easily from direct-sown seed and needs little fussing. Shearing the plants back by one-third in mid- to late summer can prolong the bloom season.

Description Calliopsis is a colorful, fast-growing, and hardy annual. Its wiry stems carry narrow green leaves and 1–2-inch (2.5–5-cm) wide, single or double, daisy-type flowers. The flowers are usually golden yellow with maroon centers but may also be all yellow or all orange. Plants can bloom from midsummer until frost.

Height and spread Height 2–3 feet (60–90 cm), depending on the cultivar; spread to 12 inches (30 cm).

Best site Full sun; average, well-drained soil. Adapts well to poor soil.

Growing guidelines Calliopsis grows quickly from seed sown directly into the garden in early to midspring. You can also sow seed ⅛ inch (3 mm) deep indoors about 6 weeks before your last frost date. Set these plants out around the last frost date. Space transplants or thin seedlings to stand about 8 inches (20 cm) apart. Push twiggy brush into the soil around young plants of tall-growing cultivars to support the stems as they grow.

Landscape uses Depend on calliopsis for adding fast, easy-care color to beds and borders. It also looks wonderful in meadow gardens. Grow some in the cutting garden for fresh arrangements.

Cosmos bipinnatus
ASTERACEAE

COSMOS

Use fast-growing cosmos to fill spaces left by early-blooming annuals and perennials. Pinch off spent flowers to encourage more bloom; leave a few to self-sow.

Description These popular half-hardy annuals are grown for their colorful blooms. The bushy plants bear many finely cut, green leaves. In late summer and fall, the stems are topped with white, pink, or rosy red flowers. The single or semidouble, daisy-type blooms can grow up to 4 inches (10 cm) across.

Height and spread Height 3–4 feet (90–120 cm); spread to 18 inches (45 cm).

Best site Full sun is best, although plants can take partial shade; average to moist, well-drained soil.

Growing guidelines For earliest blooms, buy transplants in spring or start seed indoors 3–4 weeks before your last frost date. Plant seed ¼ inch (6 mm) deep. Set plants out 12 weeks after the last frost date. You can also sow seed directly into the garden around the last frost date. Pinch off stem tips in early summer to promote branching and more flowers.

Landscape uses Cosmos adds height and color to flower beds, borders, and meadows. It looks great in cottage gardens. Grow a few in the cutting garden for arrangements.

Cosmos sulphureus
ASTERACEAE

YELLOW COSMOS

Yellow cosmos is generally trouble-free throughout the growing season. Add it to the cutting garden; the colorful blooms lend a cheerful touch to fresh arrangements.

Description Yellow cosmos is a half-hardy annual that forms bushy mounds of deeply lobed, dark green leaves. The thin stems carry showy, single or semidouble, daisy-type flowers from late summer until frost. The yellow, orange, or red blooms are 1–2 inches (2.5–5 cm) wide.

Height and spread Height 24–36 inches (60–90 cm); spread to 18 inches (45 cm).

Best site Full sun; average, well-drained soil.

Growing guidelines To get the earliest flowers, start seed indoors 4–6 weeks before your last frost date. Plant seed ¼ inch (6 mm) deep. Set plants out after the last frost date. Yellow cosmos also grows easily from seed sown directly into the garden around the last frost date. Set plants or thin seedlings to about 12 inches (30 cm) apart. Pinching off spent flowers can prolong the bloom season. If you leave a few flowers to mature at the end of the season, plants will self-sow.

Landscape uses Yellow cosmos is good for bright late-season color in flower beds, borders, and container gardens. The bushy plants make great fillers in spaces left by spring-blooming annuals and perennials.

Other common names Klondike cosmos.

Dianthus barbatus
CARYOPHYLLACEAE

SWEET WILLIAM

Sweet Williams may rebloom the following year if you shear them back after flowering, but you'll generally get a better show by starting new plants each year.

Description This short-lived perennial is grown as a hardy biennial or annual. It forms clumps of narrow, lance-shaped, green leaves and the stems are topped with dense, slightly rounded clusters of five-petaled flowers in early to midsummer. Each bloom is ¼–½ inch (6–12 mm) wide and fragrant. Red, pink, and white are the most common colors; some flowers have eyes, or zones of contrasting colors.

Height and spread Height 12–18 inches (30–45 cm); spread 8–12 inches (20–30 cm).

Best site Full sun to partial shade; average, well-drained soil.

Growing guidelines For earliest bloom, grow as a biennial. Sow seed outdoors in pots or in a nursery bed in summer, then move plants to their garden position in fall. For bloom the same year, sow seed indoors (just barely covering it) about 8 weeks before your last frost date. Set plants out 2–3 weeks before the last frost date. Space transplants 8–10 inches (20–25 cm) apart. Sweet William will self-sow if you leave a few flowers to form seeds.

Landscape uses Sweet William looks super as an early-summer filler for beds and borders. It is ideal for fresh arrangements.

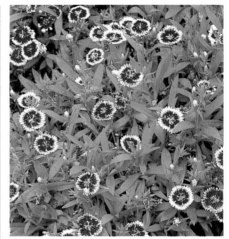

Dianthus chinensis
CARYOPHYLLACEAE

CHINA PINK

China pinks look equally lovely in beds, borders, and container plantings. Pinching off spent flowers can be time-consuming, but it will prolong the bloom season.

Description This biennial or short-lived perennial is usually grown as an annual. Plants form tufts of narrow, green leaves. The upright stems bear 1-inch (2.5-cm) wide, flat flowers with broad petals that are fringed at the tips. The white, pink, or red flowers bloom through the summer. China pinks have also been hybridized to produce more colorful and larger flowers over a longer season.

Height and spread Height 8–12 inches (20–30 cm); similar spread.

Best site Full sun (afternoon shade is needed in hot-summer areas); average, well-drained soil.

Growing guidelines Buy plants in spring, or start seed indoors (just barely cover it) 6–8 weeks before your last frost date. You can also sow seed directly into the garden 2–3 weeks before the last frost date. Thin seedlings or set transplants to stand 6–8 inches (15–20 cm) apart.

Landscape uses China pinks are a natural choice for cottage gardens. They also make colorful edging plants for flower beds and walkways. Try growing a few in container gardens, too.

Other common names Rainbow pink.

Digitalis purpurea
SCROPHULARIACEAE

COMMON FOXGLOVE

Cut down the spent flower stems of common foxgloves after bloom to keep the garden tidy, or allow the seeds (which add interest to the fall garden) to form so plants can self-sow.

Description This beautiful biennial or short-lived perennial is grown for its showy blooms. During the first year, plants form mounds of velvety, grayish green leaves. In early to midsummer of the following year, the rosettes send up long, graceful spikes topped with thimble-shaped flowers. The 2–3-inch (5–7.5-cm) blooms may be white, cream, pink, or pinkish purple and often have contrasting spots on the inside.

Height and spread Height 3–5 feet (90–150 cm); spread to 2 feet (60 cm).

Best site Full sun to partial shade (afternoon shade in hot-summer areas); average, well-drained soil with added organic matter.

Growing guidelines Grow most foxgloves as biennials by sowing outdoors in pots or in a nursery bed in late summer. Sow the seed on the soil surface, press it in lightly, and keep the soil moist until seedlings appear. Move plants to their position in the garden in fall. Space them about 12 inches (30 cm) apart. Tall cultivars may need staking.

Landscape uses Grow them in the back of borders, where other plants will fill the space left in midsummer. They look super in masses in lightly shaded woodlands.

Erysimum cheiri
BRASSICACEAE

WALLFLOWER

The fragrant blooms of wallflowers are normally orange or yellow, but they also bloom in shades of red, pink, or creamy white. The flowers are ideal for spring arrangements.

Description This perennial is commonly grown as a half-hardy annual or biennial. The bushy clumps of slender green leaves are topped with clusters of 1-inch (2.5-cm) wide four-petaled flowers from midspring to early summer.

Height and spread Height 12–24 inches (30–60 cm); spread to 12 inches (30 cm).

Best site Full sun to partial shade; average to moist, well-drained soil, ideally with a neutral to slightly alkaline pH.

Growing guidelines Sow outdoors in early spring or indoors about 8 weeks before your last frost date. Plant seed ¼ inch (6 mm) deep. Set plants 8–12 inches (20–30 cm) apart around the last frost date. In frost-free areas, grow wallflowers as biennials. Sow seed in pots or in a nursery bed in early summer; move plants to their flowering position in early fall. Water during dry spells to keep the soil evenly moist. Pull out and compost plants when they have finished blooming.

Landscape uses Grow in masses or in flower beds for spots of early color. One classic combination is orange wallflowers underplanted with blue forget-me-nots (*Myosotis sylvatica*). Wallflowers also combine beautifully with tulips.

Eschscholzia californica
PAPAVERACEAE

CALIFORNIA POPPY

The cup-shaped flowers of California poppy open during sunny days but close in cloudy weather and at night. Pinch off developing seedpods to prolong the bloom season.

Description This tender perennial is usually grown as a hardy annual. Plants form loose clumps of deeply cut, blue-green leaves. The thin stems are topped with pointed buds that unfurl into single, semi-double, or double flowers up to 3 inches (7.5 cm) across in early summer through early fall. The silky-looking petals are usually orange or yellow, but they can also bloom in white, pink, or red.

Height and spread Height 12–18 inches (30–45 cm); spread 6–12 inches (15–30 cm).

Best site Full sun; average to sandy, well-drained soil.

Growing guidelines They transplant poorly, so it's usually not worth starting seed indoors. Plants will grow quickly from seed sown directly into the garden in very early spring (or even in fall in frost-free areas). Scatter the seed over the soil surface and rake it in lightly. Thin the seedlings to stand 6 inches (15 cm) apart. If blooms are sparse by midsummer, cut plants back by about one-third to promote a new flush of flowers. Plants usually self-sow in mild-winter areas.

Landscape uses Grow as fillers for flower beds and borders and in meadow gardens.

Euphorbia marginata
EUPHORBIACEAE

SNOW ON THE MOUNTAIN

Shrubby snow on the mountain forms showy clumps of white-marked leaves by late summer. Use this old-fashioned favorite as a filler or accent plant in beds and borders.

Description This half-hardy annual is grown for its showy foliage. In mid- to late summer, the upright stems begin to branch more, and the leaves produced on the upper parts of the branches are edged with white. At the branch tips, clusters of tiny flowers are surrounded by white-edged, petal-like bracts.

Height and spread Height 2–4 feet (60–120 cm); spread 12–18 inches (30–45 cm).

Best site Full sun; average, well-drained soil.

Growing guidelines For earliest color, start seed ½ inch (12 mm) deep indoors 4–6 weeks before your last frost date. After the last frost date, set plants out or sow seed directly into the garden. Thin seedlings or space out transplants to stand 12 inches (30 cm) apart. Stake plants in early to midsummer, while they're still young. Plants often self-sow.

Landscape uses Use as a shrubby filler or accent in flower beds and borders. The showy leaves are especially nice in arrangements, so include a few in the cutting garden. Handle cut stems carefully, though; they will leak a milky sap that can irritate your skin, eyes, and mouth.

Eustoma grandiflorum
GENTIANACEAE

PRAIRIE GENTIAN

Prairie gentian looks lovely planted in masses with shrubs or alone in a container. The gorgeous blooms can last several weeks in fresh arrangements.

Description This beautiful but slow-growing biennial is generally grown as a half-hardy annual. Its slender, upright stems carry oblong, gray-green leaves and are topped with pointed buds. The buds unfurl to produce long-lasting, single or double flowers that resemble poppies or roses. The 2–3-inch (5–7.5-cm) flowers bloom in white and shades of cream, pink, rose, and purple-blue.

Height and spread Height 12–24 inches (30–60 cm); spread to 12 inches (30 cm).

Best site Full sun to partial shade; average, well-drained soil.

Growing guidelines For quickest results, buy transplants in spring. If you want to try raising your own, sow them indoors in January. Scatter the seed over the pot surface, press it lightly into the soil, and enclose the pot in a plastic bag until seedlings appear. Set transplants out 12 weeks after the last frost. Space them about 6 inches (15 cm) apart in clumps of three or more plants. Pinching off stem tips once or twice in early summer will promote branching and more blooms. Remove spent blooms to prolong flowering.

Landscape uses An elegant addition to any flower bed or border.

Gaillardia pulchella
ASTERACEAE

BLANKET FLOWER

Blanket flower blooms are often orange-red with yellow tips, but they may also be red, yellow, or orange around a reddish purple center. They provide vivid color all summer long.

Description Blanket flower is a fast-growing hardy annual. Plants produce clumps of gray-green leaves highlighted all summer by bright flowers. The single or double, daisy-type blooms may be up to 3 inches (7.5 cm) wide, with toothed petals that give them a fringed appearance.

Height and spread Height 12–24 inches (30–60 cm); similar spread.

Best site Full sun; average, well-drained to dry soil. Blanket flowers are heat- and drought-tolerant.

Growing guidelines In most areas, you'll get best results by sowing seed directly into the garden. Plant seed ⅛ inch (3 mm) deep in spring around your last frost date (or even in fall in mild-winter areas). If your summers are short and cool, get an early start by sowing seed indoors 4–6 weeks before the last frost date. Space transplants or thin seedlings to stand about 12 inches (30 cm) apart. Stick short pieces of twiggy brush into the ground around young plants to support the stems. Pinch off the spent blooms to prolong the flowering season. Plants will self-sow if flowers set seed.

Landscape uses Blanket flowers add loads of summer color to flower beds and borders. Grow a few in the cutting garden.

Gazania hybrids
ASTERACEAE

TREASURE FLOWER

Treasure flowers usually bloom in red, orange, or yellow but can also be pink, purplish, or white. They tend to close up at night and also during cloudy weather.

Description This eye-catching tender perennial is grown as a half-hardy annual. Plants form low mats of green leaves that are silvery underneath. From midsummer until the first frost, plants are topped with brilliantly colored daisy-type flowers to 3 inches (7.5) across. The petals may have a contrasting center stripe and usually have a dark brown or green spot at the base.

Height and spread Height 8–12 inches (20–30 cm); spread to 12 inches (30 cm).

Best site Full sun; average, well-drained soil.

Growing guidelines For earliest bloom, buy transplants or start seed indoors 6–8 weeks before your last frost date. Plant seed ⅛ inch (3 mm) deep. Set transplants out after the last frost date. Or sow seed directly into the garden 12 weeks after the last frost date for late-summer bloom. Thin seedlings to 8 inches (20 cm) apart. Pinch off spent flowers to prolong the bloom season. Dig up a few plants before frost and bring them indoors for winter bloom.

Landscape uses Treasure flower adds an explosion of color to beds and borders. Use it as an edging plant, or grow it in masses for an eye-opening annual groundcover. Try a few in containers, too.

Gomphrena globosa
AMARANTHACEAE

GLOBE AMARANTH

Globe amaranth is generally trouble-free. Grow it in the cutting garden for use in fresh or dried arrangements; try the compact cultivars as edgings or in containers.

Description This tender annual is grown for its long-lasting flower heads. Tiny, yellow flowers peek out from between layers of colorful, papery bracts that make up the clover-like flower heads. The magenta, pink, or creamy white, 1-inch (2.5-cm) wide flower heads bloom from midsummer until frost.

Height and spread Height 8–18 inches (20–45 cm); spread 8–12 inches (20–30 cm).

Best site Full sun; average, well-drained to dry soil.

Growing guidelines Buy transplants in spring, or start your own by sowing seed indoors 4–6 weeks before your last frost date. Plant the seed ⅛–¼ inch (3–6 mm) deep. Place in a warm place (about 75°F [24°C]) until seedlings appear; then move them back to normal room temperature. Set transplants out 2–3 weeks after the last frost date. You can also sow seed directly into the garden after the last frost date, when the soil is warm. Space transplants to stand 8–10 inches (20–25 cm) apart.

Landscape uses Tuck a few plants into beds and borders for a colorful accent. The flower heads keep their color well after being air-dried.

Gypsophila elegans
CARYOPHYLLACEAE

ANNUAL BABY'S BREATH

Sowing seed of annual baby's breath every few weeks from early to late spring can extend the bloom season well into summer. Pull out plants that have finished flowering.

Description This hardy annual is grown for its airy sprays of dainty flowers. Plants form loose clumps of slender stems with pairs of narrow, gray-green leaves. Loose clusters of many five-petaled flowers bloom atop the stems for as long as 2 months in spring and early summer. The ¼–½-inch (6–12-mm) wide flowers are usually white or light pink; some cultivars have deeper pink flowers.

Height and spread Height 18–24 inches (45–60 cm); spread 6–12 inches (15–30 cm).

Best site Full sun (afternoon shade in hot areas); average, well-drained soil.

Growing guidelines Plant seed directly into the garden where you want plants to grow; cover it with ⅛ inch (3 mm) of soil. Sow seed in early spring (or in fall in mild-winter areas). Thin seedlings to stand 6 inches (15 cm) apart. Push twiggy brush into the soil around the young plants to support the stems as they grow.

Landscape uses Makes a nice filler for flower beds and borders. It looks especially charming planted in masses with other cool-loving annuals, such as rocket larkspur (*Consolida ambigua*) and sweet peas (*Lathyrus odoratus*).

Helianthus annuus
ASTERACEAE

COMMON SUNFLOWER

Common sunflowers are much-loved hardy annuals grown for their large, showy blooms (and often for their tasty seeds as well). Tall cultivars will usually need staking.

Description This easy-to-grow plant produces large, sturdy stalks with coarse, heart-shaped leaves. From midsummer through midfall, the stems are topped with flat, daisy-type flower heads to 12 inches (30 cm) wide or more. The flower heads normally have a purple-brown center, with bright yellow, bronze, mahogany red, or orange petals.
Height and spread Height 2–8 feet (60–240 cm) or more; spread 12–18 inches (30–45 cm).
Best site Thrives in full sun; needs average, well-drained soil.
Growing guidelines Common sunflowers grow so quickly that it's easiest to sow seed directly into the garden after your last frost date. Plant seed ½ inch (12 mm) deep. Thin seedlings to stand 12 inches (30 cm) apart. Unless you're growing plants for the edible seeds, remove spent flowers to prolong the bloom season.
Landscape uses Sunflowers tend to drop their leaves along the bottom half of their stem, so place them in the middle or back of the border where other plants will hide their bare ankles. Small-flowered types are excellent as cut flowers. Plant seed-producing types in the vegetable garden.

Helichrysum petiolatum
ASTERACEAE

LICORICE PLANT

Licorice plant has soft, silvery leaves that complement both pale pastels and bold, bright hues. It's a perfect choice for cascading over the edges of borders, banks, and containers.

Description Licorice plant has a shrubby form that's partly upright and partly trailing. The woody stems carry oval, felted, white-green-gray foliage. Small, yellow-white blooms may appear. Licorice plant is generally grown as an annual, since it is winter-hardy only south of Zone 9.
Height and spread Height to 2 feet (60 cm); spread to 4 feet (1.2 m).
Best site Full sun, though well-adapted to shade and tolerates dry conditions; sandy, well-drained soil.
Growing guidelines Sow seed indoors or outdoors in late spring or early summer. Take cuttings during the growing season. When planting, space the plants well to allow for spread. Allow the soil to dry somewhat between waterings. Pinch off the shoot tips every few weeks to encourage bushy growth and to avoid the stems becoming leggy. This plant makes a good summer container plant in cold climates; bring it indoors for overwintering.
Landscape uses Licorice plant combines well with almost any colorful companion. It's especially good with dark-leaved plants, such as 'Palace Purple' heuchera (*Heuchera micrantha* var. *diversifolia*). Use in flower beds, on slopes, or in containers.

Heliotropium arborescens
BORAGINACEAE

COMMON HELIOTROPE

The violet, purple-blue, or white flowers of common heliotrope may have a vanilla- or cherry-like scent. Sniff the flowers before you buy to find the most fragrant ones.

Description This tender perennial is usually grown as a tender annual. Plants produce shrubby clumps of sturdy stems and hairy, deep to medium green, heavily veined, oval leaves. Clusters of ¼-inch (6-mm) wide, tubular flowers bloom atop the stems from summer until frost.
Height and spread Height usually 24–36 inches (60–90 cm); spread 12–24 inches (30–60 cm).
Best site Full sun (or afternoon shade in hot-summer climates); average, well-drained soil with added organic matter.
Growing guidelines Easiest to start from nursery-grown or overwintered plants. If you want to grow your own, sow seed indoors 10–12 weeks before your last frost date. Seed may take several weeks to germinate. Set plants out about 12 inches (30 cm) apart, 2–3 weeks after the last frost date. Pinch off the stem tips in early summer to promote branching and more flowers. Remove spent flower clusters. To overwinter plants, cut them back, then dig and pot them up before the first fall frost; or take stem cuttings in late summer.
Landscape uses Grow in flower beds and borders or containers.
Other common names Cherry pie.

Iberis umbellata
BRASSICACEAE

ANNUAL CANDYTUFT

Annual candytuft needs little care and tends to self-sow. In hot-summer areas, pull out plants after bloom and replace them with summer- to fall-blooming annuals.

Description This dependable, hardy annual forms mounds of narrow, green leaves on many-branched stems. The mounds are covered with dense, slightly rounded flower clusters approximately 2 inches (5 cm) across from late spring through midsummer. Each cluster contains many ¼–½-inch (6–12-mm) wide, four-petaled blooms. Flowers may be white, pink, pinkish purple, rose, or red.
Height and spread Height 8–12 inches (20–30 cm); spread 8–10 inches (20–25 cm).
Best site Full sun to partial shade; average, well-drained soil.
Growing guidelines To have the earliest flowers, sow seed indoors 6–8 weeks before your last frost date. Plant seed ¼ inch (6 mm) deep. Set plants out around the last frost date. Annual candytuft also grows easily from seed sown directly into the garden. Make the first sowing in early to midspring, sowing again every 3–4 weeks. Thin seedlings or space plants to stand 6–8 inches (15–20 cm) apart.
Landscape uses Annual candytuft makes a colorful edging or filler for flower beds and borders.
Other common names Globe candytuft.

Impatiens balsamina
BALSAMINACEAE

GARDEN BALSAM

The bright flowers of garden balsam bloom near the tops of the stems, among the lance-shaped, green leaves. This old-fashioned favorite can grow in sun if the soil is moist.

Description This tender annual has a bushy, upright habit. The 1–2-inch (2.5–5-cm) wide, single or double flowers bloom from midsummer until frost, usually in white or shades of pink, purple-pink, rose, or red.
Height and spread Height 24–30 inches (60–75 cm); spread to 18 inches (45 cm).
Best site Full sun to partial shade; average to moist, well-drained soil with added organic matter.
Growing guidelines Garden balsam is sometimes sold as transplants. To grow your own, sow seed indoors 6–8 weeks before your last frost date. Press the seed lightly into the soil surface and enclose the pot in a plastic bag until seedlings appear. Set plants out 12 weeks after the last frost date. Or sow seed directly into the garden after the last frost date; plant ⅛ inch (3 mm) deep and keep the soil moist until seedlings appear. Space transplants 12–16 inches (30–40 cm) apart. Water during dry spells. Plants often self-sow.
Landscape uses The lovely flowers and foliage of garden balsam add height and color to shady beds and borders. For the best show, set out three or more plants in each area to form lush clumps.

Impatiens New Guinea hybrids
BALSAMINACEAE

NEW GUINEA IMPATIENS

If you want a particular flower or leaf color, buy New Guinea impatiens as plants in spring. You can also grow plants from cuttings, or start certain types from seed.

Description These tender perennials are usually grown as tender annuals. The bushy plants have large, pointed, green or reddish bronze leaves; the leaves are sometimes striped with pink, red, or yellow. Vibrant pink, red, orange, purple, or white flowers to 3 inches (7.5 cm) across bloom atop the plants from June until frost.
Height and spread Height 12–24 inches (30–60 cm); spread 12–18 inches (30–45 cm).
Best site Full sun to partial shade; average to moist, well-drained soil with added organic matter.
Growing guidelines Most New Guinea impatiens are grown from cuttings, so you can buy plants with the colors you like best in spring. Some are available from seed; sow indoors (just barely cover with soil) 6–8 weeks before your last frost date. Set plants out 12–18 inches (30–45 cm) apart 12 weeks after your last frost date. They may be difficult to overwinter indoors, but try taking stem cuttings in summer. Pot up rooted cuttings and keep them in a sunny window until the following spring.
Landscape uses Enjoy the showy leaves and jewel-like flowers in beds, borders, and containers.

Impatiens wallerana
BALSAMINACEAE

IMPATIENS

A mixed planting of impatiens makes a colorful annual groundcover under trees and shrubs. For good growth, they need moist soil; mulch and water them during dry spells.

Description Plants form neat, shrubby mounds of well-branched, succulent stems; the lance-shaped, green or bronze-brown leaves have slightly scalloped edges. The plants are covered with flat, spurred flowers up to 2 inches (5 cm) wide from late spring until frost. The single or double blooms may come in white, pink, red, orange, or lavender; some have an eye, or swirls of contrasting colors.

Height and spread Height 6–24 inches (15–60 cm); similar spread.

Best site Shade; average to moist, well-drained soil with added organic matter.

Growing guidelines Buy transplants in spring or sow seed indoors 8–10 weeks before your last frost date. Don't cover the seed; just press it lightly into the soil surface. Enclose the pot in a plastic bag and store it in a warm place until the seedlings appear. Young seedlings tend to grow slowly. Set transplants out about 2 weeks after your last frost date.

Landscape uses Impatiens are the stars of shady gardens. Mix them with other annuals and perennials in beds and borders, or grow them alone in masses under trees.

Other common names Busy Lizzie, patient Lucy, patience, sultana.

Ipomoea alba
CONVOLVULACEAE

MOONFLOWER

Before planting moonflowers, set up some kind of support, such as vertical wires or a trellis. Other than watering during dry spells, the plants need little care.

Description This tender perennial vine is usually grown as a tender annual. The twining stems produce funnel-shaped to flat, white blooms up to 6 inches (15 cm) across. The fragrant summer flowers open in the evening and may stay open through the next morning.

Height and spread Height to 10 feet (3 m) or more; ultimate height and spread depend on the size of the vine's support.

Best site Full sun; well-drained soil.

Growing guidelines For earliest flowers, start seed indoors 4–6 weeks before your last frost date. Soak seed in warm water overnight, then plant it 1 inch (2.5 cm) deep in peat pots (two or three seeds per pot). When seedlings appear, keep the strongest one in each pot. Set plants out 12 weeks after the last frost date. You could sow seed directly into the garden after the last frost date, when the soil is warm. Set plants to stand 12 inches (30 cm) apart.

Landscape uses Use as a fast-growing screen for shade or privacy. Its night-blooming habit makes it an excellent choice for planting around decks and patios where you sit on summer evenings.

Other names It is also listed in seed catalogs as *Calonyction aculeatum*.

Ipomoea tricolor
CONVOLVULACEAE

MORNING GLORY

Morning glories grow slowly at first, then really take off when the weather heats up in midsummer. Established vines are generally problem-free; they often self-sow freely.

Description A tender perennial vine grown as a tender annual. The pointed buds of this fast-growing climber open in early morning to reveal showy, trumpet-shaped flowers up to 5 inches (12.5 cm) across. Each flower lasts for only a day, but new buds open every day through summer.

Height and spread Height 8 feet (2.4 m) or more; ultimate height and spread depend on the size of the vine's support.

Best site Full sun; well-drained soil.

Growing guidelines Before planting, make sure you have a sturdy trellis for the vines to climb. For earliest flowers, sow seed indoors 4 weeks before your last frost date. Soak seed in warm water overnight, then sow it ½ inch (12 mm) deep in peat pots. Plant two or three seeds in each pot, then thin to one seedling per pot. Set plants out 2 weeks after the last frost date. You can also start morning glories from seed sown directly into the garden after the last frost. Set plants or thin seedlings to stand 8–12 inches (20–30 cm) apart.

Landscape uses Morning glory makes a good quick-growing screen for shade or privacy. It also looks great climbing through large shrubs or roses or on a trellis or wall behind a cottage garden.

Lablab purpureus
PAPILIONACEAE

HYACINTH BEAN

Once established, hyacinth bean is usually trouble-free. It makes an eye-catching garden accent when trained to grow up a trellis or climb a tripod of stakes in a border.

Description This tender perennial climber is grown as a tender annual. The twining stems have pinkish purple or white summer flowers ¾ inch (18 mm) long in spiky clusters. The lightly scented flowers are followed by glossy, purple seedpods.
Height and spread Height to 15 feet (4.5 m) or more; ultimate height and spread depend on the size of the support.
Best site Full sun; well-drained soil.
Growing guidelines Before planting, install a support for the vine to climb. Hyacinth beans grow quickly from seed sown directly in the garden 2 weeks after the last frost date, when the soil is warm. Plant the seed ½ inch (12 mm) deep, with the white eye facing down. Soaking seed in water overnight before planting can help speed up germination. You can get an earlier start in cool-summer areas by sowing indoors 4–6 weeks before your last frost date. Set plants out after the last frost date; space 8–12 inches (20–30 cm) apart.
Landscape uses Use this fast-growing vine to provide quick shade or privacy, or grow it as a backdrop for a flower bed along a wall or arbor.
Other names Hyacinth bean is also sold as *Dolichos lablab* and *Dipogon lablab*.

Lathyrus odoratus
PAPILIONACEAE

SWEET PEA

Dozens of sweet pea cultivars are available in a range of heights and colors. Many modern cultivars aren't very fragrant; check catalog descriptions to find scented types.

Description These old-fashioned hardy annuals are grown for their charming flowers. Plants produce leafy vines with dainty, pea-type flowers to 2 inches (5 cm) long, which bloom on long, slender flower stems from midspring into summer. Flower colors are usually white or bright or pastel shades of pink, red, or purple. The flowers often have crimped or ruffled petals.
Height and spread Height usually 4–6 feet (1.2–1.8 m); spread 6–12 inches (15–30 cm).
Best site Full sun (or afternoon shade in hot-summer areas); loose, evenly moist soil enriched with organic matter.
Growing guidelines Before planting, set up some sort of string or netting trellis for the vines to climb. Start seed indoors 6–8 weeks before your last frost date. Soak seed in warm water overnight, then plant ½ inch (12 mm) deep in peat pots. Set plants out in midspring, after danger of frost, or sow seed directly into the garden in early spring.
Landscape uses Train sweet peas to climb a tripod of stakes as an early-season accent for beds, borders, and cottage gardens. Also include these lovely flowers in the cutting garden.

Limonium sinuatum
PLUMBAGINACEAE

ANNUAL STATICE

Annual statice is a natural for fresh or dried arrangements. To dry it, pick stems when the clusters are about three-quarters open; hang them upside down in a dark, airy place.

Description This biennial or tender perennial is usually grown as a half-hardy annual. Plants form low rosettes of wavy-edged, green leaves that send up sturdy, winged stems in summer. The loosely branched stems are topped with flattened clusters of ¼-inch (6-mm) wide, white flowers, each surrounded by a papery, tubular calyx—the colorful part of the flower head. Annual statice comes in many colors, including white, pink, peach, red, orange, yellow, purple, and blue.
Height and spread Height 12–24 inches (30–60 cm); spread to 12 inches (30 cm).
Best site Needs full sun; average, well-drained soil.
Growing guidelines Buy transplants in spring, or sow seed indoors 6–8 weeks before your last frost date. Plant the seed ¼ inch (6 mm) deep. Move seedlings to individual pots when they have two or three sets of leaves. Plant them in the garden around the last frost date, or sow seed directly into the garden after the last frost date. Space transplants or thin seedlings to stand 8–10 inches (20–25 cm) apart. Established plants need little care.
Landscape uses An attractive filler for flower beds and borders.

Lobelia erinus
CAMPANULACEAE

EDGING LOBELIA

If you grow edging lobelia from seed or buy seedlings in trays, transplant them in clumps (rather than separating them into individual plants) to avoid damaging the stems.

Description This tender perennial is usually grown as a half-hardy annual. Plants form trailing or mounding clumps of slender stems with small, narrow, green leaves. Plants are covered with ½–¾-inch (12–18-mm) wide flowers from late spring until frost. The five-petaled flowers bloom in white and shades of blue, purple, and pinkish red.
Height and spread Height 6–8 inches (15–20 cm); spread 6–10 inches (15–25 cm).
Best site Full sun to partial shade (especially in hot-summer areas); average, well-drained soil with added compost.
Growing guidelines Buy transplants in spring, or start your own by sowing seed indoors 8–10 weeks before your last frost date. Don't cover the seed; just press it lightly into the soil and enclose the pot in a plastic bag until seedlings appear. Set plants out 6–8 inches (15–20 cm) apart after the last frost date. Water during dry spells. Shear plants back by half after each flush of bloom and fertilize for rebloom.
Landscape uses Looks great along the front of beds and borders or as a filler among taller plants. Cascading types make attractive fillers for container gardens.

Lobularia maritima
BRASSICACEAE

SWEET ALYSSUM

Sweet alyssum may stop blooming during summer heat but will start again when cool weather returns. Shear off spent flowers and water thoroughly to promote new growth.

Description Sweet alyssum is a tender perennial grown as a hardy annual. Plants form low mounds of many-branched stems and narrow, green leaves. Domed clusters of many ¼-inch (6-mm) blooms cover plants in summer and fall. The sweetly scented, four-petaled flowers bloom in white and shades of pink and purple.
Height and spread Height 4–8 inches (10–20 cm); spread 10–12 inches (25–30 cm).
Best site Full sun to partial shade (especially in hot-summer areas); average, well-drained soil.
Growing guidelines Buy transplants in spring, or sow seed indoors 6–8 weeks before your last frost date. Just barely cover the seed with soil. Set plants out around the last frost date. It also grows easily from seed sown directly into the garden in mid- to late spring. Space transplants or thin seedlings to stand 6 inches (15 cm) apart.
Landscape uses Grow as an edging or filler in flower beds and borders or as a groundcover under roses and shrubs. It also grows well in container gardens.
Other names Sweet alyssum is also listed in seed catalogs as *Alyssum maritimum*.

Lunaria annua
BRASSICACEAE

HONESTY

Honesty is a hardy biennial grown for its pretty flowers and showy dried seedpods. Leave a few plants in the garden to self-sow; harvest the rest for arrangements.

Description First-year plants form clumps of coarse, heart-shaped, hairy, green leaves. In the second spring, the clumps have elongated clusters of ½-inch (12-mm) wide, four-petaled flowers. The lightly fragrant, purple-pink blooms are followed by flat, circular seedpods with papery outer skins and a satiny white central disk.
Height and spread Height 18–36 inches (45–90 cm) in bloom; spread to 12 inches (30 cm).
Best site Partial shade; average, well-drained soil (added organic matter a plus).
Growing guidelines Buy and set out nursery-grown plants in early spring for bloom the same year, or start your own from seed for bloom next year. Sow the seed directly into the garden, ⅛–¼ inch (3–6 mm) deep, in spring or late summer. Set transplants or thin seedlings to stand about 12 inches (30 cm) apart.
Landscape uses The flowers add color to spring beds and borders. The white-flowered forms look especially nice in woodland gardens. Honesty is also a traditional favorite in cutting gardens for its dried seedpods.
Other common names Money plant, silver dollar.

Malcomia maritima
BRASSICACEAE

VIRGINIA STOCK

Virginia stock can bloom in as little as four weeks from seed sown directly into the garden. Sow every few weeks through midsummer to have flowers from summer until frost.

Description The upright, branching stems of this fast-growing hardy annual carry small, pointed, grayish green leaves. Flat, four-petaled, lightly fragrant flowers bloom in loose clusters atop the stems. The pink, purple, or white flowers are ¼–½ inch (6–12 mm) wide.
Height and spread Height 6–8 inches (15–20 cm); spread to 4 inches (10 cm).
Best site Full sun to partial shade (in hot-summer areas); average, well-drained soil.
Growing guidelines Grows best from seed sown directly in the garden. For the longest bloom season, sow at 3–4 week intervals from early spring through midsummer. (In mild-winter areas, you can sow in fall for even earlier spring bloom.) Rake the seedbed to cover the seed lightly, then keep the soil moist until seedlings appear. Thin seedlings so they stand 3–4 inches (7.5–10 cm) apart. Plants will often self-sow freely.
Landscape uses Virginia stock makes a nice filler or edging annual for flower beds and borders. The flowers are very popular with bees.

Matthiola incana
BRASSICACEAE

COMMON STOCK

The fragrant, single or double flowers of common stock bloom in white and shades of pink, red, yellow, and purple. They are wonderful in the garden or in arrangements.

Description This biennial or short-lived perennial is usually grown as a hardy annual. The fast-growing, bushy plants have upright stems and lance-shaped, grayish leaves. The stems are topped with spikes of four-petaled, 1-inch (2.5-cm) wide flowers in summer.
Height and spread Height 12–24 inches (30–60 cm); spread to 12 inches (30 cm).
Best site Full sun; average, well-drained soil with added organic matter.
Growing guidelines Grows easily from seed sown directly into the garden. Make the first sowing about a month before your last frost date. To extend the bloom season, make another sowing in late spring or early summer. (In mild-winter areas, you can also sow in late summer for winter and early-spring bloom.) Scatter seed on the soil surface, then rake lightly to just cover the seed. Keep the seedbed moist until seedlings appear. Thin seedlings to stand 6–8 inches (15–20 cm) apart. Mulch plants to keep the roots cool and moist. Water during dry spells.
Landscape uses Use as a filler in beds and borders near your house or outdoor sitting areas, where you can enjoy the sweet fragrance.

Mimulus x hybridus
SCROPHULARIACEAE

MONKEY FLOWER

You can overwinter monkey flowers indoors by digging and potting up plants before frost or by rooting stem cuttings in late summer; grow them in a cool, sunny room.

Description This tender perennial is grown as a half-hardy annual. Plants form clumps of green to reddish stems with oval, light green leaves that have toothed edges. Velvety, tubular flowers with flat faces bloom atop the plants through summer. The 1–2-inch (2.5–5-cm) flowers are usually yellow, orange, or red, often dotted or splashed with other colors in the center.
Height and spread Height 6–12 inches (15–30 cm); similar spread.
Best site Partial shade; moist soil. Plants can take full sun in evenly moist soil.
Growing guidelines Start seed indoors 8–10 weeks before your last frost date. Scatter the dust-like seed over the soil surface, press lightly into the soil, and enclose the pot in a plastic bag until seedlings appear. Set transplants out 6 inches (15 cm) apart after the last frost date. Water during dry spells. If plants stop blooming in hot weather, cut them back halfway and water thoroughly.
Landscape uses Monkey flowers add glowing color to moist-soil beds and borders. Try them as a groundcover in wet spots to fill in after spring-blooming primroses. They also look great in containers, but need frequent watering.

Mirabilis jalapa
NYCTAGINACEAE

FOUR O'CLOCK

Four o'clocks have fragrant flowers that open in the late afternoon. They tend to close the next morning, unless the weather is cloudy. Grow them in the garden or in pots.

Description These tender perennials are usually grown as half-hardy annuals. The bushy, fast-growing plants have trumpet-shaped, 1-inch (2.5-cm) wide flowers, which bloom from midsummer until frost in white or shades of pink, magenta, red, and yellow; sometimes different colors appear on the same plant.

Height and spread Height usually 2–3 feet (60–90 cm); spread to 2 feet (60 cm).

Best site Full sun to partial shade; average, well-drained soil.

Growing guidelines Four o'clocks are easy to grow from seed. For earliest bloom, start them indoors 4–6 weeks before your last frost date. Soak the seed in warm water overnight, and plant ¼–½ inch (6–12 mm) deep in peat pots. Transplant seedlings about 2 weeks after the last frost date. Or sow seed directly into the garden after the last frost date. Space plants 12–18 inches (30–45 cm) apart. Four o'clocks may self-sow in mild areas.

Landscape uses Plant clumps in flower beds and borders for a colorful filler. Grow a few around an outdoor sitting area, where you can enjoy the flowers and fragrance.

Other common names Marvel-of-Peru.

Myosotis sylvatica
BORAGINACEAE

FORGET-ME-NOT

Forget-me-not blooms are often sky blue with white or yellow centers, but they can also be pink or white. They are ideal companions for spring bulbs and other early annuals.

Description These short-lived perennials are usually grown as hardy biennials or annuals. Plants form dense clumps of narrow, lance-shaped, hairy leaves. Sprays of many ⅓-inch (8-mm) wide, sky blue flowers with white or yellow centers bloom from midspring through early summer.

Height and spread Height usually 12–18 inches (30–45 cm); spread 8–10 inches (20–25 cm).

Best site Partial shade; average to moist, well-drained soil with added compost.

Growing guidelines To grow forget-me-nots as biennials, sow seed outdoors in pots or in a nursery bed in spring or summer. Plant seed ⅛ inch (3 mm) deep. Move plants to the garden in early fall. For bloom the same year, buy plants in early spring, or start seed indoors 4–6 weeks before your last frost date. Set plants out 12 weeks before the last frost date. Space plants or thin seedlings to stand 6 inches (15 cm) apart. Water during dry spells. Shearing off spent flowers often promotes rebloom. Plants often self-sow freely.

Landscape uses Forget-me-nots are invaluable for spring color in shady gardens. Try them as an early-season groundcover under shrubs.

Nemesia strumosa
SCROPHULARIACEAE

NEMESIA

Nemesia usually stops flowering in warm weather, but plants may recover and rebloom if you cut them back by half, water thoroughly, and give them a dose of fertilizer.

Description Nemesia is a tender, cool-weather annual grown for its beautiful flowers. Plants form clumps of branched stems. Clusters of trumpet-shaped, lipped flowers bloom atop the stems in summer. The 1-inch (2.5-cm) wide flowers come in a range of colors, including white, pink, red, orange, yellow, lilac, and even light blue.

Height and spread Height 12–24 inches (30–60 cm); spread 6–8 inches (15–20 cm).

Best site Full sun to partial shade (in warm- and hot-summer areas especially); evenly moist, well-drained soil enriched with added organic matter. Nemesia needs a long, cool growing season; it does not tolerate heat or humidity.

Growing guidelines Start seed indoors 6–8 weeks before your last frost date. (In mild-winter areas, you can also sow in fall for winter bloom.) Sow seed ⅛ inch (3 mm) deep. Set plants out 4–6 inches (10–15 cm) apart after the last frost date.

Landscape uses Nemesia makes an attractive edging for flower beds and borders. It is also showy when planted in masses for early-summer color. Try a few in containers and window boxes.

Nemophila menziesii
HYDROPHYLLACEAE

BABY BLUE-EYES

Sow baby blue-eyes among the emerging shoots of spring bulbs to form a colorful, fast-growing carpet that will cover the ripening bulb foliage after bloom.

Description Baby blue-eyes is a hardy annual that forms a sprawling mound. The 1-inch (2.5-cm) wide, bowl-shaped, summer-blooming flowers are sky blue with a white center.

Height and spread Height 6–8 inches (15–20 cm); spread to 12 inches (30 cm).

Best site Full sun to partial shade (morning sun and afternoon shade are ideal); moist, well-drained soil with added organic matter.

Growing guidelines For an extra-early start, sow seed indoors 4–6 weeks before your last frost date. Plant seed ⅛ inch (3 mm) deep. Set plants out 12 weeks after the last frost date. Baby blue-eyes also grows quickly from seed sown directly into the garden. Make the first sowing in early spring (or even in fall in mild-winter areas). Sow seed again every 2–3 weeks from spring through to early summer to extend the bloom season through summer. Set plants 6 inches (15 cm) apart. If plants stop blooming in midsummer, shear them back halfway and water to encourage rebloom. Plants often self-sow.

Landscape uses A charming filler or edging for shady flower beds and borders, or trailing out of pots and planters.

Nicotiana alata
SOLANACEAE

FLOWERING TOBACCO

Hybrids and red-flowered types of flowering tobacco often have little or no scent, but old-fashioned, white-flowered types tend to be quite fragrant, especially at night.

Description This tender perennial is usually grown as a half-hardy annual. Plants form lush rosettes of broad, oval to pointed, green leaves and many-branched stems; both the stems and leaves are sticky and hairy. Trumpet-shaped flowers up to 2 inches (5 cm) across bloom atop the stems from midsummer until frost. Flowers come in a range of colors, including white, pink, purple, and red.

Height and spread Height 18–36 inches (45–90 cm); spread to 12 inches (30 cm).

Best site Full sun to partial shade; average to moist, well-drained soil with added organic matter.

Growing guidelines Buy transplants in spring, or start seed indoors 6–8 weeks before your last frost date. Don't cover the fine seed; just press it into the soil and enclose the pot in a plastic bag until seedlings appear. Set the seedlings out 10–12 inches (25–30 cm) apart after the last frost date. Water during dry spells. Cut out spent stems to prolong the bloom season. Plants may self-sow.

Landscape uses Excellent as a filler or accent in beds and borders. Grow some in the cutting garden and plant fragrant types around outdoor sitting areas.

Nigella damascena
RANUNCULACEAE

LOVE-IN-A-MIST

Sowing every few weeks from early spring to early summer can extend the bloom season of love-in-a-mist right through the summer and possibly into fall.

Description A fast-growing, hardy annual that forms bushy mounds of slender stems and thread-like, bright green leaves. Single or double, 1–2-inch (2.5–5-cm) wide flowers are nestled into the leaves at the tops of the stems. The blue, pink, or white flowers are followed by swollen, striped seedpods with short, pointed horns.

Height and spread Height 18–24 inches (45–60 cm); spread 6–8 inches (15–20 cm).

Best site Full sun to partial shade; average, well-drained soil.

Growing guidelines For the earliest flowers, start seed indoors 6–8 weeks before your last frost date. Sow seed (just barely cover it with soil) in peat pots. Move plants to the garden after the last frost date. In most cases, you'll get better results by sowing directly into the garden in early spring. Space transplants or thin seedlings to 6 inches (15 cm) apart. Established plants are care-free. Plants may self-sow.

Landscape uses Grow as a filler in beds, borders, and cottage gardens. It's also a natural for the cutting garden. Leave some plants to mature into the puffy seedpods.

Other common names Fennel flower, devil-in-the-bush.

Papaver nudicaule
PAPAVERACEAE

ICELAND POPPY

Removing spent flower stems can prolong Iceland poppy's bloom season. As summer approaches and new growth slows, leave a few flowers to mature so plants can self-sow.

Description This short-lived perennial is usually grown as a hardy biennial or annual. Plants form compact rosettes of hairy, deeply cut, gray-green leaves. Long, slender, leafless stems are topped with plump, hairy, nodding buds that open to bowl-shaped, four-petaled flowers. The 2–4-inch (5–10-cm) wide, lightly fragrant flowers have crinkled petals. They bloom mainly in early to midsummer in white and a range of vibrant colors, including pink, red, orange, and yellow.
Height and spread Height 12–18 inches (30–45 cm); spread 4–6 inches (10–15 cm).
Best site Full sun; average, well-drained to dry soil. Grows poorly in hot weather.
Growing guidelines Easiest to grow from seed sown directly into the garden. Plant in late fall or very early spring for summer bloom. (In hot-summer areas, sow this cool-loving plant in late summer to early fall for spring bloom.) Scatter the fine seed over the soil and rake it in lightly. Thin seedlings to about 6 inches (15 cm) apart.
Landscape uses Plant Iceland poppies for early color in beds and borders; follow them with summer-blooming annuals. Grow some in the cutting garden, too, for fresh cut flowers.

Papaver rhoeas
PAPAVERACEAE

CORN POPPY

Corn poppy is a hardy annual grown for its summer flowers. Remove spent blooms at the base of the stem to extend the flowering season through most of the summer.

Description Plants form clumps of ferny, blue-green leaves. Bowl-shaped flowers have four silky, crinkled petals. The 2–4-inch (5–10-cm) wide summer blooms are most often a glowing scarlet. Shirley poppy is a strain that has been selected for single or double flowers in white, pink, red, and bicolors.
Height and spread Height 24–36 inches (60–90 cm); spread 6–8 inches (15–20 cm).
Best site Full sun; well-drained soil.
Growing guidelines Corn poppy is easy to grow from seed sown directly into the garden in late fall or early spring. A second sowing in midspring can help extend the bloom season. Scatter the fine seed over the soil surface, then rake in lightly. Thin seedlings to stand 6–8 inches (15–20 cm) apart. Leave a few flowers at the season's end and plants will self-sow.
Landscape uses Corn poppies are natural choices for adding sparkle to meadow gardens. They also look good as fillers in beds and borders, and in arrangements, too. Pick them just as the buds are starting to open, then sear the ends in a gas flame or in boiling water to prolong their vase life.
Other common names Flanders poppy, Shirley poppy.

Pelargonium peltatum
GERANIACEAE

IVY GERANIUM

Ivy geranium is an excellent choice for hanging baskets and window boxes. It offers bright green, ivy-like leaves, gracefully cascading stems, and delicately marked blooms.

Description Ivy geraniums are shrubby plants with long, trailing stems and glossy, green leaves. Clusters of single or double white, pink, red, or lavender flowers appear all summer. These geraniums are always grown as annuals, except in frost-free areas.
Height and spread Height 1 foot (30 cm); spread 2–4 feet (60–120 cm).
Best site Full sun to light shade; average, well-drained soil.
Growing guidelines Take cuttings from overwintered ivy geraniums in spring or from outdoor plants in late summer to early autumn. Start seed indoors 10 weeks before the last frost date. Space plants well when transplanting. Allow the soil to dry somewhat between waterings, but note that lack of water can cause wilting and leaf drop. Deadhead faded flowers and pinch back growing tips several times in late spring and early summer to encourage branching. To keep container-grown plants from year to year in frost-prone areas, bring them indoors for the winter.
Landscape uses Ivy geranium makes a good groundcover or spillover planting. It can be used in cottage gardens and looks lovely in container gardens, hanging baskets, and window boxes, too.

Pelargonium x hortorum
GERANIACEAE

ZONAL GERANIUM

Colorful and dependable, zonal geraniums are a mainstay of summer flower gardens. You can also bring them indoors in the fall and enjoy their flowers through the winter.

Description The sturdy, branched stems carry hairy, rounded, bright to dark green leaves with scalloped margins. The leaves are pungent and often marked with dark green or brown, curved bands (zones). Plants produce rounded clusters of many 2-inch (5-cm) wide flowers. The single or double flowers bloom from late spring until frost in white or shades of pink, salmon, red, and bicolors.

Height and spread Height 12–24 inches (30–60 cm); spread 12–18 inches (30–45 cm).

Best site Full sun to partial shade; average, well-drained soil.

Growing guidelines Zonal geraniums are grown as annuals except in Zone 10, where they are grown as perennials. If you just need a few geraniums or if you want special kinds (such as those with double flowers or fancy leaves), start with a few purchased plants in spring. During the summer, pinch off spent flower stems to promote rebloom. To save special plants, dig them up in fall, move them into pots, and grow them on a sunny windowsill. Take 4-inch (10-cm) long cuttings from the shoot tips in spring.

Landscape uses Grow them alone, in masses, or tuck them into beds and borders.

Petunia x hybrida
SOLANACEAE

PETUNIA

Petunias are tender perennials usually grown as half-hardy annuals for a lovely display in beds and borders. They may self-sow, but the seedlings seldom resemble the parent plants.

Description Plants form clumps of upright or trailing stems with funnel-shaped, single or double flowers. They bloom from early summer until frost in nearly every color of the rainbow; some have stripes, streaks, or bands of contrasting colors.

Height and spread Height 6–10 inches (15–25 cm); spread to 12 inches (30 cm).

Best site Full sun (can take light shade); average to moist, well-drained soil.

Growing guidelines Petunias are among the most popular annuals, and many types are sold as transplants each spring. You can also grow your own from seed, although the fine, dust-like seed can be hard to handle. If you want to try, sow the seed indoors 8–10 weeks before your last frost date. Don't cover the seed; just press it lightly into the soil and enclose the pot in a plastic bag until seedlings appear. Move plants to the garden after the last frost date; space them 8–12 inches (20–30 cm) apart. Water during dry spells.

Landscape uses Petunias—especially the multiflora and floribunda types—are favorites for flower beds and borders, planted alone in masses or mixed with other plants. They are particularly good for filling in gaps in the garden.

Phaseolus coccineus
PAPILIONACEAE

SCARLET RUNNER BEAN

Scarlet runner beans are equally at home in the flower garden and the vegetable garden. The fast-growing vines produce showy orange-red blooms and edible seedpods.

Description This tender perennial climber is grown as a half-hardy annual. The twining stems carry showy clusters of 1-inch (2.5-cm) long, orange-red flowers from midsummer until frost. The pea-type flowers are followed by long, silvery green pods that are quite tasty when young (cook them like snap beans).

Height and spread Height usually 6–8 feet (1.8–2.4 m); ultimate height and spread depend on the size of the support that scarlet runner bean is growing on.

Best site Full sun; well-drained soil.

Growing guidelines Before planting, make sure you have a sturdy support already in place. This fast-growing vine is easy to start from seed sown directly into the garden. Wait until 12 weeks after the last frost date, when the soil is warm, then plant the seed 1 inch (2.5 cm) deep. Thin seedlings to stand 8 inches (20 cm) apart. Water during dry spells.

Landscape uses Scarlet runner bean is an ideal vine to grow as a screen for quick shade or privacy. It makes a good garden accent when trained on a tripod of sturdy posts. It's also excellent as a temporary solution for covering an ugly section of fence or screening an unpleasant view.

Phlox drummondii
POLEMONIACEAE

ANNUAL PHLOX

Annual phlox is a hardy annual grown for its colorful flowers. If plants stop blooming, cut them back by half and water thoroughly; they should resprout and rebloom in fall.

Description Plants form bushy clumps of narrow, lance-shaped, green leaves. From midsummer to fall, the leafy stems are topped with clusters of flat, five-petaled flowers, each ½–1 inch (1.2–2.5 cm) across. The flowers bloom in a wide range of colors, including white, pink, red, pale yellow, blue, and purple; some have a contrasting eye.
Height and spread Height 6–18 inches (15–45 cm), depending on the cultivar; spread 6–8 inches (15–20 cm).
Best site Needs full sun; average, well-drained soil.
Growing guidelines For the earliest flowers, buy transplants in spring, or start seed indoors 6–8 weeks before the last frost date. Sow seed ⅛ inch (3 mm) deep in individual pots. Set plants out around the last frost date. You can also sow seed directly into the garden around the last frost date. Set plants or thin seedlings to stand 6 inches (15 cm) apart. Pinching off spent flowers and watering during dry spells can prolong the bloom season.
Landscape uses An excellent filler for flower beds and borders. Try the compact cultivars in container gardens. The tall cultivars are excellent cut flowers.

Portulaca grandiflora
PORTULACACEAE

ROSE MOSS

Rose moss comes in many vibrant colors, including white, pink, red, orange, yellow, and magenta. The flowers tend to close by afternoon and stay closed on cloudy days.

Description A low-growing, tender annual, rose moss forms creeping mats of fleshy, many-branched stems with small, thick, almost needle-like leaves. Single or double, 1-inch (2.5-cm) wide flowers bloom from early summer through fall.
Height and spread Height to 6 inches (15 cm); spread 6–8 inches (15–20 cm).
Best site Full sun; average, well-drained to dry soil.
Growing guidelines For earliest bloom, buy transplants in spring, or sow seed indoors 6–8 weeks before your last frost date. For easy transplanting later, sow the seed in cell packs or small pots. Do not cover the seed; just press it lightly into the soil and enclose the container in a plastic bag until seedlings appear. Set plants out after the last frost date; space them about 6 inches (15 cm) apart. Or sow the seed directly into the garden after the last frost date; keep the soil moist until seedlings appear. Thin seedlings only if they're crowded. Plants may self-sow.
Landscape uses Rose moss makes a great groundcover for dry, rocky slopes. It also looks charming as an edging for sunny beds and borders, or in containers.
Other common names Sun plant.

Ricinus communis
EUPHORBIACEAE

CASTOR BEAN

Castor beans add a touch of the tropics to any garden. Stake the tall plants to keep them upright, especially in windy or exposed sites, and water them during dry spells.

Description This tender perennial is usually grown as a half-hardy annual. The huge, fast-growing plants produce small, ½-inch (12-mm) wide, creamy-looking, petal-less flowers in spiky clusters along the upper stems. These summer flowers are followed by showy, reddish burs.
Height and spread Height usually to 6 feet (1.8 m) or more; spread 3–4 feet (90–120 cm).
Best site Full sun; average to moist, well-drained soil.
Growing guidelines For an early start, sow seed indoors 6–8 weeks before your last frost date. Soak the seeds in warm water overnight, then sow ¾ inch (18 mm) deep in individual pots (two or three per pot). If all of the seeds germinate, thin to one per pot. Set plants out after the last frost date. Or sow seed directly into the garden after the last frost date. Space plants or thin seedlings to about 3 feet (90 cm) apart. Plants may self-sow.
Landscape uses Grow castor beans as accents or backgrounds for beds and borders or as a temporary but fast-growing screen or hedge. The seeds are poisonous if eaten, so avoid planting castor beans around children's play areas.

Rudbeckia hirta
ASTERACEAE

BLACK-EYED SUSAN

The daisy-type blooms of black-eyed Susans have golden yellow outer petals and a purple-brown or black, raised center. They make excellent cut flowers.

Description This short-lived perennial or biennial is usually grown as a hardy annual. Plants form clumps of long, hairy leaves that taper to a point. Stiff, hairy stems are topped with 2–3-inch (5–7.5-cm) wide flowers from summer into fall.

Height and spread Height 24–36 inches (60–90 cm); spread to about 12 inches (30 cm).

Best site Full sun (can take light shade); average, well-drained to dry soil.

Growing guidelines For earliest bloom, sow seed indoors 8–10 weeks before your last frost date. Just barely cover the seed. Set plants out 2 weeks before the last frost date (protect plants if there's a chance of heavy frost). You can also sow seed directly into the garden after the last frost date, although the plants probably won't bloom until the following year. Space plants or thin seedlings to stand 12 inches (30 cm) apart. Plants often self-sow; if this becomes a problem, remove the spent flower heads before they set seed.

Landscape uses Black-eyed Susans look bright and cheerful in flower beds and borders. They're also a natural choice for meadow gardens.

Other common names Gloriosa daisy.

Salvia farinacea
LAMIACEAE

MEALY-CUP SAGE

Mealy-cup sage is fairly drought-tolerant but appreciates watering during extended dry spells. The plants sometimes live through mild winters; they may also self-sow.

Description This tender perennial is usually grown as a half-hardy annual. Plants produce bushy clumps of narrow, lance-shaped, green leaves with slightly toothed edges. Stiff, purple-blue stem tips are topped with long spikes of dusty blue buds from midsummer until frost. These buds open to ½-inch (12 mm) long, blue flowers.

Height and spread Height 18–24 inches (45–60 cm); spread to 12 inches (30 cm).

Best site Full sun; well-drained soil.

Growing guidelines Buy transplants in spring, or grow your own by starting seed indoors 8–10 weeks before your last frost date. Soaking the seed overnight before planting can promote quicker sprouting. Don't cover the sown seed; just press it lightly into the soil and enclose the pot in a plastic bag until seedlings appear. Set plants out after the last frost date; space them 12 inches (30 cm) apart.

Landscape uses Grow alone in masses or mix with other annuals, perennials, and roses in beds, borders, and cottage gardens. The neat, shrubby plants are ideal for containers, too. The spiky blooms are useful for fresh or dried arrangements.

Other common names Blue salvia.

Salvia splendens
LAMIACEAE

SCARLET SAGE

Compact cultivars of scarlet sage tend to flower mostly in summer; taller types generally start blooming in midsummer and last until frost. Pinch off faded spikes.

Description This tender perennial is grown as a half-hardy annual. Plants form clumps of upright stems with oval, deep green leaves that have pointed tips and slightly toothed edges. The stems are topped with thick, showy spikes of colorful, petal-like bracts and 1½-inch (3.7-cm) long tubular flowers. The flowers are most often red, but they are also available in white, pink, salmon, and purple.

Height and spread Height 12–24 inches (30–60 cm); spread to 12 inches (30 cm).

Best site Needs full sun; average, well-drained soil.

Growing guidelines Widely sold as transplants in spring. If you really want to grow your own, sow indoors 8–10 weeks before your last frost date. Don't cover the seed; just press it lightly into the soil and enclose the pot in a plastic bag until seedlings appear. Set plants out after the last frost date; space them 8–12 inches (20–30 cm) apart. Fertilize several times during the summer.

Landscape uses If you enjoy mixing bright colors, grow scarlet sage as an edging or filler for flower beds and borders. For a somewhat more restrained effect, surround scarlet sage with leafy green herbs.

Sanvitalia procumbens
ASTERACEAE

CREEPING ZINNIA

Plant creeping zinnia where it can trail over walls, screening unsightly views with its brilliant flowers. Or allow it to cascade out of containers, raised beds, window boxes, and hanging baskets.

Description Creeping zinnia is usually grown as a half-hardy annual for its colorful flowers. Plants form spreading or trailing mounds, which are covered with many ¾-inch (18-mm) wide flowers that look like miniature black-eyed Susans from midsummer until frost. The raised, purple-brown centers are surrounded by a ring of golden yellow petals.

Height and spread Height to 6 inches (15 cm); spread to 18 inches (45 cm).

Best site Full sun; average, well-drained to dry soil.

Growing guidelines For earliest bloom, sow seed indoors 6–8 weeks before your last frost date. Sow in individual pots so you minimize root disturbance at transplanting time. Don't cover the fine seed; just press it lightly into the soil and enclose the pots in a plastic bag until seedlings appear. Set the plants out after the last frost date. You can also sow seed directly into the garden after the last frost date. Space plants or thin seedlings to stand 8–12 inches (20–30 cm) apart. Established plants are care-free.

Landscape uses Creeping zinnia is a great groundcover in dry, sunny spots. It's useful as an edging or filler for beds and borders.

Senecio cineraria
ASTERACEAE

DUSTY MILLER

Dusty miller can live through mild winters, but second-year plants tend to be more open. Where uniformity is important (as in an edging), start with new plants each year.

Description This tender perennial is usually grown as a half-hardy annual. Plants form shrubby mounds of deeply lobed leaves that are covered with matted, white hairs. The plants may produce clusters of daisy-type yellow flowers in summer, but these are usually removed so they won't detract from the silvery foliage.

Height and spread Height 8–24 inches (20–60 cm); spread to 12 inches (30 cm).

Best site Needs full sun; average, well-drained soil.

Growing guidelines Buy transplants in spring. They grow slowly from seed, but if you want to raise your own, sow seed indoors 8–10 weeks before your last frost date. Don't cover the seed; just press it lightly into the soil and enclose the pot in a plastic bag until seedlings appear. Set plants out after the last frost date; space them 8 inches (20 cm) apart. Pinch out stem tips in early summer for bushy growth.

Landscape uses Dusty miller's silvery foliage is invaluable as an edging or accent for flower beds, borders, and all kinds of container plantings. The silvery leaves and stems also dry well.

Other names Dusty miller is also listed in seed catalogs as *Cineraria maritima*.

Solenostemon scutellarioides
LAMIACEAE

COLEUS

Keep favorite coleus plants from year to year by taking cuttings in summer; they'll root quickly in water. Pot up the cuttings for winter; then put them outdoors in spring.

Description These tender perennials are grown as bushy, tender annuals. Their sturdy, square stems carry showy, patterned leaves with scalloped or ruffled edges. Each leaf can have several different colors, with zones, edges, or splashes in shades of red, pink, orange, yellow, and cream.

Height and spread Height 6–24 inches (15–60 cm); spread 8–12 inches (20–30 cm).

Best site Partial shade; average to moist, well-drained soil with added well-rotted organic matter.

Growing guidelines Buy transplants in spring, or start your own by sowing seed indoors 8–10 weeks before your last frost date. Don't cover the seed; just press it lightly into the soil and enclose the pot in a plastic bag until seedlings appear. Set plants out 8–12 inches (20–30 cm) apart after the last frost. Water during dry spells. Pinch off the spikes of the pale blue flowers to promote more leafy growth.

Landscape uses Coleus are great for adding all-season color to beds, borders, and container plantings. Groups of mixed leaf patterns can look too busy when combined with flowering plants, so grow them alone in masses.

Tagetes hybrids
ASTERACEAE

MARIGOLDS

Marigolds can add bright color to any sunny spot. Mix them with other annuals and perennials, or grow them alone in masses. Tall-stemmed types may need staking.

Description These half-hardy annuals are grown for their bright, 2–4-inch (5–10-cm) wide summer flowers and bushy mounds of lacy, green leaves. African or American marigolds (*T. erecta*) tend to be large plants, with 18–36-inch (45–90-cm) stems and large, usually double, yellow or orange flowers. French marigolds (*T. patula*) tend to be much daintier, with many smaller, single or double flowers in yellow, orange, or red on 12-inch (30-cm) tall plants.
Height and spread Height 6–36 inches (15–90 cm); spread 6–18 inches (15–45 cm).
Best site Full sun; average, well-drained soil. Light afternoon shade can help prolong bloom in hot-summer areas, especially for creamy-flowered cultivars.
Growing guidelines For earliest bloom (especially for tall-growing types), start seed indoors 4–6 weeks before your last frost date. Plant seed ⅛–¼ inch (3–6 mm) deep. Set plants out after your last frost date. You can also sow seed of small, early-blooming types directly into the garden after the last frost date.
Landscape uses Grow as summer fillers or edgings for flower beds and borders.

Tanacetum parthenium
ASTERACEAE

FEVERFEW

Feverfew is pretty but can become a pest by dropping lots of seed. Cutting off bloom stalks after the flowers fade will prevent this problem and promote new leafy growth.

Description This short-lived perennial or biennial is often grown as a hardy annual. The plants form ferny mounds of deeply cut, aromatic, green leaves. The leafy stems are topped with 1-inch (2.5-cm) wide, single or double flowers, mainly in early to midsummer. The white or yellow, daisy-type flowers have yellow centers.
Height and spread Height 12–30 inches (30–75 cm); spread 12–18 inches (30–45 cm).
Best site Full sun to partial shade; average, well-drained soil.
Growing guidelines Starts easily from seed sown in the garden in mid- to late spring. You can also start seed indoors 6–8 weeks before your last frost date. Plant the fine seed in a pot, press it lightly into the soil, and enclose the pot in a plastic bag until seedlings appear. Move young plants outdoors after the last frost date. Space plants or thin seedlings to stand 8–12 inches (20–30 cm) apart.
Landscape uses Grow feverfew in flower beds and borders, herb gardens, and also container gardens. It looks particularly charming with roses in cottage gardens. The sprays of small flowers are great in fresh arrangements, too.

Thunbergia alata
ACANTHACEAE

BLACK-EYED SUSAN VINE

If you plan to grow bright and cheerful black-eyed Susan vine as a climber, install a support—such as plastic netting or a trellis—before planting seeds or transplants.

Description This tender perennial is grown as a tender annual. Plants produce twining vines with pointed buds, which open to rounded, flattened, 3-inch (7.5-cm) wide flowers. The orange-yellow flowers have a deep purple to black center. They may bloom from late summer until frost, but they usually put on their best show in late summer to early fall.
Height and spread Height to about 6 feet (1.8 m); ultimate height and spread depend on the support the vine is growing on.
Best site Full sun to partial shade; average to moist, well-drained soil.
Growing guidelines For earliest flowers, start seed indoors 6–8 weeks before your last frost date. Sow seed ¼ inch (6 mm) deep in peat pots (two or three per pot); thin to one seedling per pot. Set plants out after the last frost date. You can also start plants from seed sown directly into the garden after the last frost date. Set plants or thin seedlings out to stand 12 inches (30 cm) apart. Mulch plants to keep the roots cool. Water during dry spells.
Landscape uses This vine is a good fast-growing screen for shade or privacy. It also makes a feature in a hanging basket.
Other common names Clock vine.

Tithonia rotundifolia
ASTERACEAE

MEXICAN SUNFLOWER

Mexican sunflowers are popular with bees and butterflies, and they make good cut flowers. Pinch off spent blooms to encourage reblooming and extend the flowering season.

Description Mexican sunflower is a half-hardy annual with colorful blooms. Plants produce tall, sturdy, hairy stems with velvety, lobed or broadly oval, pointed, dark green leaves. During summer, the shrubby clumps are accented with many 3-inch (7.5-cm) wide, glowing orange, daisy-type flowers.

Height and spread Height 4–6 feet (1.2–1.8 m); spread 18–24 inches (45–60 cm).

Best site Full sun; average, well-drained soil with added organic matter.

Growing guidelines For earliest flowers, start seed indoors 6–8 weeks before your last frost date. Sow seed ¼ inch (6 mm) deep in individual pots (two or three seeds per pot); thin to one seedling per pot. Set plants out after the last frost date. Or grow from seed sown directly into the garden about 2 weeks after the last frost date. Set plants or thin seedlings to stand 18 inches (45 cm) apart. Water during dry spells. Plants growing in exposed sites may become floppy; stake if necessary.

Landscape uses Makes an attractive flowering screen or hedge. It also looks great as a tall accent or background plant.

Other common names Torch flower.

Torenia fournieri
SCROPHULARIACEAE

WISHBONE FLOWER

Wishbone flowers are usually purplish blue with a yellow throat; they may also be white or pink. The mouth of each bloom has two short, curved stamens that resemble a wishbone.

Description This tender, shade-loving annual forms clumps of upright, many-branched stems with oval, pointed to narrow, toothed, green leaves that take on reddish purple tints in fall. The stems are topped with trumpet-shaped, purplish blue blooms to 1 inch (2.5 cm) long from early summer through fall.

Height and spread Height to 12 inches (30 cm); spread 6–8 inches (15–20 cm).

Best site Partial shade; moist, well-drained soil. Plants can take more sun in cool Northern gardens.

Growing guidelines Sow seed indoors 8–10 weeks before your last frost date. Don't cover the seed; just press it lightly into the soil. Enclose the pot in a plastic bag, and set it in a warm, dark place. When seedlings appear (in about a week), remove the bag and set the pot in a bright place. Set plants out after the last frost date; space them 6 inches (15 cm) apart. Water during dry spells. If plants start to flop, shear them back by about half to promote branching.

Landscape uses Use as an edging or filler for shady beds and borders. It also looks good in containers and window boxes.

Other common names Bluewings.

Tropaeolum majus
TROPAEOLACEAE

GARDEN NASTURTIUM

Garden nasturtiums are half-hardy annuals with brightly colored flowers. Bushy types are great as edgings or fillers for beds and borders. These prolific bloomers may self-sow.

Description Garden nasturtiums grow either as a climbing or trailing vine or as a bushy mound. The plants bear showy, fragrant, five-petaled blooms to 2 inches (5 cm) wide from early summer through fall. They bloom in colors ranging from cream, rose, red, orange, to yellow.

Height and spread Height of vining types up to about 8 feet (2.4 m), bushy types up to about 12 inches (30 cm); spread usually 6–12 inches (15–30 cm).

Best site Full sun; average, well-drained to dry soil.

Growing guidelines Sow seed indoors 4–6 weeks before your last frost date. Soak the seed overnight before planting, then sow it ¼–½ inch (6–12 mm) deep in peat pots. Set plants out after the last frost date. They will also grow easily from seed sown directly into the garden 12 weeks before your last frost date. If you're growing vining types, put up some kind of support before planting. Watch for aphids; use a strong spray of water to wash them off.

Landscape uses Use climbing types to quickly cover trellises; grow the compact types in containers or as edgings or fillers.

Viola x wittrockiana
VIOLACEAE

PANSY

To keep pansies happy, mulch the soil around them and water during dry spells to keep the roots moist. Pinching off spent flowers can prolong bloom; leave a few to self-sow.

Description These short-lived perennials are usually grown as hardy annuals or as biennials. Plants form tidy clumps of oval to narrow, green leaves. Flat, five-petaled flowers bloom just above the clumps, mainly in spring but also sometimes in fall. The 2–5-inch (5–12.5-cm) wide flowers bloom in a range of colors, including white, pink, red, orange, yellow, purple, blue, and near black; they often have contrasting faces.

Height and spread Height 6–8 inches (15–20 cm); spread 8–12 inches (20–30 cm).

Best site Full sun to partial shade; moist, well-drained soil.

Growing guidelines For bloom the same year, buy plants in early spring or start seed indoors 8–10 weeks before your last frost date. Sow seed ⅛ inch (3 mm) deep. Set the pot in a refrigerator for 12 weeks, then move it to a bright place. Set seedlings out after your last frost date. If you wish to grow pansies as biennials for earlier spring bloom, sow the seed outdoors in a nursery bed in late spring; move plants to the garden in midfall.

Landscape uses Use them as fillers or as an edging. They are also cute in containers.

Zinnia angustifolia
ASTERACEAE

NARROW-LEAVED ZINNIA

Narrow-leaved zinnia is a tender annual that is grown for its colorful flowers. Established plants are trouble-free; they are also quite disease- and drought-resistant.

Description Plants form loose mounds of slender, dark green leaves. The mounds are covered with open, daisy-type blooms to 1½ inches (3.7 cm) wide from midsummer until frost. The flowers are most often bright orange with a gold stripe in the center of each petal; white- and yellow-flowered types are also available.

Height and spread Height 8–12 inches (20–30 cm); spread to 12 inches (30 cm).

Best site Full sun; average, well-drained to dry soil.

Growing guidelines For earliest flowers, sow seed indoors 3–4 weeks before your last frost date. Plant seed ¼–½ inch (6–12 mm) deep in peat pots (two or three seeds per pot). Thin seedlings to leave one per pot. Set plants out after the last frost date. It's easy to start these fast growers from seed sown directly into the garden 12 weeks after the last frost date, when the soil is warm. Space plants or thin seedlings to stand 10–12 inches (25–30 cm) apart.

Landscape uses Grow in masses as a groundcover, or combine it with other plants as an edging or filler for beds and borders. It also looks super in pots.

Other common names Classic zinnia; also listed in catalogs under *Z. linearis.*

Zinnia elegans
ASTERACEAE

COMMON ZINNIA

Common zinnias are excellent for replacing early-blooming annuals and filling in gaps left by dormant spring-flowering bulbs and perennials. They are also great cut flowers.

Description Plants produce stiff, sturdy stems with pairs of oval to pointed, green leaves. The stems are topped with blooms from midsummer until frost in nearly every color of the rainbow (except true blue). Common zinnias come in a range of flower forms, from 1–6 inches (2.5–15 cm) across. The petals of the single or double blooms may be quilled (curled), ruffled, or flat.

Height and spread Height 6–36 inches (15–90 cm), depending on the cultivar; spread usually 12–24 inches (30–60 cm).

Best site Full sun; average, well-drained soil with added organic matter.

Growing guidelines Buy transplants in spring, or sow seed indoors 3–4 weeks before your last frost date. Plant seed ¼–½ inch (6–12 mm) deep in peat pots (two or three seeds per pot). Thin seedlings to one per pot. Set plants out after the last frost date. Common zinnias also grow quickly from seed sown directly into the garden 1–2 weeks after the last frost date, when the soil is warm. Mulch plants to keep the roots moist. Tall cultivars may need staking.

Landscape uses Grow them alone in masses, or mix them with other plants in flower beds, borders, and cottage gardens.

A Guide to Popular Perennials

You may want to re-create a classic English perennial border,
an informal cottage garden, a lush meadow, or a shady woodland garden.
With the thousands of perennial species and cultivars available, there's
a good chance that you'll find the plant forms, leaf textures, and flower
colors to fit the garden you have in mind. This guide to some of the best-
known perennials is designed to help you make your selections.

Plants are arranged alphabetically by their botanical names, with their most
often-used common name displayed prominently. Each plant is illustrated
with a color photograph to make identification easy. There are plant
descriptions, cultivation tips, and a guide to the right climate zone, too.
With this guide, you can start to explore the many possibilities offered
when incorporating perennials into your garden.

Acanthus mollis
ACANTHACEAE

BEAR'S BREECH

Bear's breech is a robust plant with lustrous evergreen leaves, 1–2 feet (30–60 cm) long and edged with jagged teeth. It grows from a stout crown with thick, fleshy roots.

Flower color Unusual 1-inch (2.5-cm) flowers with three white petals and overarching purple hoods are carried in tall spikes.

Flowering time Late spring or summer; flowers open sequentially up the spike.

Height and spread 2½–4 feet (75–120 cm) tall; 3 feet (90 cm) wide. Spreads to form broad clumps.

Temperature requirements Zones 8–10. Sensitive to humidity.

Position Evenly moist, humus-rich soil. Partial shade to full shade.

Cultivation Mulch after the ground freezes in winter and remove the mulch gradually in spring to protect plants from heaving. Keep moist; dry soil will reduce the size of the leaves.

Propagation Divide plants in spring when they first emerge. Alternatively, take root cuttings in spring or late fall. Roots left in the ground when plants are divided will form new shoots.

Pest and disease prevention Bait slugs with pans of beer set flush with the surface of the soil.

Landscape uses Use bear's breech as foundation plantings or as bold accents in formal and informal gardens.

Achillea filipendulina
ASTERACEAE

FERN-LEAVED YARROW

Fern-leaved yarrow bears flat-topped heads of tiny flowers on dozens of tall, leafy stems. This aromatic herb grows from fibrous roots and has deeply incised, ferny, olive green leaves.

Flower color Dozens of tightly packed golden yellow flowers cluster in heads 4–5 inches (10–12.5 cm) across.

Flowering time Summer. Flowers last for several weeks and rebloom if deadheaded.

Height and spread 3–4 feet (90–120 cm) tall; 3 feet (90 cm) wide.

Temperature requirements Zones 3–9. Thrives in moderate summer humidity.

Position Average, dry to moist, well-drained soil. Full sun to light shade.

Cultivation Plants spread rapidly and need frequent division. Lift and divide clumps every 3 years to keep vigorous.

Propagation Take tip cuttings in spring or early summer. Divide in early spring or fall. Replant healthy divisions into soil enriched with organic matter.

Pest and disease prevention Plants develop powdery mildew, a cottony white coating on the leaves, especially in areas with warm humid nights. Rot causes stems to blacken and topple over. Remove and destroy all affected parts and dust the remaining plants with sulfur.

Landscape uses Plant at the front or middle of formal perennial borders or with grasses in wildflower meadows. Use them in cutting gardens or on dry, sunny banks.

Achillea millefolium
ASTERACEAE

COMMON YARROW

Summer-blooming common yarrow offers finely cut, deep green foliage and colorful flowers. It can be invasive in the border; try it in a meadow or informal garden.

Flower color Numerous tiny white, pink, or red florets in dense, flat clusters 2–3 inches (5–7.5 cm) across are produced on stout stems.

Flowering time June to September. To extend flowering, pick blossoms often.

Height and spread 1–1½ feet (30–45 cm) tall; 3 feet (90 cm) wide.

Temperature requirements Zones 2–8.

Position Ordinary, well-drained soil. Full sun, but shade is tolerated.

Cultivation This hardy, easy-care perennial spreads rapidly and can become invasive. Lift and divide regularly to keep plants vigorous and also to stop them from spreading out of control.

Propagation Sow seed shallowly indoors in early spring, or outdoors in late spring. Divide established plants in early spring or autumn.

Pest and disease prevention Provide well-drained soil to avoid powdery mildew. Said to attract beneficial insects.

Landscape uses Use in meadows, informal gardens, or herb gardens.

Other common names Milfoil.

Aconitum carmichaelii
RANUNCULACEAE

AZURE MONKSHOOD

Azure monkshood is a graceful plant with lush, three-lobed, dissected leaves, sturdy stems, and hooded flowers. All parts of the plant are poisonous when ingested.

Flower color Deep blue hooded flowers in dense spikes.
Flowering time Late summer and fall.
Height and spread 2–3 feet (60–90 cm) tall; 2 feet (60 cm) wide. Open and somewhat vase-shaped, especially in shade.
Temperature requirements Zones 3–7. Prefers climates with cool summer nights and warm days with low humidity.
Position Fertile, humus-rich, moist but well-drained soil. Full sun to light shade; afternoon shade in warmer zones.
Cultivation Dislikes disturbance once established. Space 2–3 feet (60–90 cm) apart with the crowns just below the surface. Take care not to damage the brittle roots. Divide if plants become overcrowded.
Propagation Divide crowns in fall or early spring. Replant strong, healthy divisions into soil enriched with organic matter.
Pest and disease prevention Crowns will rot if soil is wet and temperatures are hot. Site plants properly to avoid problems.
Landscape uses Plant azure monkshood near the middle or rear of borders with other fall-blooming perennials and ornamental grasses or in groups with fruiting shrubs like the *Viburnum* species.

Aconitum x *cammarum* 'Bicolor'
RANUNCULACEAE

BICOLOR MONKSHOOD

Bicolor monkshood is a showy, fall-flowering perennial for borders or informal gardens. It thrives in climates with cool summer nights and warm days with low humidity.

Flower color The dark blue or two-toned flower spikes have protruding helmet-like hoods above three lower petals.
Flowering time Late summer and fall.
Height and spread 3–4 feet (90–120 cm) tall; 2 feet (60 cm) wide. Habit is variable, but generally open and vase-shaped, especially in shade.
Temperature requirements Zones 3–7.
Position Plant in fertile, humus-rich, moist but well-drained soil in full sun or light shade. Afternoon shade is advised in warmer zones.
Cultivation Space plants 2–3 feet (60–90 cm) apart, with the crowns just below the surface. Divide in fall or early spring only if plants become overcrowded and bloom diminishes.
Propagation Divide in fall or early spring.
Pest and disease prevention Crowns will rot if soil is wet and temperatures are hot. Site plants properly to avoid problems.
Landscape uses Plant near the middle or rear of perennial borders, in informal settings like open woodlands and meadows, or as a mass planting in front of trees and shrubs. Combine with other fall-blooming perennials and ornamental grasses.

Actaea alba
RANUNCULACEAE

WHITE BANEBERRY

Mature clumps of white baneberry in full fruit provide a stunning highlight in the fall garden. The red-stalked berries are poisonous to people but savored by birds.

Flower color The white flowers are composed of a fuzzy cluster of broad stamens. The showy oval white fruits for which this plant is noted are ¼ inch (6 mm) long and borne on stalks.
Flowering time Spring bloom; late summer to fall for berries.
Height and spread 2–4 feet (60–120 cm) tall. Mature clumps may reach 3 feet (90 cm) across.
Temperature requirements Zones 3–9.
Position Plant in moist, humus-rich soil in partial to full shade.
Cultivation Top-dress clumps with compost or shredded leaves in spring or fall. Plants seldom need division.
Propagation Sow fresh seed outdoors in early fall to midfall after removing the pulp from ripe berries.
Pest and disease prevention No serious pests or diseases.
Landscape uses Plant baneberries for dramatic accent at the edge of the path in a woodland garden or at the end of a shady walk. Mass plantings are breathtaking among ferns and foliage plants. Combine with wild bleeding heart (*Dicentra eximia*) and violets.

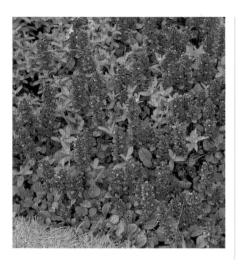

Ajuga reptans
LAMIACEAE

AJUGA

Ajuga is a low, rosette-forming groundcover that spreads by creeping aboveground stems to form broad, dense mats. The spoon-shaped leaves are evergreen in mild climates.

Flower color Tiered whorls of small, intense blue flowers on stalks.
Flowering time Late spring and early summer.
Height and spread 4–10 inches (10–25 cm) tall; 8–10 inches (20–25 cm) wide. Clumps may spread to several feet across from a single plant.
Temperature requirements Zones 3–9. Tolerates heat, humidity, and cold.
Position Average to humus-rich, moist but well-drained soil. Will not tolerate extended drought or excessive moisture. Full sun to light shade.
Cultivation Plant in spring or fall. Ajuga spreads rapidly to form a dense weed-proof groundcover and may become somewhat invasive, especially in lawns.
Propagation Divide anytime during the growing season or sow seed in spring.
Pest and disease prevention Provide good drainage and air circulation to prevent crown rot, which causes patches to wither and die out.
Landscape uses Use as a groundcover under trees and shrubs or for edging beds.
Other common names Common bugleweed.

Alchemilla mollis
ROSACEAE

LADY'S MANTLE

Lady's mantles form mounded clumps of pleated foliage. The 4–6-inch (10–15-cm) pale green leaves are covered in soft hair that collects beads of water like jewels on velvet.

Flower color Foamy clusters of small greenish yellow flowers.
Flowering time Spring and early summer.
Height and spread 6–8 inches (15–20 cm) tall; 1–2 feet (30–60 cm) wide.
Temperature requirements Zones 4–8. Excessive heat and humidity can damage the foliage.
Position Humus-rich, evenly moist soil. Full sun; provide afternoon shade where summer heat and humidity are excessive.
Cultivation Set the stout crowns at the soil surface. Mulch with organic matter to keep the soil evenly moist. Cut tattered foliage to the ground; fresh leaves will quickly appear again.
Propagation Divide crowns in spring or fall. Sow fresh seed outdoors in summer. Plants often self-sow.
Pest and disease prevention No serious pests or diseases.
Landscape uses Choose lady's mantle for the front of formal and informal beds and borders or for edging walks. The greenish yellow flowers add light to the garden in evening. Combine with other plants that enjoy moist soil like Siberian iris (*Iris sibirica*), astilbe, and hosta.
Cultivars 'Auslese' has erect flower stems.

Allium christophii
LILIACEAE

STAR OF PERSIA

Star of Persia produces 1½-foot (45-cm) strap-like blue-green leaves that arch outward from the bulbs. Starry flowers radiate from stout 1–1½-foot (30–45-cm) stalks.

Flower color Lilac-pink flowers carried in 10-inch (25-cm) globose heads.
Flowering time Early to midsummer.
Height and spread 1–1½ feet (30–45 cm) tall; 1 foot (30 cm) wide.
Temperature requirements Zones 4–8.
Position Humus-rich, well-drained soil. Full sun.
Cultivation New bulbs planted in fall multiply slowly to form spectacular flowering clumps. Plants go dormant after flowering.
Propagation Divide in mid- to late summer as plants go dormant. Sow ripe seed outdoors in summer or fall.
Pest and disease prevention No serious pests or diseases. Mulch with organic matter to keep the soil evenly moist.
Landscape uses Plant bulbs at the front of borders where their stalks will explode into bloom above mounding plants like cranesbills (*Geranium* spp.). Combine with shrubs and overplant with a groundcover.

Allium giganteum
LILIACEAE

GIANT ONION

The large bulbs of giant onion produce showy flower heads in early summer. Plant perennials or summer-blooming annuals at the base to fill in when the bulbs go dormant.

Flower color A 6-inch (15-cm) globe that is densely packed with many small, reddish purple flowers tops each tall, slender stem.
Flowering time Early to midsummer.
Height and spread Height of leaves usually 6–12 inches (15–30 cm); flower stems grow to 5 feet (1.5 m). Spread to about 12 inches (30 cm).
Temperature requirements Zones 5–8.
Position Full sun, but tolerates light shade; average, well-drained soil.
Cultivation Plant bulbs in early to midfall or in early spring. Set them in individual holes or larger planting areas dug 8 inches (20 cm) deep. In Zones 5 and 6, protect bulbs over winter with a loose mulch; remove this in spring. Cut down spent flower stems, unless you want to collect seed or use the attractive dried seed heads for arrangements. Leave established bulbs undisturbed in the garden.
Propagation Divide bulbs in fall.
Pest and disease prevention No serious pests or diseases.
Landscape uses A showstopping accent for the back of flower beds and borders.

Alstroemeria aurea
AMARYLLIDACEAE

PERUVIAN LILY

Peruvian lilies have tall, leafy stems crowned by open clusters of flaring, saucer-shaped flowers. The gray-green leaves are narrow and pointed. Plants grow from thick, fibrous roots.

Flower color Showy orange or yellow flowers with brownish purple flares on the upper petals.
Flowering time Throughout summer.
Height and spread 2–3 feet (60–90 cm) tall; 2 feet (60 cm) wide.
Temperature requirements Zones 7–10.
Position Full sun to partial shade; protect from strong winds. Evenly moist but well-drained, humus-rich soil.
Cultivation Plant dormant roots in early spring or fall. Growth begins early in the season, and plants may be damaged by late frost. Mulch with organic matter in fall to avoid frost heaving. It achieves its best performance after the third year.
Propagation Divide clumps in early spring or fall. Take care not to damage the brittle roots. Sow fresh seed indoors after 4–6 weeks of cold (35°–40°F [4°–5°C]), moist stratification. To stratify, mix seed with damp peat moss or seed-starting medium in a plastic bag and close with a twist-tie. Place the bag in the refrigerator for the appropriate time period, then sow the mixture as you would other seed.
Pest and disease prevention No serious pests or diseases.
Landscape uses Use in beds and borders.

Amsonia tabernaemontana
APOCYNACEAE

WILLOW BLUE STAR

Willow blue star is a tough, shrubby plant with lance-shaped leaves, stout stems, and terminal clusters of tiny blue flowers. Plants grow from a woody, fibrous-rooted crown.

Flower color Steel blue, ½-inch (12-mm), five-petaled starry flowers.
Flowering time Spring, with some blooming in early summer.
Height and spread 1–3 feet (30–90 cm) tall; 3 feet (90 cm) wide.
Temperature requirements Zones 3–9. Heat- and cold-tolerant.
Position Average to humus-rich, moist, well-drained soil. Full sun to light shade.
Cultivation A single plant will reach shrub-like proportions with age. Plants in shade may be floppy. If necessary, prune stems back to 6–8 inches (15–20 cm) after flowering. New shoots will form an attractive, compact mound. Leaves turn bright orange to golden yellow in fall.
Propagation Divide plants in early spring or fall. Take 4–6-inch (10–15-cm) stem cuttings in early summer. Sow ripe seed outdoors in fall or indoors after soaking in hot water for several hours before planting.
Pest and disease prevention No serious pests or diseases. Mulch with organic matter to keep the soil evenly moist.
Landscape uses Use to add structure to the garden, either alone as a mass planting or combined with other perennials.
Other common names Willow amsonia.

Anaphalis triplinervis
ASTERACEAE

THREE-VEINED EVERLASTING

Unlike most silver-leaved plants, three-veined everlasting grows well in moist soil. The papery white flowers and soft leaves add bright spots to the late-summer garden.

Flower color Papery, white, double flowers with dark centers borne in open, flattened clusters. The flowers dry on the plant and persist for weeks.
Flowering time A profusion of flowers in July, August, and September.
Height and spread 1–1½ feet (30–45 cm) tall; 1 foot (30 cm) wide.
Temperature requirements Zones 3–8.
Position Plant three-veined everlasting in moist, average to humus-rich soil in full sun to partial shade.
Cultivation This easy-care perennial spreads to form large clumps in moist soil. Divide the vigorous clumps every 2–4 years to control their spread.
Propagation Cuttings root freely in early summer.
Pest and disease prevention No serious pests or diseases.
Landscape uses Grow them in the front or middle of beds and borders or plant in informal gardens and meadow plantings. Combine with Siberian iris (*Iris sibirica*) or sweet flag (*Acorus calamus*). Ornamental grasses also make excellent companion plants, as do astilbes, daylilies, and garden phlox (*Phlox paniculata*).

Anchusa azurea
BORAGINACEAE

ITALIAN BUGLOSS

Italian bugloss has lush oblong leaves covered in stiff hair. Long branches bear terminal clusters of flowers. This fibrous-rooted plant may reach 5 feet (1.5 m) in height.

Flower color Brilliant blue, ¾-inch (18-mm), five-petaled flowers.
Flowering time Late spring.
Height and spread 2–5 feet (60–150 cm) tall; 2 feet (60 cm) wide.
Temperature requirements Zones 3–8.
Position Humus-rich, well-drained soil. Full sun to light shade.
Cultivation Since seed-grown plants may be short-lived, choose a named cultivar for better performance and longevity. Cut plants back after blooming to encourage more flowers. Divide every 2–3 years to keep plants vigorous.
Propagation Divide clumps of Italian bugloss after flowering. Replant strong, healthy divisions into soil enriched with added organic matter. Take root cuttings in early spring. Plants freely self-sow.
Pest and disease prevention No serious pests or diseases.
Landscape uses Plant among bright flowers such as yarrows and shasta daisies (*Leucanthemum* x *superbum*) or use in mass plantings with flowering shrubs.
Cultivars 'Dropmore' is a compact, 4-foot (1.2-m) selection with deep blue flowers. 'Loddon Royalist' is 3 feet (90 cm) tall with gentian blue flowers.

Anemone blanda
RANUNCULACEAE

GRECIAN WINDFLOWER

Grecian windflowers bloom in mid- to late spring in most areas; in warm Southern gardens, they may appear in late winter or early spring. They thrive in sun or light shade.

Flower color Daisy-like blue, pink, or white flowers to 2 inches (5 cm) across bloom just above ferny leaves.
Flowering time Spring.
Height and spread 6 inches (15 cm) tall; 4–6 inches (10–15 cm) wide.
Temperature requirements Zones 5–8.
Position Full sun to partial shade (ideally under deciduous trees and shrubs); average to moist, well-drained soil.
Cultivation Buy and plant the tubers in late spring through early fall. Soak them overnight before planting, and set them in individual holes or larger planting areas dug about 2 inches (5 cm) deep. If you can see a shallow depression on one side, plant with that side up; otherwise, plant the tubers on their sides or simply drop them into the hole. Space the tubers 4–6 inches (10–15 cm) apart. Windflowers propagate themselves by spreading and self-sowing.
Propagation Divide the tubers in spring, before planting.
Pest and disease prevention No serious pests or diseases.
Landscape uses Naturalize masses of Grecian windflowers under trees. They combine well with daffodils. Try them in pots and window boxes, too.

Anemone x hybrida
RANUNCULACEAE

JAPANESE ANEMONE

Japanese anemone produces clouds of flowers on slender stems. The deeply divided, hairy leaves are mostly basal. Stem leaves have fewer dissections. Plants grow from thick, tuberous roots.

Flower color Ranges from white to pink and rose; single or double blooms.
Flowering time Late summer and fall.
Height and spread 3–5 feet (90–150 cm) tall; 2–3 feet (60–90 cm) wide.
Temperature requirements Zones 5–8.
Position Humus-rich, evenly moist soil. Full sun to light shade. Protect from hot afternoon sun in warmer zones.
Cultivation Plants spread by creeping underground stems to form broad clumps once established. Thin overgrown clumps in spring if bloom wanes. Replant into soil that has been enriched with added organic matter. Mulch plants in colder zones.
Propagation Take root cuttings after plants go dormant in fall. Sow fresh seed outdoors in summer or fall. Divide mature plants in early spring.
Pest and disease prevention No serious pests or diseases.
Landscape uses Group with other late-season perennials and ornamental grasses. Combine with shrubs or ferns to provide color in moist, open shade areas.
Cultivars 'Honorine Jobert' bears pure white single blooms. 'Margarete' has deep pink semidouble flowers. 'Max Vogel' has large pink single flowers.

Antennaria dioica
ASTERACEAE

PUSSY TOES

Pussy toes is a charming little groundcover for a dry, sunny site. The rosettes of hairy, silver-green leaves are topped with pink-tipped, off-white flowers in early summer.

Flower color Pussy toes gets its name from the tiny, off-white, pink-tipped flowers that resemble a cat's foot. The blooms appear atop leafless stalks above rosettes of hairy, silver-green, 1-inch (2.5-cm) wide leaves.
Flowering time Early summer.
Height and spread Height of foliage to 10 inches (25 cm); spreads over a wide area in time. Flower height to 1 foot (30 cm).
Temperature requirements Zones 4–7.
Position Dry, sandy, poor soil. Full sun.
Cultivation Set plants 6 inches (15 cm) or more apart in light soil in spring or fall. Plants are generally maintenance-free, but they self-sow readily and tend to become invasive, so cut off the flowers before they form seed if you wish to prevent spreading.
Propagation Pussy toes is very easy to propagate; sow seed or divide in spring.
Pest and disease prevention No serious pests or diseases.
Landscape uses Pussy toes will spread to form a good cover for hot, dry spots in sunny wild areas or rock gardens. The flowers dry well for winter bouquets.
Cultivars 'Rosea' has rosy pink flower heads and whitish leaves.

Aquilegia canadensis
RANUNCULACEAE

WILD COLUMBINE

Wild columbines may be short-lived in the garden, but self-sown seedlings are plentiful and will replenish your plantings. The flowers are popular with hummingbirds.

Flower color The red-and-yellow blooms of these wildflowers nod atop delicate stalks with divided, gray-green leaflets.
Flowering time Early spring to midspring.
Height and spread 1–3 feet (30–90 cm) tall; 1 foot (30 cm) wide.
Temperature requirements Zones 3–8.
Position Plant in poor to average, well-drained soil in full sun or partial shade. Established plants are drought-tolerant.
Cultivation Set out young plants in spring or fall.
Propagation Divide or sow seed in fall or spring; they self-seed readily.
Pest and disease prevention Columbines are plagued by leafminers, which form pale tunnels and blotches in the leaves. Remove and destroy affected foliage; in severe cases, spray weekly with insecticidal soap.
Landscape uses Plant as an airy group in beds, borders, woodlands, and open meadows. Use them as a mass planting with flowering shrubs and small trees. Combine them with ferns and woodland wildflowers such as wild ginger (*Asarum canadense*) and foamflower (*Tiarella cordifolia*). In sunny meadows, plant them with wild geranium (*Geranium maculatum*) and ornamental grasses.

Aquilegia McKana hybrids
RANUNCULACEAE

HYBRID COLUMBINE

Hybrid columbines are graceful plants with curious nodding flowers. Each flower has five spurred petals surrounded by five petal-like sepals. Plants grow from a thick taproot.

Flower color Single- or bicolored variable flowers. Yellow, red, blue, purple, pink, and white are common. The spurs may be ½–4 inches (1.2–10 cm) long.
Flowering time Spring and early summer.
Height and spread 2–3 feet (60–90 cm) tall; 1–2 feet (30–60 cm) wide.
Temperature requirements Zones 3–9. Tolerates heat and cold.
Position Light, average to humus-rich, well-drained soil. Full sun to partial shade.
Cultivation They generally live 2–4 years, rewarding the gardener with a month or more of bloom. Self-sowing.
Propagation Sow seed outdoors in spring or summer. Sow indoors in winter after dry storing them in a refrigerator for 4–6 weeks.
Pest and disease prevention Leafminers create pale tunnels and blotches in the leaves. Remove and destroy damaged foliage. In severe cases spray weekly with insecticidal soap. Borers cause plants to collapse dramatically. Remove and destroy all portions of affected plants.
Landscape uses They look best in groups or drifts. Plant with spring and early-summer perennials, tulips, and daffodils. Combine with wildflowers in light shade.

Arabis caucasica
BRASSICACEAE

WALL ROCK CRESS

Wall rock cress is an attractive evergreen groundcover only 4–6 inches (10–15 cm) high. The 1-inch (2.5-cm) leaves are clothed in soft hair and are often obscured by the spring flowers.

Flower color White or pink.
Flowering time Late winter and early spring.
Height and spread 6–10 inches (15–25 cm) tall; 12–18 inches (30–45 cm) wide.
Temperature requirements Zones 3–7. Plants languish in warmer zones.
Position Average, well-drained soil. Full sun to light shade. Tolerates a wide range of soil moisture and fertility.
Cultivation Spreads quickly to form loose mats of foliage. Cut plants back after flowering to encourage new shoots and to keep them neat. Divide every 2–4 years to keep plants healthy.
Propagation Take cuttings in spring. Layer by burying 6 inches (15 cm) of a low-growing stem and leaving the leafy tip exposed. Divide in spring or fall.
Pest and disease prevention No serious pests or diseases.
Landscape uses Rock cress looks great tumbling over a stone wall or in a rock garden. Interplant with spring bulbs and early perennials along borders.
Cultivars 'Snow Cap' is a robust plant with profuse white flowers. 'Rosabella' has rose pink flowers.

Arenaria montana
CARYOPHYLLACEAE

MOUNTAIN SANDWORT

Mountain sandwort is a dense, mat-forming groundcover with tiny needle-like leaves and flat, white, five-petaled flowers. Plants grow from thin, fibrous roots.

Flower color White.
Flowering time Spring and early summer.
Height and spread 2–4 inches (5–10 cm) tall; 12 inches (30 cm) tall in flower; 10–12 inches (25–30 cm) wide; they grow larger with age.
Temperature requirements Zones 4–8.
Position Average sandy or loamy, well-drained soil. Full sun. These plants dislike acid soil.
Cultivation Spreads slowly to form low, moss-like mats of foliage. Shallow-rooted; keep moist during dry spells.
Propagation Divide in spring or fall. Sow seed outdoors in fall or inside in early spring.
Pest and disease prevention No serious pests or diseases.
Landscape uses Plant between pavers in walkways or among the rocks in loosely constructed walls. Mountain sandwort is excellent in rock gardens and perfect for pot or trough culture.

Arisaema triphyllum
ARACEAE

JACK-IN-THE-PULPIT

Jack-in-the-pulpits are spring wildflowers. The unusual flower hides beneath single or paired leaves, each with three broad leaflets. Plants grow from a button-like tuber.

Flower color Green flowers striped with yellow or purple. Glossy red berries ripen in late summer.
Flowering time Spring.
Height and spread 1–3 feet (30–90 cm) tall; 1–1½ feet (30–45 cm) wide.
Temperature requirements Zones 3–9.
Position Evenly moist, humus-rich soil. Partial to full shade. Tolerates wet soil.
Cultivation Easy to grow and long-lived. Clumps grow slowly from offsets or seed.
Propagation Remove the pulp from ripe berries and sow the seed outdoors in spring or fall. Seedlings develop slowly and may take several years to bloom. Propagate from natural offsets in spring.
Pest and disease prevention No serious pests or diseases.
Landscape uses Plant among low wildflowers for an eye-catching vertical accent. Combine with fringed bleeding heart (*Dicentra eximia*), hostas, bloodroot (*Sanguinaria canadensis*), and ferns. Plant under shrubs or flowering trees.

Armeria maritima
PLUMBAGINACEAE

THRIFT

Thrift forms dense tufts of grass-like, gray-green evergreen leaves. These are topped by delicate flowers, which arise from the centers of the tightly packed clumps.

Flower color Small, pink flowers crowded into rounded 1-inch (2.5-cm) heads.
Flowering time Late spring and summer.
Height and spread 10–14 inches (25–35 cm) tall; 8–10 inches (20–25 cm) wide.
Temperature requirements Zones 4–8.
Position Average to humus-rich, moist but well-drained soil. Full sun. Prefers cool nights and low humidity.
Cultivation Drought-tolerant once established; will grow in rock crevices where water is scarce. Tolerates air- and soilborne salt; perfect for seaside gardens.
Propagation Divide clumps in early spring or fall. Sow seed indoors in winter on a warm (70°F [21°C]) seedbed.
Pest and disease prevention No serious pests or diseases.
Landscape uses Plant in rock and wall gardens or along paths.
Other common names Sea pink.
Cultivars 'Alba' has white flowers on 5-inch (12.5-cm) stems. 'Vindictive' is only 6 inches (15 cm) tall with bright rose pink flowers. 'Dusseldorf Pride' has wine red flowers on 6–8-inch (15–20-cm) stems. 'Robusta' has large pink flower heads on 12–15-inch (30–37.5-cm) stems.

Artemisia absinthium
ASTERACEAE

COMMON WORMWOOD

Common wormwood is a stout, shrubby perennial with stems that become woody with age. Soft hair on the deeply lobed, aromatic foliage gives the plant a muted gray-green tone.

Flower color Inconspicuous yellow flowers borne in terminal clusters.
Flowering time Late summer and fall.
Height and spread 2–3 feet (60–90 cm) tall; 2 feet (60 cm) wide.
Temperature requirements Zones 3–9.
Position Average sandy or loamy, well-drained soil. Full sun.
Cultivation Thrives in all but the most inhospitable garden spots. Overly rich soils result in weak growth. Encourage compact growth by pruning back untidy plants by at least half.
Propagation Grow from stem cuttings taken in late summer or spring. Dust the cut surfaces with a rooting hormone to speed production of new roots.
Pest and disease prevention No serious pests or diseases.
Landscape uses Combine common wormwood with yarrows and other drought-tolerant perennials. The soft foliage looks lovely when planted with ornamental grasses.
Cultivars 'Lambrook Silver' has beautiful deeply cut silver-gray foliage.

Artemisia lactiflora
ASTERACEAE

WHITE MUGWORT

White mugwort bears showy plumes of fragrant white flowers in late summer. Unlike its silver-leaved relatives, white mugwort needs moist soil and can take light shade.

Flower color A spectacular show of graceful, 2-foot (60-cm) long plumes of fragrant white flowers.

Flowering time Late summer.

Height and spread 4–6 feet (1.2–1.8 m) tall; up to 4 feet (1.2 m) wide.

Temperature requirements Zones 5–8.

Position Does best in full sun but will tolerate light shade; moist, fertile soil.

Cultivation Give plenty of space when planting seedlings. Fertilize lightly in spring and prune back lightly to stimulate growth. Water during drought.

Propagation Propagate by cuttings in summer or by division in spring.

Pest and disease prevention Plants are generally problem-free.

Landscape uses White mugwort makes a nice background plant in a flower border, especially when highlighted by lower-growing coneflowers (*Rudbeckia* spp.), daylilies, or asters.

Arum italicum
ARACEAE

ITALIAN ARUM

By late summer, the spring flowers of Italian arum mature into columns of reddish orange berries. These colorful spikes add interest until the new leaves appear in fall.

Flower color Italian arum has a greenish white, hood-like spathe sheltering a narrow column known as the spadix. These unusual flowers are interesting, but the plant is mainly grown for its arrowhead-shaped, semiglossy, dark green leaves that are marked with creamy white.

Flowering time Mid- to late spring.

Height and spread Height 12–18 inches (30–45 cm); spread to 12 inches (30 cm).

Temperature requirements Zones 6–10.

Position Partial shade; average, well-drained soil with organic matter.

Cultivation Plant in late summer or early fall. Set the tubers into individual holes or larger planting areas dug 2–3 inches (5–7.5 cm) deep. Space the tubers 8–12 inches (20–30 cm) apart. The leaves emerge in fall and last through the winter, finally dying in summer. Keep the soil moist during leaf growth and flowering.

Propagation Divide plants in early fall.

Pest and disease prevention No serious pests or diseases.

Landscape uses Italian arum looks marvelous in masses along streams and in woodland gardens. It also adds multiseason interest when planted under trees.

Aruncus dioicus
ROSACEAE

GOAT'S BEARD

Goat's beards are showy, shrub-like perennials with large, three-lobed leaves and airy plumes of flowers. Male and female flowers are borne on separate plants.

Flower color Creamy white flowers with small petals.

Flowering time Late spring and early summer.

Height and spread 3–6 feet (90–180 cm) tall; 3–5 feet (90–150 cm) wide.

Temperature requirements Zones 3–7; unsuitable for areas with hot nights.

Position Moist, humus-rich soil. Full sun (in cooler zones) to partial shade.

Cultivation Plant 4–5 feet (1.2–1.5 m) apart to allow for the plant's impressive mature size. The tough rootstocks are difficult to move once established. Divide plants only if necessary to revitalize the clumps. Lift in early spring and replant strong, healthy divisions into soil that has been enriched with organic matter.

Propagation Sow seed in summer outdoors. Alternatively, sow inside on a warm (70°F [21°C]) seedbed.

Pest and disease prevention No serious pests or diseases.

Landscape uses Use with wildflowers, ferns, and hostas in a lightly shaded woodland garden or as an accent with flowering shrubs. It combines well with other perennials in beds and borders.

Asarum europaeum
ARISTOLOCHIACEAE

EUROPEAN WILD GINGER

European wild ginger is a slow-creeping evergreen groundcover. The glossy, kidney-shaped leaves are mottled along the veins. The aromatic rhizomes creep at or just below the soil surface.

Flower color Jug-like, dull brown flowers are usually hidden under the foliage.
Flowering time Spring.
Height and spread 6–12 inches (15–30 cm) tall; 12 inches (30 cm) wide. Forms broad clumps with age.
Temperature requirements Zones 4–8.
Position Moist, humus-rich soil. Partial to full shade. This plant is drought-tolerant once established but does best when moisture is adequate.
Cultivation An exceptional groundcover. Clumps spread steadily to form tight mats of weed-proof foliage. Divide crowded plants in early spring or fall.
Propagation Divide in spring. Sow fresh seed outdoors in summer.
Pest and disease prevention No serious pests or diseases.
Landscape uses Plant along a garden path with ferns and wildflowers or in a shaded rock garden.

Asclepias tuberosa
ASCLEPIADACEAE

BUTTERFLY WEED

The bright flowers of butterfly weed are perfect for enlivening borders, cottage gardens, meadows, and container plantings. These plants can even tolerate seaside conditions.

Flower color Butterflies adore the masses of brilliant orange flowers that crown the mounded, shrub-like clumps in summer.
Flowering time May and June.
Height and spread 2–3 feet (60–90 cm) tall; 2 feet (60 cm) wide.
Temperature requirements Zones 3–9.
Position Plant in poor to average, well-drained soil in full sun or light shade. Plants thrive in sandy soil and tolerate seaside conditions.
Cultivation Established plants are extremely drought-tolerant and thrive for years with little care.
Propagation Take tip cuttings in late spring or early summer; they root quickly. Sow fresh seed outdoors in fall.
Pest and disease prevention No serious pests or diseases.
Landscape uses Grow butterfly weed in formal borders, rock gardens, and meadow plantings. Combine with blue and purple flowers such as sages (*Salvia* spp.) and lavenders (*Lavandula* spp.) for a lively display. Ornamental grasses, asters, and goldenrods (*Solidago* spp.) are natural companions in meadows.

Aster novae-angliae
ASTERACEAE

NEW ENGLAND ASTER

New England aster is a tall, stately plant with hairy stems and clasping, lance-shaped leaves. Most selections are best planted at the back of the perennial border.

Flower color Lavender to purple, 1½–2-inch (3.7–5-cm) flowers with bright yellow centers. Flowers may vary in color from white to pink and rose.
Flowering time Late summer through fall.
Height and spread 3–6 feet (90–180 cm) tall; 3 feet (90 cm) wide. Matures into broad clumps.
Temperature requirements Zones 3–8.
Position Moist, humus-rich soil. Full sun to light shade.
Cultivation Clumps become quite large with age. Divide every 3–4 years in spring. Plants may need staking.
Propagation Take 4–6-inch (10–15-cm) stem cuttings in late spring or early summer. Divide in early spring or fall.
Pest and disease prevention Powdery mildew turns leaves dull gray. Thin stems to promote air circulation. Dust affected plants with sulfur.
Landscape uses Plant with fall perennials like sunflowers (*Helianthus* spp.), Japanese anemones (*Anemone* x *hybrida*), and ornamental grasses.
Cultivars 'Alma Potschke' has dark salmon-pink flowers on 2–4-foot (60–120-cm) plants. 'Purple Dome' is a dwarf selection with royal purple flowers.

Aster novi-belgii
ASTERACEAE

NEW YORK ASTER

Late-blooming New York aster is a colorful addition to the fall garden. Divide clumps every year or two to keep them vigorous; pinch in early summer to promote strong stems.

Flower color White, blue, purple, or pink single or double flowers, 1¼–2½ inches (3–6 cm) wide, with bright yellow centers.
Flowering time Late summer and early fall.
Height and spread Depending on the cultivar, 1–6 feet (30–180 cm) tall; 1–3 feet (30–90 cm) wide.
Temperature requirements Zones 3–8.
Position Sun; moist, well-drained soil of moderate fertility.
Cultivation Pinch asters once or twice before June 15 to make them bushier and less likely to need staking. Divide every 1–2 years to renew the plant. Mulch during winter in Zone 4.
Propagation Divide in early spring.
Pest and disease prevention Don't overcrowd; this plant needs plenty of fresh air to avoid mildew.
Landscape uses Use in clumps or masses in flower or mixed borders. Asters look good with chrysanthemums and goldenrods (*Solidago* spp.).

Aster x frikartii
ASTERACEAE

FRIKART'S ASTER

Frikart's aster produces open clusters of yellow-centered flowers on loosely branched stems. Plants grow from short, slow-creeping rhizomes with fibrous roots.

Flower color Lavender-blue, 2½-inch (6-cm) flowers with bright yellow centers.
Flowering time Midsummer through fall.
Height and spread 2–3 feet (60–90 cm) tall; 2–3 feet (60–90 cm) wide. Stems often lean on other plants for support.
Temperature requirements Zones 5–8; Zone 4 with mulch protection or consistent winter snow.
Position Moist but well-drained soil. Full sun to light shade. Plants will rot in sodden soil, especially in winter.
Cultivation Frikart's aster may be short-lived. Clumps spread slowly. Divide plants as necessary in spring or fall.
Propagation Take stem cuttings in spring. Divide in early spring or fall.
Pest and disease prevention Plant in a well-drained position to deter root rot.
Landscape uses Combine Frikart's asters with late-summer and fall perennials like coneflowers (*Rudbeckia* spp.), garden phlox (*Phlox paniculata*), and ornamental grasses. They grow well in containers in Zones 6–8.
Cultivars 'Monch' has erect stems and lavender-blue flowers. 'Wonder of Staffa' is more open in habit with paler flowers.

Astilbe x arendsii
SAXIFRAGACEAE

ASTILBE

Astilbes have dense, showy flower clusters and ferny, dissected leaves with shiny broad leaflets. The emerging spring shoots are often tinged with red.

Flower color Upright, often-plumed flower clusters bear tightly packed, fuzzy blooms in shades of red, pink, rose, lilac, cream, and white.
Flowering time Spring and early summer.
Height and spread 2–4 feet (60–120 cm) tall; 2–3 feet (60–90 cm) wide. Leafy clumps spread steadily outward.
Temperature requirements Zones 3–9.
Position Moist, slightly acid, humus-rich soil. Full to partial shade; tolerates more sun in cool-summer areas.
Cultivation Benefits from an annual application of balanced organic fertilizer. Top-dress with compost or lift and replant the clumps if crowns rise above the soil. Divide clumps every 3–4 years and replant into soil enriched with organic matter. Keep plants well watered.
Propagation Propagate the true species by sowing fresh seed outdoors in summer or early fall. Propagate cultivars by spring or fall division only.
Pest and disease prevention Spray spider mites with insecticidal soap as necessary. Control root rot with good drainage and good air circulation.
Landscape uses Plant by streams or ponds and in borders.

Astrantia major
APIACEAE

MASTERWORT

Masterwort is a showy perennial with bold, deeply lobed palmate leaves on a stout, fibrous-rooted crown. Leafy branched flower stalks rise from the center of the foliage clumps.

Flower color Creamy white, button-like flower heads are surrounded by a whorl of starry, pointed bracts. The stiff bracts remain after the flowers fade, prolonging the display.
Flowering time Early to late summer. Reblooms frequently if deadheaded.
Height and spread 2–3 feet (60–90 cm) tall; 1–2 feet (30–60 cm) wide. Clumps become quite large with age.
Temperature requirements Zones 4–7. Does not tolerate high temperatures, especially at night.
Position Evenly moist, humus-rich soil. Full sun to partial shade. Tolerates wet soil.
Cultivation Clumps increase by creeping underground stems and may outgrow their position. Divide mature plants to control their size and spread.
Propagation Divide plants in fall or early spring or remove runners from the main clump at the same time of year. Sow fresh seed outdoors in late summer.
Pest and disease prevention No serious pests or diseases.
Landscape uses Plant along borders or use beside ponds with irises and ferns.

Aubrieta deltoidea
BRASSICACEAE

ROCK CRESS

Rock cress is a low, mounding, spring-blooming plant with weak stems clothed in sparsely toothed evergreen leaves. Plants spread by thin rhizomes to form broad clumps.

Flower color Four-petaled, ¾-inch (18-mm) flowers in white, rose, or purple.
Flowering time Early spring.
Height and spread 6–8 inches (15–20 cm) tall; 8–12 inches (20–30 cm) wide. Forms tight mounds of foliage smothered in flowers.
Temperature requirements Zones 4–8. Grows best where summer humidity and temperatures are not excessive.
Position Average, well-drained, sandy or loamy, neutral soil. Full sun to light shade.
Cultivation Plants tend to flop after flowering. Shear clumps at that time to promote compact growth and to encourage repeat bloom.
Propagation Divide in fall. Take stem cuttings after flowering. Sow seed indoors or outdoors from spring to fall.
Pest and disease prevention Plant in well-drained soil to avoid root rot, especially in areas where nighttime temperatures are high.
Landscape uses Rock cress is at home in the cracks and crevices of walls and rock gardens. Plant at the edge of walks or at the front of beds and borders.
Cultivars 'Aurea Variegata' has yellow-variegated leaves and blue-violet flowers.

Aurinia saxatilis
BRASSICACEAE

BASKET OF GOLD

Basket of gold produces mounds of 6-inch (15-cm) oblong gray-green leaves from a thick crown. Hairy leaves and deep roots help the plant endure dry soil and warm temperatures.

Flower color Brilliant yellow flowers have four rounded petals and are carried in upright, branched clusters.
Flowering time Early spring.
Height and spread 10–12 inches (25–30 cm) tall; 12 inches (30 cm) wide.
Temperature requirements Zones 3–7. Tolerates hot, dry conditions, but not suitable for hot and humid climates.
Position Average, well-drained, loamy or sandy soil. Full sun.
Cultivation Clumps spread by creeping stems and may flop after flowering. Cut stems back by two-thirds after flowering to encourage compact growth.
Propagation Divide in fall. Take stem cuttings in spring or fall. Sow seed in fall.
Pest and disease prevention Heavy, moist soils along with high humidity will encourage root rot. To avoid this problem, plant in well-drained soils only.
Landscape uses Basket of gold lends color to rock walls, rock gardens, and walkways. Combine with rock cresses (*Aubrieta* spp.) and pinks (*Dianthus* spp.).
Cultivars 'Citrinum' has clear lemon yellow flowers. 'Compactum' forms tight clumps only 8 inches (20 cm) tall. 'Sunny Border Apricot' has peach-colored flowers.

Baptisia australis
FABACEAE

BLUE FALSE INDIGO

Blue false indigo is a spectacular perennial that reaches shrub-like proportions. Mature plants form dense, rounded mounds of three-lobed, blue-green leaves.

Flower color Deep blue, 1-inch (2.5-cm) flowers are carried in narrow, open clusters and resemble lupines. The dried gray pods are showy in fall and winter.

Flowering time Late spring and early summer.

Height and spread 2–4 feet (60–120 cm) tall; 3–4 feet (90–120 cm) wide.

Temperature requirements Zones 3–9. Tolerant of heat and cold.

Position Average to humus-rich, moist, well-drained soil. Full sun to partial shade.

Cultivation Grows slowly until its taproot establishes. Mature plants have massive, tough root systems that resent disturbance. Space young plants 3–4 feet (90–120 cm) apart. Division is seldom necessary.

Propagation Take cuttings after flowering or sow fresh seed outdoors in fall. Treat stored seed by pouring near-boiling water over and soaking for 12–24 hours. Divide clumps in fall, late winter, or early spring.

Pest and disease prevention No serious pests or diseases.

Landscape uses Plant toward the rear of borders with Siberian iris (*Iris sibirica*), peonies, and other bold-textured plants. Use them in meadow and prairie plantings.

Other common names Baptisia.

Begonia Tuberhybrida hybrids
BEGONIACEAE

HYBRID TUBEROUS BEGONIAS

Hybrid tuberous begonias bloom in a wide range of colors, except for blues and purples; many are edged or shaded with other colors. Pinch off spent flowers to keep plants tidy.

Flower color The bushy plants produce an abundance of gorgeous single or double flowers up to 4 inches (10 cm) wide in almost every color except blue.

Flowering time Summer through fall.

Height and spread Height to 18 inches (45 cm); spread 12–18 inches (30–45 cm).

Temperature requirements Hardy in Zone 10; elsewhere, grown as annuals or stored indoors in winter.

Position Evenly moist but well-drained soil that has been enriched with added organic matter. Partial shade.

Cultivation Buy thick tubers that are 1½–2 inches (3.7–5 cm) across. Start growing indoors about 4 weeks before your last frost date. Give developing plants bright light, and keep the soil evenly moist. Set plants out when night temperatures stay above 50°F (10°C). Water and mulch to keep the soil evenly moist. Fertilize several times during the season.

Propagation Divide tubers in spring, after bringing them out of winter storage.

Pest and disease prevention Prevent powdery mildew by giving plants a site with good air circulation.

Landscape uses Plant in shaded beds and borders, containers, and hanging baskets.

Belamcanda chinensis
IRIDACEAE

BLACKBERRY LILY

Blackberry lilies produce showy, curved fans of foliage that resemble irises. Branched clumps grow from creeping rhizomes and may produce dozens of orange flowers.

Flower color Six-petaled, 2-inch (5-cm), orange flowers are speckled with red. Inflated seed capsules split in fall to expose the berry-like clusters of black seeds that give the plant its common name.

Flowering time Mid- to late summer.

Height and spread 2–4 feet (60–120 cm) tall; 1–2 feet (30–60 cm) wide.

Temperature requirements Zones 4–10. May need winter protection in the colder areas of Zone 4.

Position Average to humus-rich, well-drained soil. Full sun to light shade. Afternoon shade may prolong the life of individual flowers.

Cultivation Plants spread by creeping rhizomes to form dense clumps. Divide as necessary to control their spread. Self-sown seedlings often appear.

Propagation Divide in late summer or sow fresh seed outdoors in spring.

Pest and disease prevention No serious pests or diseases.

Landscape uses Plant with garden phlox (*Phlox paniculata*), daylilies, and other plants with large flowers that will contrast with blackberry lily's small, starry flowers.

Bergenia cordifolia
SAXIFRAGACEAE

HEART-LEAVED BERGENIA

Heart-leaved bergenias are handsome plants with broad, oval, leathery, evergreen foliage. The 10–12-inch (25–30-cm) leaves emerge in a whorl from a stout, creeping rhizome.

Flower color Nodding pink or rose flowers are carried above the foliage on thick, branched stems.
Flowering time Late winter and early spring.
Height and spread 12–14 inches (30–35 cm) tall; 12 inches (30 cm) wide.
Temperature requirements Zones 3–9. Foliage benefits from winter protection where snowfall is not consistent.
Position Moist, humus-rich soil. Full sun to partial shade; afternoon shade in warmer zones to protect leaves from burning.
Cultivation As clumps age, they become bare in the center. Lift plants in spring and remove old portions of the rhizome with a sharp knife. Replant in soil enriched with organic matter. Protect with winter mulch.
Propagation Divide in spring. Sow ripe seed indoors on a warm (70°F [21°C]) seedbed. Leave seed uncovered. Young plants develop slowly.
Pest and disease prevention Exclude slugs with barrier strips of wood ashes or sand, or bait them with shallow pans of beer set flush with the soil surface.
Landscape uses Use as accents at the base of rock walls or along a path. Plant under shrubs for a glossy groundcover.

Boltonia asteroides
ASTERACEAE

BOLTONIA

Boltonias are tall, late-season perennials with masses of flowers smothering the gray-green willow-like foliage. The mounded plants are lovely for their foliage; the flowers are a bonus.

Flower color A profusion of 1-inch (2.5-cm) white daisies with bright yellow centers is carried in open clusters.
Flowering time Late summer through fall.
Height and spread 4–6 feet (1.2–1.8 m) tall; 4 feet (1.2 m) wide.
Temperature requirements Zones 3–9.
Position Moist, humus-rich soil. Full sun to light shade. Dry soil produces much smaller plants.
Cultivation These easy-to-grow plants form sturdy, dense clumps with stems that will seldom need staking.
Propagation Divide oversized clumps in spring. Take cuttings in early summer. Seed collected from cultivars will produce seedlings unlike the parent plants and, in most cases, inferior to them.
Pest and disease prevention No serious pests or diseases.
Landscape uses Combine with fall-blooming perennials like asters, Japanese anemones (*Anemone* x *hybrida*), goldenrods (*Solidago* spp.), Joe-Pye weeds (*Eupatorium* spp.), and ornamental grasses.
Cultivars 'Pink Beauty' sports soft pink flowers in open clusters. Cool summers produce brighter colors. 'Snowbank' is a compact selection with white flowers.

Brunnera macrophylla
BORAGINACEAE

SIBERIAN BUGLOSS

Siberian bugloss is grown for both its flowers and its foliage. The bold, 8-inch (20-cm), heart-shaped leaves rise in a tight mound from a short, fibrous-rooted rhizome.

Flower color Sprays of ¼-inch (6-mm), forget-me-not-blue flowers cover the plants before the leaves emerge.
Flowering time Early spring. Flowering often continues for 3–4 weeks.
Height and spread 1–1½ feet (30–45 cm) tall; 2 feet (60 cm) wide. Foliage reaches mature size in summer.
Temperature requirements Zones 3–8.
Position Evenly moist, humus-rich soil. Partial to full shade; full sun in cooler zones. This plant tolerates short dry spells once established.
Cultivation Plants are tough, increase slowly, and seldom need division. Self-sown seedlings appear regularly around the parent clumps. Keep soil moist; plants will go dormant in persistent drought.
Propagation Divide clumps in early spring or fall. Take 3–4-inch (7.5–10-cm) root cuttings either in fall or early winter. Transplant seedlings that have self-sown to the desired position.
Pest and disease prevention No serious pests or diseases.
Landscape uses Plant as a groundcover under trees or shrubs with spring bulbs, wildflowers, and ferns.

Caladium bicolor
ARACEAE

CALADIUM

Caladiums are grown for their showy leaves; pinch off any of the small, hooded flowers that appear in summer. These shade-loving plants thrive in heat and humidity.

Flower color Caladiums are grown for their foliage, producing bushy clumps of usually heart-shaped leaves that are shaded and veined with combinations of green, white, pink, and red.

Flowering time Late spring until frost.

Height and spread 1–2 feet (30–60 cm) tall; 2 feet (60 cm) wide.

Temperature requirements Hardy in Zone 10; elsewhere, grown as annuals or stored indoors for winter.

Position Partial shade; moist but well-drained soil with added organic matter.

Cultivation Start the tubers indoors in early spring. Set them with the knobby side up in pots of moist potting mix and cover with 2 inches (5 cm) mix. Keep in a warm, bright spot with soil evenly moist. Move out to the garden when night temperatures stay above 60°F (16°C). Keep soil moist until late summer. When leaves die, dig up the tubers and store in a warm place.

Propagation Divide tubers in spring, after bringing them out of winter storage.

Pest and disease prevention No serious pests or diseases.

Landscape uses Caladiums provide summer color in shady beds and borders, especially in warm- and hot-summer areas.

Calluna vulgaris
ERICACEAE

HEATHER

Heather thrives in full sun and infertile, acid soil. In cold climates, protect plants from winter winds by covering them with a light mulch or a layer of evergreen branches.

Flower color Tiny, pinkish, bell-shaped flowers bloom along the shoot tips.

Flowering time Late summer to fall.

Height and spread Up to 2 feet (60 cm) tall but varies according to cultivar; 2–4 feet (60–120 cm) wide.

Temperature requirements Zones 5–7.

Position Acid, well-drained, poor soil; does not grow well in alkaline or fertile conditions. Full sun is necessary to produce flowers, though the plant will also grow in partial shade.

Cultivation Set plants 12–18 inches (30–45 cm) apart in spring or early fall. Prune off the shoots from the previous season in early spring to encourage tight, compact growth.

Propagation Propagate by seed anytime, by cuttings in early summer, or by layering in spring (cover part of a low-growing stem with soil until new roots form, then separate it from the parent plant).

Pest and disease prevention No serious pests or diseases.

Landscape uses Heather looks great with other shrubs or in masses that use several different cultivars. It is also excellent for dried arrangements.

Caltha palustris
RANUNCULACEAE

MARSH MARIGOLD

Marsh marigolds grow in moist soil and shallow wetlands. They produce yellow spring flowers over mounds of rounded leaves from a thick crown with fleshy white roots.

Flower color Butter yellow, 1½-inch (3.7-cm) flowers have five shiny petals and are carried in open clusters.

Flowering time Early to midspring.

Height and spread 1–2 feet (30–60 cm) tall; up to 2 feet (60 cm) wide.

Temperature requirements Zones 2–8.

Position Wet, humus-rich or loamy soil. Full sun to partial shade. This plant grows even when covered with 1–4 inches (2.5–10 cm) of water. Once flowering is complete, moisture is less critical.

Cultivation Divide overgrown plants a month after flowering, when dormant.

Propagation Divide in summer. Sow fresh seed outdoors immediately upon ripening; these plants will not germinate, however, until the following spring.

Pest and disease prevention No serious pests or diseases.

Landscape uses Marsh marigolds are perfect for water gardens or along the low banks of streams. Plant with primroses, irises, and ferns in bog gardens.

Other common names Cowslip.

Cultivars 'Flore Pleno' ('Multiplex') has double flowers that last for a week or more.

Camassia quamash
HYACINTHACEAE

COMMON CAMASS

In full sun, steady soil moisture is critical for growing common camass successfully. In lightly shaded spots, the bulbs, which usually like good moisture levels, can withstand drier conditions.

Flower color Grassy clumps send up leafless stems topped with dense, spiky flower clusters. These spikes are made up of many 1–2-inch (2.5–5-cm) wide, starry flowers in white or pale to deep blue.
Flowering time Late spring.
Height and spread 2–2½ feet (60–75 cm) tall; 1 foot (30 cm) wide.
Temperature requirements Zones 4–8.
Position Full sun to partial shade; moist but not waterlogged soil.
Cultivation The bulbs usually aren't available for sale at garden centers, so you'll probably have to buy them from a mail-order source. Plant the bulbs in fall, in individual holes or in larger planting areas dug about 4 inches (10 cm) deep. Space 8–10 inches (20–25 cm) apart. Cut down faded flower stems after bloom.
Propagation Divide bulbs once foliage has died back in mid- to late summer.
Pest and disease prevention No serious pests or diseases.
Landscape uses Plant in low spots, along streams and ponds, or with moisture-loving shrubs and perennials.
Other common names Quamash, wild hyacinth. Common camass may also be sold as *C. esculenta*.

Campanula carpatica
CAMPANULACEAE

CARPATHIAN HAREBELL

Adaptable Carpathian harebell spreads to form tidy mounds of dark green leaves topped with cup-shaped, blue-purple flowers. Mulch to keep the roots cool in warm climates.

Flower color Clumps of lively blue-purple or white flowers.
Flowering time Early summer.
Height and spread 9 inches (22.5 cm) tall; slightly wider spread.
Temperature requirements Zones 3–8.
Position Well-drained, moist, fertile soil. Full sun; light shade in hotter sites.
Cultivation Mulch with compost during summer. Water in drought.
Propagation Carpathian harebells are short-lived unless you divide and renew plants every couple of years. Deadhead for an extended bloom period or leave a few flowers on so the plant can self-sow.
Pest and disease prevention Exclude snails and slugs with barrier strips of diatomaceous earth, wood ashes, or sand. Alternatively, bait them with shallow pans of beer set flush with the soil surface.
Landscape uses Set in clumps or rows at the front of a flower or shrub border. Or use plants individually in a rock garden or beside a stone patio.
Cultivars 'Alba' has pure white flowers.

Campanula persicifolia
CAMPANULACEAE

PEACH-LEAVED BELLFLOWER

Peach-leaved bellflower produces mounds of narrow, 8-inch (20-cm), evergreen leaves from a fibrous-rooted crown. The summer blooms make long-lasting cut flowers.

Flower color Open, bell-shaped flowers, lavender-blue in color, are carried on tall, narrow stalks.
Flowering time Summer.
Height and spread 1–3 feet (30–90 cm) tall; 2 feet (60 cm) wide.
Temperature requirements Zones 3–8. Prefers cooler summer temperatures.
Position Moist but well-drained, humus-rich soil. Full sun to partial shade; protect from hot afternoon sun in warmer zones.
Cultivation Peach-leaved bellflower is a tough, easy-care plant that spreads slowly by sideshoots from the central crown. Division is seldom necessary. Plants may be short-lived in warmer zones.
Propagation Take tip cuttings in early summer. Divide clumps in early spring.
Pest and disease prevention Exclude slugs with barrier strips of diatomaceous earth, wood ashes, or sand. Alternatively, bait them with shallow pans of beer set flush with the soil surface.
Landscape uses Plant toward the middle or rear of borders. The showy flowers combine well with yarrows, Russian sage (*Perovskia atriplicifolia*), and other fine-textured plants. Use them in drifts as an accent along a stone wall or garden fence.

Campanula portenschlagiana
CAMPANULACEAE

DALMATIAN BELLFLOWER

Dalmatian bellflower is a free-flowering, easy-care groundcover that spreads over soil and rocks to form extensive clumps. It also looks great cascading over walls.

Flower color Creeping mats of small, triangular leaves are practically obscured by starry, blue-purple, bell-shaped flowers.
Flowering time Spring and early summer.
Height and spread 3–6 inches (7.5–15 cm) tall; 10–12 inches (25–30 cm) wide.
Temperature requirements Zones 4–8.
Position Plant in average to rich, well-drained soil in full sun or partial shade. Tolerates drought and heat.
Cultivation Plants grow from fibrous-rooted crowns and root along the spreading stems as they rest on the ground. Protect from drying winds.
Propagation Divide plants in spring or fall or take tip cuttings in late spring. Plants are also easy to grow from seed sown indoors or outdoors.
Pest and disease prevention Set shallow pans of beer flush with the soil surface to drown slugs, which can be a problem.
Landscape uses Dalmatian bellflowers are perfect for rock and wall gardens: Plant them in crevices and watch them spread to form breathtaking clumps. Also use them at the front of borders or as edging for beds.

Canna x generalis
CANNACEAE

CANNA

Cannas grow from thick rhizomes. They produce tall, sturdy stems with large, oval, green or reddish purple leaves from spring until frost. Tall flower stalks are topped with showy flowers.

Flower color Showy clusters of broad-petaled flowers up to 5 inches (12.5 cm) across, which bloom in shades of pink, red, orange, and yellow, as well as bicolors.
Flowering time Mid- to late summer.
Height and spread 2–6 feet (60–180 cm) tall; 1–2 feet (30–60 cm) wide.
Temperature requirements Usually hardy in Zones 7–10; elsewhere, grow as annuals.
Position Full sun to partial shade; average to moist, well-drained soil with added organic matter.
Cultivation Start rhizomes indoors about a month before your last frost date. Set out 2–3 weeks after the last frost date. Or plant rhizomes directly into the garden at that time, setting them 3–4 inches (7.5–10 cm) deep and 12–18 inches (30–45 cm) apart. Cannas are drought-tolerant, but mulch and water during dry spells. Pinch off spent flowers to prolong bloom.
Propagation Divide canna clumps in spring; divide the rhizomes into pieces about 6 inches (15 cm) square, making sure each has at least one growth bud.
Pest and disease prevention No serious pests or diseases.
Landscape uses Alone in masses, or with annuals and perennials in beds and borders.

Catananche caerulea
ASTERACEAE

CUPID'S DART

Cupid's dart produces tufts of narrow, woolly leaves from a fibrous rootstock. The straw-like flowers look great in the summer garden and dry easily for flower arrangements.

Flower color Blue, 2-inch (5-cm) flowers resemble asters but lack the bold yellow center. Carried singly on wiry stems.
Flowering time Summer.
Height and spread 18–24 inches (45–60 cm) tall; 10–12 inches (25–30 cm) wide.
Temperature requirements Zones 4–9. Cupid's dart is heat-tolerant.
Position Light, well-drained, humus-rich soil. Full sun. Good drainage is imperative for healthy growth.
Cultivation Plants may be short-lived, especially in heavy soil. Divide plants every year to promote longevity.
Propagation Divide in fall. Take 2–3-inch (5–7.5-cm) root cuttings in fall or winter. Sow seed indoors in early spring. Plants will bloom the first year.
Pest and disease prevention No serious pests or diseases.
Landscape uses Use in mass plantings in rock gardens or at the front of a dry, sunny perennial garden. Combine with yarrows and sundrops (*Oenothera* spp.).
Cultivars 'Blue Giant' is a stout cultivar with dark blue flowers. 'Major' has single lavender-blue flowers that open on 3-foot (90-cm) stems.

Centaurea hypoleuca
ASTERACEAE

KNAPWEED

Knapweeds have lobed leaves with woolly divisions. The leaves clothe thick, weakly upright stems over fibrous-rooted crowns. Use the blooms as fresh cut flowers or for drying.

Flower color The delicately fringed pink flowers have broad white centers. They resemble cornflowers and are borne one to a stem.
Flowering time Late spring and early summer.
Height and spread 1½–2½ feet (45–75 cm) tall; 1½ feet (45 cm) wide.
Temperature requirements Zones 3–7.
Position Moist but well-drained, humus-rich soil. Full sun.
Cultivation Remove flower heads as they fade to promote rebloom. Cut plants back to remove floppy stems when flower production wanes. Divide clumps every 2–3 years to keep plants vigorous.
Propagation Divide mature plants in spring or fall. Sow seed outdoors in fall or indoors in late winter.
Pest and disease prevention No serious pests or diseases.
Landscape uses Combine knapweeds with ornamental grasses, coneflowers (*Rudbeckia* spp.), and yarrows in informal gardens and meadow plantings.
Other common names Persian cornflower.

Centranthus ruber
VALERIANACEAE

RED VALERIAN

Red valerian is an upright perennial with opposite, gray-green, oval leaves and white, pink, or red flowers on branching stems. Plants grow from a fibrous-rooted crown.

Flower color Small flowers are carried in domed, branched clusters. Colors range from white to pink, rose, or coral red.
Flowering time Spring and summer.
Height and spread 1–3 feet (30–90 cm) tall; 2 feet (60 cm) wide.
Temperature requirements Zones 4–8. Plants perform best in cool-summer areas.
Position Average, sandy or loamy, neutral or alkaline soil. Full sun. Grows readily in rock crevices where soil is limited.
Cultivation Plants may become floppy after blooming. Shear them back to promote compact growth and reblooming.
Propagation Sow seed outdoors in summer. Plants often self-sow prolifically if spent flowers are not removed. To produce plants of a specific color, remove basal shoots and treat them like cuttings.
Pest and disease prevention No serious pests or diseases.
Landscape uses Perfect for wall and rock gardens. The striking coral red flowers combine well with the neutral colors of stone or with creamy yellow flowers.
Other common names Jupiter's beard.

Cerastium tomentosum
CARYOPHYLLACEAE

SNOW-IN-SUMMER

Snow-in-summer is a low-mounding plant with small, woolly leaves and clusters of white flowers on wiry stems. Plants grow from a dense tangle of fibrous roots.

Flower color Snow white 1-inch (2.5-cm) flowers have five deeply notched petals that give the impression of a ten-petaled flower. They are borne in open clusters held well above the foliage.
Flowering time Late spring and early summer.
Height and spread 6–10 inches (15–25 cm) tall; 12 inches (30 cm) wide.
Temperature requirements Zones 2–7; extremely cold-tolerant.
Position Average, sandy or loamy, well-drained soil. Full sun.
Cultivation Shear plants to the ground after flowering to promote fresh, compact growth. Clumps spread easily and may overgrow their position.
Propagation Divide in spring or fall and replant vigorous portions. Take tip cuttings in early summer.
Pest and disease prevention Relatively pest-free. May suffer from fungal rots that blacken the leaves and stems. Remove and destroy infected foliage. Well-drained soil and cool summer temperatures are best.
Landscape uses Choose for cascading over a wall, planting in a rock garden, or edging a path. The profusion of flowers is a bright addition to the spring garden.

Ceratostigma plumbaginoides
PLUMBAGINACEAE

PLUMBAGO

Plumbago is a creeping, semiwoody perennial with russet stems and sparse, wedge-shaped leaves. Plants die back to the ground each year; prune out winter-damaged stems by late spring.

Flower color Deep gentian blue flowers are carried in clusters at the stems tips.
Flowering time Mid- to late summer, often into fall.
Height and spread 6–12 inches (15–30 cm) tall; 12–18 inches (30–45 cm) wide, growing wider with age.
Temperature requirements Zones 5–9; quite heat-tolerant.
Position Average to humus-rich, moist but well-drained soil. Full sun to partial shade. Plants will survive on dry, sunny banks or under shrubs, but not in the dense, dry shade of large trees.
Cultivation Prune stems back to the ground in fall or spring. New growth emerges in late spring. The foliage often turns orange in fall.
Propagation Divide in early spring. Take tip cuttings in early summer.
Pest and disease prevention No serious pests or diseases.
Landscape uses Plant as a groundcover under flowering shrubs, along walks, in rock walls, or at the front of the perennial garden. Interplant the creeping stems with spring- and fall-flowering bulbs to hide the declining bulb foliage.
Other common names Leadwort.

Chamaemelum nobile
ASTERACEAE

ROMAN CHAMOMILE

Herb gardens of yesterday often included a lush lawn of chamomile that released a sweet, apple-like scent when walked upon. Tea made from the flowers is relaxing after a stressful day.

Flower color White, daisy-type flowers with yellow centers.
Flowering time Summer.
Height and spread 6–9 inches (15–22.5 cm) tall; 6–12 inches (15–30 cm) wide.
Temperature requirements Zones 6–9.
Position Full sun to partial shade. Light, moist but well-drained garden soil.
Cultivation Plant seed or transplants in spring. In the first year, clip to prevent flowering and encourage vegetative growth while it becomes established. Chamomile is a poor competitor, so weed often. Once established, it can self-sow. Established lawns can be mowed like grass.
Propagation Sow seed indoors or out in spring or fall; thin to 6 inches (15 cm). Alternatively, take cuttings or divide older plants in early spring.
Pest and disease prevention Usually free from pests and diseases.
Landscape uses This low-growing perennial with aromatic lacy foliage is ideal in a herb or cottage garden, or growing in borders or beds.
Other common names Garden chamomile, ground apple, Russian chamomile.

Chelone lyonii
SCROPHULARIACEAE

PINK TURTLEHEAD

Pink turtleheads are bushy perennials with tall, leafy stems from a stout, fibrous-rooted crown. The 4–7-inch (10–17.5-cm) leaves are broadly ovate with toothed margins.

Flower color Rose pink, inflated, tubular flowers resemble the head of a turtle with its jaws open, hence the common name.
Flowering time Late summer into fall.
Height and spread 1–3 feet (30–90 cm) tall; 1–2 feet (30–60 cm) wide.
Temperature requirements Zones 3–8; intolerant of excessive heat.
Position Evenly moist, humus-rich soil. Full sun to partial shade. Tolerates drier soil once established.
Cultivation Divide the crowns to reduce large clumps in aged plants.
Propagation Divide established plants in spring or after flowering. Take stem cuttings in early summer; remove any flower buds. Sow seed outdoors in fall or indoors in late winter after stratification. To stratify, mix seed with moist peat moss or seed-starting medium in a plastic bag. Close the bag with a twist-tie and refrigerate for 4–6 weeks. Then sow the mixture as you would normal seed.
Pest and disease prevention No serious pests or diseases.
Landscape uses Combine with asters, phlox, and goldenrods (*Solidago* spp.) for late-summer color.

Chrysanthemum x *morifolium*
ASTERACEAE

GARDEN MUM

Hardy garden mums have stout stems clothed in lobed leaves. They grow from creeping stems with tangled fibrous roots. Most garden mums bloom in late summer and fall.

Flower color Garden mums bloom in a wide variety of colors from white to pale pink, rose, burgundy, red, golden brown, gold, yellow, and cream.
Flowering time Late summer through fall.
Height and spread 1½–5 feet (45–150 cm) tall; 1–3 feet (30–90 cm) wide.
Temperature requirements Garden mums vary in their hardiness. Zones 3–9.
Position Light, humus-rich, well-drained soil. Full sun to light shade.
Cultivation Pinch the stems once or twice in May or June to promote compact growth. Divide the fast-growing clumps every 1–2 years. Replant vigorous shoots into soil enriched with organic matter.
Propagation Divide mature plants in spring. Tip cuttings taken in late spring or early summer root quickly and often bloom in the first season.
Pest and disease prevention Spray aphids or spider mites with insecticidal soap or an insecticide such as pyrethrin.
Landscape uses Use for annual displays or a showy fall display.
Other common names Hardy mum, mum, florist's chrysanthemum, hardy chrysanthemum.

Chrysogonum virginianum
ASTERACEAE

GREEN AND GOLD

Green and gold is a low-growing plant with dark green leaves and bright golden blooms. It's a natural choice for woodland gardens and for growing beneath trees and shrubs.

Flower color The 1–2-inch (2.5–5-cm), five-petaled flowers are golden yellow.
Flowering time Spring, then intermittently all summer.
Height and spread 8–12 inches (20–30 cm) tall; up to 1 foot (30 cm) wide.
Temperature requirements Zones 5–8.
Position Well-drained, light-textured, moist, slightly acid soil, with humus and nutrients. Partial shade in the North; full shade in the South.
Cultivation Plant 12–18 inches (30–45 cm) apart in spring. Green and gold forms rosettes of oval, deep green, slightly hairy leaves and spreads quickly by underground runners and prostrate stems that root where they touch the soil. Do not overfertilize or plants tend to become floppy and produce fewer blooms. Provide winter protection in Zone 5.
Propagation Propagate by division in spring or fall.
Pest and disease prevention No serious pests or diseases.
Landscape uses Green and gold is attractive under trees and shrubs and in wild areas or rock gardens. It makes a low-maintenance groundcover at the edge of woodlands or against rocks or stone walls.

Cimicifuga racemosa
RANUNCULACEAE

BLACK SNAKEROOT

The wand-like spires of black snakeroot wave above an open cluster of large compound leaves with toothed leaflets. Plants grow from a stout, fibrous-rooted crown.

Flower color The small, ½-inch (12-mm), creamy white flowers have a dense whorl of fuzzy stamens and no petals.
Flowering time Early to midsummer.
Height and spread 4–7 feet (1.2–2.1 m) tall; 3–4 feet (90–120 cm) wide.
Temperature requirements Zones 3–8.
Position Moist, humus-rich soil. Full sun to partial shade. Protect from afternoon sun in warmer zones. Dense shade may produce sparse flowers. Somewhat drought-tolerant once established.
Cultivation An extremely long-lived perennial. Young plants take several years to reach flowering size. Clumps increase gradually each year and may have 10–15 bloom stalks at maturity.
Propagation Divide clumps with a sharp knife in fall or spring. Leave at least one bud per division. Sow fresh seed outdoors in fall. It may take 2 seasons to germinate.
Pest and disease prevention No serious pests or diseases.
Landscape uses Place at the rear of borders with bold flowers like phlox and daylilies. In the woodland garden, combine with ferns, hostas, and wildflowers.
Other common names Black cohosh, bugbane.

Clematis integrifolia
RANUNCULACEAE

SOLITARY CLEMATIS

Unlike most other clematis, which grow as vines, solitary clematis forms a sprawling mound that makes an unusual, attractive, and long-blooming flowering groundcover.

Flower color Bell-shaped, lavender-blue flowers bloom over a long period, followed by charming silvery seed heads.
Flowering time Midsummer.
Height and spread 2–3 feet (60–90 cm) tall; similar spread.
Temperature requirements Zones 4–9.
Position Light, loamy, alkaline soil, which should be cool and moist. Full sun.
Cultivation Set plants out 2–3 feet (60–90 cm) apart in spring or fall. They form bushy mounds of egg-shaped leaves, which are deciduous. Maintain an organic mulch (such as compost or shredded leaves) to keep the soil cool and moist; otherwise, plants need no special care.
Propagation Propagate by seed in late summer or cuttings in late spring.
Pest and disease prevention No serious pests or diseases.
Landscape uses Solitary clematis is not especially showy, but the flowers and seed heads can provide several months of subtle interest. It looks best combined with other plants, as part of a border, or as an accent with other low-growing groundcovers.
Cultivars 'Rosea' has pink flowers.

Colchicum speciosum
COLCHICACEAE

SHOWY AUTUMN CROCUS

Showy autumn crocus grows from large, plump corms. Once established, each corm will produce vibrant clumps of rosy pink flowers in late summer through to early fall.

Flower color The 4-inch (10-cm) wide, goblet-shaped, stemless flowers are rosy pink with white throats.
Flowering time Late summer to early fall.
Height and spread Leaves up to about 8 inches (20 cm) tall; flowers 4–6 inches (10–15 cm) tall. Spread to about 6 inches (15 cm) wide.
Temperature requirements Zones 4–9.
Position Full sun to partial shade; average, well-drained soil.
Cultivation Plant corms in mid- to late summer, as soon as they are available; they may begin to bloom even before you plant them if you delay. Set in individual holes or in larger planting areas dug about 4 inches (10 cm) deep. Space 6 inches (15 cm) apart. The wide, flat, glossy green leaves turn yellow and die to the ground in early summer, then the flowers appear.
Propagation Divide just after the leaves have died down.
Pest and disease prevention Crocus corms interplanted with daffodil bulbs may discourage mice.
Landscape uses Usually best coming up through low groundcovers or under shrubs, where the coarse spring leaves won't detract from or smother other flowers.

Convallaria majalis
CONVALLARIACEAE

LILY-OF-THE-VALLEY

Established clumps of lily-of-the-valley compete well with weeds and can thrive in the same spot for decades with little or no care. They spread quickly by creeping roots.

Flower color Lily-of-the-valley has fragrant, bell-shaped, waxy, white flowers. The flowers may be followed by glossy, orange-red berries in summer.
Flowering time Late spring.
Height and spread Foliage 6–8 inches (15–20 cm) tall; flowers 8–10 inches (20–25 cm) tall. Spread unlimited.
Temperature requirements Zones 2–8.
Position Partial to full shade. Moist, well-drained, fertile soil with organic matter.
Cultivation Set out plants 4–6 inches (10–15 cm) apart in late fall or very early spring. The deciduous leaves turn brown in mid- to late summer; place them where their unsightly appearance won't be a problem. If desired, you can cut down the brown leaves to tidy up the planting. Apply compost or leaf mold each fall if the area isn't fertile. Thin out crowded plantings if they stop blooming well.
Propagation Propagate by division after flowering or in fall.
Pest and disease prevention Avoid hot, dry sites to discourage spider mites.
Landscape uses Clumps of lily-of-the-valley are ideal groundcovers in shady borders and foundation plantings and under shrubs and deciduous trees.

Coreopsis verticillata
ASTERACEAE

THREAD-LEAVED COREOPSIS

Thread-leaved coreopsis is an airy, rounded plant with thread-like, three-lobed leaves and masses of bright yellow summer flowers. Plants grow from a fibrous-rooted crown.

Flower color The 1–2-inch (2.5–5-cm), starry flowers are butter to golden yellow.
Flowering time Throughout summer.
Height and spread 1–3 feet (30–90 cm) tall; 2–3 feet (60–90 cm) wide.
Temperature requirements Zones 3–9.
Position Average to rich, moist but well-drained soil. Full sun or light shade; drought-tolerant once established.
Cultivation Thread-leaved coreopsis is an easy-care perennial that demands very little attention once established. Plants eventually die out at the center. Divide old clumps and replant in enriched soil.
Propagation Divide in spring or fall. Take stem cuttings in early summer.
Pest and disease prevention No serious pests or diseases.
Landscape uses These plants are perfect for the front of the border with cranesbills (*Geranium* spp.), yarrows, daylilies, and coneflowers (*Rudbeckia* and *Echinacea* spp.). Combine them with ornamental grasses or use a mass planting with shrubs.
Cultivars 'Golden Showers' grows 2 feet (60 cm) tall with golden yellow flowers. 'Moonbeam' is a spreading plant with pale yellow flowers. 'Zagreb' is a compact selection similar to 'Golden Showers.'

Coronilla varia
FABACEAE

CROWN VETCH

Crown vetch is a pretty and tough groundcover, which makes it ideal for difficult sites such as steep slopes. It can be invasive, so keep it away from flower gardens.

Flower color Clover-like clusters of pink and white flowers bloom at the top of sprawling, vine-like stems.
Flowering time Summer.
Height and spread Up to 18 inches (45 cm) tall; up to 4 feet (1.2 m) wide.
Temperature requirements Zones 3–9.
Position Full sun; dry, sandy, and well-drained soil.
Cultivation Plant 1–2 feet (30–60 cm) apart in spring. Crown vetch spreads by rhizomes, producing feathery, deciduous leaflets on the sprawling stems. Once plants are established and start to spread, mow the stems each spring to encourage compact growth.
Propagation Propagate by division or seed in spring.
Pest and disease prevention No serious pests or diseases.
Landscape uses Crown vetch is an excellent groundcover for banks that are difficult to mow. It's also a good choice for erosion control and for stabilizing the soil in large, dry areas. Plants will become invasive in conditions they like, so be wary about putting them near flower borders or rock gardens; they can easily overpower less vigorous plants.

Crocosmia x crocosmiiflora
IRIDACEAE

CROCOSMIA

Crocosmia is a brightly colored perennial with vivid red or orange summer flowers and fans of sword-like leaves that resemble gladiolus. They grow from button-like corms.

Flower color Tubular orange or red flowers are carried on erect, sparsely branched, zigzagging stems.
Flowering time Summer and early fall; varies with individual cultivars.
Height and spread 2–3 feet (60–90 cm) tall; 1–2 feet (30–60 cm) wide.
Temperature requirements Zones 6–9. In colder zones, lift corms in fall and store in a cool, dry place.
Position Moist, humus-rich soil. Full sun.
Cultivation Crocosmias spread to form broad clumps of tightly packed foliage fans. Remove the spent stalks after flowering. Divide overgrown clumps in spring. If you store corms over winter, replant them when temperatures are moderate.
Propagation Remove corms from the outside of the clump in spring.
Pest and disease prevention Spider mites and thrips cause white or brown stippling or streaks on the leaves. Spray with insecticidal soap or an insecticide such as pyrethrin. Cut badly damaged plants to the ground and destroy the infested portions.
Landscape uses Plant with summer perennials like phlox and daylilies. Use as accents along walls or with shrubs.

Crocus vernus
IRIDACEAE

DUTCH CROCUS

Dutch crocus are one of the earliest spring flowers, a welcome sight after a long, cold winter. After bloom, the leaves continue to elongate until they ripen and die back to the ground in early summer.

Flower color Goblet-shaped, stemless flowers up to 3 inches (7.5 cm) across bloom just above the leaves. The flowers are white, lavender, purple, or yellow; they may be striped with contrasting colors.
Flowering time Late winter to early spring.
Height and spread Leaves to 8 inches (20 cm) tall; flowers usually to 4 inches (10 cm). Spread 1–3 inches (2.5–7.5 cm).
Temperature requirements Zones 3–8.
Position Full sun to partial shade (under deciduous trees and shrubs); average, well-drained soil.
Cultivation Plant the corms in fall, pointed side up, in individual holes or larger areas dug 2–4 inches (5–10 cm) deep. Space 2 inches (5 cm) apart. Dutch crocus usually return year after year and spread to form showy clumps.
Propagation Divide the corms after the foliage has died back in late summer.
Pest and disease prevention Interplant corms with daffodil bulbs (which are toxic if eaten) to help discourage mice.
Landscape uses Include them in beds and borders for early color. Grow them in containers for outdoor spring bloom.

Cyclamen hederifolium
PRIMULACEAE

HARDY CYCLAMEN

Hardy cyclamen bloom in early fall, then handsome, heart-shaped, silver-marked green leaves emerge shortly after the blooms finish. They are attractive through most of the year.

Flower color Leafless flower stalks are topped with pink or white, nodding flowers that have upward-pointing petals.
Flowering time Early fall.
Height and spread Height and spread of flowers and foliage 4–6 inches (10–15 cm).
Temperature requirements Zones 5–9.
Position Partial shade; average, well-drained soil.
Cultivation Many commercial cyclamen sources sell wild-collected tubers. Avoid supporting this irresponsible practice by buying nursery-propagated tubers, or start your own from seed. Set plants into the garden in spring or summer, or plant dormant tubers shallowly in summer, making sure the smooth, unmarked side is on the bottom. Top-dress with a thin layer of compost in late summer.
Propagation Divide tubers in summer or grow from seeds; soak the seed overnight, then sow ¼ inch (6 mm) deep in a pot. Enclose the pot in a plastic bag, then place in a dark place.
Pest and disease prevention No serious pests or diseases.
Landscape uses Hardy cyclamen look good in shady spots with ferns and hellebores (*Helleborus* spp.).

Dahlia hybrids
ASTERACEAE

DAHLIAS

Some types, known as bedding dahlias, form compact, bushy plants; others produce the tall, large-flowered border favorites. Both types have upright stems with divided, green leaves.

Flower color Flowers come in almost every color but true blue—even in near black and bicolors.
Flowering time Midsummer through fall.
Height and spread Height varies from 1 foot (30 cm) for bedding types to 5 feet (1.5 m) for border types. Spread to 1 foot (30 cm) and 4 feet (1.2 m) respectively.
Temperature requirements Hardy in Zones 9–10; elsewhere, grow as annuals.
Position Full sun; well-drained soil.
Cultivation Start bedding types from seed sown indoors 6–8 weeks before your last frost date. In Northern areas, start tuberous roots indoors 2–3 weeks before. Set plants out 1–2 weeks after the last frost date. Elsewhere, plant the roots directly into the garden around the last frost date. Water regularly and fertilize in late summer with a complete organic fertilizer. Pinch stem tips in early summer.
Propagation Grow bedding types from seed. Divide tuberous roots in spring, just before planting. Cut the roots apart at the stem end, so each root has at least one bud.
Pest and disease prevention Prone to many pests; keep plants healthy to offset.
Landscape uses Plant in beds and borders and in the cutting garden.

Delphinium x *elatum* hybrids
RANUNCULACEAE

HYBRID DELPHINIUM

Hybrid delphiniums are stately border plants with dense flower clusters atop tall stems with deeply cut, palmately lobed leaves. Plants grow from stout crowns with thick, fleshy roots.

Flower color White through all shades of true blue to lavender and purple.
Flowering time Late spring through summer. Plants may rebloom in fall.
Height and spread 4½–6 feet (1.35–1.8 m) tall; 2–3 feet (60–90 cm) wide.
Temperature requirements Zones 4–7.
Position Evenly moist but well-drained, fertile, humus-rich soil. Full sun.
Cultivation Delphiniums are often short-lived in warm climates. They benefit from an annual spring top-dressing of organic fertilizer. Set out new plants in spring; thin the clumps to three to five stems as they emerge. To encourage plants to rebloom, cut off old flowering stems above the foliage and below the flower spike. Divide overgrown plants.
Propagation Divide in spring. Sow fresh seed in summer or fall. Take cuttings in spring from the new shoots; use the stems removed from thinning for propagation.
Pest and disease prevention Powdery mildew may cause white blotches on the leaves. Dust affected parts with sulfur.
Landscape uses Plant at the rear of borders where their showy spires will tower over other summer-blooming perennials.

Dianthus gratianopolitanus
CARYOPHYLLACEAE

CHEDDAR PINKS

Cheddar pinks bear sweet-scented flowers you'll enjoy outdoors in the garden or indoors as cut flowers. They grow well in sunny rock gardens or cascading over walls.

Flower color The fragrant white, rose, or pink flowers are borne on wiry stems.
Flowering time Early to midsummer.
Height and spread 9–12 inches (22.5–30 cm) tall; 12 inches (30 cm) wide.
Temperature requirements Zones 3–9.
Position Plant in average, well-drained, sandy or loamy soil in full sun. The soil should be neutral or only slightly acid for the best growth.
Cultivation Divide clumps every 2–3 years to keep them vigorous. Remove flowers as they fade to promote continued bloom.
Propagation Take stem cuttings from the foliage rosettes in summer.
Pest and disease prevention Pinks are susceptible to rust, a fungus that causes yellow blotches on the upper leaf surfaces and raised orange spots on the lower. Thin clumps to promote air circulation and dust affected plants with sulfur.
Landscape uses Place cheddar pinks at the front of borders or use them as an edging along paths. Combine with other front-of-the-border plants such as sedums, thyme, and lamb's ears (*Stachys byzantina*). Interplant them with spiky foliage such as yuccas (*Yucca* spp.) and grasses.

Dianthus plumarius
CARYOPHYLLACEAE

COTTAGE PINKS

Cottage pinks are popular, sweet-scented plants for the garden or for cutting. The broad, mounded plants produce dense clusters of 3-inch (7.5-cm), blue-green, grass-like leaves.

Flower color Fragrant white or pink flowers are borne in clusters on wiry stems.
Flowering time Early to midsummer.
Height and spread 1½–2 feet (45–60 cm) tall; 1 foot (30 cm) wide.
Temperature requirements Zones 3–9. Tolerates extreme heat and cold.
Position Average, well-drained, sandy or loamy soil. Full sun. The soil should be neutral or only slightly acid for best growth. Plants tolerate alkaline soil.
Cultivation Plants may be short-lived, especially when grown in warmer zones. Divide clumps every 2–3 years.
Propagation Layer or take stem cuttings from the foliage rosettes in summer. Strip leaves from the lower third of a 2–3-inch (5–7.5-cm) cutting. Place cutting in a medium of one part vermiculite and two parts sand or perlite to allow excellent drainage and air circulation.
Pest and disease prevention Rust causes yellow blotches on the upper surface of the leaves and raised orange spots on the lower surface. To discourage rust, thin clumps for better air circulation and dust with sulfur.
Landscape uses Plant at the front of borders or use them as an edging along paths. Grow them in sunny rock gardens.

Dicentra eximia
FUMARIACEAE

FRINGED BLEEDING HEART

Fringed bleeding hearts bloom mostly in spring, but flowers can appear at any time during the growing season. The ferny foliage looks great from spring through fall.

Flower color Fringed bleeding hearts bear a profusion of small clusters of pink, heart-shaped flowers held above finely divided, blue-green foliage.

Flowering time Early spring to early summer, with sporadic bloom throughout the season.

Height and spread 1–2½ feet (30–75 cm) tall; 2–3 feet (60–90 cm) wide.

Temperature requirements Zones 3–9. Protect plants with a winter mulch in colder zones.

Position Plant in evenly moist, humus-rich soil in partial shade. Plants tolerate full sun in Northern gardens.

Cultivation Top-dress with compost in early spring. If plants lose their vigor, lift and divide clumps and replant into soil enriched with organic matter.

Propagation For propagation, sow fresh seed outdoors in summer or divide plants in fall. Self-sown seedlings are common.

Pest and disease prevention No serious pests or diseases.

Landscape uses Plant in formal and informal gardens, in rockeries, or in masses along garden paths. The flowers and foliage are exquisite and delicate, so place them where they are easy to admire.

Dicentra spectabilis
FUMARIACEAE

COMMON BLEEDING HEART

Common bleeding hearts are beloved, old-fashioned perennials with strings of heart-shaped flowers held above deeply divided, blue-green foliage. Plants grow from thick, fleshy roots.

Flower color Bright pink, heart-shaped flowers consist of two reflexed lobes with a central column that resembles a dangling drop of blood.

Flowering time Early spring to early summer.

Height and spread 1–2½ feet (30–75 cm) tall; 2–3 feet (60–90 cm) wide.

Temperature requirements Zones 2–9. Extremely tolerant of heat and cold. Mulch in winter in colder zones.

Position Evenly moist, humus-rich soil. Partial shade; full sun in cooler zones.

Cultivation Bleeding hearts will bloom for 4–6 weeks in spring. In warm climates or if the soil is dry, plants will go dormant after blooming. Top-dress with well-rotted manure in early spring to maintain soil fertility. If plants lose vigor, lift and divide.

Propagation Divide clumps in fall. Sow fresh seed in summer. Take root cuttings in late summer.

Pest and disease prevention No serious pests or diseases.

Landscape uses Plant common bleeding hearts with spring bulbs, primroses, and wildflowers for a striking spring display. In warm zones combine them with hostas to fill the void left by the declining foliage.

Dictamnus albus
RUTACEAE

GAS PLANT

Gas plant forms shrub-like clumps of stout stems with deep green, pinnately lobed leaves and erect flower spikes. Plants grow from thick, woody crowns with fibrous roots.

Flower color The 1-inch (2.5-cm), showy white flowers have five starry petals and ten long, curled stamens that protrude from the flower. The starry seed capsules are attractive throughout summer.

Flowering time Late spring or early summer.

Height and spread 1–4 feet (30–120 cm) tall; 1–3 feet (30–90 cm) wide.

Temperature requirements Zones 3–8.

Position Well-drained, average to humus-rich soil. Full sun to light shade.

Cultivation Gas plants are long-lived perennials that are slow to establish and resent disturbance once planted. Established plants are trouble-free.

Propagation Sow fresh seed outdoors in late summer. Seedlings appear the next season but grow slowly. Transplant young plants to their permanent position after 3 years of growth.

Pest and disease prevention Avoid soggy soils, which will encourage root rot. Destroy infected plants.

Landscape uses Combine gas plants with other perennials that need good drainage, such as oriental poppies (*Papaver orientale*), yarrows, and sundrops (*Oenothera* spp.).

Other common names Dittany.

Digitalis x *mertonensis*
SCROPHULARIACEAE

STRAWBERRY FOXGLOVE

The popular strawberry foxglove has fuzzy, broad, lance-shaped leaves. Rosettes of foliage form at the base of the flowering stems and persist over winter.

Flower color The 2–3-inch (5–7.5-cm) tubular flowers are flushed with pink, rose, or purple on the outside and heavily spotted with dark purple or brown on the inside. Some selections are pure white.

Flowering time Plants flower throughout summer and often rebloom.

Height and spread 3–4 feet (90–120 cm) tall; 1 foot (30 cm) wide.

Temperature requirements Zones 3–8.

Position Moist but well-drained, humus-rich soil. Full sun to partial shade.

Cultivation Strawberry foxgloves are easy-care perennials that bloom tirelessly with little care. Divide overgrown clumps and replant into soil enriched with organic matter. Remove spent bloom stalks to promote rebloom, leaving one to self-sow.

Propagation Divide in spring or fall. Sow fresh seed outdoors in fall or allow to self-sow. Seedlings emerge the next spring and will bloom the second year.

Pest and disease prevention No serious pests or diseases.

Landscape uses Plant at the middle or rear of perennial gardens, and also in informal and cottage gardens. Use mass plantings along a wall or fence.

Dodecatheon meadia
PRIMULACEAE

SHOOTING STAR

Shooting stars spread slowly to form thick clumps with many bloom stalks. Plants go dormant after flowering, so grow them with bushy perennials that will fill the gap.

Flower color The bloom stalk is crowned with a cluster of pink or white flowers. Each flower resembles a dart, with a forward-pointing cluster of stamens and five reflexed petals.

Flowering time Spring.

Height and spread Flowers 1–2 feet (30–60 cm) tall; leaves to 1 foot (30 cm) tall. Up to 1 foot (30 cm) wide.

Temperature requirements Zones 4–8.

Position Average to humus-rich, moist soil with a near-neutral or slightly alkaline pH. Plant in sun or shade; direct sun in spring is necessary for best bloom.

Cultivation Plants go dormant after flowering, so the soil can be allowed to go somewhat dry.

Propagation Divide established clumps in summer or fall. Lift plants and tease the crowns apart; replant.

Pest and disease prevention No serious pests or diseases.

Landscape uses Plant shooting stars in shade and woodland gardens or at the edge of a moist meadow or prairie garden. Use them in drifts under shrubs and spring-flowering trees. Combine with spring wildflowers. In a shaded corner, plant them with anemones and ferns.

Doronicum orientale
ASTERACEAE

LEOPARD'S BANE

Leopard's bane is a brightly colored daisy with deep green, triangular leaves. It emerges early in spring, growing in dense, open clusters from a fibrous-rooted crown.

Flower color Dozens of 1–2-inch (2.5–5-cm), vivid yellow, single, daisy-type flowers are borne on slender, leafless stems.

Flowering time Spring and early summer.

Height and spread 1–2 feet (30–60 cm) tall; 1 foot (30 cm) wide.

Temperature requirements Zones 3–8.

Position Moist, humus-rich soil. Full sun to shade. Soil must not dry out while plants are actively growing.

Cultivation Leopard's banes emerge early in spring and may be damaged by late frosts. Plants go dormant after flowering in warmer zones. In colder zones, the foliage remains all season, so moist soil in those zones is imperative. Mulch will help to keep the soil cool. Divide clumps every 2–3 years to keep them vigorous.

Propagation Divide in spring or fall. Sow seed indoors in late winter or early spring.

Pest and disease prevention No serious pests or diseases.

Landscape uses Combine with clustered bellflowers (*Campanula glomerata*), Virginia bluebells (*Mertensia virginica*), spring bulbs, and wildflowers. Plant with foliage plants such as hostas to fill the voids when the leopard's banes go dormant.

Echinacea purpurea
ASTERACEAE

PURPLE CONEFLOWER

Purple coneflowers are showy summer flowers with sparse, 6-inch (15-cm), oval or broadly lance-shaped leaves on stout, hairy stems. Plants grow from thick, deep taproots.

Flower color Red-violet to rose pink flowers have broad, drooping rays (petal-like structures) surrounding raised, bristly centers, or cones.

Flowering time Mid- to late summer.

Height and spread 2–4 feet (60–120 cm) tall; 1–2 feet (30–60 cm) wide.

Temperature requirements Zones 3–8. Extremely heat-tolerant.

Position Average to humus-rich, moist but well-drained soil. Full sun. Drought-tolerant once established.

Cultivation Plants increase from basal buds to form broad, long-lived clumps. Division is seldom necessary and is not recommended.

Propagation Sow seed outdoors in fall or indoors after stratification. To stratify, mix seed with moist peat moss or seed-starting medium in a plastic bag. Close with a twist-tie and place in the refrigerator for 4–6 weeks. Sow the mixture as you would normal seed. Alternatively, take root cuttings in fall.

Pest and disease prevention No serious pests or diseases.

Landscape uses Plant in formal perennial gardens or meadow and prairie gardens.

Echinops ritro
ASTERACEAE

GLOBE THISTLE

Globe thistles are stout perennials that make an arresting display with their spiky, round flower heads, erect stems, and spiny, lobed leaves. They grow from thick, deep-branched taproots.

Flower color Multiple small, steel blue flowers are packed into 1–2-inch (2.5–5-cm) spherical heads.

Flowering time Midsummer.

Height and spread 2–4 feet (60–120 cm) tall; 2–3 feet (60–90 cm) wide.

Temperature requirements Zones 3–8. This plant is heat-tolerant.

Position Average to humus-rich, well-drained soil. Full sun. Good drainage is essential, especially in winter.

Cultivation Globe thistles are tough, long-lived perennials. They are drought-tolerant once established and thrive for many years without staking or division.

Propagation Remove sideshoots from the main clump without disturbing the crown in fall or late winter. Take root cuttings in spring or fall.

Pest and disease prevention Plant in well-drained soil to avoid root rot.

Landscape uses Combine showy globe thistles with other drought-tolerant perennials like Russian sages (*Perovskia* spp.), sedums, catmints (*Nepeta* spp.), and oriental poppies (*Papaver orientale*). Position them near the middle or rear of borders. The flowers are also perfect for cutting fresh or for drying.

Epimedium x rubrum
BERBERIDACEAE

RED EPIMEDIUM

Epimediums make a great woodland groundcover that will grow happily for years with little attention. They perform well under adverse conditions, even in dry shade under trees.

Flower color The unusual flowers have four red, petal-like sepals and four spurred, ivory petals. They are held in clusters above the emerging new leaves.

Flowering time Early to midspring.

Height and spread 10–12 inches (25–30 cm) tall; 12 inches (30 cm) wide.

Temperature requirements Zones 4–8.

Position Plant in moist, humus-rich soil in partial to full shade. Avoid waterlogged soil, especially during the winter.

Cultivation Mulch plants in winter to protect the crowns when growing them at the edge of their range. Cut foliage to the ground in early spring to allow the flowers to emerge unobscured. Divide overgrown clumps in late summer.

Propagation Propagate from ripe seed or division in late summer or fall.

Pest and disease prevention No serious pests or diseases.

Landscape uses Plant in drifts in woodland gardens, along paths, or under shrubs and trees. Combine with spring bulbs, Lenten roses (*Helleborus* spp.), primroses, hostas, wildflowers, and ferns. Plant them under spring-flowering shrubs.

Epimedium x versicolor
BERBERIDACEAE

PERSIAN EPIMEDIUM

Persian epimedium is a woodland groundcover with semi-evergreen leaves divided into glossy, heart-shaped leaflets. The wiry, trailing stems have matted, fibrous roots.

Flower color The unusual flowers have eight yellow, petal-like sepals and four spurred petals tinged with red. They are held above the new leaves as they emerge.
Flowering time Early to midspring.
Height and spread 10–12 inches (25–30 cm) tall; 12 inches (30 cm) wide.
Temperature requirements Zones 5–8.
Position Moist, humus-rich soil. Partial to full shade. Avoid waterlogged soil, especially during winter.
Cultivation Persian epimediums thrive for years with little attention. They perform well under adverse conditions, even in the dry shade of mature trees. Mulch plants in winter. Cut foliage to the ground in early spring so flowers can emerge unobscured.
Propagation Divide overgrown clumps in late summer or spring.
Pest and disease prevention No serious pests or diseases.
Landscape uses Plant in woodland gardens with hostas, wildflowers, and ferns. Combine them with spring bulbs, Lenten roses (*Helleborus* spp.), and primroses.
Other common names Bicolor barrenwort.

Eremurus stenophyllus
ASPHODELACEAE

FOXTAIL LILY

Foxtail lilies are robust, stately perennials with tall flower spikes and clumps of strap-like foliage. Plants grow from a thickened crown with brittle, spreading roots.

Flower color Starry, 1-inch (2.5-cm), six-petaled flowers densely cover tall, pointed spikes.
Flowering time Spring and summer.
Height and spread 2–3 feet (60–90 cm) tall; 2 feet (60 cm) wide.
Temperature requirements Zones 5–9.
Position Moist but well-drained, humus-rich soil. Full sun to light shade.
Cultivation Plant crowns 4–6 inches (10–15 cm) deep. Do not allow them to dry out. Mulch to protect emerging leaves from late frosts. Divide clumps if they become crowded or if bloom wanes.
Propagation Divide in fall. Sow fresh seed outdoors in fall or indoors after it has been stratified. To stratify, mix seed with moist peat moss or seed-starting medium in a plastic bag. Close the bag with a twist-tie and place in the refrigerator for 4–6 weeks. Sow the mixture as you would normal seed.
Pest and disease prevention Soggy soil, especially in winter, promotes root rot; to avoid, plant in well-drained soil.
Landscape uses Plant among perennials or against a wall or hedge. Surround with bold poppies (*Papaver* spp.), daylilies (*Hemerocallis* spp.), and irises.

Erigeron karvinskianus
ASTERACEAE

FLEABANE

Fleabane bears many tiny, dainty, daisy-type flowers that are white when they open and then change color to dark pink with age. In warm climates they flower all year round.

Flower color Masses of small, 1-inch (2.5-cm), daisy-type flowers with yellow centers open white, then age to various shades of pink and purple.
Flowering time Spring until late summer.
Height and spread 6–10 inches (15–25 cm) high with an indefinite spread.
Temperature requirements Zones 6–10.
Position Full sun; dry soil.
Cultivation Fleabane is hardy and will thrive with little water. Space plants 8–10 inches (20–25 cm) apart when planting. Cut back after flowering to encourage compact growth and also to discourage self-seeding.
Propagation Sow seeds or divide mature plants in spring.
Pest and disease prevention Plants are generally problem-free.
Landscape uses Plant in rock gardens or on dry banks.

Erigeron speciosus
ASTERACEAE

DAISY FLEABANE

Daisy fleabane forms leafy clumps of hairy, 6-inch (15-cm), lance-shaped leaves that spring from fibrous-rooted crowns. The colorful flowers bloom in summer.

Flower color The pretty 1½-inch (3.7-cm), aster-like flowers have white, pink, rose, or purple rays, which surround bright yellow centers.
Flowering time Early to midsummer; occasional rebloom.
Height and spread 1½–2½ feet (45–75 cm) tall; 1–2 feet (30–60 cm) wide.
Temperature requirements Zones 2–9. Tolerant of heat and cold.
Position Moist but well-drained, average to humus-rich soil. Full sun to light shade.
Cultivation Fleabanes are long-lived, easy-care perennials that benefit from division every 2–3 years.
Propagation Divide in fall. Take cuttings in spring before the flower buds form. Sow seed outdoors in fall or indoors in spring.
Pest and disease prevention No serious pests or diseases.
Landscape uses Plant at the front of beds and borders along with summer-blooming perennials like cranesbills (*Geranium* spp.), cinquefoils (*Potentilla* spp.), evening primroses (*Oenothera* spp.), and phlox. Daisy fleabanes make long-lasting and delightful cut flowers.

Eryngium amethystinum
APIACEAE

AMETHYST SEA HOLLY

Amethyst sea holly is a dramatic architectural plant with stiff flowering stems and mostly basal, pinnately divided leaves. The plants grow from thick taproots.

Flower color Small, steel blue globose flower heads surrounded by thin, spiny bracts make for a striking display.
Flowering time Summer.
Height and spread 1–1½ feet (30–45 cm) tall; 1–2 feet (30–60 cm) wide.
Temperature requirements Zones 2–8. Heat- and cold-tolerant.
Position Average, well-drained soil. Full sun. Sea holly is extremely drought-tolerant once established.
Cultivation Set plants out in their permanent location while they are young. Older plants resent disturbance. Division is seldom necessary.
Propagation Sow fresh seed outdoors in fall or indoors after stratification. To stratify, mix seed with moist peat moss or seed-starting medium in a plastic bag. Close the bag with a twist-tie and place it in the refrigerator for 4–6 weeks. Then sow the mixture as you would normal seed.
Pest and disease prevention No serious pests or diseases.
Landscape uses Plant in the middle of borders with goldenrods (*Solidago* spp.), asters, phlox, and ornamental grasses.

Eupatorium maculatum
ASTERACEAE

SPOTTED JOE-PYE WEED

Spotted Joe-Pye weed is a tall, stately perennial that's perfect for moist borders and meadow plantings. The flowers will attract bees and butterflies to your garden.

Flower color The showy terminal flower clusters are domed to rounded and consist of hundreds of small, fuzzy, rose-purple flowers.
Flowering time Mid- to late summer.
Height and spread 4–6 feet (1.2–1.8 m) tall; 3–4 feet (90–120 cm) tall.
Temperature requirements Zones 2–8.
Position Moist, humus-rich soil in full sun or light shade.
Cultivation Plants take 2–3 years to mature, so leave ample room when planting small transplants.
Propagation For propagation, divide plants in early spring or fall, or take stem cuttings in early summer.
Pest and disease prevention Leafminers may cause large pale patches on the leaves; remove and destroy the affected foliage.
Landscape uses Choose spotted Joe-Pye weeds for the middle or back of the border for a bold accent. Plant them as a screen with ornamental grasses. Combine with tall perennials such as asters, rose mallow (*Hibiscus* spp.), ironweed (*Vernonia* spp.), goldenrods (*Solidago* spp.), and grasses.

Eupatorium purpureum
ASTERACEAE

JOE-PYE WEED

Joe-Pye weed is anything but a weed in the late summer perennial border. Its tall stems are topped with showy domed clusters of purplish flowers that are popular with butterflies.

Flower color Topped by rounded clusters of purple or white flowers that grow to 18 inches (45 cm) across.
Flowering time Late summer.
Height and spread 3–6 feet (90–180 cm) tall; 4 feet (1.2 m) wide or more.
Temperature requirements Zones 4–9, but avoid hot sites.
Position Full sun—it will flop in shade; constantly moist soil.
Cultivation Leave plenty of room when planting small transplants. Prune lightly in spring or after flowering, and deadhead to prevent self-sowing. Water during drought.
Propagation Propagate from seed in spring, from cuttings in summer, or by division in early spring or fall.
Pest and disease prevention Plants are generally problem-free.
Landscape uses This is a natural for a boggy area, or grow it in a moist meadow, flower border, or cutting garden.

Eupatorium rugosum
ASTERACEAE

WHITE SNAKEROOT

Brighten up late-season shade gardens with the fall flowers of white snakeroot. These perennials are easy to care for and grow quickly to form multistemmed clumps.

Flower color White snakeroot is a late-blooming perennial with foamy terminal clusters of white flowers.
Flowering time Early fall bloom. The silvery seed heads are showy into winter.
Height and spread 3–4 feet (90–120 cm) tall; 1–2 feet (30–60 cm) wide.
Temperature requirements Zones 3–7.
Position Partial sun or shade; average to rich, most soil.
Cultivation White snakeroot is easy to grow; self-sown seedlings may be numerous.
Propagation To propagate, divide in early spring or after flowering.
Pest and disease prevention No serious pests or diseases.
Landscape uses Plant white snakeroot in informal situations, such as along woodland paths or in meadow gardens. Grow them in groups in shaded recesses where few other plants will grow. Combine with other late-season plants such as asters, grasses, and goldenrods (*Solidago* spp.). In shaded areas, plant them with Solomon's seals (*Polygonatum* spp.), astilbes, and ferns.

Euphorbia epithymoides
EUPHORBIACEAE

CUSHION SPURGE

Cushion spurge blooms at the same time as tulips, so you can create many striking color combinations. The plants are long-lived garden residents that need little care.

Flower color The unusual flower heads consist of tiny yellow flowers surrounded by showy, funnel-shaped, yellow bracts.
Flowering time Spring.
Height and spread 6–10 inches (15–25 cm) tall; 1–2 feet (30–60 cm) wide.
Temperature requirements Zones 3–8.
Position Average to rich, well-drained soil in full sun or light shade. Plants will grow in poor, gravelly soil.
Cultivation Divide the congested clumps if they overgrow their position.
Propagation Propagate by taking stem cuttings in summer; quickly place the cuttings in a well-drained medium, before the cut end dries out.
Pest and disease prevention No serious pests or diseases.
Landscape uses Plant at the front of the border, in a sunny rock garden, or in a rock wall. Combine with early-blooming perennials such as columbines (*Aquilegia* spp.), rock cress (*Arabis* and *Aubrieta* spp.), creeping phlox (*Phlox stolonifera*), and daisy fleabane (*Erigeron speciosus*). Use them with bulbs such as ornamental onions (*Allium* spp.), fritillaries (*Fritillaria* spp.), and daffodils.

Euphorbia myrsinites
EUPHORBIACEAE

MYRTLE EUPHORBIA

Myrtle euphorbia is a creeping plant with thick stems and succulent, blue-gray, wedge-shaped leaves. It grows from fleshy, fibrous roots and is a striking addition to the spring garden.

Flower color Unusual flower heads have tiny yellow flowers surrounded by showy, funnel-shaped, yellow bracts.
Flowering time Spring.
Height and spread 6–10 inches (15–25 cm) tall; 1–2 feet (30–60 cm) wide.
Temperature requirements Zones 5–9.
Position Average to humus-rich, well-drained soil. Full sun to light shade. Plants will grow in poor, gravelly soils.
Cultivation Myrtle euphorbias are long-lived, easy-care garden residents. They thrive on neglect. Divide the clumps if they overgrow their position.
Propagation Take stem cuttings after flowering in spring; place the cuttings in a well-drained medium before the cut end dries out. Divide mature plants in spring or fall. Sow seed outdoors in fall or spring or indoors in early spring.
Pest and disease prevention No serious pests or diseases.
Landscape uses Plant in a sunny rock garden, in a rock wall, or at the front of borders. Combine with early-blooming perennials like rock cresses (*Arabis* and *Aubrieta* spp.), phlox, and bulbs.

Filipendula rubra
ROSACEAE

QUEEN-OF-THE-PRAIRIE

Queen-of-the-prairie is a towering perennial with huge flower heads on stout, leafy stalks. The showy 1-foot (30-cm) leaves are deeply lobed and star-like. Plants grow from creeping stems.

Flower color Small, five-petaled, pink flowers are crowded into large heads that resemble cotton candy.
Flowering time Late spring and early summer.
Height and spread 4–6 feet (1.2–1.8 m) tall; 2–4 feet (60–120 cm) wide.
Temperature requirements Zones 3–9.
Position Evenly moist, humus-rich soil. Full sun to light shade. Plants will not tolerate prolonged dryness.
Cultivation Established clumps make an arresting display when in bloom. If leaves become tattered after flowering has finished, cut plants to the ground; new leaves will emerge. Plants spread quickly in moist soil. Divide every 3–4 years to keep them from overtaking their neighbors.
Propagation Division is the best method. Lift clumps in spring or fall, or dig crowns from the edge of the clump. Sow seed indoors in spring.
Pest and disease prevention No serious pests or diseases.
Landscape uses Plant queen-of-the-prairie at the rear of borders with shrub roses, irises, daylilies, and phlox. Use them at the side of ponds with ferns and ornamental grasses.

Fritillaria imperialis
LILIACEAE

CROWN IMPERIAL

Crown imperial's sturdy shoots of green stems and glossy green leaves emerge in early spring and elongate for several weeks, to be followed by a striking circlet of flowers.

Flower color Tall stems are topped with a tuft of green leaves and hanging, bell-shaped, yellow, orange, or red flowers about 2 inches (5 cm) long.
Flowering time Mid- to late spring.
Height and spread 2–4 feet (60–120 cm) tall; 12 inches (30 cm) wide.
Temperature requirements Zones 5–9.
Position Full spring sun; average to sandy, well-drained soil.
Cultivation Plant the bulbs in late summer or early fall. Dig a large hole for each bulb or prepare a large planting area; make either about 8 inches (20 cm) deep. Loosen the soil at the base of the hole to promote good drainage. When you plant the bulb, tilt it slightly to one side to discourage water from collecting in the depression at the top. Crown imperials may take a few seasons to get established; mature clumps can live for many years.
Propagation Divide bulbs after the foliage has died back to the ground in midsummer.
Pest and disease prevention No serious pests or diseases.
Landscape uses Crown imperials make striking spring accents for beds and borders. All parts of the plant have a musky (some say skunk-like) odor.

Fritillaria meleagris
LILIACEAE

CHECKERED LILY

The slender, arching stems with narrow, gray-green leaves and pretty, nodding flowers of checkered lilies add a charming touch to spring gardens. Clumps will spread to give large sweeps of color.

Flower color Broad, nodding, bell-like blooms dangle from the ends of the thin, nodding stems. The 1–2-inch (2.5–5-cm) long flowers range in color from white to deep purple; many are marked with a checkered pattern.
Flowering time Midspring.
Height and spread Up to 1 foot (30 cm) tall; 2–4 inches (5–10 cm) wide.
Temperature requirements Zones 3–8.
Position Partial shade; average, well-drained soil.
Cultivation Plant in early fall. Dig holes or planting areas 2–3 inches (5–7.5 cm) deep. Space bulbs 4–6 inches (10–15 cm) apart when planting. Leave established clumps undisturbed to form large sweeps of spring color.
Propagation Divide the bulbs after the foliage has died back in midsummer.
Pest and disease prevention No serious pests or diseases.
Landscape uses Checkered lilies look lovely when naturalized in masses in woodland or meadow gardens. Grow them in beds and borders under deciduous trees.
Other common names Guinea-hen flower, snake's-head lily.

Gaillardia x grandiflora
ASTERACEAE

BLANKET FLOWER

The showy hybrid blanket flower blooms throughout the summer on loose stems with hairy, lobed leaves. Plants grow from fibrous-rooted crowns and may be short-lived.

Flower color Ragged, yellow-and-orange, 3-inch (7.5-cm), daisy-type flowers have single or double rows of toothed, petal-like rays surrounding a raised yellow center.
Flowering time Throughout summer.
Height and spread 2–3 feet (60–90 cm) tall; 2 feet (60 cm) wide.
Temperature requirements Zones 4–9.
Position Average to poor, well-drained soil. Full sun. Rich, moist soil causes plants to overgrow and flop.
Cultivation Blanket flowers are drought-tolerant and thrive in seaside conditions. Divide every 2–3 years.
Propagation Divide in early spring. Sow seed outdoors in fall or indoors in spring after stratification. To stratify, mix seed with moist peat moss or seed-starting medium in a plastic bag. Close the bag with a twist-tie and place it in the refrigerator for 4–6 weeks. Then sow the mixture as you would normal seed. Seedlings often bloom the first year.
Pest and disease prevention No serious pests or diseases.
Landscape uses Blanket flowers are an excellent choice for rock gardens, seaside gardens, or borders.

Galanthus nivalis
AMARYLLIDACEAE

COMMON SNOWDROP

Common snowdrops are among the earliest flowers to bloom in the spring garden. Established bulbs are trouble-free; they will spread and reseed freely, giving a lovely sweep of delicate white blooms.

Flower color Dainty, nodding flowers to 1 inch (2.5 cm) long bloom at the tips of arching green flower stems. The single or double flowers are white; each of the shorter, inner petals has a green tip.
Flowering time Late winter or early spring.
Height and spread Flowers and foliage to 6 inches (15 cm) tall; 2–3 inches (5–7.5 cm) wide.
Temperature requirements Zones 3–9.
Position Full sun to partial shade; average to moist, well-drained soil with added organic matter.
Cultivation Plant bulbs in fall. Set them in individual holes or larger planting areas dug 3–4 inches (7.5–10 cm) deep. Space each bulb 3–4 inches (7.5–10 cm) apart.
Propagation Divide bulbs while plants are in bloom or after plants have died back to the ground in early summer.
Pest and disease prevention No serious pests or diseases.
Landscape uses Grow clumps in the garden with other early flowers. Naturalize them in lawns, groundcovers, and low-maintenance areas or under deciduous trees and shrubs. (In lawns, you'll have to wait until the leaves have died before mowing.)

Galium odoratum
RUBIACEAE

SWEET WOODRUFF

Sweet woodruff produces whorls of light to dark green leaves that form an enchanting groundcover in shady gardens. The dainty, white spring flowers are an added bonus.

Flower color Small, white flowers are carried at the tip of each stem.
Flowering time Spring.
Height and spread 4–10 inches (10–25 cm) tall; 1–2 feet (30–60 cm) wide.
Temperature requirements Zones 3–9.
Position Average to rich, moist soil in partial sun to shade.
Cultivation Plants spread by creeping stems to form broad clumps.
Propagation Propagate by dividing overgrown plants in early spring or after flowering. Alternatively, take stem cuttings in early summer.
Pest and disease prevention No serious pests or diseases.
Landscape uses Plant sweet woodruff in shade or woodland gardens, as an edging for paths, or as a groundcover under trees and shrubs. Combine with large-leaved plants such as hostas, wild gingers (*Asarum* spp.), lungworts (*Pulmonaria* spp.), and bergenia. Plant with spring bulbs, bleeding hearts (*Dicentra* spp.), primroses, and ferns.

Gaura lindheimeri
ONAGRACEAE

WHITE GAURA

White gaura is a shrubby perennial with airy flower clusters on wiry stems and small, hairy leaves. This dependable, long-blooming plant grows from a thick, deep taproot.

Flower color Unusual white flowers are tinged with pink. They have four triangular petals and long, curled stamens on slender spikes above the foliage.
Flowering time Throughout summer.
Height and spread 3–4 feet (90–120 cm) tall; 3 feet (90 cm) wide.
Temperature requirements Zones 5–9. Extremely heat-tolerant.
Position Moist, well-drained, average to rich soil. Full sun.
Cultivation White gaura is an easy-care perennial that thrives for years with little care or attention. Plants bloom nonstop all summer despite high heat and humidity. Remove old bloom stalks to make way for the new ones.
Propagation Sow seed outdoors in spring or fall. Self-sown seedlings are likely.
Pest and disease prevention No serious pests or diseases.
Landscape uses White gaura is a lovely addition to formal and informal gardens alike. The flower clusters look like a swirl of dancing butterflies. Combine them with low-mounding perennials like verbenas (*Verbena* spp.), cranesbills (*Geranium* spp.), and sedums.

Gentiana asclepiadea
GENTIANACEAE

WILLOW GENTIAN

Willow gentian is a late-blooming perennial with leafy, arching stems that grow from a crown with thick, fleshy roots. The lance-shaped, opposite leaves have prominent veins.

Flower color Deep blue flowers are carried in pairs along the stems. Each flower is tubular, with five flaring, starry lobes.
Flowering time Late summer and fall.
Height and spread 1½–2 feet (45–60 cm) tall; 2–3 feet (60–90 cm) wide.
Temperature requirements Zones 5–7.
Position Evenly moist, humus-rich soil. Full sun to partial shade. Provide shade from hot afternoon sun to avoid leaf browning, especially in warmer zones.
Cultivation These long-lived perennials thrive with little care. Plants seldom need division and dislike root disturbance.
Propagation Divide carefully in spring. Sow fresh seed outside in late fall or indoors in late winter after stratification. To stratify, mix seed with moist peat moss or seed-starting medium in a plastic bag. Close the bag with a twist-tie and place it in the refrigerator for 4–6 weeks. Then sow the mixture as you would normal seed.
Pest and disease prevention No serious pests or diseases.
Landscape uses Plant in borders or use with ferns and wildflowers in the wild garden. Combine with asters, goldenrods, and other fall-blooming plants.

Geranium macrorrhizum
GERANIACEAE

BIGROOT CRANESBILL

Bigroot cranesbill grows in spreading clumps to form lush mats of aromatic, lobed, green leaves. The foliage turns reddish in fall and may hold its color into early winter.

Flower color Bigroot cranesbill bears 1-inch (2.5-cm), pink or reddish purple flowers on fine stems.

Flowering time Early summer.

Height and spread 1–1½ feet (30–45 cm) tall; 2–3 feet (60–90 cm) wide.

Temperature requirements Zones 3–8.

Position Sun or light shade. (These plants prefer not to be in hot sunlight all day, particularly in the South.) Well-drained, fairly rich, moist soil; plants will tolerate dry soil once they are established.

Cultivation This slow-spreading perennial is one of many versatile species of hardy geranium (*Geranium* spp.)—not to be confused with *Pelargonium* spp., the common houseplant geraniums. Plant about 2 feet (60 cm) apart in early spring. They need little maintenance, but divide them whenever they become too large and stop blooming well.

Propagation Propagate by division in spring or fall.

Pest and disease prevention No serious pests or diseases.

Landscape uses Grow bigroot cranesbill in borders, rock gardens, wild gardens, and on slopes. It can even take dry shade.

Geranium sanguineum
GERANIACEAE

BLOOD-RED CRANESBILL

Blood-red cranesbill is an adaptable, easy-care perennial that looks equally wonderful dotted about beds and borders or planted in masses as a flowering groundcover.

Flower color Five-petaled, 1-inch (2.5-cm) blossoms, ranging from pink to magenta, cover the plant.

Flowering time Late spring to mid-summer, with some flowers thereafter.

Height and spread 9–18 inches (22.5–45 cm) tall; 2–3 feet (60–90 cm) wide.

Temperature requirements Zones 3–8.

Position Sun to light shade; prefers well-drained, rich, moist soil; will adapt to most soil types.

Cultivation This adaptable, dependable perennial needs virtually no care. Plant about 2 feet (60 cm) apart in spring or fall. Divide plants when they overgrow their position; lift clumps in spring or fall, tease stems apart, and replant into improved soil.

Propagation Propagate by division in spring or fall.

Pest and disease prevention No serious pests or diseases.

Landscape uses Blood-red cranesbill is a fine specimen plant in the perennial border, rock garden, or woodland planting. It is also spectacular in masses, alone, or combined with other *Geranium* species.

Gillenia trifoliata
ROSACEAE

BOWMAN'S ROOT

Grow Bowman's root in borders and meadows, along driveways and roadsides, and at the edges of woodlands. Be patient; it will take several years to form large clumps.

Flower color The white flowers have five slender, twisted petals and are carried in loose terminal clusters.

Flowering time Summer.

Height and spread 3–4 feet (90–120 cm) tall; 2–3 feet (60–90 cm) wide.

Temperature requirements Zones 3–9. Tolerates heat and cold.

Position Near-neutral to alkaline, moist, humus-rich soil in full sun or light shade.

Cultivation Set out young transplants, as mature plants resent disturbance. Clumps seldom need division.

Propagation Take stem cuttings in spring or sow seed when it ripens.

Pest and disease prevention No serious pests or diseases.

Landscape uses Choose Bowman's root for an airy accent in beds and borders. Use it as a "weaver" plant in cottage gardens to link together bolder flowers such as delphiniums and poppies.

Other names Also known as *Porteranthus trifoliatus*.

Gladiolus x *hortulanus*
IRIDACEAE

GLADIOLUS

Gladioli grow from flattened corms. They produce tall fans of flat, sword-shaped, green leaves. A slender flower stem rises from the center of each fan in summer to early fall.

Flower color A flower spike with many buds produces open, funnel-shaped flowers in nearly every color but true blue; many have spots or splashes of contrasting colors.
Flowering time Summer to early fall (depending on the planting time).
Height and spread 2–5 feet (60–150 cm) tall; 6–12 inches (15–30 cm) wide.
Temperature requirements Usually hardy in Zones 8–10; elsewhere, grow as annuals.
Position Full sun; well-drained soil.
Cultivation Start planting the corms outdoors after the last frost date. Set them in individual holes or larger planting areas dug 4–6 inches (10–25 cm) deep. Extend the bloom season by planting more corms every 2 weeks until midsummer. Tall-flowering types benefit from staking. In cold areas, dig the corms before or just after the first frost and store them indoors.
Propagation Sow seed in early spring or collect cormlets from around the corms at any time, then plant in winter; the flowers will be quite small in the first season.
Pest and disease prevention Spray spider mites and thrips with insecticidal soap or a botanical insecticide as necessary.
Landscape uses Plant in beds and borders or in cutting gardens.

Gypsophila paniculata
CARYOPHYLLACEAE

BABY'S BREATH

Baby's breath is an old-fashioned perennial with airy flower clusters and sparse, smooth, blue-green foliage. The stems and basal leaves grow from a thick, deep taproot.

Flower color Small, single or double, white flowers in large, domed clusters.
Flowering time Summer.
Height and spread 3–4 feet (90–120 cm) tall; 2–3 feet (60–90 cm) wide.
Temperature requirements Zones 3–9. Heat- and cold-tolerant.
Position Near-neutral to alkaline, moist, humus-rich soil. Full sun to light shade.
Cultivation Set out in spring and do not disturb the crowns once plants are established. Good drainage is essential for longevity. Some double-flowered cultivars are grafted onto seed-grown, single root-stocks. Plant them with the crowns below the surface to encourage the stems to form roots. Tall cultivars may need staking.
Propagation Take cuttings in summer. Sow seed outdoors in spring or fall or indoors in spring.
Pest and disease prevention No serious pests or diseases.
Landscape uses Use the airy sprays to hide the yellowing foliage of bulbs and perennials such as oriental poppy (*Papaver orientale*) that go dormant in summer. Combine them with bold and spiky perennials for dramatic effect.

Helenium autumnale
ASTERACEAE

COMMON SNEEZEWEED

Common sneezeweed is a showy, late-season perennial with tall, leafy stems that spring from a fibrous-rooted crown. The hairy, lance-shaped leaves have toothed edges.

Flower color The 2-inch (5-cm), golden yellow, daisy-type flowers have broad, petal-like rays and raised, yellow centers.
Flowering time Late summer and fall.
Height and spread 3–5 feet (90–150 cm) tall; 2–3 feet (60–90 cm) wide.
Temperature requirements Zones 3–8.
Position Evenly moist, humus-rich soil. Full sun or light shade. Tolerates wet soil.
Cultivation Either stake plants or pinch the stem tips in early summer to promote compact growth. Divide the clumps every 3–4 years to keep them vigorous.
Propagation Divide in spring or fall. Take stem cuttings in early summer. Sow seed outdoors in spring or fall.
Pest and disease prevention No serious pests or diseases.
Landscape uses Common sneezeweeds offer late-season color. Combine them with asters, garden phlox (*Phlox paniculata*), and goldenrods (*Solidago* spp.).
Other common names Helen's flower.
Cultivars 'Butterpat' has bright yellow flowers on 3–4-foot (90–120-cm) stems. 'Crimson Beauty' has mahogany flowers. 'Riverton Beauty' has golden yellow flowers with bronze-red centers.

Helianthus decapetalus
ASTERACEAE

THIN-LEAVED SUNFLOWER

Thin-leaved sunflowers are showy summer flowers with stout stems clothed in wide, 8-inch (20-cm), wedge-shaped leaves. Plants grow from stout, fibrous-rooted crowns.

Flower color The 2–3-inch (5–7.5-cm) daisy-type flowers have bright yellow, petal-like rays and yellow centers.
Flowering time Mid- to late summer.
Height and spread 4–5 feet (1.2–1.5 m) tall; 2–3 feet (60–90 cm) wide.
Temperature requirements Zones 4–8.
Position Moist, average to humus-rich soil. Full sun. Plants will tolerate wet soil.
Cultivation Thin-leaved sunflowers are easy to grow but need room to spread. Divide every 3–4 years. The stems are usually self-supporting, except when plants are grown in partial shade.
Propagation Divide in fall. Take stem cuttings in early summer or sow seed outdoors in fall.
Pest and disease prevention No serious pests or diseases.
Landscape uses Sunflowers add bold splashes of color to the summer garden. Combine them with garden phlox (*Phlox paniculata*), asters, goldenrods (*Solidago* spp.), sedums, and ornamental grasses.

Helianthus x *multiflorus*
ASTERACEAE

PERENNIAL SUNFLOWER

Perennial sunflowers are easy to grow but need room to spread. Their cheerful flowers add bold splashes of colour to the summer border, meadow, or cutting garden.

Flower color Showy, 5-inch (12.5-cm), daisy-type flowers have bright yellow rays and yellow centers on long stems.
Flowering time Mid- to late summer.
Height and spread 4–5 feet (1.2–1.5 m) tall; 2–3 feet (60–90 cm) wide.
Temperature requirements Zones 4–8.
Position Moist, average to rich soil in full sun. Plants will tolerate wet soil.
Cultivation Divide in fall every 3–4 years. The stems are usually self-supporting, except when plants are grown in partial shade; then they will need staking.
Propagation Take stem cuttings in early summer or sow seed outdoors in fall.
Pest and disease prevention No serious pests or diseases.
Landscape uses Plant at the middle or rear of beds and borders, in meadow and prairie gardens, and in the cutting garden. Combine with goldenrods (*Solidago* spp.), garden phlox (*Phlox paniculata*), asters, sedums, and ornamental grasses. Plant in masses in front of evergreens and in mixed plantings of shrubby conifers and grasses.

Helleborus niger
RANUNCULACEAE

CHRISTMAS ROSE

Christmas roses are winter or early-spring perennials with deeply lobed, leathery leaves growing from a stout crown with fleshy roots. The flowers open white and turn pink with age.

Flower color White flowers have five petal-like sepals surrounded by green, leafy bracts. They turn pink with age.
Flowering time Early winter through spring.
Height and spread 1–1½ feet (30–45 cm) tall; 1–2 feet (30–60 cm) wide.
Temperature requirements Zones 3–8.
Position Evenly moist, humus-rich soil. Partial to full shade. Established plants tolerate dry soil and deep shade.
Cultivation In spring remove any damaged leaves. Plants take 2–3 years to become established and resent disturbance. Divide only to propagate.
Propagation Lift clumps after flowering in spring and separate the crowns. Replant the divisions immediately. Self-sown seedlings often appear. Sow seed outdoors in spring or early summer.
Pest and disease prevention Check for aphids; wash off with a stream of water or spray them with insecticidal soap.
Landscape uses Combine with early spring bulbs, wildflowers, and ferns. The lovely foliage is attractive all season.

Helleborus orientalis
RANUNCULACEAE

LENTEN ROSE

Lenten roses may take a couple of years to get established; after that, they'll bloom dependably every spring. Try them as a groundcover under shrubs and flowering trees.

Flower color The reddish purple, pink, or white flowers have five petal-like sepals surrounded by green, leafy bracts. The flowers fade to soft pink with age.
Flowering time Early winter through spring.
Height and spread 1–1½ feet (30–45 cm) tall; 1–2 feet (30–60 cm) wide.
Temperature requirements Zones 4–8.
Position Evenly moist, humus-rich soil in partial to full shade. Established plants tolerate dry soil and deep shade.
Cultivation In spring, remove any damaged leaves. Divide only if needed for propagation.
Propagation Lift clumps after flowering in spring and separate the crowns. Replant the divisions immediately. Plant fresh seed outdoors in late summer. Self-sown seedlings usually appear.
Pest and disease prevention Check for aphids; wash off with a stream of water or spray them with insecticidal soap.
Landscape uses Plant Lenten roses in shade gardens, along woodland walks, and in spring borders. Combine with early-spring bulbs, wildflowers, lungworts (*Pulmonaria* spp.), and ferns.

Hemerocallis hybrids
HEMEROCALLIDACEAE

DAYLILY

Daylily hybrids are among the most popular perennials. Although each flower lasts for only one day, a profusion of new buds keeps the plants in bloom for a month or more.

Flower color Daylily flowers vary in color and form. The majority of the wild species are orange or yellow with wide petals and narrow, petal-like sepals. Modern hybrids come in many colors.
Flowering time Spring through summer.
Height and spread 1–5 feet (30–150 cm) tall; 2–3 feet (60–90 cm) wide.
Temperature requirements Zones 3–9.
Position Evenly moist, average to humus-rich soil. Full sun to light shade.
Cultivation Plant container-grown or bareroot plants in spring or fall. Place the crowns just below the soil surface. Plants take a year to become established and then spread quickly to form dense clumps.
Propagation Divide hybrids in fall or spring. Seed-grown plants will be variable and are often inferior to the parent plant.
Pest and disease prevention Aphids and thrips may attack the foliage and flower buds. Wash off aphids with a stream of water or spray them with insecticidal soap. Thrips make small white lines in the foliage and may deform flower buds if damage is severe. Spray with insecticidal soap or a botanical insecticide.
Landscape uses Perfect for mass plantings in beds and borders.

Heuchera x brizoides
SAXIFRAGACEAE

HYBRID CORAL BELLS

Hybrid coral bells are attractive in foliage and in flower. The evergreen leaves may be deep green, gray-green, or mottled with silver. Plants grow from woody, fibrous-rooted crowns.

Flower color Small, fringed flowers are carried in slender, branching clusters. Colors vary from white through shades of pink and red.
Flowering time Late spring through summer. Variable according to cultivar.
Height and spread 1–2½ feet (30–75 cm) tall; 1–2 feet (30–60 cm) wide.
Temperature requirements Zones 3–8. More heat-tolerant than other coral bells.
Position Moist but well-drained, humus-rich soil. Full sun to partial shade. In warmer zones provide shade from hot afternoon sun.
Cultivation Coral bells are long-lived perennials. Remove old bloom stalks to promote reblooming. As plants grow, they rise above the soil on woody crowns. Lift plants every 3–4 years and replant the crowns into soil that has been enriched with organic matter.
Propagation Propagate by division only in spring or early fall.
Pest and disease prevention No serious pests or diseases.
Landscape uses Plant at the front of borders, along walkways, or in a lightly shaded rock garden.

Hibiscus moscheutos
MALVACEAE

COMMON ROSE MALLOW

The showy flowers of common rose mallow are borne in profusion on a shrub-like plant that grows from a thick, woody crown. The broad, oval leaves have three to five shallow lobes.

Flower color The 6–8-inch (15–20-cm) flowers have five pleated, white petals that surround a central, fuzzy column. The flowers have bright red centers.
Flowering time Throughout summer.
Height and spread 4–8 feet (1.2–2.4 m) tall; 3–5 feet (90–150 cm) wide.
Temperature requirements Zones 5–10.
Position Evenly moist, humus-rich soil. Full sun to light shade. Tolerates some dryness once established; tolerates wet soil.
Cultivation Space young plants 3–4 feet (90–120 cm) apart to accommodate their eventual spread. Once established, clumps dislike disturbance.
Propagation Take cuttings in summer. Remove the flower buds and cut the leaves back by one-half to reduce water loss. Seeds gathered from the parent plant are variable and often inferior. Sow fresh seed of the true species outdoors in fall.
Pest and disease prevention Japanese beetles may skeletonize the leaves. Pick them off and drop them in soapy water.
Landscape uses Plant rose mallows wherever you need a bold dash of color. They make great accent plants and are lovely in borders with ornamental grasses and airy summer perennials.

Hosta hybrids
HOSTACEAE

HOSTA

Hostas are indispensable foliage plants for shaded gardens. Their thick, pleated or puckered leaves are the real feature of this perennial, which grows from stout crowns with thick, fleshy roots.

Flower color Lavender, purple, or white flowers are carried on slender spikes.
Flowering time Summer or fall depending on hybrid and origin.
Height and spread ½–3 feet (15–90 cm) tall; ½–5 feet (15–150 cm) wide.
Temperature requirements Zones 3–8. Some selections are hardy to Zone 2.
Position Evenly moist, humus-rich soil. Partial to full shade. Adaptable to both dry and wet soil conditions. Filtered sun encourages the best leaf color in the gold- and blue-leaved forms. All hostas need protection from hot afternoon sun, especially in warm zones.
Cultivation Hostas take several years to reach mature form and size; allow ample room when planting. New shoots are slow to emerge in spring, so take care not to damage them during spring cleanup.
Propagation Divide in late summer.
Pest and disease prevention Set shallow pans of beer flush with the soil surface to drown slugs and snails.
Landscape uses Use the smaller cultivars to edge beds or as a groundcover under shrubs and trees. Choose giants for a mixed planting or alone as an accent.

Hyacinthoides hispanica
HYACINTHACEAE

SPANISH BLUEBELLS

Spanish bluebells grow from small bulbs. In spring, the plants form clumps of sprawling, strap-shaped, green leaves, each with a stem holding clusters of bell-shaped flowers.

Flower color Upright, leafless flower stems are topped with spikes of many bell-shaped blooms. The ¾-inch (18-mm) wide flowers come in white, pink, or shades of purple-blue.
Flowering time Late spring.
Height and spread Flowers 12–18 inches (30–45 cm) tall; leaves to 8 inches (20 cm) tall. Spread 4–6 inches (10–15 cm).
Temperature requirements Zones 4–8.
Position Full sun to partial shade; well-drained soil with added organic matter.
Cultivation Plant bulbs in fall. Set them in individual holes or larger planting areas dug 3–4 inches (7.5–10 cm) deep. Space 4–6 inches (10–25 cm) apart. Established patches of Spanish bluebells increase quickly, often to the point of becoming invasive. Remove spent flower stalks to minimize reseeding; mow unwanted plants.
Propagation Divide bulbs after mid-summer, when the plants go dormant.
Pest and disease prevention No serious pests or diseases.
Landscape uses Include in beds, borders, or woodlands, or with groundcovers.
Other names It is sold under a variety of former names, including *Scilla campanulata*, *S. hispanica*, and *Endymion hispanicus*.

Hyacinthus orientalis
HYACINTHACEAE

HYACINTH

Hyacinths grow from plump bulbs. Sturdy shoots with wide, strap-shaped, green leaves and upright flower stalks emerge in early spring, to be followed by the wonderfully fragrant flowers.

Flower color A dense spike of starry, 1-inch (2.5-cm) wide, powerfully fragrant flowers tops each stalk. The single or double flowers bloom in a wide range of colors, including white, pink, red, orange, yellow, blue, and purple.

Flowering time Midspring.

Height and spread Height 8–12 inches (20–30 cm); spread to 4 inches (15 cm).

Temperature requirements Zones 4–8.

Position Full sun; average, well-drained soil with added organic matter.

Cultivation Plant bulbs in midfall. Set them in individual holes or larger planting areas dug 5–6 inches (12.5–15 cm) deep. Space 6–10 inches (15–20 cm) apart. Double-flowered types may need staking. Remove spent flower stalks. After the first year, hyacinth bloom spikes tend to become smaller; in some cases, they may not flower at all. Plant new bulbs every year or two to ensure a good display.

Propagation Dig up and divide crowded clumps as the leaves yellow.

Pest and disease prevention Trap slugs and snails in shallow pans of beer set flush with the soil.

Landscape uses Plant for cheerful spring color in beds and borders, or in containers.

Hyssopus officinalis
LAMIACEAE

HYSSOP

Mature hyssop plants form shrubby clumps that are popular for herb and cottage gardens. The blooms are usually blue, but you may find white-and-pink flowered forms.

Flower color The tubular, two-lobed, blue flowers are carried in tight whorls. White and pink selections may also be available.

Flowering time Summer.

Height and spread 2–3 feet (60–90 cm) tall; 1–2 feet (30–60 cm) wide or more with time.

Temperature requirements Zones 3–9.

Position Average to rich, well-drained soil in full sun or light shade. Plants grow well in sandy soils and are somewhat drought-tolerant.

Cultivation Cut stems back by half after flowering to encourage repeat bloom.

Propagation Take stem cuttings in spring or summer, divide established plants in early spring or fall, or sow seed indoors or outside in spring.

Pest and disease prevention No serious pests or diseases.

Landscape uses Plant hyssop in formal and informal beds and borders, cottage gardens, and seaside areas. For indoor use, cut the stems just before the flowers open. Hang bunches upside down to dry. Combine with yarrows, balloon flowers (*Platycodon grandiflorus*), lamb's ears (*Stachys byzantina*), sages (*Salvia* spp.), and ornamental onions (*Allium* spp.).

Iberis sempervirens
BRASSICACEAE

PERENNIAL CANDYTUFT

Perennial candytuft is a floriferous, semiwoody subshrub with persistent stems tightly clothed in 1½-inch (3.5-cm), narrow, deep green leaves. Plants grow from fibrous-rooted crowns.

Flower color The tight, rounded clusters consist of many ¼-inch (6-mm), four-petaled, white flowers.

Flowering time Early spring.

Height and spread 6–12 inches (15–30 cm) tall; 1–2 feet (30–60 cm) wide.

Temperature requirements Zones 3–9.

Position Average to humus-rich, well-drained soil. Full sun to light shade.

Cultivation Space plants 1–1½ feet (30–45 cm) apart in informal plantings or 6 inches (15 cm) apart if edging a planting. Shear after flowering to promote compact growth. Mulch plants in Zones 3 and 4 to protect stems from winter damage.

Propagation Layer sideshoots or take cuttings in early summer. Sow seed outdoors in spring or fall.

Pest and disease prevention No serious pests or diseases.

Landscape uses Use perennial candytuft to edge formal plantings, walkways, or walls. Plant it in rock gardens or in combination with spring bulbs and early-blooming perennials.

Incarvillea delavayi
BIGNONIACEAE

HARDY GLOXINIA

Hardy gloxinias are showy plants with 1-foot (30-cm), pinnately divided leaves. They are slow to emerge in spring; mark their location to avoid damaging the crowns.

Flower color The 2–3-inch (5–7.5-cm), tubular, rose pink flowers have flat, five-petaled faces. They are borne in clusters 1–2 feet (30–60 cm) above the foliage.
Flowering time Spring and early summer.
Height and spread 1½–2 feet (45–60 cm) tall; 1½ feet (45 cm) wide.
Temperature requirements Zones 5–8. Intolerant of high temperatures.
Position Average to humus-rich, well-drained soil. Full sun to partial shade. Protect plants from hot afternoon sun when grown in warm zones.
Cultivation Plants are easy to grow. Good drainage is important for success. Mulch plants to protect them from winter cold.
Propagation Sow seed in spring or fall on a warm (70°F [21°C]) seedbed. Keep the soil moist and cover with clear plastic wrap to encourage humidity. Seedlings will develop in 10–20 days. Divide large plants in spring or fall.
Pest and disease prevention No serious pests or diseases.
Landscape uses Combine with ground-cover plants like rock cresses (*Arabis* spp.), candytufts (*Iberis* spp.), and sedums for a colorful spring show. In partial shade plant them with foliage plants.

Iris bearded hybrids
IRIDACEAE

BEARDED IRIS

Bearded irises are old-fashioned, cottage garden favorites. They combine well with other summer-blooming perennials such as peonies, poppies, and cranesbills (Geranium spp.).

Flower color The exceptionally beautiful flowers range in colour from white and yellow to blue, violet, and purple. They have three segments, called falls, ringing the outside of each bloom. The falls usually hang downward and bear a fringed "beard." The center of the flower boasts three slender segments called standards.
Flowering time Late spring and early summer; some cultivars rebloom.
Height and spread 1–3 feet (30–90 cm) tall; 1–2 feet (30–60 cm) wide.
Temperature requirements Zones 3–9.
Position Evenly moist, average to humus-rich soil in full sun or partial shade.
Cultivation Set out bareroot irises in late summer or container-grown plants in spring, summer, and fall. Divide every 3–4 years in mid- to late summer. Replant with the top half of the rhizome above the soil. Cut the foliage back by half. Remove dead foliage in spring and fall.
Propagation Divide rhizomes in mid- to late summer.
Pest and disease prevention No serious pests or diseases.
Landscape uses Plant bearded irises in formal or informal gardens with perennials, ornamental grasses, and shrubs.

Iris cristata
IRIDACEAE

DWARF CRESTED IRISES

Dwarf crested irises are delicate woodland wildflowers beloved for their diminutive stature, tidy foliage, and exuberant bloom. They form extensive colonies with time.

Flower color The flattened, 2-inch (5-cm) flowers are sky blue to lavender and purple with a white-and-yellow blaze.
Flowering time Early spring.
Height and spread Flowers up to 4 inches (10 cm) tall; leaves 6–8 inches (15–20 cm) tall. Each plant is 3–4 inches (7.5–10 cm) wide; clumps spread indefinitely.
Temperature requirements Zones 3–9.
Position Moist, humus-rich soil in partial to full shade. Plants bloom more heavily with some direct sun.
Cultivation Clumps may become so congested that plants bloom less. If this happens, lift plants after blooming and tease the rhizomes apart. Replant into soil enriched with organic matter.
Propagation Divide rhizomes in mid- to late summer.
Pest and disease prevention Slugs and other foliage feeders may damage the leaves. Set shallow pans of beer flush with the soil surface to drown them.
Landscape uses Plant crested iris in shade gardens, along woodland trails, or in rock gardens. Use them as a mass planting under flowering shrubs or mature trees. Combine with ferns, spring-blooming wildflowers, and small variegated hostas.

Iris reticulata
IRIDACEAE

RETICULATED IRIS

Reticulated irises return year after year to grace the garden with their delicate flowers. The grass-like, dark green leaves are short at bloom time but elongate after the flowers fade.

Flower color The dainty blue, purple, or white flowers have three upright petals (known as standards) and three outward-arching petals (known as falls). The falls have gold and/or white markings.

Flowering time Early spring.

Height and spread Flowers 4–6 inches (10–15 cm) tall; leaves to 12 inches (30 cm) tall. Spread to 2 inches (5 cm).

Temperature requirements Zones 5–9.

Position Full sun. Prefers average, well-drained soil.

Cultivation Plant the bulbs in fall. Set them in individual holes or larger planting areas dug 3–4 inches (7.5–10 cm) deep.

Propagation Lift and divide clumps after the leaves turn yellow.

Pest and disease prevention No serious pests or diseases.

Landscape uses The delicate, lightly fragrant blooms are beautiful in spring beds and borders, and rock gardens. For extra color, combine with Grecian windflowers (*Anemone blanda*) and early-flowering crocus. Reticulated irises also grow well in pots for spring bloom outdoors or winter forcing indoors.

Iris sibirica
IRIDICEAE

SIBERIAN IRIS

Siberian irises produce graceful early-summer flowers in a wide range of colors. Plants form tight fans of narrow, sword-like leaves from slow-creeping rhizomes.

Flower color Flowers range in color from pure white, cream, and yellow to all shades of blue, violet, and purple. Some cultivars come close to true red.

Flowering time Early summer; some cultivars rebloom.

Height and spread 1–3 feet (30–90 cm) tall; 1–2 feet (30–60 cm) wide.

Temperature requirements Zones 3–9. Heat- and cold-tolerant.

Position Evenly moist, humus-rich soil. Full sun to partial shade. Plant bareroot irises in fall and container-grown plants in spring, summer, and fall.

Cultivation Siberian irises thrive for many years without division. If bloom begins to wane, divide and replant.

Propagation Divide rhizomes in late summer. Seed collected from cultivars will be variable and often inferior to the parent plant. Sow fresh seed of the species outdoors in summer or fall.

Pest and disease prevention These irises are susceptible to iris borer. Smash the grubs between your fingers while they are in the leaves. Dig up affected plants and cut off affected portions of the rhizome.

Landscape uses Plant with other perennials, ornamental grasses, and ferns.

Kniphofia uvaria
ASPHODELACEAE

COMMON TORCH LILY

Common torch lily is a commanding perennial with tufts of narrow, evergreen leaves growing from a fleshy-rooted crown. The flower spikes add a dramatic accent to summer gardens.

Flower color Long, slender spikes consist of tightly packed, tubular flowers. The lowest on the spike are yellow-white; the upper ones are red.

Flowering time Late spring and summer.

Height and spread 3–5 feet (90–150 cm) tall; 2–4 feet (60–120 cm) wide.

Temperature requirements Zones 5–9.

Position Average to humus-rich, well-drained soil. Full sun. Established plants are quite drought-tolerant.

Cultivation Set out young plants 2–2½ feet (60–75 cm) apart. Leave established plants undisturbed. Plants increase to form broad, floriferous clumps.

Propagation Remove a few crowns from the edges of clumps in fall. Sow seed indoors in winter after stratification. To stratify, mix seed with moist peat moss or seed-starting medium in a plastic bag. Close the bag with a twist-tie and place it in the refrigerator for 4–6 weeks. Then sow the mixture as you would normal seed.

Pest and disease prevention Provide excellent drainage to avoid crown rot.

Landscape uses The bold, vertical form of common torch lilies adds excitement to perennial borders and rock gardens.

Other common names Red hot poker.

Lamium galeobdolon
LAMIACEAE

YELLOW ARCHANGEL

Yellow archangel is a fast-spreading perennial, with small, yellow flowers on silvery green, heart-shaped or oval leaves. These produce a strong odor when bruised.

Flower color Dense clusters of small, yellow, hooded flowers bloom in whorls along the stems.

Flowering time Late spring.

Height and spread 1–1½ feet (30–45 cm) tall; spreads quickly to cover large areas.

Temperature requirements Zones 4–9.

Position Partial to full shade; prefers moist, fertile soil but tolerates other soil types. It can cover dry, shady areas where few other plants will grow.

Cultivation Set plants 14 inches (35 cm) apart in spring. Because yellow archangel spreads so rapidly and can quickly overpower other plants, surround plantings with an edging strip and ruthlessly remove any shoots that try to sneak out.

Propagation Divide in spring or fall or take stem cuttings in summer.

Pest and disease prevention No serious pests or diseases.

Landscape uses Naturalize yellow archangel in a woodland garden or other shady area where invasiveness will not become a problem.

Lamium maculatum
LAMIACEAE

SPOTTED LAMIUM

Spotted lamium spreads quickly to form broad, ground-hugging clumps that tolerate dry soil and deep shade. White-flowered and yellow-leaved cultivars are available.

Flower color Tubular, two-lipped, pink flowers are borne in the axils of the smaller leaves at the top of the stem.

Flowering time Spring, with periods of flowering throughout the summer.

Height and spread 6–12 inches (15–30 cm) tall; 1–2 feet (30–60 cm) wide.

Temperature requirements Zones 3–8.

Position Average to rich, well-drained soil in partial to full shade.

Cultivation Set plants out at least 2 feet (60 cm) apart. Shear plants after flowering to promote fresh growth. Divide overgrown plants in early spring or fall.

Propagation Propagate by division or take stem cuttings in spring or summer. Self-sown seedlings may be abundant.

Pest and disease prevention No serious pests or diseases.

Landscape uses Choose spotted lamium as a bright groundcover along walks, in small tight corners, or under shrubs and trees. Use mass plantings on shaded banks and anywhere you need an attractive, fast-growing groundcover. Combine with spring-flowering bulbs, hostas, ferns, and astilbes.

Lavandula angustifolia
LAMIACEAE

ENGLISH LAVENDER

English lavender is a small, rounded shrub beloved for its herbal and ornamental qualities. Fragrant, gray-green leaves clothe soft, hairy stems topped with spikes of purple-blue flowers.

Flower color The ½-inch (1-cm), purple-blue flowers are carried in tight, narrow clusters along the flower stalks.

Flowering time Early to late summer.

Height and spread 2–3 feet (60–90 cm) tall; 2–3 feet (60–90 cm) wide.

Temperature requirements Zones 5–8.

Position Average to humus-rich, well-drained soil. Full sun to light shade. Neutral or slightly alkaline soil is best. Extremely drought-tolerant.

Cultivation Shoots may be partially killed in winter. Prune out any dead wood and reshape the shrubs in spring. Shear plants every few years to encourage fresh new growth and to promote bloom.

Propagation Layer or take tip cuttings in summer. Place cuttings in a well-drained medium; transplant them as soon as they root to avoid root rot.

Pest and disease prevention No serious pests or diseases.

Landscape uses Plant lavender in ornamental and herb gardens. Use as an edging plant or to configure knot gardens. In borders combine them with other plants that need excellent drainage such as yarrows and sundrops (*Oenothera* spp.).

Leucanthemum x *superbum*
ASTERACEAE

SHASTA DAISY

Shasta daisies are showy, summer-blooming plants with dense clusters of shiny, 10-inch (25-cm), deep green, toothed leaves and short, creeping, fibrous-rooted stems.

Flower color Bright white, 3-inch (7.5-cm) daisies with large, bright yellow centers are carried on stout, leafy stems.
Flowering time Throughout summer.
Height and spread 1–3 feet (30–90 cm) tall; 2 feet (60 cm) wide.
Temperature requirements Zones 3–10. Extremely cold- and heat-tolerant. Exact zones vary by cultivar.
Position Average to rich, well-drained soil. Full sun. Tolerates seaside conditions but not waterlogged soil.
Cultivation Shasta daisies are easy-care perennials. Deadhead plants to promote continued bloom. Plants grow quickly but may be short-lived, especially in warmer zones. Divide and replant clumps in organically enriched soil every 3–4 years to keep them vigorous.
Propagation Remove offsets from the main clump or divide in spring.
Pest and disease prevention No serious pests or diseases.
Landscape uses Combine with summer-blooming perennials like daylilies, irises, and poppies. In a seaside garden, plant them with blanket flowers (*Gaillardia* spp.) and coreopsis.

Leucojum aestivum
AMARYLLIDACEAE

SUMMER SNOWFLAKE

Despite their name, summer snowflakes actually bloom in spring. Plant the small bulbs in groups; over time, they'll multiply to form large clumps of nodding white bells.

Flower color Slender, green flower stems are tipped with loose clusters of nodding, bell-shaped, ¾-inch (18-mm) wide flowers. The white flowers have a green spot near the tip of each petal.
Flowering time Mid- to late spring.
Height and spread Foliage and flowers to 18 inches (45 cm) tall; spread to 6 inches (15 cm) wide.
Temperature requirements Zones 4–9.
Position Full sun to partial shade; moist but well-drained soil that has been enriched with added organic matter.
Cultivation In early fall, set bulbs in individual holes or larger planting areas dug 4 inches (10 cm) deep. Space them about 6 inches (15 cm) apart.
Propagation Divide in early fall.
Pest and disease prevention Set shallow pans of beer flush with the soil surface to drown slugs and snails.
Landscape uses Grow summer snowflakes with tulips and daffodils in flower beds and borders. Interplant with summer- and fall-blooming annuals that will fill in when the bulbs go dormant. Also naturalize in moist meadows and woodlands.
Other common names Giant snowflake.

Liatris spicata
ASTERACEAE

SPIKE GAYFEATHER

Spike gayfeather is a tall perennial with slender flower spikes. The erect stems arise from basal tufts of grass-like, medium green foliage. Plants grow from a fat corm.

Flower color Rose-purple flowers are carried in small heads that are crowded together into dense spikes. The spikes open from the top down.
Flowering time Midsummer.
Height and spread 2–3 feet (60–90 cm) tall; 1–2 feet (30–60 cm) wide.
Temperature requirements Zones 3–9.
Position Average to humus-rich, moist soil. Full sun. Plants tend to flop if grown in partial shade.
Cultivation Spike gayfeathers are long-lived perennials that offer lots of flowers for very little effort. Clumps increase slowly and seldom need division.
Propagation Divide plants in spring or early fall. Sow seed outdoors in fall or indoors in late winter after stratification. To stratify, mix seed with moist peat moss or seed-starting medium in a plastic bag. Close the bag with a twist-tie and place it in the refrigerator for 4–6 weeks. Then sow the mixture as you would normal seed.
Pest and disease prevention No serious pests or diseases.
Landscape uses Spike gayfeather is lovely in perennial gardens, meadow gardens, and prairie plantings.
Other common names Blazing star.

Ligularia dentata
ASTERACEAE

BIG-LEAVED LIGULARIA

Big-leaved ligularia has heads of bright flowers and 1–2-foot (30–60-cm), round or kidney-shaped leaves on long stalks. Plants grow from stout crowns with thick, fleshy roots.

Flower color 5-inch (12.5-cm), bright orange-yellow flowers look like spidery daisies. They are carried in open clusters.
Flowering time Late summer.
Height and spread 3–4 feet (90–120 cm) tall; 3–4 feet (90–120 cm) wide.
Temperature requirements Zones 3–8.
Position Consistently moist, humus-rich soil. Light to partial shade. These plants do not tolerate dry soil.
Cultivation The huge leaves lose water rapidly. In hot sun plants go into dramatic collapse, but they recover as temperatures moderate in the evening. Plants form big clumps but do not need frequent division.
Propagation Lift clumps in early spring or fall and cut the crowns apart with a sharp knife. Replant into soil that has been enriched with organic matter.
Pest and disease prevention Trap slugs with shallow pans of beer set flush with the soil surface, or exclude them with a ring of diatomaceous earth, wood ashes, or sand.
Landscape uses These ligularias are bold accent plants. Use by ponds or in gardens with ferns, hostas, irises, and grasses.

Lilium hybrids
LILIACEAE

LILIES

Lilies are excellent as cut flowers; pick them when the first one or two buds open. You may want to remove the orange anthers to keep them from dropping their staining pollen on furniture.

Flower color Flower buds open to showy, flat or funnel-shaped flowers in white, yellow, orange, red, pinks, and bicolors.
Flowering time Early to late summer (depending on the hybrid).
Height and spread Height 2–5 feet (60–150 cm), depending on the hybrid; spread usually 6–12 inches (15–30 cm).
Temperature requirements Zones 4–8.
Position Full sun to partial shade; average, well-drained soil.
Cultivation Plant bulbs in fall or early spring. Dig individual holes or larger planting areas 6–8 inches (15–20 cm) deep. Mulch to keep the bulbs cool and well moist, and water during dry spells, especially before flowering. Pinch off spent flowers where they join the stem. Cut stems to the ground when leaves yellow.
Propagation Divide clumps when the leaves turn yellow.
Pest and disease prevention Trap slugs and snails in saucers of beer set flush with the soil surface.
Landscape uses Lilies add height and color to any flower bed or border. They are also elegant mixed into foundation plantings, grouped with shrubs, or naturalized in woodlands.

Limonium latifolium
PLUMBAGINACEAE

SEA LAVENDER

Sea lavender has airy clusters of pink flowers above showy rosettes of spatula-shaped to narrowly oval shiny green leaves. Plants grow from stout, woody crowns.

Flower color Tiny pink flowers are carried in broad, domed clusters.
Flowering time Summer.
Height and spread 2–2½ feet (60–75 cm) tall; 2–2½ feet (60–75 cm) wide.
Temperature requirements Zones 3–9.
Position Average to humus-rich, moist but well-drained soil. Full sun. This plant is extremely drought-tolerant and grows in alkaline or saline soil.
Cultivation Plants are slow to establish and should not be disturbed after planting.
Propagation Remove small crowns from the main clump in fall. Sow seed outdoors in fall. Seedlings are slow-growing.
Pest and disease prevention Plant on a well-drained site to avoid crown rot, which is a problem in wet soil.
Landscape uses Plant in borders or seaside gardens. Combine the airy flowers with irises, phlox, yarrows, asters, and ornamental grasses.
Other common names Statice.
Cultivars 'Violetta' has dark purple-blue flowers.

Liriope spicata
CONVALLARIACEAE

CREEPING LILYTURF

Creeping lilyturf is a vigorous, spreading plant with long, narrow, grass-like leaves, perfect for low-maintenance gardening. The light lavender to white flowers are followed by black berries.

Flower color Spikes of light lavender to whitish flowers, ¼ inch (6 mm) long, bloom above the foliage.
Flowering time Mid- to late summer.
Height and spread Foliage to 10 inches (25 cm) tall, flower spikes 16–18 inches (40–45 cm) tall; 18 inches (45 cm) wide.
Temperature requirements Zones 5–10.
Position Full sun to deep shade; well-drained, moist, fertile, acid soil. This plant will tolerate drought.
Cultivation Set plants 1 foot (30 cm) apart in spring. Mow established plants in early spring to encourage new growth. It spreads by underground runners and can be extremely invasive; use where it can creep freely or contain it with an edging strip.
Propagation Propagate by division in spring or fall.
Pest and disease prevention No serious pests or diseases.
Landscape uses Creeping lilyturf forms a durable groundcover for difficult locations such as slopes or under trees and shrubs. It can also tolerate salt spray in seaside plantings. The foliage is evergreen in warm climates but often becomes yellow and unsightly during Northern winters.

Lobelia cardinalis
CAMPANULACEAE

CARDINAL FLOWER

Cardinal flowers have fiery-colored flower spikes on leafy stems. They grow from a fibrous-rooted crown, and the lance-shaped leaves may be fresh green or red-bronze.

Flower color Brilliant scarlet tubular flowers have three lower and two upper petals that look like delicate birds in flight.
Flowering time Late summer to fall.
Height and spread 2–4 feet (60–120 cm) tall; 1–2 feet (30–60 cm) wide.
Temperature requirements Zones 2–9.
Position Evenly moist, humus-rich soil. Full sun to partial shade.
Cultivation Cardinal flowers are shallow-rooted and subject to frost heaving. Where winters are cold, mulch plants to protect the crowns. In warmer zones winter mulch may rot the crowns. Replant in spring if frost has lifted them. Plants may be short-lived, but self-sown seedlings are numerous.
Propagation Divide in late fall or spring. Sow seed outdoors in fall or spring, or indoors in late winter. Seedlings grow quickly and bloom the first year from seed.
Pest and disease prevention No serious pests or diseases.
Landscape uses Cardinal flowers need even moisture so they are commonly used around pools, along streams, or in informal plantings. Combine them with irises, hostas, ligularias (*Ligularia* spp.), and ferns.

Lupinus polyphyllus
FABACEAE

WASHINGTON LUPINE

Washington lupine has conical flower spikes on stout stems with large, palmately divided leaves. Plants grow from thick roots. Lupines add a dramatic vertical accent to borders.

Flower color The ¾-inch (18-mm), blue-purple or yellow pea-type flowers are crowded into 1–2-foot (30–60-cm) spikes.
Flowering time Spring and summer.
Height and spread 3–5 feet (90–150 cm) tall; 2–3 feet (60–90 cm) wide.
Temperature requirements Zones 3–7. Sensitive to high summer temperatures.
Position Moist but well-drained, acid, humus-rich soil. Full sun to light shade.
Cultivation They are heavy feeders. Top-dress in spring with organic fertilizer. Protect plants from hot, dry winds.
Propagation Remove sideshoots from the edges of the clump in fall. Sow seed outdoors in fall or inside in winter. Before sowing indoors, soak seed overnight and then stratify. To stratify, mix seed with moist peat moss or seed-starting medium in a plastic bag. Close the bag with a twist-tie and place it in the refrigerator for 4–6 weeks. Then sow the mixture as you would normal seed.
Pest and disease prevention No serious pests or diseases.
Landscape uses Plant with border perennials like columbines (*Aquilegia* spp.), cranesbills (*Geranium* spp.), bellflowers (*Campanula* spp.), irises, and peonies.

Lychnis chalcedonica
CARYOPHYLLACEAE

MALTESE CROSS

Maltese cross is an old-fashioned perennial with brilliant flower clusters atop tall stems with opposite, oval leaves. Plants grow from fibrous-rooted crowns.

Flower color Brilliant scarlet flowers are held in compact, domed, terminal clusters.
Flowering time Midsummer.
Height and spread 2–3 feet (60–90 cm) tall; 1–1½ feet (30–45 cm) wide.
Temperature requirements Zones 4–8.
Position Average to humus-rich, moist but well-drained soil. Needs full sun to light shade.
Cultivation Maltese cross spreads quickly to form tight clumps. Divide every 2–3 years to keep it strong and healthy.
Propagation Divide in spring or fall. Sow seed outdoors in fall.
Pest and disease prevention No serious pests or diseases.
Landscape uses Use Maltese cross to create strong-colored excitement in a subdued scheme of blues and pale yellows. It is also perfect for hot color combinations with coneflowers (*Rudbeckia* spp.), blanket flowers (*Gaillardia* spp.), and sundrops (*Oenothera* spp.).

Lychnis coronaria
CARYOPHYLLACEAE

ROSE CAMPION

The soft, silver leaves and shocking magenta flowers of rose campion add excitement to beds, borders, and cottage gardens, especially when combined with softer colors.

Flower color The deep rose red, five-petaled flowers are carried in open clusters atop woolly stems.
Flowering time Late spring.
Height and spread 2–3 feet (60–90 cm) tall; 1–1½ feet (30–45 cm) wide.
Temperature requirements Zones 4–8.
Position Average to rich, moist but well-drained soil in full sun or light shade.
Cultivation Divide clumps every 2–3 years in spring or fall to keep them vigorous. Plants may be short-lived, especially in rich soil, but self-sown seedlings are numerous.
Propagation Sow seeds outdoors in fall, or remove small crowns from the edge of the clump in spring or fall.
Pest and disease prevention No serious pests or diseases.
Landscape uses Plant rose campion in formal and informal beds and borders or in rock gardens. Use the strong-colored flowers to spice up a subdued scheme of blues and pale yellows. Combine them with catmints (*Nepeta* spp), cranesbills (*Geranium* spp.), and blue-leaved grasses. Plant them in bright color combinations with yarrows, marguerites (*Argyranthemum frutescens*), and sundrops (*Oenothera* spp.).

Lycoris squamigera
AMARYLLIDACEAE

MAGIC LILY

Magic lily bulbs produce leaves in spring, which die back before leafless flower stalks appear in late summer. Some gardeners like to combine them with bushy plants to hide the bare stalks.

Flower color Slender, greenish brown, leafless flower stalks are topped with loose clusters of funnel-shaped, rosy pink flowers up to 4 inches (10 cm) long.
Flowering time Late summer to early fall.
Height and spread Flowers to 2 feet (60 cm) tall; leaves to 1 foot (30 cm). Spread to 6 inches (15 cm).
Temperature requirements Zones 5–9.
Position Full sun to partial shade; average, well-drained soil that's dry in summer.
Cultivation Plant bulbs in midsummer. Set them in individual holes or larger planting areas 4–5 inches (10–12.5 cm) deep. Space bulbs about 8 inches (20 cm) apart. Water during dry spells in fall and spring. Protect the leaves over winter with a loose mulch such as evergreen branches, pine needles, or straw.
Propagation Divide bulbs after flowering, before the leaves begin to re-emerge several weeks after the blooms fade.
Pest and disease prevention No serious pests or diseases.
Landscape uses Magic lilies grow best naturalized on slopes, among groundcovers, or in low-maintenance areas.

Lysimachia nummularia
PRIMULACEAE

CREEPING JENNY

Creeping Jenny is an attractive groundcover for moist-soil areas. It has shiny, round leaves that resemble coins, and bears a mass of brilliant cupped flowers.

Flower color Trailing stems bear bright yellow flowers, 1 inch (2.5 cm) across.
Flowering time Throughout summer.
Height and spread 4–8 inches (10–20 cm) tall; 3 feet (90 cm) wide.
Temperature requirements Zones 3–8.
Position Full sun (in cool climates) to full shade (in warm climates). Provide moist, fertile soil.
Cultivation Set plants 8 inches (20 cm) apart in spring or fall. Creeping Jenny can be very invasive, particularly in dry soil, and it rapidly becomes a weed problem when it spreads into lawn areas.
Propagation Propagate by division in spring or fall.
Pest and disease prevention No serious pests or diseases.
Landscape uses Creeping Jenny is an effective groundcover around ponds and streams. Its spread is not a problem in such moist-soil areas.
Other common names Moneywort.
Cultivars 'Aurea', golden creeping Jenny, grows 2 inches (5 cm) tall with golden yellow spring foliage that turns lime green in summer. It is a vigorous mat-forming creeper but not as invasive as the species.

Lysimachia punctata
PRIMULACEAE

YELLOW LOOSESTRIFE

Grow yellow loosestrife in informal gardens, where it can spread happily without crowding out less vigorous plants. It also thrives in the moist to wet soil beside ponds and streams.

Flower color The bright yellow, five-petaled flowers are carried in whorls among the leaves on the top one-third of the stem.
Flowering time Summer.
Height and spread 1–2½ feet (30–75 cm) tall; 2–3 feet (60–90 cm) wide.
Temperature requirements Zones 4–8.
Position Average to rich, evenly moist soil in full sun to partial shade. It grows well in wet soil. The leaf margins turn crispy if the soil is too dry.
Cultivation Plants need dividing every 2–3 years to keep them from engulfing the garden. Lift clumps in early spring or fall and discard the less vigorous portions; replant the remaining divisions.
Propagation Propagate by division or take cuttings in early summer.
Pest and disease prevention No serious pests or diseases.
Landscape uses Choose yellow loosestrife for cottage gardens and informal plantings. Use large clumps by ponds or alongside streams. Combine with Siberian iris (*Iris sibirica*), rose mallow (*Hibiscus* spp.), meadowsweets (*Filipendula* spp.), grasses, ferns, and hostas.

Macleaya cordata
PAPAVERACEAE

PLUME POPPY

The imposing plume poppy is tree-like in stature, with 10-inch (25-cm) lobed leaves clothing erect stems. Plants grow from stout, creeping roots that can quickly become invasive.

Flower color The 12-inch (30-cm) plumes consist of small, cream-colored flowers that give way to showy, flat, rose-colored seedpods.
Flowering time Summer.
Height and spread 6–10 feet (1.8–3 m) tall; 4–8 feet (1.2–2.4 m) wide.
Temperature requirements Zones 3–8.
Position Moist, average to humus-rich soil. Full sun to partial shade. Stems are not as sturdy on shade-grown plants.
Cultivation Established clumps can double in size each season. Control is necessary to avert a total takeover. Chop off the creeping roots with a spade as soon as you see new stems emerging.
Propagation Remove new offsets in fall or spring or take root cuttings in winter.
Pest and disease prevention No serious pests or diseases.
Landscape uses Place plume poppies at the rear of borders where there is ample room for them to grow; a mature clump is a lovely sight. Also plant them as accents along stairs or fences or use them like shrubs as a focal point.

Mazus reptans
SCROPHULARIACEAE

MAZUS

This creeping plant from the Himalayas forms ground-hugging mats of small leaves topped by a mass of delicate, lipped flowers in spring and early summer.

Flower color The lovely light blue-violet flowers, ¾ inch (18 mm) long, have a lower lip spotted in white, greenish yellow, and purple.

Flowering time Spring and early summer.

Height and spread 1–2 inches (2.5–5 cm) tall; 1¼–1½ feet (37.5–45 cm) wide.

Temperature requirements Zones 5–8.

Position Full sun to partial shade; well-drained, moist, rich soil.

Cultivation Set plants 12 inches (30 cm) apart in spring. They can be invasive; surround plantings with edging strips if spreading is a problem.

Propagation Propagate by division in spring or fall or by cuttings in summer.

Pest and disease prevention No serious pests or diseases.

Landscape uses Plant mazus in crevices between flagstones on pathways; it mingles happily with creeping thyme and similar low-growing plants. Grow it in rock gardens as a carpet for small bulbs like crocuses. Mazus is competitive with grass and will invade lawns.

Cultivars 'Alba' has white flowers.

Melissa officinalis
LAMIACEAE

LEMON BALM

Fresh-smelling lemon balm forms attractive clumps in herb gardens and informal plantings. Plant it along paths so you can frequently brush by, releasing the scent, or pick the foliage.

Flower color Lemon balm is a fragrant perennial herb grown for its lemon-scented foliage. Small white flowers are produced among the leaves at the tops of the stems.

Flowering time Late summer and fall.

Height and spread 1½–2 feet (45–60 cm) tall; 2 feet (60 cm) wide.

Temperature requirements Zones 4–9.

Position Average to rich, well-drained soil in full sun to partial shade.

Cultivation Plants have an open, often rangy appearance, especially in shade. If plants flop, cut them back by two-thirds to encourage fresh growth.

Propagation Divide plants in spring or fall, or take cuttings in early summer.

Pest and disease prevention No serious pests and diseases.

Landscape uses Choose lemon balm for cottage and herb gardens or informal settings such as meadow gardens. Combine with herbs, shasta daisies (*Leucanthemum* x *superbum*), artemisias, ornamental onions (*Allium* spp.), and grasses.

Cultivars 'All Gold' has yellow foliage that turns greenish during summer. Shear to 6 inches (15 cm) in midsummer to promote colorful leaves.

Mertensia pulmonarioides
BORAGINACEAE

VIRGINIA BLUEBELL

Virginia bluebells are lovely spring wildflowers with graceful flowers on arching stems clothed with thin, blue-green leaves. Plants grow from thick roots and go dormant after flowering.

Flower color Nodding, sky blue, bell-shaped flowers open from pink buds.

Flowering time Spring.

Height and spread 1–2 feet (30–60 cm) tall; 1–2 feet (30–60 cm) wide.

Temperature requirements Zones 3–9.

Position Consistently moist, well-drained, humus-rich soil. Full sun to shade.

Cultivation Virginia bluebells emerge early in spring and go dormant soon after flowering. Sun is essential for plants to bloom but they are shade-tolerant once dormant. Place where you will not dig into them by accident.

Propagation Divide large clumps after flowering or in fall; leave at least one bud per division. Self-sown seedlings are usually abundant. They will bloom in the second or third year.

Pest and disease prevention No serious pests or diseases.

Landscape uses Plant along a woodland path with spring bulbs like daffodils and squills (*Scilla* spp.), as well as wildflowers such as spring beauty (*Claytonia virginica*), and bloodroot (*Sanguinaria canadensis*). Interplant clumps with foliage plants such as ferns and hostas to fill the gaps left by plants when they become dormant.

Monarda didyma
LAMIACEAE

BEE BALM

Bee balm is a lovely perennial with bright flowers on sturdy stems that grow from fast-creeping runners. The pointed oval leaves give Earl Grey tea its distinctive aroma and flavor.

Flower color Tight heads of tubular, red flowers are surrounded by a whorl of colored leafy bracts (modified leaves).
Flowering time Summer.
Height and spread 2–4 feet (60–120 cm) tall; 2–3 feet (60–90 cm) wide.
Temperature requirements Zones 4–8.
Position Evenly moist, humus-rich soil. Full sun to partial shade. If plants dry out, the lower foliage will be shed.
Cultivation Plants spread quickly; divide every 2–3 years.
Propagation Divide in spring or fall. Sow seed indoors or outdoors in spring.
Pest and disease prevention Powdery mildew causes white blotches on the foliage and may cover the entire plant. Thin the stems for good air circulation. Cut affected plants to the ground.
Landscape uses Plant bee balm in formal or informal gardens. The lovely flowers add brilliant color to the summer garden and are favored by hummingbirds.
Other common names Bergamot, oswego tea.
Cultivars 'Blue Stocking' has violet flowers. 'Cambridge Scarlet' has brilliant scarlet flowers. 'Croftway Pink' is soft pink. 'Mahogany' has ruby red flowers.

Muscari armeniacum
HYACINTHACEAE

GRAPE HYACINTH

Once planted and established, grape hyacinths are trouble-free. They naturalize well under trees and shrubs, and they look also attractive combined with groundcovers.

Flower color The dense spikes of grape-like blooms have individual purple-blue, white-rimmed flowers that are only ¼ inch (6 mm) wide.
Flowering time Early spring.
Height and spread 6–8 inches (15–20 cm) tall; 3–4 inches (7.5–10 cm) wide.
Temperature requirements Zones 4–8.
Position Full sun to partial shade (under deciduous trees and shrubs); average, well-drained soil.
Cultivation Plant bulbs in early to mid-fall, as soon as they are available. Set them in individual holes or larger planting areas dug 2–3 inches (5–7.5 cm) deep. Space the bulbs about 4 inches (10 cm) apart. Leave the bulbs undisturbed unless propagating; they will form sweeps of spring color.
Propagation Divide just after the leaves die back in early summer.
Pest and disease prevention No serious pests or diseases.
Landscape uses Scatter the bulbs liberally throughout flower beds and borders. Mix them with primroses, pansies, daffodils, and tulips for an unforgettable spring show.

Narcissus hybrids
AMARYLLIDACEAE

DAFFODILS

It's hard to imagine a garden without at least a few daffodils for spring color. Grow them in borders, plant them under trees, or naturalize them in low-maintenance areas.

Flower color The sometimes-fragrant flowers have a cup or trumpet and an outer ring of petals. The single or double blooms are commonly white or yellow but may also have pink, green, or orange markings.
Flowering time Early, mid-, or late spring.
Height and spread 6–20 inches (15–50 cm) tall; usually 4–8 inches (10–20 cm) wide.
Temperature requirements Zones 4–8.
Position Full sun to partial shade; average, well-drained soil enriched with added organic matter.
Cultivation Plant the bulbs in early to midfall. Set them in individual holes or larger planting areas dug 4–8 inches (10–20 cm) deep. Allow the leaves to turn yellow before cutting them back or pulling them out. Fertilize in early spring with a complete organic fertilizer.
Propagation Divide bulbs after the foliage has died back in late spring.
Pest and disease prevention Plant in a well-drained position to deter root rot. Trap slugs and snails in saucers of beer set shallowly in the ground near the plants.
Landscape uses Create unforgettable combinations by grouping daffodils with other early bloomers.

Nepeta racemosa
LAMIACEAE

PERSIAN NEPETA

Persian nepeta is an easy-to-grow, old-fashioned, trouble-free garden perennial. Cutting it back after flowering promotes compact growth and also encourages rebloom.

Flower color Light blue or white flowers, ¼ inch (6 mm) long.
Flowering time Early summer.
Height and spread Foliage to about 1 foot (30 cm) tall; 20 inches (50 cm) wide. Flowers to 1½ feet (45 cm) tall.
Temperature requirements Zones 3–8.
Position Full sun. Light-textured, average, well-drained soil; plants can tolerate poor (infertile) soil.
Cultivation Set plants 20 inches (50 cm) apart in spring. Trim back halfway after blooming for compact appearance and to encourage reblooming. Plants that are 2 years old or more are not as vigorous as young ones and don't bloom as readily, so you may need to divide or replace them.
Propagation Propagate by division in spring or by cuttings in summer.
Pest and disease prevention No serious pests or diseases.
Landscape uses Persian nepeta is a good choice for rock gardens or when grown in borders and edgings.

Nepeta x faassenii
LAMIACEAE

CATMINT

Catmint produces terminal flower clusters in spring and early summer. The wiry stems are clothed in soft, hairy, gray-green oval leaves and grow from fibrous-rooted crowns.

Flower color Violet-blue flowers are carried in whorls on slender spikes.
Flowering time Spring through midsummer.
Height and spread 1½–3 feet (45–90 cm) tall; 2–3 feet (60–90 cm) wide.
Temperature requirements Zones 3–8.
Position Average to humus-rich, moist but well-drained soil. Full sun to light shade. Plants tolerate poor, dry soil.
Cultivation Clumps get quite rangy after bloom. Cut back finished flower stalks to encourage fresh growth and repeat bloom.
Propagation Divide plants in spring or fall. Take cuttings in early summer.
Pest and disease prevention No serious pests or diseases.
Landscape uses Catmints are perfect for edging walks and beds or for planting along rock walls. In borders, combine them with bellflowers (*Campanula* spp.), cranesbills (*Geranium* spp.), coreopsis, peonies, and ornamental grasses.
Cultivars 'Six Hills Giant' has purple-blue flowers on 3-foot (90-cm) stems.

Oenothera fruticosa subsp. Glauca
ONAGRACEAE

COMMON SUNDROPS

The young plants of common sundrops start out small but quickly form large clumps, so leave ample space when planting. Cut them back after flowering to promote rebloom.

Flower color The bright lemon yellow flowers are saucer-shaped and 3–4 inches (7.5–10 cm) wide.
Flowering time Late spring and early summer; may rebloom sporadically throughout the season if cut back.
Height and spread 1–2 feet (30–60 cm) tall; 1–3 feet (30–90 cm) wide.
Temperature requirements Zones 3–9.
Position Average to rich, well-drained soil in full sun. Established plants are extremely drought- and heat-tolerant.
Cultivation Plants grow from fibrous roots and spread by creeping stems, which root as they spread. Plants form large clumps with age, so space them at least 30 inches (75 cm) apart when planting.
Propagation Divide rosettes in early spring. Take stem cuttings in early summer.
Pest and disease prevention No serious pests or diseases.
Landscape uses Use common sundrops in the front or middle of borders. They are perfect for cottage gardens, and perform well in rock gardens and meadows. Choose them for an open groundcover in a sunny spot. Combine with wild sweet William (*Phlox maculata*), cranesbills (*Geranium* spp.), catmints (*Nepeta* spp.), and yarrows.

Oenothera macrocarpa
ONAGRACEAE

OZARK SUNDROPS

Ozark sundrops are showy perennials with yellow flowers and narrow, pale green leaves on sprawling stems. Plants grow from a deep taproot and spread by creeping stems.

Flower color The bright lemon yellow flowers are saucer-shaped and 3–4 inches (7.5–10 cm) wide.

Flowering time Late spring and early summer, sporadically through the season.

Height and spread 6–12 inches (15–30 cm) tall; 1–3 feet (30–90 cm) wide.

Temperature requirements Zones 4–8.

Position Average to humus-rich, well-drained soil. Full sun. Established plants are extremely drought- and heat-tolerant.

Cultivation Plants form large clumps with age, so space at least 30 inches (75 cm) apart. Stems root as they spread.

Propagation Divide rosettes in early spring. Take stem cuttings in early summer. Sow seed outdoors in fall or indoors in early spring.

Pest and disease prevention No serious pests or diseases.

Landscape uses Use Ozark sundrops at the front of borders with phlox, cranesbills (*Geranium* spp.), catmints (*Nepeta* spp.), yarrows, and other early-season perennials. They perform well in rock gardens and look lovely in meadow plantings.

Cultivars 'Greencourt Lemon' has 2-inch (5-cm), soft sulfur yellow flowers.

Oenothera speciosa
ONAGRACEAE

SHOWY SUNDROPS

Showy sundrops spread quickly by underground runners, the stems clothed in green leaves. They flower during the day, unlike the many night-blooming species of the Oenothera *genus.*

Flower color White, cup-shaped flowers, 2 inches (5 cm) across, fade to soft pink and turn toward the sun.

Flowering time Early summer, only during the day.

Height and spread 18 inches (45 cm) tall; 2 feet (60 cm) or more wide.

Temperature requirements Zones 3–8.

Position Full sun to very light shade; well-drained, average soil.

Cultivation Set plants about 2 feet (60 cm) apart in spring or fall. Showy sundrops can be invasive, especially in moist, fertile soil; plant where the spread won't become a problem, or surround the planting with an edging strip that extends a few inches below the ground.

Propagation Propagate by division or seed in spring or fall.

Pest and disease prevention No serious pests or diseases.

Landscape uses Showy sundrops look wonderful massed in low-maintenance areas, such as dry, sunny slopes.

Cultivars 'Rosea' grows to 15 inches (37.5 cm) and has clear pink, 3-inch (7.5-cm) blooms.

Omphalodes verna
BORAGINACEAE

BLUE-EYED MARY

Blue-eyed Mary is a charming little groundcover, ideal for a moist site in partial shade. The oval, dark green, textured leaves are evergreen in warm climates.

Flower color Blue-eyed Mary is sometimes called creeping forget-me-not because its loose clusters of lavender-blue, ½-inch (12-mm) flowers resemble the flowers of that well-known plant.

Flowering time Spring.

Height and spread 8 inches (20 cm) tall; 2 feet (60 cm) wide.

Temperature requirements Zones 5–8.

Position Partial shade; cool, moist, humus-rich soil.

Cultivation Set these easy-to-grow plants 1 foot (30 cm) apart in spring or fall. The plant spreads quickly by runners that root as they travel over the soil. Mulch in hot climates to lengthen the bloom period.

Propagation Propagate by division in spring or by seed in summer.

Pest and disease prevention No serious pests or diseases.

Landscape uses Blue-eyed Mary naturalizes easily on banks or alongside streams. It is also effective used as an underplanting for spring bulbs such as crocuses and dwarf daffodils.

Pachysandra procumbens
BUXACEAE

ALLEGHENY PACHYSANDRA

The new spring leaves of Allegheny pachysandra are upright and light green. By winter, they are dark green mottled with silver, and they tend to rest on the ground.

Flower color Brush-like spikes of white or purplish flowers spring from the base of the plant.
Flowering time Early spring.
Height and spread 6–10 inches (15–25 cm) tall; 1 foot (30 cm) or more wide.
Temperature requirements Zones 5–9.
Position Partial to full shade. Moist, cool, fertile, somewhat acid soil; established plants are drought-tolerant.
Cultivation Set out plants 6–12 inches (15–30 cm) apart in spring. Mulch with compost or top-dress with aged manure in fall. Mow or cut down all of the leaves in early spring to clean up the planting and make it easier to see the flowers.
Propagation Propagate by division in early spring or by cuttings in summer.
Pest and disease prevention No serious pests or diseases.
Landscape uses Allegheny pachysandra makes an attractive groundcover on shady slopes, beneath trees, or in woodland plantings. Combine with spring-blooming bulbs and wildflowers for extra interest.

Pachysandra terminalis
BUXACEAE

JAPANESE PACHYSANDRA

Japanese pachysandra is one of the most common evergreen groundcovers for shady spots, especially in the North. Established plantings need very little maintenance.

Flower color Clusters of fragrant, creamy white flowers bloom at the stem tips.
Flowering time Spring.
Height and spread 8–10 inches (20–25 cm) tall; spread unlimited.
Temperature requirements Zones 4–8.
Position Partial to deep shade; fertile, moist, neutral to slightly acid soil.
Cultivation Set plants 8–12 inches (20–30 cm) apart in spring. The leaves may turn yellow if plants get too much sun or if the soil lacks nutrients. Top-dress plantings yearly with compost or organic fertilizer. Prune back or mow every few years in spring to renew the planting.
Propagation Propagate by division in spring or by cuttings in summer.
Pest and disease prevention Euonymus scale can be a problem; destroy infested plants that have pear-shaped, white-and-gray scales on the leaves.
Landscape uses Japanese pachysandra is a dependable, easy-care groundcover for planting under deciduous or evergreen trees or in any shady area. It forms a good covering for slopes or banks.

Paeonia lactiflora
RANUNCULACEAE

COMMON GARDEN PEONY

Common garden peonies are shrub-like, with sturdy stalks clothed in compound, shiny green leaves. Plants grow from thick, fleshy roots and may live for 100 years or more.

Flower color White, cream, yellow, pink, rose, burgundy, or scarlet flowers may be single, semidouble, or double. Peonies with single or semidouble flowers tend to be more resistant to wind and water damage.
Flowering time Common garden peonies are classified by their bloom time; early-May blooming (April in the South); mid-May blooming; and late-May blooming (early June in the North).
Height and spread 1½–3 feet (45–90 cm) tall; 3–4 feet (90–120 cm) wide.
Temperature requirements Zones 2–8.
Position Moist, humus-rich soil. Full sun to light shade. Good drainage is important.
Cultivation Plant container-grown peonies in spring or fall. Plant bareroot plants in September and October. Mulch new plants to protect from frost heaving. Taller selections and those with double flowers may need staking. Lift plants in fall, divide the roots, leaving at least one eye (bud) per division, and replant.
Propagation Divide in fall.
Pest and disease prevention Spray or dust foliage with an organically acceptable fungicide to discourage Botrytis.
Landscape uses Combine with early spring bulbs like snowdrops and squills.

Papaver orientale
PAPAVERACEAE

ORIENTAL POPPY

Oriental poppies are prized for their colorful, crêpe-paper-like flowers. Plants produce rosettes of coarse, hairy, lobed foliage from a thick taproot. They often go dormant after flowering.

Flower color The 3–4-inch (7.5–10-cm) flowers have crinkled petals in shades of pink through to scarlet-red, with black spots at their base. The petals surround the seedpod.
Flowering time Early summer.
Height and spread 2–3 feet (60–90 cm) tall; 2–feet (60–90 cm) wide.
Temperature requirements Zones 2–7.
Position Average to rich, well-drained, humus-rich soil. Full sun to light shade. Established plants are long-lived.
Cultivation In warm zones plants go dormant after flowering, leaving a bare spot. In fall new foliage rosettes emerge. Divide overgrown plants at this time.
Propagation Divide in fall. Take root cuttings in late summer, fall, or winter.
Pest and disease prevention No serious pests or diseases.
Landscape uses Plant showy oriental poppies with border perennials and ornamental grasses. Combine them with bushy plants like catmints (*Nepeta* spp.) or asters, which will fill the gap left by the declining foliage.
Cultivars 'Bonfire' has brilliant red flowers. 'Helen Elizabeth' has pale salmon-pink flowers without spots.

Patrinia scabiosifolia
VALERIANACEAE

PATRINIA

Patrinia's tall-stemmed, bright yellow flower clusters add height and color to late-summer borders. Avoid planting them near paths, though—the flowers have a strong odor.

Flower color The stems are topped with branched clusters of small, yellow flowers.
Flowering time Late summer and fall.
Height and spread 3–6 feet (90–180 cm) tall; 3–4 feet (90–120 cm) wide.
Temperature requirements Zones 4–9.
Position Average to rich, moist but well-drained soil. Full sun or light shade.
Cultivation Patrinia is a tough and long-lived plant that seldom needs division. Self-sown seedlings may be plentiful. To reduce self-seeding, remove heads after the flowers fade.
Propagation Propagate by division in spring or after flowering, or sow seed outdoors in fall.
Pest and disease prevention No serious pests or diseases.
Landscape uses Choose patrinia for the middle or back of beds and borders, cottage gardens, and informal plantings along a woodland edge. Combine patrinia with New England asters (*Aster novae-angliae*), butterfly bush (*Buddleia davidii*), sedums, and ornamental grasses. Use the airy flowers as a foil for bold textures such as the leaves of cannas (*Canna* x *generalis*).

Penstemon barbatus
SCROPHULARIACEAE

COMMON BEARDTONGUE

Common beardtongue is a showy plant with erect flower spikes clothed in shiny, broadly lance-shaped leaves. Flowering stems and basal foliage rosettes grow from fibrous-rooted crowns.

Flower color 1–1½-inch (2.5–3.7-cm), irregular, tubular, pink flowers have two upper and three lower lips.
Flowering time Late spring to early summer.
Height and spread 1½–3 feet (45–90 cm) tall; 1–2 feet (30–60 cm) wide.
Temperature requirements Zones 3–8.
Position Average to humus-rich, well-drained soil. Full sun to light shade. Good drainage is essential for success.
Cultivation Plants form dense clumps with maturity and benefit from division every 4–6 years. More frequent division is required in rich soil.
Propagation Divide in spring. Sow seed outdoors in fall or indoors in winter after stratification. To stratify, mix seed with moist peat moss or seed-starting medium in a plastic bag. Close the bag with a twist-tie and place in the refrigerator for 4–6 weeks. Then sow the mixture as you would normal seed. Seedlings may bloom the first year.
Pest and disease prevention No serious pests or diseases.
Landscape uses Plant in formal borders, informal gardens, and rock gardens.

Penstemon digitalis
SCROPHULARIACEAE

FOXGLOVE PENSTEMON

Foxglove penstemons are a natural choice for meadow gardens, and they also blend well into formal borders. Enjoy the flowers in late spring and the seed heads in winter.

Flower color Foxglove penstemon is a showy plant with upright flower spikes. The 1–1½-inch (2.5–3.7-cm), irregular, tubular flowers are white with purple lines. They have two upper and three lower lips.
Flowering time Late spring to early summer.
Height and spread 2–4 feet (60–120 cm) tall, sometimes larger; 1–2 feet (30–60 cm).
Temperature requirements Zones 4–8.
Position Average to rich, moist but well-drained soil in full sun or light shade. This species of penstemon tolerates wet soil; good drainage is essential for success with most other species.
Cultivation Plants benefit from division every 4–6 years, although they may need more frequent division if they are growing in rich, moist soil.
Propagation Divide in spring or sow seed outdoors in fall.
Pest and disease prevention No serious pests or diseases.
Landscape uses Use in formal borders, informal gardens, and rock gardens. They grow well in low meadows and in light shade at the edge of a woodland. Combine the spiky flowers with rounded plants such as cranesbills, yarrows, and coral bells.

Perovskia atriplicifolia
LAMIACEAE

RUSSIAN SAGE

Russian sage is a shrubby, branching summer-blooming perennial with erect stems clothed in gray-green, deeply lobed leaves. Plants grow from fibrous-rooted crowns.

Flower color Small, irregularly shaped, blue flowers are carried in slender 12–15-inch (30–37.5-cm) sprays.
Flowering time Mid- to late summer.
Height and spread 3–5 feet (90–150 cm) tall; 3–5 feet (90–150 cm) wide.
Temperature requirements Zones 4–9.
Position Average to rich, well-drained soil. Full sun. Good drainage is essential.
Cultivation The stems of Russian sage become woody with age. After hard frost, cut the stems back to 1 foot (30 cm). In cooler zones plants die back to the soil line but resprout from the roots. Division is seldom necessary.
Propagation Take stem cuttings in early summer.
Pest and disease prevention No serious pests or diseases.
Landscape uses Plant toward the middle or back of borders where the airy, gray flower buds and soft blue flowers mix well with yellow, pink, deep blue, and purple flowers. Combine with yarrows, gayfeathers (*Liatris* spp.), sedum, phlox, balloon flower (*Platycodon grandiflorus*), and grasses.
Cultivars 'Blue Spire' has violet-blue flowers on strong, upright stems.

Phlox divaricata
POLEMONIACEAE

WILD BLUE PHLOX

Wild blue phlox is a sweet-scented woodland species with blue spring flowers and creeping stems clothed in evergreen, oval leaves. The plants have fibrous, white roots.

Flower color The soft blue to sky blue flowers are borne in open, domed clusters on upright stems.
Flowering time Spring.
Height and spread 10–15 inches (25–37.5 cm) tall; 1–2 feet (30–60 cm) wide.
Temperature requirements Zones 3–9.
Position Evenly moist, humus-rich soil. Partial to full shade. Sun is necessary in spring, but protection from summer sun is critical.
Cultivation Plants spread to form clumps of lovely flowers. Divide as necessary to control spread.
Propagation Divide after flowering. Take cuttings in late spring or early summer from nonblooming stems. Sow seed in spring or fall. Self-sown seedlings often appear.
Pest and disease prevention Powdery mildew may attack, causing white patches on leaves. Spray with wettable sulfur to keep the disease from spreading.
Landscape uses Plant in shade or wild gardens with spring bulbs, hellebores (*Helleborus* spp.), wildflowers, and ferns. Wild blue phlox also grows well under flowering shrubs as a groundcover.

Phlox paniculata
POLEMONIACEAE

GARDEN PHLOX

Garden phlox is a popular summer-blooming perennial with domed clusters of fragrant, richly colored flowers atop stiff, leafy stems. Plants grow from fibrous-rooted crowns.

Flower color Varies from magenta to pink and white. Hybrids have a wide color range, including purples, reds, and oranges. There are also bicolored and "eyed" forms.
Flowering time Mid- to late summer.
Height and spread 3–4 feet (90–120 cm) tall; 2–4 feet (60–120 cm) wide.
Temperature requirements Zones 3–8. Cold hardiness varies with cultivars.
Position Moist but well-drained, humus-rich soil. Full sun to light shade.
Cultivation Divide clumps every 3–4 years for vigor. To keep garden phlox looking its best, cut off the spent flower clusters.
Propagation Divide in spring. Take stem cuttings in late spring or early summer. Take root cuttings in the fall.
Pest and disease prevention Powdery mildew causes white patches on the leaves or, in bad cases, turns entire leaves white. Thin the stems before plants bloom to increase air circulation, and spray with wettable sulfur to keep the disease from spreading. Select resistant cultivars, especially hybrids with *P. maculata*.
Landscape uses Garden phlox is a beautiful and versatile garden perennial. Combine with summer daisies, bee balms (*Monarda* spp.), daylilies, and asters.

Phlox stolonifera
POLEMONIACEAE

CREEPING PHLOX

Creeping phlox spreads to form broad clumps of lovely spring flowers. The mats of evergreen foliage make a good groundcover after the bloom stalks have faded.

Flower color The pink to lilac-blue flowers bloom in open clusters. Each flower has an orange eye.
Flowering time Spring.
Height and spread Flowers 6–8 inches (15–20 cm) tall, leaves 1–2 inches (2.5–5 cm) tall; 1–2 feet (30–60 cm) wide.
Temperature requirements Zones 2–8.
Position Evenly moist, humus-rich soil in partial sun to full shade. Sun is necessary in spring, but plants can tolerate quite dense shade in summer.
Cultivation Divide the clumps as necessary to control their spread.
Propagation Divide or take tip cuttings from nonblooming stems in late spring or early summer. Self-sown seedlings will usually appear.
Pest and disease prevention Powdery mildew may cause white patches on leaves; spray with wettable sulfur to keep the disease from spreading.
Landscape uses Use creeping phlox in shaded and wild gardens, along a woodland path, or at the edge of a meadow. It also grows well under flowering shrubs and trees as a groundcover.

Physostegia virginiana
LAMIACEAE

OBEDIENT PLANT

Fast-spreading obedient plant is named for the tendency of its flowers to remain where positioned when shifted within their four-ranked clusters. Plants grow from creeping stems.

Flower color The tubular, bilobed flowers are rose pink to lilac-pink.
Flowering time Late summer.
Height and spread 3–4 feet (90–120 cm) tall; 2–4 feet (60–120 cm) wide.
Temperature requirements Zones 3–9.
Position Moist, average to humus-rich soil. Full sun to light shade. Grows well in moist to wet soil.
Cultivation Wild forms of obedient plant tend to flop in rich soil. Stake the plants or choose a compact cultivar. Divide every 2–4 years to control their spread.
Propagation Divide in spring. Take stem cuttings in early summer.
Pest and disease prevention No serious pests or diseases.
Landscape uses Use cultivars of obedient plant in formal gardens with garden phlox (*Phlox paniculata*), goldenrods (*Solidago* spp.), boltonia (*Boltonia asteroides*), asters, and ornamental grasses. The wild form is lovely in informal plantings.
Other common names False dragonhead.
Cultivars 'Pink Bouquet' has bright pink flowers on 3–4-foot (90–120-cm) stems. 'Summer Snow' has white flowers on 3-foot (90-cm) stems. 'Vivid' has vibrant rose pink flowers.

Platycodon grandiflora
CAMPANULACEAE

BALLOON FLOWER

Balloon flowers are showy, summer-blooming plants with saucer-shaped flowers on succulent stems clothed in toothed, triangular leaves. The plants grow from thick, fleshy roots.

Flower color The rich blue flowers have five-pointed petals that open from inflated buds, which resemble balloons.
Flowering time Summer.
Height and spread 2–3 feet (60–90 cm) tall; 1–2 feet (30–60 cm) wide.
Temperature requirements Zones 3–8.
Position Well-drained, average to humus-rich soil. Full sun to light shade. Plants, once established, are drought-tolerant.
Cultivation New shoots are slow to emerge in spring. Take care not to damage them by mistake. Remove spent flowers to encourage more bloom. Established clumps seldom need division.
Propagation Lift and divide clumps in spring or early fall; dig deeply to avoid root damage. Take basal cuttings from non-flowering shoots in summer, preferably with a piece of root attached. Sow seed outdoors in fall. Self-sown seedlings occur.
Pest and disease prevention No serious pests or diseases.
Landscape uses Plant balloon flowers with summer perennials like yellow yarrows (*Achillea* spp.), bee balms (*Monarda* spp.), sages (*Salvia* spp.), and phlox.

Polemonium caeruleum
POLEMONIACEAE

JACOB'S LADDER

Jacob's ladder has tall, leafy stems crowned with loose clusters of nodding flowers. The showy leaves are pinnately divided with many leaflets. Plants grow from fibrous-rooted crowns.

Flower color Saucer-shaped, blue or white flowers with five overlapping petals.
Flowering time Throughout summer.
Height and spread 1½–2½ feet (45–75 cm) tall; 1–1½ feet (30–45 cm) wide.
Temperature requirements Zones 3–7. Sensitive to high temperatures.
Position Evenly moist, humus-rich soil. Full sun to partial shade.
Cultivation Remove spent flowers to encourage reblooming. Plants are easy-care and seldom need division.
Propagation Sow seed outdoors in fall. Self-sown seedlings may appear.
Pest and disease prevention No serious pests or diseases.
Landscape uses Plant in formal gardens with goat's beard (*Aruncus dioicus*), Russian sage (*Perovskia atriplicifolia*), phlox, and ornamental grasses. Massed plantings are effective in informal gardens with ferns or under flowering trees.

Polygonatum odoratum
CONVALLARIACEAE

FRAGRANT SOLOMON'S SEAL

Fragrant Solomon's seal has graceful, arching stems with broad, oval, blue-green leaves arranged like stairs up the stem. The cultivar 'Variegatum' has white-edged leaves.

Flower color Tubular, pale green, fragrant flowers are carried in clusters at the nodes. Showy, blue-black fruit is produced in late summer.
Flowering time Spring.
Height and spread 1½–2½ feet (45–75 cm) tall; 2–4 feet (60–120 cm) wide.
Temperature requirements Zones 3–9.
Position Moist, humus-rich soil. Partial to full shade. Tolerates dry soil.
Cultivation Spreads from thick, creeping rhizomes to form wide clumps. Divide to control its spread.
Propagation Divide clumps in spring or fall or sow fresh seed outdoors in fall. Seedlings may not appear for 2 years and take several years to bloom.
Pest and disease prevention No serious pests or diseases.
Landscape uses Fragrant Solomon's seal provides grace and beauty in the shade garden. Combine it with hostas, lungworts (*Pulmonaria* spp.), irises, wildflowers, and ferns. Use massed plantings under shrubs or in the dry shade of mature trees.
Other common names Japanese Solomon's seal.

Polygonum affine
POLYGONACEAE

HIMALAYAN FLEECEFLOWER

Himalayan fleeceflower produces masses of pink flower spikes in early summer. It makes an excellent fast-spreading groundcover for moist sites, and creates a lovely display in borders.

Flower color Himalayan fleeceflower has small, pink flowers tightly packed into narrow, erect spikes.

Flowering time Early summer.

Height and spread Flowers 6–8 inches (15–20 cm) tall, leaves to about 4 inches (10 cm) tall. Clumps spread 1–3 feet (30–90 cm) wide.

Temperature requirements Zones 3–8.

Position Moist, humus-rich soil in full sun or partial shade.

Cultivation Plants spread rapidly to form wide clumps; frequent division in spring or fall will keep them from taking over.

Propagation Divide by removing sideshoots from the clump.

Pest and disease prevention No serious pests or diseases.

Landscape uses Himalayan fleeceflower is perfect when you need a fast-spreading, showy groundcover. Choose it for the front of the border, along walks, or in rock gardens. Combine with irises, astilbes, hostas, ferns, and ornamental grasses.

Cultivars 'Border Jewel' has rose pink flowers. 'Darjeeling Red' has crimson pink flowers. 'Dimity' has light pink flowers.

Polygonum bistorta
POLYGONACEAE

SNAKEWEED

Snakeweed is a vigorous perennial with upright flower spikes and pointed, broadly lance-shaped leaves with prominent central veins. The plants grow from creeping stems.

Flower color Small, pink flowers are tightly packed into erect spikes.

Flowering time Early summer.

Height and spread 1½–2½ feet (45–75 cm) tall; 1–3 feet (30–90 cm) wide.

Temperature requirements Zones 3–8.

Position Constantly moist, humus-rich soil. Full sun to partial shade. Plants tolerate wet soil.

Cultivation Plants spread rapidly to form wide clumps. Frequent removal of some plants is necessary to keep them from taking over.

Propagation Divide in fall or spring. Sow seed outdoors in fall or spring or indoors in late winter.

Pest and disease prevention No serious pests or diseases.

Landscape uses Snakeweed is a showy, fast-spreading groundcover. Combine it with irises, astilbes, hostas, ferns, and ornamental grasses.

Other common names Bistort.

Cultivars 'Superbum' has thick, showy flower spikes.

Primula denticulata
PRIMULACEAE

DRUMSTICK PRIMROSE

Drumstick primroses have distinctive flowers that add a fun touch to the early-spring garden. Combine them with ferns and moisture-loving perennials for all-season interest.

Flower color The leafless flower stems bear tight, globe-shaped clusters of lavender or pink flowers.

Flowering time Early spring.

Height and spread Flowers 6–12 inches (15–30 cm) tall, leaves 6–8 inches (15–20 cm) tall; clumps 10–12 inches (25–30 cm) wide.

Temperature requirements Zones 3–8.

Position Humus-rich, moist soil in light to partial shade.

Cultivation Drumstick primroses grow slowly to form dense clumps with many flowering stalks. They are heavy feeders, so mulch them with compost or well-rotted manure in early spring or summer to provide extra nutrients.

Propagation Divide after flowering. Alternatively, sow seed outdoors in fall or indoors in early spring.

Pest and disease prevention No serious pests or diseases.

Landscape uses Plant along a stream, at poolside, or in a moist shade garden. In a low spot, use drumstick primroses in mass plantings with moisture-tolerant shrubs, such as red-osier dogwood (*Cornus sericea*). Combine with astilbes, ferns, wildflowers, and other primroses.

Primula japonica
PRIMULACEAE

JAPANESE PRIMROSE

Japanese primrose is grown mainly for its delicate, tiered blooms. It is a tough, hardy, easy-to-grow plant in conditions of light shade with a very moist soil that's rich in organic matter.

Flower color The flowers are up to 1 inch (2.5 cm) wide and bloom one tier above the other on strong, upright stems over large clumps of oblong, 10-inch (25-cm) leaves. Cultivars come in many flower colors, including pink, rose, red, purple, and white, with "eyes" of varying shades.
Flowering time Late spring and early summer.
Height and spread 1 foot (30 cm) tall; 1½ feet (45 cm) wide. Flowers 1½–2 feet (45–60 cm) tall.
Temperature requirements Zones 4–8.
Position Light shade; well-drained, very moist, fertile soil.
Cultivation Set plants 12–20 inches (30–50 cm) apart in spring. Top-dress every year with leaf mold, aged manure, or compost. Plants self-sow to form large colonies in moist soil. Divide overcrowded clumps every 3–5 years for better flowering.
Propagation Divide or sow seed in spring.
Pest and disease prevention No serious pests or diseases.
Landscape uses Plant in moist borders and bog gardens, beside streams and ponds, and in woodland plantings.
Other common names Candelabra primrose.

Primula x polyantha
PRIMULACEAE

POLYANTHUS PRIMROSE

Polyanthus primroses are hybrids with large, showy flowers in a rainbow of colors. The broad, crinkled leaves rise directly from stout crowns with thick, fibrous roots.

Flower color Flat, five-petaled flowers vary in color from white, cream, and yellow to pink, rose, red, and purple. Many bicolored and eyed forms are available.
Flowering time Spring and early summer.
Height and spread 8–12 inches (20–30 cm) tall; 1 foot (30 cm) wide.
Temperature requirements Zones 3–8.
Position Evenly moist, humus-rich soil. Light to partial shade. Plants can tolerate dryness in the summer if they go dormant.
Cultivation In cooler zones mulch plants to avoid frost heaving and crown damage. Divide overgrown clumps after flowering and replant into soil enriched with organic matter.
Propagation Divide in fall to increase your stock or grow from fresh seed sown outdoors or indoors in early spring.
Pest and disease prevention No serious pests or diseases.
Landscape uses Plant drifts of primroses with spring bulbs like daffodils, Spanish bluebells (*Hyacinthoides hispanica*), and tulips. Combine them with early-blooming perennials like hellebores (*Helleborus* spp.), lungworts (*Pulmonaria* spp.), forget-me-nots (*Myosotis* spp.), and cranesbills (*Geranium* spp.).

Primula vulgaris
PRIMULACEAE

ENGLISH PRIMROSE

The pale yellow flowers of English primroses are excellent companions for spring-blooming bulbs and wildflowers in woodland gardens and under shrubs and trees.

Flower color English primroses have flat, five-petaled, pale yellow flowers.
Flowering time Spring and early summer.
Height and spread 6–9 inches (15–22.5 cm) tall; 1 foot (30 cm) wide.
Temperature requirements Zones 4–8.
Position Evenly moist, humus-rich soil in light to partial shade. Plants may become dormant if the soil dries out in summer.
Cultivation In Northern zones, mulch plants in winter to minimize the alternate freezing and thawing that can cause frost heaving.
Propagation Divide overgrown clumps after flowering. English primroses are easy to grow from fresh seed sown outdoors or indoors in early spring.
Pest and disease prevention No serious pests or diseases.
Landscape uses Grow primroses in light shade in woodland and informal gardens. Plant scattered clumps and drifts with spring bulbs such as daffodils, tulips, and Spanish bluebells (*Hyacinthoides hispanica*). Combine them with early-blooming perennials such as hellebores (*Helleborus* spp.), forget-me-nots (*Myosotis* spp.), lungworts (*Pulmonaria* spp.), cranesbills (*Geranium* spp.), and wildflowers.

Pulmonaria saccharata
BORAGINACEAE

BETHLEHEM SAGE

Bethlehem sage is a lovely spring-blooming foliage plant with wide, hairy leaves variously spotted and blotched with silver. Plants grow from crowns with thick, fibrous roots.

Flower color The nodding, five-petaled flowers vary from pink to medium blue. Some buds open pink and change to blue.
Flowering time Spring.
Height and spread 9–18 inches (22.5–45 cm) tall; 1–2 feet (30–60 cm) wide.
Temperature requirements Zones 3–8.
Position Moist, humus-rich soil. Partial to full shade.
Cultivation The foliage of Bethlehem sage remains attractive all season unless the soil remains dry for an extended period. Plants seldom need division.
Propagation Divide in spring after flowering or in fall.
Pest and disease prevention Trap slugs in shallow pans of beer set flush with the soil surface.
Landscape uses Plant Bethlehem sage with spring bulbs, primroses, bleeding hearts (*Dicentra* spp.), foamflowers (*Tiarella* spp.), wildflowers, and ferns.
Other common names Lungwort.
Cultivars 'Janet Fisk' has densely spotted, white leaves and lavender-pink flowers. 'Mrs. Moon' has spotted leaves and pink flowers. 'Sissinghurst White' is a hybrid with white flowers.

Pulsatilla vulgaris
RANUNCULACEAE

PASQUE FLOWER

Pasque flowers are early-blooming perennials with cupped flowers over rosettes of deeply incised, lobed leaves clothed in soft hairs. Plants grow from deep, fibrous roots.

Flower color The purple flowers have five starry petals surrounding a central ring of fuzzy, orange-yellow stamens. The flowers are followed by clusters of fuzzy seeds.
Flowering time Early to midspring.
Height and spread 6–12 inches (15–30 cm) tall; 10–12 inches (25–30 cm) wide.
Temperature requirements Zones 3–8.
Position Average to humus-rich, well-drained soil. Full sun to light shade. Does not tolerate soggy soil.
Cultivation Pasque flowers begin blooming in spring and continue for several weeks. After seed is set, plants go dormant unless conditions are cool. They seldom need division.
Propagation Divide clumps in spring (after flowering) or fall. Sow seed outdoors in fall or spring. Plants will also self-sow.
Pest and disease prevention No serious pests or diseases.
Landscape uses Perfect for rock gardens with bulbs, rock cresses (*Arabis* spp.), perennial candytuft (*Iberis sempervirens*), basket of gold (*Aurinia saxatilis*), and columbines (*Aquilegia* spp.).

Rhodanthe anthemoides
ASTERACEAE

PAPER DAISY

The small, white flowers of paper daisies are especially well-suited to mixed plantings in rockeries. Deadheading regularly will encourage more flowers to bloom.

Flower color Masses of stiff, white, papery, daisy-type flowers, each 1 inch (2.5 cm) wide, with a yellow center.
Flowering time Virtually thoughout the entire year.
Height and spread 8 inches (25 cm) tall; 1 foot (30 cm) wide.
Temperature requirements Zones 9–10.
Position Full sun; well-drained soils. Will grow in poor soils.
Cultivation Deadhead paper daisies regularly to stimulate more flowers. Cut back occasionally to maintain dense growth. It is often treated as an annual.
Propagation Sow seed in spring. Propagate cultivars from spring cuttings.
Pest and disease prevention No serious pests or diseases.
Landscape uses Paper daisies are an attractive choice for rockeries, dry banks, and meadow plantings.
Cultivars The cultivar 'Paper Cascade' is good for hanging baskets or rockeries.

Rodgersia pinnata
SAXIFRAGACEAE

RODGERSIA

Rodgersias are bold perennials with pinkish red flowers and large, pinnately compound leaves. These moisture-loving plants grow from stout, fibrous-rooted crowns.

Flower color The small, rose red flowers are carried in 1–2-foot (30–60-cm), plume-like clusters.
Flowering time Late spring and early summer.
Height and spread 3–4 feet (90–120 cm) tall; 4 feet (1.2 m) wide.
Temperature requirements Zones 4–7.
Position Constantly moist, humus-rich soil. Partial to full shade. Protect from hot afternoon sun in warm zones.
Cultivation Rodgersias form huge clumps from large crowns that can remain in place for years. Make sure you provide at least 3–4 feet (90–120 cm) for each plant.
Propagation Propagate by division in fall or spring. Sow seed outdoors in fall or indoors in spring.
Pest and disease prevention No serious pests or diseases.
Landscape uses Plant rodgersias in bog and water gardens or alongside streams. Combine with hostas, irises, astilbes, ferns, ligularias (*Ligularia* spp.), and primroses.
Other common names Rodger's flower.

Rudbeckia fulgida
ASTERACEAE

ORANGE CONEFLOWER

Orange coneflowers are cheery summer daisies with oval to broadly lance-shaped, rough, hairy foliage on stiff stems. Plants grow in clumps from fibrous-rooted crowns.

Flower color The daisy-type flowers have yellow-orange rays (petal-like structures) and raised, dark brown centers.
Flowering time Mid- to late summer.
Height and spread 1½–3 feet (45–90 cm) tall; 2–4 feet (60–120 cm) wide.
Temperature requirements Zones 3–9. Extremely heat-tolerant.
Position Average, moist but well-drained soil. Full sun to light shade. Good drainage is important.
Cultivation Orange coneflowers are tough, long-lived perennials. They spread outward to form large clumps. The edges of the clumps are the most vigorous. Divide every 2–4 years and replant into soil that has been enriched with organic matter.
Propagation Divide in spring or fall. Sow seed outdoors in fall or spring, or indoors in late winter.
Pest and disease prevention No serious pests or diseases.
Landscape uses Plant orange coneflowers with other daisies, phlox, chrysanthemums, sedums, bee balms (*Monarda* spp.), and ornamental grasses.
Other common names Black-eyed Susan.

Ruta graveolens
RUTACEAE

RUE

Rue is a traditional favorite for herb gardens, but its lacy, blue-gray foliage also looks lovely in ornamental plantings, especially alongside bold, colorful flowers.

Flower color Small, yellow flowers are carried in open clusters above the aromatic, blue-gray foliage.
Flowering time Summer.
Height and spread 1–3 feet (30–90 cm) tall; 2–3 feet (60–90 cm) wide.
Temperature requirements Zones 4–9.
Position Average to rich, well-drained soil in full sun or light shade. Plants tolerate dry, sandy soil.
Cultivation Rue forms broad, dense clumps that seldom need division.
Propagation Propagate by stem cuttings in summer and fall.
Pest and disease prevention No serious pests or diseases.
Landscape uses Choose rue for herb and knot gardens or for the front or middle of beds and borders. Think twice about planting rue where people will have to brush by it; it produces an oil that can irritate the skin of some people. Combine with hyssop (*Hyssopus officinalis*), yarrows, ornamental onions (*Allium* spp.), and ornamental grasses. Contrast the delicate-textured foliage with bold flowers such as balloon flower (*Platycodon grandiflorus*), orange coneflowers (*Rudbeckia* spp.), and blanket flowers (*Gaillardia* spp.).

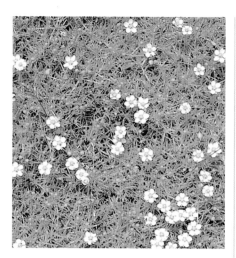

Sagina subulata
CARYOPHYLLACEAE

PEARLWORT

Pearlwort is a dainty, little, moss-like evergreen that makes a lovely groundcover in partial shade. It can withstand some foot traffic and looks great growing between stepping stones.

Flower color Numerous small, translucent white flowers.
Flowering time Midsummer.
Height and spread Foliage 1–2 inches (2.5–5 cm) tall; 1 foot (30 cm) wide. Flowers to 5 inches (12.5 cm) tall.
Temperature requirements Zones 5–7.
Position Partial shade; prefers well-drained, moist, fertile soil; tolerates dry, sandy soil.
Cultivation Set plants 1 foot (30 cm) apart in spring.
Propagation Divide in spring.
Pest and disease prevention Slugs and snails can be problems; trap in shallow pans of beer set flush with the soil surface.
Landscape uses Grow pearlwort in lightly shaded rock gardens and between flagstones since it tolerates foot traffic.
Other common names Irish moss.
Cultivars 'Aurea', commonly called Scotch moss, has yellow-green foliage.

Salvia officinalis
LAMIACEAE

SAGE

Sage is an aromatic herb that blends equally well into flower gardens and herb gardens. You can even dry the foliage and enjoy it in cooking and crafts all year.

Flower color The pink or purple flowers are less showy than those of other sages but are an added bonus to the sea green to purple-green leaves.
Flowering time Summer.
Height and spread 1–2½ feet (30–75 cm) tall; 2–3 feet (60–90 cm) wide.
Temperature requirements Zones 4–9.
Position Light, sandy or loamy, well-drained soil in full sun or light shade.
Cultivation Sage grows to form a small shrub, with persistent woody growth in warmer zones. Cut plants back in spring to remove winter-damaged growth and to reshape the plants.
Propagation Propagate by taking stem cuttings in summer.
Pest and disease prevention No serious pests or diseases.
Landscape uses Use sage in herb and cottage gardens or for winter structure and foliage interest in formal beds and borders. Combine with blue-, yellow-, or orange-flowered plants for exciting complements: Consider yarrows, ornamental onions (*Allium* spp.), butterfly weed (*Asclepias tuberosa*), and balloon flower (*Platycodon grandiflorus*). Sage also blends naturally with many other herbs.

Salvia x superba
LAMIACEAE

VIOLET SAGE

Violet sage is covered with colorful flower spikes in summer. The bushy, well-branched plants have aromatic, triangular leaves. They grow from a fibrous-rooted crown.

Flower color The violet-blue flowers are carried in narrow spikes. Below each flower is a leaf-like bract.
Flowering time Early to midsummer. Plants often rebloom.
Height and spread 1½–3½ feet (45–105 cm) tall; 2–3 feet (60–90 cm) wide.
Temperature requirements Zones 4–7.
Position Average to humus-rich, moist but well-drained soil. Full sun to light shade. Drought-tolerant once established.
Cultivation After flowering wanes, shear back flowering stems to promote fresh growth and renewed bloom. Plants seldom need division.
Propagation Divide in spring or fall. Take cuttings in late spring or early summer; remove the flower buds.
Pest and disease prevention No serious pests or diseases.
Landscape uses Plant violet sages in borders or rock gardens with early summer perennials such as yarrows, lamb's ears (*Stachys byzantina*), daylilies, coreopsis (*Coreopsis* spp.), and ornamental grasses.

Sanguinaria canadensis
PAPAVERACEAE

BLOODROOT

Bloodroot is a bright spring wildflower with a single, deeply cut, seven-lobed leaf that emerges wrapped around the single flower bud. Plants grow from a thick, creeping rhizome.

Flower color The snow-white flowers have 8–11 narrow petals surrounding a cluster of yellow-orange stamens. The flowers last only a few days.
Flowering time Early to midspring.
Height and spread 4–6 inches (10–15 cm) tall; 6–8 inches (15–20 cm) wide.
Temperature requirements Zones 3–9.
Position Moist, humus-rich soil. Light to full shade. Spring sun is important but summer shade is essential. Plants will go dormant during prolonged dry spells, with no ill effects.
Cultivation Bloodroot foliage remains attractive all summer when ample moisture is available. Plants form dense clumps that can be divided.
Propagation Divide in late summer. Sow fresh seed outdoors in summer. Self-sown seedlings often appear.
Pest and disease prevention No serious pests or diseases.
Landscape uses Bloodroot is a good choice in woodland gardens. Combine with spring bulbs, wildflowers, and hostas. Use as a groundcover under shrubs.

Sanguisorba canadensis
ROSACEAE

CANADIAN BURNET

The tall bottlebrushes of Canadian burnet bloom in late summer atop stout stems clothed in pinnately divided leaves with oblong leaflets. Plants grow from thick, fleshy roots.

Flower color The fuzzy, white flowers lack petals. They are packed into dense spikes.
Flowering time Late summer and early fall.
Height and spread 4–5 feet (1.2–1.5 m) tall; 4 feet (1.2 m) wide.
Temperature requirements Zones 3–8. Plants do not tolerate excessive summer heat.
Position Evenly moist, humus-rich soil. Full sun to partial shade.
Cultivation Mulch plants to help keep the soil cool and moist. Plants form stout clumps with age. Divide clumps when they become overgrown.
Propagation Divide in spring. Sow seed outdoors in fall.
Pest and disease prevention No serious pests or diseases.
Landscape uses Plant Canadian burnet at the rear of informal borders with phlox, monkshoods (*Aconitum* spp.), boltonia (*Boltonia asteroides*), sedums, asters, and ornamental grasses.

Santolina chamaecyparissus
ASTERACEAE

LAVENDER COTTON

Lavender cotton is a compact, semiwoody plant with small, white, woolly, pinnately divided leaves topped with yellow flowers in summer. Plants grow from fibrous-rooted crowns.

Flower color Button-like, yellow flowers are held above the foliage on thin stalks.
Flowering time Summer.
Height and spread 1–2 feet (30–60 cm) tall; 2 feet (60 cm) wide.
Temperature requirements Zones 6–8.
Position Average, well-drained soil. Full sun. Tolerates drought, poor soil, and salt.
Cultivation Plants need winter protection in cold areas. Cut back in early spring to promote strong, healthy growth.
Propagation Layer in spring. Take cuttings in summer.
Pest and disease prevention No serious pests or diseases.
Landscape uses Use lavender cotton to edge walks and beds or to configure intricate knot garden designs. Combine with other perennials that need good drainage like pinks (*Dianthus* spp.), rock cresses (*Arabis* spp.), and sedums.

Saponaria ocymoides
CARYOPHYLLACEAE

ROCK SOAPWORT

Plant rock soapworts where they can tumble over rocks or walls. After their main flush of early summer bloom, cut the plants back by half to promote compact new growth.

Flower color A profusion of ¼-inch (6-mm), pink flowers smothers the plants for nearly a month.
Flowering time Early summer.
Height and spread 4–6 inches (10–15 cm) tall; 1–2 feet (30–60 cm) wide.
Temperature requirements Zones 3–7.
Position Average to rich, well-drained soil in full sun or light shade. Plants also grow well in sandy soils.
Cultivation Clumps spread quickly and may die out in the center after a few years. To keep them looking good, divide plants every 2–3 years in spring or fall, especially if you grow them in rich soil.
Propagation Take cuttings in summer.
Pest and disease prevention No serious pests or diseases.
Landscape uses Plant rock soapwort as an edging to beds and borders or along the path in a cottage garden. Choose it for rock gardens and unmortared walls as well as for edging walkways.
Cultivars 'Rubra Compacta' has deep pink flowers on compact plants. 'Splendens' is rosy red. 'Alba' has white flowers.

Saponaria x lempergii
CARYOPHYLLACEAE

SOAPWORT

Soapworts have mounds of flowers on sprawling stems with oval leaves. Plants grow from fibrous-rooted crowns. They are ideal for planting on walls or in rock gardens.

Flower color The 1-inch (2.5-cm), pink flowers have five squared petals.
Flowering time Summer.
Height and spread 4–6 inches (10–15 cm) tall; 12–14 inches (30–35 cm) wide.
Temperature requirements Zones 5–8.
Position Average, well-drained soil. Full sun to light shade.
Cultivation Soapworts form broad clumps from creeping stems. Divide to control their spread. Cut back after flowering to encourage new growth.
Propagation Divide in spring or fall. Take cuttings in early summer.
Pest and disease prevention No serious pests or diseases.
Landscape uses Plant soapworts along walks, along the edges of beds, at the front of borders, or in rock gardens.
Cultivars 'Max Frei' is a compact grower with rich pink flowers.

Saxifraga stolonifera
SAXIFRAGACEAE

STRAWBERRY GERANIUM

Strawberry geranium is not a true geranium but an attractive groundcover with round leaves that resembles bedding geraniums. The evergreen leaves are attractively veined with silver.

Flower color The small, white flowers have five petals, two of which are longer than the others.
Flowering time Spring.
Height and spread 10–12 inches (25–30 cm) tall; 1 foot (30 cm) wide.
Temperature requirements Zones 6–9.
Position Moist, humus-rich soil. Partial to full shade.
Cultivation Plants spread quickly to form dense, weed-proof mats. Plants are easily pulled if they spread out of bounds.
Propagation Remove and replant rooted offsets in spring or fall. Alternatively, sow seed outdoors in fall.
Pest and disease prevention No serious pests or diseases.
Landscape uses Plant as a groundcover under flowering shrubs and small trees. In the shaded garden, use the silvery foliage to complement hostas, bulbs, wildflowers, and ferns. Plants perform admirably in pots.
Cultivars 'Tricolor' has pink and cream variegation but is less hardy.

Scabiosa caucasica
DIPSACACEAE

PINCUSHION FLOWER

Pincushion flowers are old-fashioned perennials that are regaining the popularity they had in Victorian gardens. The stems are loosely clothed in lance-shaped to three-lobed leaves.

Flower color The unusual soft blue flowers are packed into flat, 2–3-inch (5–7.5-cm) heads. The flowers increase in size as they near the margins of the heads.
Flowering time Summer.
Height and spread 1½–2 feet (45–60 cm) tall; 1–1½ feet (30–45 cm) wide.
Temperature requirements Zones 3–7.
Position Average to humus-rich, moist but well-drained soil. Full sun to light shade. Sensitive to high temperatures. Does not tolerate wet soil.
Cultivation Plants form good-sized clumps in 1–2 years. Divide when overcrowded. Deadheading promotes continued bloom.
Propagation Propagate by division in spring. Alternatively, sow fresh seed outdoors in fall or indoors in late winter.
Pest and disease prevention No serious pests or diseases.
Landscape uses Plant pincushion flowers in groups to increase their visual impact. The airy flowers stand tall above low, mounded plants like phlox, yarrows, and pinks (*Dianthus* spp.). They combine well with daylilies, bee balms (*Monarda* spp.), and columbines (*Aquilegia* spp.).

Scilla sibirica
HYACINTHACEAE

SIBERIAN SQUILL

The deep blue blooms of Siberian squill look marvelous in masses. They also combine beautifully with many other spring-flowering bulbs, annuals, and perennials.

Flower color Flower stems are topped with clusters of nodding, starry or bell-shaped, blue flowers, ½ inch (12 mm) wide.
Flowering time Early to midspring.
Height and spread 6 inches (15 cm) tall; 2–3 inches (5–7.5 cm) wide.
Temperature requirements Zones 3–8.
Position Full sun to partial shade; average, well-drained soil.
Cultivation Plant bulbs in early to midfall, as soon as they are available. Set them in individual holes or larger planting areas dug 3–4 inches (7.5–10 cm) deep. Once established, bulbs are trouble-free. Leave them undisturbed to spread into large clumps unless propagating.
Propagation Divide bulbs after the leaves turn yellow.
Pest and disease prevention No serious pests or diseases.
Landscape uses Tuck Siberian squill into beds and borders with pansies, primroses, and daffodils. They are also excellent for naturalizing in lawns and low-maintenance areas and under trees and shrubs; wait until the bulb leaves have turned yellow to mow.

Sedum spectabile
CRASSULACEAE

SHOWY STONECROP

Showy stonecrops are late summer perennials with clusters of pink flowers atop thick stems clothed in broad, gray-green leaves. Plants grow from fibrous-rooted crowns.

Flower color Small, bright pink flowers are borne in 4–6-inch (10–15-cm), domed clusters. The pale green buds are attractive in summer and the brown seed heads hold their shape all winter.
Flowering time Mid- to late summer.
Height and spread 1–2 feet (30–60 cm) tall; 2 feet (60 cm) wide.
Temperature requirements Zones 3–9. Plants are heat-tolerant.
Position Average to humus-rich, well-drained soil. Full sun. Extremely drought-tolerant.
Cultivation Clumps get quite full with age and may fall open. To counteract this, divide overgrown plants.
Propagation Propagate by division any time from spring to midsummer. Take cuttings of nonflowering shoots in summer. Sow seed in spring or fall.
Pest and disease prevention No serious pests or diseases.
Landscape uses Plant in formal borders, informal gardens, and rock gardens. Grow with purple coneflowers (*Echinacea* spp.), cranesbills (*Geranium* spp.), coreopsis, yarrows, and ornamental grasses.

Sedum spurium
CRASSULACEAE

TWO-ROW SEDUM

Two-row sedum is an adaptable, low-growing perennial that makes a great groundcover or edging. The leaves age from green to red; the pink flowers bloom in summer.

Flower color Starry flowers in big, rounded flowerheads range from rose pink to white.
Flowering time Summer.
Height and spread 2–6 inches (5–15 cm) tall; 1–2 feet (30–60 cm) wide.
Temperature requirements Zones 3–8.
Position Average, sandy or loamy, well-drained soil in full sun or partial shade.
Cultivation Divide overgrown plants in spring or fall.
Propagation Propagate by division or take cuttings in summer.
Pest and disease prevention No serious pests or diseases.
Landscape uses Two-row sedum is a tough groundcover. Plant it as an edging for beds and borders or in rock gardens. It grows well in the tight crevices of rock walls. Also use it as a groundcover on a dry bank or under high-branched trees.

Smilacina racemosa
CONVALLARIACEAE

SOLOMON'S PLUME

Solomon's plume is a showy woodland wildflower. The erect, arching stems bear broad, glossy, green leaves arranged like ascending stairs. Plants grow from a thick, creeping rhizome.

Flower color Small, starry, creamy white flowers are borne in terminal, plume-like clusters. Red berries ripen in late summer.
Flowering time Spring.
Height and spread 2–4 feet (60–120 cm) tall; 2–3 feet (60–90 cm) or more wide.
Temperature requirements Zones 3–8.
Position Evenly moist, humus-rich, neutral to acid soil in light to full shade. Plants burn in full sun.
Cultivation Divide the tangled rhizomes if plants overgrow their position.
Propagation Divide in spring or fall. Sow fresh seed outdoors in fall.
Pest and disease prevention No serious pests or diseases.
Landscape uses Plant Solomon's plumes in woodland gardens with bleeding hearts (*Dicentra* spp.), lungworts (*Pulmonaria* spp.), columbines (*Aquilegia* spp.), hostas, wildflowers, and ferns. Also use them under shrubs and flowering trees.
Other common names False Solomon's seal.

Solidago rigida
ASTERACEAE

STIFF GOLDENROD

Stiff goldenrod is a common roadside wildflower with plumed flower clusters and oval- to lance-shaped leaves. Plants grow from a crown with thick roots, and can become invasive.

Flower color Stiff goldenrod is a showy wildflower with flattened clusters of bright yellow, fuzzy flowers on leafy stalks. The foliage is attractive in summer and turns ruby red in fall. The seed heads are silvery.
Flowering time Late summer and fall.
Height and spread 3–5 feet (90–150 cm) tall; 1–2 feet (30–60 cm) wide.
Temperature requirements Zones 3–9.
Position Average, sandy or loamy, well-drained soil in full sun or light shade. When planted in rich soil, stiff goldenrod produces weak, floppy growth.
Cultivation Stiff goldenrod spreads rapidly and needs frequent division.
Propagation Divide in spring or after flowering, or take stem cuttings in early summer. Self-sown seedlings may appear.
Pest and disease prevention No serious pests or diseases.
Landscape uses Plant stiff goldenrod in beds and borders, along walls and fences, or in meadows and prairies. The stiff, upright form and showy blooms make them suitable for formal settings, too. Combine with fall flowers such as chrysanthemums, anemones (*Anemone* spp.), sneezeweeds (*Helenium autumnale*), and asters.

Stachys byzantina (syn. *S. lanata*)
LAMIACEAE

LAMB'S EARS

Lamb's ears are eye-catching foliage plants with basal rosettes of elongated, densely white, woolly leaves. These sun-loving plants grow from slow-creeping stems.

Flower color Small, two-lipped, rose-purple flowers are carried on woolly flower stalks. Many people consider the flowers unattractive and remove them.
Flowering time Early summer.
Height and spread 6–15 inches (15–37.5 cm) tall; 1–2 feet (30–60 cm) wide.
Temperature requirements Zones 4–8. Plants are sensitive to hot, humid weather.
Position Well-drained, sandy or loamy soil. Full sun to light shade. Intolerant of heavy, soggy soil.
Cultivation Lamb's ears form dense, broad clumps of tightly packed foliage. Divide overgrown clumps to control their spread.
Propagation Propagate by division in spring or fall.
Pest and disease prevention In wet, humid weather rot may occur. Cut back affected plants. Proper siting is the best defense against this problem.
Landscape uses Plant at the front of formal and informal gardens with irises, coral bells (*Heuchera* spp.), yuccas, alliums (*Allium* spp.), and sedums.
Cultivars 'Primrose Heron' has soft, primrose yellow foliage in spring. 'Sheila McQueen' has larger, less woolly leaves.

Stokesia laevis
ASTERACEAE

STOKE'S ASTER

Stoke's aster is attractive in foliage and flower. The broad, lance-shaped leaves are deep green with a white midvein. The leaves form a rosette from a crown with thick, fibrous roots.

Flower color The 2–3-inch (5–7.5-cm), daisy-type flowers have ragged, pale blue rays and fuzzy white centers.
Flowering time Summer.
Height and spread 1–2 feet (30–60 cm) tall; 2 feet (60 cm) wide.
Temperature requirements Zones 5–9.
Position Average to humus-rich, moist but well drained soil. Full sun to light shade. Established plants tolerate dry soil.
Cultivation Plants can grow undisturbed for many years. Divide in spring or fall.
Propagation Divide in early spring. Sow seed outdoors in fall or indoors in winter after stratification. To stratify, mix seed with moist peat moss or seed-starting medium in a plastic bag. Close bag with a twist-tie and place in the refrigerator for 4–6 weeks. Then sow the mixture as you would normal seed.
Pest and disease prevention No serious pests or diseases.
Landscape uses Combine with verbenas (*Verbena* spp.), phlox, goldenrods (*Solidago* spp.), columbines (*Aquilegia* spp.), and ornamental grasses.
Cultivars 'Alba' has white flowers. 'Blue Danube' has lavender-blue flowers. 'Klaus Jelitto' has deep blue flowers.

Symphytum ibericum
BORAGINACEAE

YELLOW COMFREY

Yellow comfrey is an excellent, easy-care groundcover for dry, shady spots. It produces dense, spreading clumps that tend to crowd out most weeds.

Flower color Clusters of white to creamy yellow, tubular flowers, ¾ inch (18 mm) long, rise above the foliage.
Flowering time Spring.
Height and spread Foliage to 1 foot (30 cm) tall; 2 feet (60 cm) wide. Flowers to 1½ feet (45 cm) tall.
Temperature requirements Zones 3–8.
Position Sun or partial shade, light-textured, well-drained soil; tolerates dry, poor soil.
Cultivation Set plants 18–24 inches (45–60 cm) apart in spring or fall. Once established, plants need virtually no care.
Propagation Propagate by division in spring or fall.
Pest and disease prevention No serious pests or diseases.
Landscape uses Yellow comfrey is an excellent, easy-care, weed-suppressing groundcover for dry, shaded spots.
Cultivars 'Variegatum' has green leaves variegated with yellow and cream.

Tellima grandiflora
SAXIFRAGACEAE

FRINGE CUPS

*Fringe cups are ideal for lightly shaded gardens.
They form tidy clumps of heart-shaped, cupped
green leaves, which spread slowly but steadily
and turn reddish in fall.*

Flower color Loose clusters of small,
bell-shaped, nodding flowers with fringed
petals, which are greenish white when
they open, then turn reddish.
Flowering time Spring.
Height and spread Foliage to 1 foot
(30 cm) tall; 20 inches (50 cm) wide.
Flowers to 2 feet (60 cm) tall.
Temperature requirements Zones 5–8
Position Light shade; fertile, well-drained,
slightly acid, cool soil.
Cultivation Set plants 18–24 inches
(45–60 cm) apart in spring. They may
self-sow in ideal conditions. Divide when
plants become overcrowded.
Propagation Divide in spring.
Pest and disease prevention No serious
pests or diseases.
Landscape uses This slow-spreading
plant makes an attractive, dense cover for
rock gardens or woodland gardens. It is
evergreen in warm climates and deciduous
in cool zones.
Cultivars 'Rubra' has maroon leaves.

Thalictrum aquilegifolium
RANUNCULACEAE

COLUMBINE MEADOW RUE

*Columbine meadow rue has billowy plumes
crowning erect stalks clothed in intricately divided
leaves that resemble those of columbines. Plants
grow from fibrous-rooted crowns.*

Flower color The ½-inch (12-mm),
lavender or white flowers consist of many
fuzzy stamens in dense, branched clusters.
Flowering time Late spring and early
summer.
Height and spread 2–3 feet (60–90 cm)
tall; 1–2 feet (30–60 cm) wide.
Temperature requirements Zones 5–8.
Position Evenly moist, humus-rich soil.
Full sun or partial shade. Plants tolerate
wet soil.
Cultivation Clumps spread slowly and
seldom outgrow their position. Can be
divided if necessary.
Propagation Propagate by division in
spring or fall. Sow seed outdoors in fall
or indoors in early spring.
Pest and disease prevention No serious
pests or diseases.
Landscape uses Plant columbine meadow
rue in formal or informal gardens. It grows
well beside ponds or along streams with
irises, hostas, hibiscuses (*Hibiscus* spp.),
daylilies, and ferns.
Cultivars 'Album' has white flowers.
'Atropurpureum' has violet flowers.
'Thundercloud' has deep purple flowers.

Thermopsis villosa
LEGUMINOSAE

CAROLINA LUPINE

*Carolina lupine produces upright flower spikes
atop stout stems clothed in three-part, gray-
green leaves. Plants grow from stout, fibrous-
rooted crowns.*

Flower color Lemon yellow, pea-shaped
flowers are tightly packed into 8–12-inch
(20–30-cm) clusters.
Flowering time Late spring or early
summer.
Height and spread 3–5 feet (90–150 cm)
tall; 2–4 feet (60–120 cm) wide.
Temperature requirements Zones 3–9.
Heat-tolerant.
Position Average to humus-rich, moist,
acid soil. Full sun to light shade.
Cultivation Clumps grow to shrub-like
proportions but seldom need division if
ample space is allotted. If foliage declines
after bloom, cut it to the ground.
Propagation Take cuttings in early
summer from sideshoots. Sow seed
outdoors in fall. Sow seed indoors in early
spring after soaking it in hot water for
12–24 hours.
Pest and disease prevention No serious
pests or diseases.
Landscape uses Plant toward the rear of
the garden with peonies, willow blue star
(*Amsonia tabernae-montana*), cranesbills
(*Geranium* spp.), and other rounded or
mounding plants. Lovely with shrubs or in
meadows or lightly shaded wild gardens.
Other names Carolina thermopsis.

Thymus serpyllum
LAMIACEAE

MOTHER OF THYME

Aromatic mother of thyme tolerates light foot traffic, making it ideal for a small-scale lawn substitute. Underplant it with small bulbs, such as crocuses, for spring interest.

Flower color Small, ½-inch (12-mm), rose-purple flowers bloom in clusters atop 4-inch (10-cm) stems.
Flowering time Summer.
Height and spread Foliage to 2 inches (5 cm) tall; spread unlimited. Flowers 3–4 inches (7.5–10 cm) tall.
Temperature requirements Zones 4–7; grows well in Zone 3 with snow cover.
Position Full sun; well-drained, dry soil that is not too fertile.
Cultivation Set plants about 8 inches (20 cm) apart in spring.
Propagation Propagate by division or seed in spring or by cuttings in early summer.
Pest and disease prevention As long as it grows in full sun, mother of thyme is remarkably free of pests and diseases.
Landscape uses The creeping habit of this plant makes it a natural for climbing over rocks in rock gardens or filling spaces between rocks in a terrace or pathway.
Cultivars 'Album' has white flowers in early summer. 'Coccineum' has reddish purple flowers in early summer over dense mats of green leaves that turn bronze in fall. Zones 3–9.

Tiarella cordifolia
SAXIFRAGACEAE

FOAMFLOWER

Foamflowers are elegant woodland wildflowers with fuzzy flowers and rosettes of triangular, three-lobed hairy leaves. Plants grow from fibrous-rooted crowns and creeping stems.

Flower color The small, starry, white flowers are borne in spike-like clusters. They are often tinged with pink.
Flowering time Spring.
Height and spread 6–10 inches (15–25 cm) tall; 1–2 feet (30–60 cm) wide.
Temperature requirements Zones 3–8.
Position Evenly moist, humus-rich, slightly acid soil. Partial to full shade.
Cultivation Foamflowers spread by creeping stems to form broad mats. Divide plants to control their spread.
Propagation Remove runners in summer and treat them as cuttings if they lack roots of their own. Sow seed in spring.
Pest and disease prevention No serious pests or diseases.
Landscape uses Foamflowers are good groundcovers. Their tight foliage mats discourage weeds under shrubs and flowering trees. In woodland gardens combine them with bulbs, ferns, and wildflowers like bloodroot (*Sanguinaria canadensis*), fringed bleeding heart (*Dicentra eximia*), hostas, and irises.

Tradescantia x andersoniana
COMMELINACEAE

COMMON SPIDERWORT

Common spiderworts have satiny flowers that open in the morning and fade in the afternoon. They are borne in clusters at the tips of the stems. Plants grow from thick, spidery roots.

Flower color 1–1½-inch (2.5–3.7-cm) flowers have three rounded, blue, purple, or white petals.
Flowering time Spring and early summer.
Height and spread 1–2 feet (30–60 cm) tall; 2 feet (60 cm) wide.
Temperature requirements Zones 3–9.
Position Moist but well-drained, average to humus-rich soil. Grow in full sun to partial shade.
Cultivation After flowering, plants tend to look shabby. Cut them to the ground to encourage new growth. Plants in dry situations go dormant in summer.
Propagation Divide in fall. Self-sown seedlings often appear.
Pest and disease prevention No serious pests or diseases.
Landscape uses Plant in informal gardens with bellflowers (*Campanula* spp.), hostas, columbines (*Aquilegia* spp.), and ferns. In formal gardens, combine with tulips and spring-blooming perennials.
Cultivars 'Blue Stone' has rich medium blue flowers. 'James C. Weguelin' has sky blue flowers. 'Pauline' has orchid pink flowers. 'Red Cloud' has maroon flowers. 'Zwanenberg Blue' has purple-blue flowers.

Tricyrtis formosana
CONVALLARIACEAE

FORMOSA TOAD LILY

The creeping stems of toad lilies spread to form handsome clumps that seldom need division. Their curious flowers add interest to the late-summer and fall shade garden.

Flower color Toad lilies have 1-inch (2.5-cm), upward-facing, purple-spotted flowers, with three petals and three petal-like sepals around a central column.
Flowering time Late summer and fall.
Height and spread 2–3 feet (60–90 cm) tall; 1–3 feet (30–90 cm) wide.
Temperature requirements Zones 4–9.
Position Evenly moist, humus-rich soil in light to partial shade. Full sun will damage the foliage.
Cultivation Plants spread by creeping stems to form handsome clumps that rarely need division. In Northern gardens, plants may be damaged by frost just as they are beginning to bloom in fall.
Propagation Divide clumps in spring or remove shoots from the edge of the clump and plant. Sow seed outdoors in fall.
Pest and disease prevention No serious pests or diseases.
Landscape uses Formosa toad lily flowers are subtle and best used where you can appreciate them at close range. Plant along a lightly shaded path or near the edge of a shade garden. The stiff stems make an interesting accent in the garden. Large clumps are effective combined with astilbes, hostas, ferns, and woodland plants.

Trollius x cultorum
RANUNCULACEAE

HYBRID GLOBEFLOWER

The glorious cup-shaped blooms of globeflowers add masses of color to spring gardens. These showy perennials need steady soil moisture and enriched soil to really look their best.

Flower color Globeflowers are showy spring perennials with waxy, cup-shaped flowers. Instead of petals, they have yellow or orange petal-like sepals.
Flowering time Spring.
Height and spread 2–3 feet (60–90 cm) tall; 1–2 feet (30–60 cm) wide.
Temperature requirements Zones 3–6.
Position Humus-rich, moist soil in full sun or partial shade. Plants are intolerant of dry soil and high night temperatures.
Cultivation The clumps increase from slow-spreading roots to form many crowns.
Propagation Divide in early spring or fall. Sow fresh seed outside as soon as it ripens; stored seed usually germinates poorly.
Pest and disease prevention No serious pests or diseases.
Landscape uses Plant globeflowers beside ponds and streams or in beds and borders where the soil stays evenly moist. Combine globeflowers with Siberian iris (*Iris sibirica*), lady's mantle (*Alchemilla mollis*), cardinal flower (*Lobelia cardinalis*), and primroses. Plants may go dormant after flowering, so plant them with foliage plants such as hostas, ferns, and grasses to fill the void.

Tulipa hybrids
LILIACEAE

TULIP

Hybrid tulips often bloom poorly after the first year. For a great show each year, pull them out after flowering and replace them with summer annuals; plant new tulips in fall.

Flower color Showy, single or double flowers, to 4 inches (10 cm) across, come in almost every color: white, yellow, red, orange, pink, purple, lilac, violet, blue, green, brown, bronze, black, and bicolors.
Flowering time Early to midspring.
Height and spread ½–2½ feet (15–90 cm) tall, depending on the cultivar; 6–10 inches (15–25 cm) wide.
Temperature requirements Usually best in Zones 3–8; in Zones 9 and 10, treat as annuals and plant precooled bulbs each year in late fall or early winter.
Position Full sun to partial shade; average, well-drained soil that's dry in summer.
Cultivation Plant bulbs in mid- to late fall. Set them in individual holes or larger planting areas dug 4–6 inches (10–15 cm) deep. Pinch off developing seedpods after flowering. Allow leaves to yellow before removing or pull out bulbs after bloom.
Propagation Divide bulbs after the foliage has died back.
Pest and disease prevention Trap slugs and snails in saucers of beer set flush with the soil surface. Spray aphids and thrips with insecticidal soap.
Landscape uses Indispensable in the spring garden; also charming as cut flowers.

Uvularia grandiflora
CONVALLARIACEAE

GREAT MERRYBELLS

Great merrybells is a graceful wildflower with nodding, bell-shaped flowers on slender stalks clothed in gray-green leaves. Plants grow from rhizomes with brittle, white roots.

Flower color The nodding, lemon yellow flowers have three petals and three petal-like sepals that twist in the middle.
Flowering time Spring.
Height and spread 1–1½ feet (30–45 cm) tall; 1–2 feet (30–60 cm) wide.
Temperature requirements Zones 3–8.
Position Moist, humus-rich soil. Partial to full shade. Spring sun is important for bloom but summer shade is mandatory.
Cultivation Great merrybells spread to form tight, attractive clumps. When the flowers fade, the foliage expands to form an attractive summer-long groundcover.
Propagation Divide plants before flowering in early spring or in fall.
Pest and disease prevention No serious pests or diseases.
Landscape uses Plant great merrybells in woodland gardens with wildflowers like fringed bleeding heart (*Dicentra eximia*), bloodroot (*Sanguinaria canadensis*), and wild gingers (*Asarum* spp.). Ferns and hostas are also good companions.
Other common names Large-flowered bellwort.

Vancouveria hexandra
BERBERIDACEAE

AMERICAN BARRENWORT

American barrenwort may look delicate, but it is a tough and vigorous perennial that spreads by underground stems. It prefers moist soil but can adapt to dry conditions.

Flower color Tiny, ½-inch (12-mm), white flowers bloom in drooping clusters just above the leaves.
Flowering time Late spring or early summer.
Height and spread 1 foot (30 cm) tall; 2 feet (60 cm) or more wide.
Temperature requirements Zones 5–8.
Position Prefers partial shade but will tolerate full shade. Moist, well-drained, fertile soil, rich in leaf mold; can adapt to dry conditions.
Cultivation Set plants 18–24 inches (45–60 cm) apart in spring. They may be slow getting started but will begin to spread by the second growing season. Mulch to keep them moist and cool in summer. If the soil is sandy, feed them once a year with compost or leaf mold.
Propagation Divide in spring.
Pest and disease prevention No serious pests or diseases.
Landscape uses American barrenwort makes an attractive groundcover beneath trees, in shady rock gardens, and in wild gardens. It's also a nice edging plant for shady beds of hostas.

Verbascum chaixii
SCROPHULARIACEAE

NETTLE-LEAVED MULLEIN

Nettle-leaved mullein has thick flower spikes and stout stems with broadly oval, pointed leaves. The species has yellow flowers; the cultivar 'Album' has white flowers.

Flower color The small, five-petaled, yellow flowers are tightly packed into dense clusters.
Flowering time Summer.
Height and spread 2–3 feet (60–90 cm) tall; 1–2 feet (30–60 cm) wide.
Temperature requirements Zones 4–8.
Position Average, well-drained soil. Full sun to light shade.
Cultivation Established plants are quite attractive. Plants spread slowly and seldom need division.
Propagation Sow seed outdoors in fall or spring or indoors in spring. Take root cuttings in late winter or early spring. Plants often self-sow.
Pest and disease prevention No serious pests or diseases.
Landscape uses Plant nettle-leaved mulleins in borders with fine-textured perennials like cranesbills (*Geranium* spp.), meadow rues (*Thalictrum* spp.), and thread-leaved coreopsis (*Coreopsis verticillata*). Combine them with mounded plants such as catmints (*Nepeta* spp.) and ornamental grasses in informal gardens.
Cultivars 'Album' has white flowers with purple eyes.

Verbena canadensis
VERBENACEAE

ROSE VERBENA

Rose verbena has deeply lobed leaves and circular, flat flower clusters at the ends of the stems. Plants grow from fibrous-rooted crowns but also root along the trailing stems.

Flower color The tubular lavender to rose pink flowers have flat, five-petaled faces.
Flowering time Late spring through fall.
Height and spread 8–18 inches (20–45 cm) tall; 1–3 feet (30–90 cm) wide.
Temperature requirements Zones 4–10.
Position Poor to humus-rich, well-drained soil. Full sun. These plants are heat- and drought-tolerant.
Cultivation Plants spread quickly to form broad clumps. Prune or divide plants that overgrow their position.
Propagation Take stem cuttings in summer.
Pest and disease prevention Powdery mildew may cause white blotches on the foliage. Spray infected plants with wettable sulfur to control the spread of the disease.
Landscape uses Rose verbena is an excellent "weaver." Use it to tie mixed plantings together at the front of the border. The stems will cover bare ground between yuccas (*Yucca* spp.), mulleins (*Verbascum* spp.), and ornamental grasses.

Veronica prostrata
SCROPHULARIACEAE

ROCK SPEEDWELL

The spreading foliage mats of rock speedwell are accented by spikes of blue flowers in late spring. This plant is a perfect choice for sunny slopes and rock gardens.

Flower color Spikes of deep blue flowers bloom on upright stems above creeping mats of green leaves.
Flowering time Late spring.
Height and spread 8–10 inches (20–25 cm) tall; 18 inches (45 cm) or more wide.
Temperature requirements Zones 4–8.
Position Prefers full sun, but tolerates partial shade; moist but well-drained, average soil.
Cultivation Set plants at least 2 feet (60 cm) apart in spring or fall. If needed, surround plantings with an edging strip to keep them in bounds.
Propagation Propagate by division in spring or fall, by stem cuttings in summer, or by seed in spring.
Pest and disease prevention No serious pests or diseases.
Landscape uses Rock speedwell makes a charming groundcover in rock gardens and on rocky slopes.
Other common names Hungarian speedwell, harebell speedwell.
Cultivars 'Alba' has white flowers that bloom over a long season. 'Mrs. Holt' has rose pink flowers.

Veronica spicata
SCROPHULARIACEAE

SPIKE SPEEDWELL

Spike speedwell has pointed flower clusters atop leafy stems. The opposite leaves are oval to oblong and clothed in soft hair. Plants grow from fibrous-rooted crowns.

Flower color The small, two-lipped, pink, blue, or white flowers are tightly packed into erect spikes.
Flowering time Summer.
Height and spread 1–3 feet (30–90 cm) tall; 1½–2½ feet (45–75 cm) wide.
Temperature requirements Zones 3–8.
Position Average to humus-rich, moist, well-drained soil. Full sun to light shade.
Cultivation Plants grow slowly to form neat, attractive clumps. Cut plants back if they get rangy and also to encourage fresh growth and continued bloom.
Propagation Divide in spring or fall. Take stem cuttings in late spring or early summer; remove any flower buds.
Pest and disease prevention No serious pests or diseases.
Landscape uses Plant spike speedwells with summer perennials that need good drainage like yarrows, catmints (*Nepeta* spp.), sundrops (*Oenothera* spp.), and ornamental grasses. Their spiky forms are perfect for adding excitement to plantings.
Cultivars 'Barcarolle' has rose pink flowers and gray-green leaves. 'Blue Fox' has lavender-blue flowers. 'Blue Peter' has dark blue flowers.

Viola odorata
VIOLACEAE

SWEET VIOLET

Sweet violets are beloved for their delicate, fragrant, early-season flowers. They produce rosettes of heart-shaped leaves from creeping rhizomes and make an ideal groundcover for a shady site.

Flower color The deep purple or blue flowers have five petals. Two point upward and three point outward and down. The two outfacing petals have fuzzy beards.
Flowering time Spring.
Height and spread 2–8 inches (5–20 cm) tall; 4–8 inches (10–20 cm) wide.
Temperature requirements Zones 6–9.
Position Moist, humus-rich soil. Sun or shade. Widely tolerant of varying soil and moisture conditions.
Cultivation Violets are prolific spreaders, at home in any garden.
Propagation Divide plants after flowering or in fall. Plants often self-sow.
Pest and disease prevention No serious pests or diseases.
Landscape uses Violets form attractive groundcovers under shrubs and flowering trees. In informal gardens plant them with bulbs, wildflowers, hostas, as well as early-blooming perennials.
Cultivars 'Deloris' has deep purple flowers. 'White Queen' has white flowers.

Waldsteinia fragarioides
ROSACEAE

BARREN STRAWBERRY

Barren strawberry has shiny, evergreen leaves that take on a purplish color in cold weather. It grows well in partial shade but needs moist soil in sunlight. The spring flowers are followed by inedible fruits.

Flower color Clusters of five-petaled, yellow flowers, ½ inch (12 mm) wide, appear on the stems.
Flowering time Late spring.
Height and spread 6 inches (15 cm) tall; spread unlimited.
Temperature requirements Zones 5–8.
Position Prefers partial shade but will tolerate sunny spots if kept moist; well-drained, fertile soil.
Cultivation Set plants about 2 feet (60 cm) apart in spring. Keep watered in dry periods and divide when overcrowded.
Propagation Propagate by division in early spring or fall or by seed in spring.
Pest and disease prevention No serious pests or diseases.
Landscape uses Grow barren strawberry in rock gardens, on banks and rocky ledges, or cascading over walls.

Yucca filamentosa
AGAVACEAE

ADAM'S NEEDLE

Adam's needle produces tall, oval clusters of bell-like, white flowers and rosettes of sword-shaped, blue-green leaves. It grows from a woody crown with fleshy roots.

Flower color Nodding, creamy white flowers have three petals and three petal-like sepals that form a bell.
Flowering time Summer.
Height and spread 5–15 feet (1.5–4.5 m) tall (5 feet [1.5 m] is average); 3–6 feet (90–180 cm) wide.
Temperature requirements Zones 3–10.
Position Average to humus-rich, well-drained soil. Full sun to light shade.
Cultivation Plants thrive for years with little care. After flowering the main crown dies but auxiliary crowns keep growing.
Propagation Remove young sideshoots from the clump in spring or fall.
Pest and disease prevention No serious pests or diseases.
Landscape uses Plant in dry borders or rock gardens as accents, or use in seaside gardens. Contrast the stiff foliage with soft or delicate plants like lamb's ears (*Stachys byzantina*), sedums, and verbenas.

USDA Plant Hardiness Zone Map

These maps of the United States, Canada, and Europe are divided into ten zones. Each zone is based on a 10°F (5.6°C) difference in average annual minimum temperature. Some areas are considered too high in elevation for plant cultivation and so are not assigned to any zone. There are also island zones that are warmer or cooler than surrounding areas because of differences in elevation; they have been given a zone different from the surrounding areas. Many large urban areas, for example, are in a warmer zone than the surrounding land.

Plants grow best within an optimum range of temperatures. The range may be wide for some species and narrow for others. Plants also differ in their ability to survive frost and in their sun or shade requirements. The zone ratings indicate conditions where designated plants will grow well and not merely survive. Many plants may survive in zones warmer or colder than their recommended zone range. Remember that other factors, including wind, soil type, soil moisture, humidity, snow, and winter sunshine may have a great effect on growth.

Some nursery plants have been grown in greenhouses and they might not survive in your garden, so it's a waste of money, and a cause of heartache, to buy plants that aren't right for your climate zone.

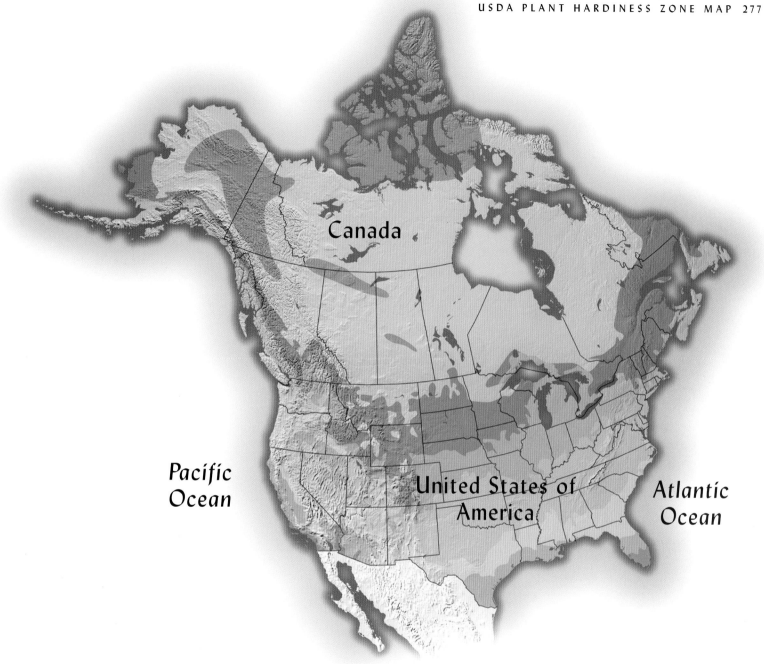

Canada

Pacific
Ocean

United States of
America

Atlantic
Ocean

Average annual minimum temperature °F (°C)

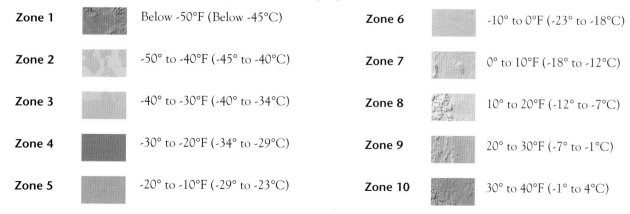

Zone 1	Below -50°F (Below -45°C)	**Zone 6**	-10° to 0°F (-23° to -18°C)
Zone 2	-50° to -40°F (-45° to -40°C)	**Zone 7**	0° to 10°F (-18° to -12°C)
Zone 3	-40° to -30°F (-40° to -34°C)	**Zone 8**	10° to 20°F (-12° to -7°C)
Zone 4	-30° to -20°F (-34° to -29°C)	**Zone 9**	20° to 30°F (-7° to -1°C)
Zone 5	-20° to -10°F (-29° to -23°C)	**Zone 10**	30° to 40°F (-1° to 4°C)

Index

Page numbers in *italics* indicate illustrations and photos.

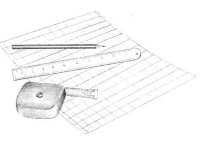

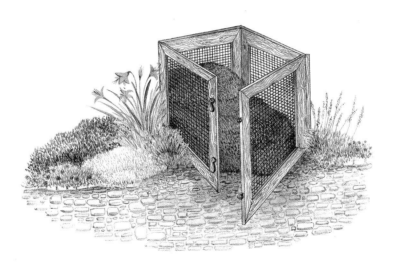

Credits and Acknowledgments

KEY l=left, r=right, c=center, t=top, b=bottom, f=far

APL=Australian Picture Library; BC=Bruce Coleman; CN=Clive Nichols; COR=Corel Corp.; DW=David Wallace; GPL=Garden Picture Library; HEM=Hemera Studio; HS=Harry Smith Collection; HSI=Holt Studios Int.; GB=Gillian Beckett; GPL=Garden Picture Library; JP=Jerry Pavia; LC=Leigh Clapp; PH=Photos Horticultural; PL=photolibrary.com; SO=S & O Matthews; TE=Thomas Eltzroth; WO=Weldon Owen.

1 Corbis Images 2c LC 4 LC 6 LC 10 APL 12b APL/Corbis 13tr PhotoDisc 14tl COR; cl GPL/John Glover; b COR 15t COR 16t APL/Jessie Walker; b GPL/Lynne Brotchie 17tl Clive Nichols; tr SO; b COR 18t APL/Corbis; c PhotoDisc 19t COR; b Corbis 20tl APL/Corbis; tr Clive Nichols; br SO 21t GPL/Gary Rogers 22t PL/Robin Smith; br Corbis; bl SO 23t APL; b APL/Corbis 24tl CN; tr CN; b PhotoDisc 25t TE; br APL/Corbis; bl CN 26tl APL/Jessie Walker Associates; cr JP; b PhotoDisc 27t JP; br CN; bl Graham Strong 28t PhotoDisc; b PL/Hiroshi Higuchi 29tl COR; tr CN 30t PL/Hiroshi Higuchi; c CN; cb CN; cr CN 31tr PhotoDisc; tl CN; bc Joanna Pavia 32–33c APL/Corbis 34tr, cr, br Derek Fell; bl PL/Robin Smith 35tl Derek Fell; bl BC; cr, br GPL/Michael Homes 36tl PhotoDisc; br GPL/Roger Hyam 37bl JP 38t PhotoDisc; bl Getty Images/Tony Stone Images; br JP 39t COR; bl PH; br JP 40tr CN ; tl JP; l APL/Corbis; b APL/Jessie Walker 41tr GPL/Steve Wooster 42b APL/John Baker 43tl HEM; tr CN ; b GPL/Steven Wooster 44tl LC; tr GPL/Brian Carter; br HEM; bc Joanna Pavia 45c PhotoDisc 46–47c APL/Corbis 48t WO; b APL/Corbis 49tr JP; tl SO 50b CN 51tr PhotoDisc; b JP 52b JP 53c APL/Corbis 54t JP; b CN 55t JP; b CN 56t GPL/S. Harte; b PhotoDisc 57t HEM; tr PhotoDisc; br APL/Corbis; bl CN 58 APL/Corbis 59t JP; cr, br CN 60t SO; b CN 61t, b APL/Corbis; 62tr HEM; cl GPL/Brian Carter; br JP 63t COR; bl GPL/Zara McCalmont 64t SO; b APL/Corbis 65tr APL/Corbis; c, bl PhotoDisc; br EWA Photo Library 66t GPL/JP; br CN; bl BC/Hans Rein-

hard 67tl JP; tr GPL/JP; br WO 68t APL/Corbis; bl PhotoDisc; br GPL/CN 69t APL/Corbis; br GPL/Brian Carter; bl BC/John Shaw 70t Artville; br Derek Fell; bl BC/Eric Chricton 71tr APL/Corbis; tl CN; b Artville 72t PhotoDisc; br CN; bl JP 73tr HEM; tl CN 74bl CN; br GPL/Jane Legate 75tl, bc PhotoDisc; br CN 76tr JP; bl COR; br Getty Images/Tony Stone 77tl Corbis; cl PhotoDisc; bc SO 78t COR; br Holt Studios/Bob Gibbons; bl JP 79tr BC/Hans Reinhard; b HEM 80tr PhotoDisc; tl PH; b JP 81tl COR; tr PL/Hiroshi Higuchi 82tl, tr APL/Corbis; b JP 83tl TE; tr JP; br SO 84br CN; bl JP 85tl APL/Corbis; tr PhotoDisc 86t APL/Corbis; bl HEM; br Andrew Larson 87tl GPL Brian Carter; br PL/Claver Carroll; bl CN 88–89c PL/Nigel Hicks 90tr SO; bl BC/Hans Reinhard 91t PhotoDisc; bl PH; br CN 92tl HEM; tr CN 93t JP; b GPL/John Glover 94tl PhotoDisc 95tr GPL/Vaughan Fleming; tl Corel; bl HEM 96tl, tr PhotoDisc; bl Derek Fell; br PL/Norman Wong 97t COR 98t PhotoDisc; b JP 99t GPL Zara McCalmont; bl HEM; br CN 100bl PhotoDisc; br Auscape/Jerry Harpur 101tr PH; tl JP; r PhotoDisc 102t PhotoDisc; br HEM; bl LC 103tr GPL/JP; br PH 104–105c LC 106tr WO; bl Gardener's Supply Co., Burlington, VT; br Derek Fell 107tr JP; bl COR; br PhotoDisc 108t APL/Corbis; b PH 109t LC; b WO 110t LC; b Getty Images/Tony Stone 111tl PhotoDisc; tr LC 112tl PH; br COR; cl DW 113br GPL/J. S. Siva; bl GPL Mayer/Le Scanff 114tl GPL Mayer/Le Scanff; tr GPL/Zara McCalmont; bl LC 115t PhotoDisc; br GPL/Michael Howes 116t DW; br PhotoDisc 117tl LC 118t HEM; bl PhotoDisc 119t COR; b LC 120tl APL/Geoff Woods; cr Artville; br Derek Fell 121tr PhotoDisc; b PH 122–123c LC 124tr APL/Corbis; bl APL/Premium-Houses 125tl, tr, cl WO; bl David Aldous 126t GPL Lynn Brotchie; br APL/ZEFA 127t PH 128 APL/Premium-Houses 129t PhotoDisc; b APL/Corbis 130tl HS; tr DW; b Auscape/Rob Walls 131t GPL/Brian Carter; b LC 132tr BC/Norbet Rosing; br DW; bl LC 133tl PhotoDisc 134t BC/Eric Chricton; b COR 135tl PH; tr PhotoDisc; b APL/Corbis 136tr GPL/CN 137t LC; b Rodale Stock Images 138t LC; fbl WO; bl Derek

Fell; bc WO; br BC/Peter Ward 139tc, tr WO; tl BC/Eric Chricton; ftl BC/Kim Taylor 140br BC/Dr. Frieder Sauer; bl Ron West 141t LC 142tl, tr WO; br COR; bl Holt Studios; ftl Derek Fell; tc Michael Dir 143tl WO; tr WO; br BC/Hans Reinhard 144tr PhotoDisc; tl Andrew Larson; b GPL/Michael Howes 145tl GPL/Brigitte Thomas; tr GPL/Lamontagne; bl APL/Corbis 146t PH; tr PhotoDisc; br COR 147t PH; cl Photo-Disc; br JP 148tr PL/Claver Carroll; tl CN 149t LC; b PH 150t Heather Angel; b LC 151t TE; cr PhotoDisc; b GPL/Linda Burgess; 152t COR; br GPL/Brian Carter; bl CN 153tr GPL/Lamontagne; br LC 154tr BC/R. Glover; tl Photo Essentials; b Corbis 155c LC 156t Corbis; br Andrew Lawson 157t LC; b Photo-Disc 158c APL/J. P. & E. S. Baker 160 COR 161t PhotoDisc; bl HEM; br PH 162tr CN 163t PhotoDisc; br Corbis Images; bl GPL/Lamontagne 164tr COR; bl GPL/Brian Carter; c Heather Angel 165tr DW; bl APL/Corbis; r DW 166tl BC/Eric Crichton 167bl Corbis Images; r DW 168l David Wallace; br LC 169tl Andrew Lawson 170bl Corbis Images; br GPL/Jane Legate 171tl PhotoDisc; tr BC; b COR 172c APL/Corbis 174tr, tl, tc TE 175tr Joanne Pavia; tc PH; tl TE 176tr HS; tl, tc TE 177tr HS; tl PH; tc SO 178tr PH; tl SO; tc TE 179tl, tc, tr TE 180tl JP; tc, tr TE 181tl HS; tc, tr TE 182tr JP; tl, tc TE 183tl JP; tc GPL/Lamontagne; tr TE 184tl, tc, tr TE 185tl Stirling Macoby; tc, tr TE 186tl WO; tc JP; tr TE 187tr GB; tl JP; tc TE 188tc Derek Fell; tl GPL/Lamontagne; tr TE 189tl JP; tr GPL/Lynne Brotchie; tc SO 190tr HS; tl JP; tc HSI/Nigel Cattlin 191tl HS; tr GB; tc TE 192tl HS; tc CN; tr TE 193tr GPL/John Glover; tc Stirling Macoboy; tl TE 194tc COR; tc HS; tl TE 195tl COR; tc GPL/Lamontagne; tr TE 196tr GB; tl, tc TE 197tc JP; tl, tr TE 198tc PH; tr S. & O. Mathews; tl TE 199tl COR; tc CN; tr TE 200tl HS; tc, tr TE 201tl, tr COR; tc TE 202c APL/Corbis 204tr Corbis Royalty Free; tl John Callanan 205tc HS; tr unknown; tl Tony Rodd 206tc John Callanan; tl Tony Rodd 207tr PH; tc TE 208tl PH; tr S. & O. Matthews; tc TE 209tl PH; tc GB 210tc GB; tr TE 211tc PH; tl Nancy J. Ondra; tr TE 212tl PH; tr GBt; tc GPL/Jane Legate 213tl PH; tc HS; tr

Allan Armitage 214 TE 215tl CN; tr John Callanan; tc TE 216tl HS; tc Andrew Lawson; tr Stirling Macoby 21t HSI; tr PH; tc Derek Fell 218tl HS; tr PH; tc GB 219tl, tc HS; tr GB 220tl HS; tr JP; tc TE 221tl, tc HS; tr TE 222tr Anita Sabrese; tc Stirling Macoby; tl TE 223tl GPL; tc JP; tr GPL/Roger Hyam 224tl HS; tc CN; tr SO 225tl CN; tc, tr TE 226tr HS; tc GB; tl SO 227tl DW; tc JP; tr John Callanan 228tc PH; tl SO; tr TE 229tl PH; tr Allan Armitage; tc GB 230tc PH; tr GPL/J. S. Sira; tl JP 231tr Stirling Macoby; tl, tc TE 232tc PH; tr HS; tl JP 233tr GB; tl GPL/Ron Sutherland 234tc PH; tr SO; tl Tony Rodd 235tc HS; tl, tr CN 236tr PH; tl JP; tc John Callanan 237tl PH; tc, tr TE 238tr JP; tl GPL/Michael Howes; tc TE 23 tr Corbis Corp.; tl John J. Smith; tc A–Z Botanical Collection/Peter Jousiffe 240tc HS; tr Allan Armitage; tl SO 241tl Rodale Stock Images; tc GPL/Didier Willery; tr SO 242tl CN; tc SO; tl TE 243tr PH; tr BC/John Shaw; tc SO 244tl CN; tc JP; tr Tony Rodd 245tl, tc, tr GB 246tl, tc, tr TE 247tl HS; tc SO; tr Tony Rodd 248tr PH; tl, tc TE 249tr Derek Fell; tl Lorna Rose; tc TE 250tl HSI; tr GPL/Brian Carter; tc TE 251tc Joanne Pavia; tl Malcom Richards; tr TE 252c CN; r JP; l SO 253r HS; l GB; c TE 254r HS; l, c TE 255l HS; r JP; c TE 256c Ardea London/A. P. Paterson; r John Callanan; l SO 257l HS; c PH; r Derek Fell 258c HS; r JP; l Stirling Macoby 259l HS; c John Callanan; r SO 260l CN; c, r SO 261c PH; l CN; r GB 262c PH; l GB; r Stirling Macoby 263c CN; r G.R. "Dick" Roberts Photo Library; l JP 264r HS; c, l CN 265r HS; l, c John J. Smith 266r HS; l, c TE 267l HS; c SO; r TE 268r CN; l, c SO 269l CN; r GB; c TE 270r HS; l GB; c John Callanan 271l HS; c GB; r TE 272r COR; l GB; c SO 273c, r GB; l SO 274c HS; l JP; r TE 275c GB; l, r TE.

All illustrations by Barbara Rodanska except the following:
Tony Britt-Lewis 84t. Mike Gorman 63b, 7br, 45b, 97b. Stuart McVicar 277, 276. Edwina Riddell l, 42c, 45tr, 49br, 49bl, 50, 73 74, 79, 97,107, 114, 115, 117, 127, 133t, 133t, 140t, 153l, 162l, 166r, 169b, 170tr. Genevieve Wallace 85b.

With special thanks to Geoffrey Burnie, horticultural consultant; Kate Brady, for editorial assistance; Debbie Duncan, Diana Grivas, and Angela Handley, for proofreading; Caroline Colton & Associates, for indexing.